Football: A College History

Football
A College History

by

Tom Perrin

McFarland & Company, Inc., Publishers
Jefferson, North Carolina, and London

Library of Congress Cataloguing-in-Publication Data

Perrin, Tom, 1928–
Football : a college history.

Includes index.
1. Football — United States — History.   I. Title.
GV950.P47   1987   796.332'63'0973   87-43029

ISBN 0-89950-294-6 (acid-free natural paper)

Printed in the United States of America.

McFarland & Company, Inc., Publishers
Box 611, Jefferson, North Carolina 28640

To
my daughter, Terri,
who loves the game
as much as I do

Table of Contents

Foreword

Knute Rockne once said that "All football comes from Yale." More than any other person, Walter Camp of Yale changed the game from its English origins and made it uniquely American.

In the first football game between Princeton and Rutgers in 1869 there were 25 men on each side, the rules were adapted from the London Football Association (the game was often called soccer), no running with the ball was permitted, and the 6–4 Rutgers win was made on kicks between the soccer-style goal posts. The game was preceded by a Princeton cheer of three hurrahs and "Siss! Boom! Ah!" It was taken from a yell by the Seventh New York Regiment which went through Princeton during the Civil War. The Rutgers side replied by singing "Oh, Susanna" and "Wait for the Wagon." The toss of a coin determined who got the ball or the wind, and it ended with a nineteenth-century version of a tailgate party, a supper for both teams.

In 1874, Harvard played McGill University of Montreal in a rugby scrummage in which the ball was thrown between two opposing lines who tried to heel it out, or kick it back to one of the men in the rear. The back ran with the ball until he was downed, an innovation which began in 1823 at Rugby, England, when William Webb Ellis ran with the ball for the first time. After the back was tackled the ball was thrown between the two lines, and play began again by heeling it back. Control of the ball could change on every play, since it depended on which way it squirted back.

In the next year, 1875, Harvard introduced Yale to the rugby game with a 4–0 whitewash, and one year later Camp made his first appearance on a Yale team. That fall at the Massasoit House in Springfield, Massachusetts, the Intercollegiate Football Association was formed and they adopted a modified Rugby Union Code.

Camp continued the suggestion of Yale captain Gene Baker to change the number of players from 15 to 11, and in 1880 he was successful. With the introduction of Camp's scrimmage line and a center who snapped the ball with his foot that year, American football began. From this came ball control and signals which allowed planned plays to be run. In 1881, Camp was instrumental in reducing the size of the field from 140 by 70 yards to 110 by 53 yards. In the following year, Camp proposed a first down by gaining five yards in three attempts and using yard lines to mark the field. One year later, he introduced the modern scoring system.

It was also Yale which gave the game the deeper values of team play, team spirit, and physical self-sacrifice for the good of the team. The society of strained ligaments, lost teeth, and broken bones can be shared only by those who are willing to deny themselves for the good of all. It is not by accident that "The battle of Waterloo was won on the playing fields of Eton," as the Duke of Wellington said, for freedom has been won on a thousand other playing fields and gridirons which have taught its meaning.

In this book the top teams and events have been discussed, but it could easily be dedicated to the also-rans. Many thanks are due the NCAA for their statistics beginning with the 1937 season, the schools which provided the photos for this book, and the librarians, sports information directors, and their secretaries and assistants who answered my countless questions.

I. The Early Years

1883

Yale (8-0-0)			Princeton (7-1-0)		
60	Wesleyan	0	20	Rutgers	0
90	Wesleyan	0	54	Lafayette	7
48	Stevens	0	15	Stevens	5
98	Rutgers	0	61	Rutgers	0
93	Columbia	0	39	Penn	6
64	Michigan	0	24	Wesleyan	0
6	Princeton	0	26	Harvard	7
23	Harvard	2	0	Yale	6
482		2	239		31

American football began with the scrimmage line of 1880 and a quarter-back who handled the ball first on every play, including punts and field goal attempts. It was hindered by a safety rule which took the ball out to the 25-yard line when a team retreated behind its goal. If the ball wasn't fumbled away, it could be kept indefinitely. In the "block" game of 1881, Princeton held the ball for the entire first half and moved it only a few yards. In the last half, Yale did the same thing. Newspapers derided a game in which each side did nothing but block the other's efforts.

In 1882, a system of downs with its endless struggle between offense and defense changed the American game. If a team didn't gain five yards in three tries, the ball went over to the other side. The field was lined every five yards, and a gridiron was born. One thing still stood in the way, for the scoring system had a rule which would defy Einstein: "A match shall be decided by a majority of touchdowns; a goal shall be equal to four touchdowns; but in case of a tie a goal kicked from a touchdown shall take precedence over four touchdowns."

The Harvard-Princeton game of 1882 brought things to a head. Harvard's Frank Mason made a touchdown, missed the goal after it, but kicked a goal from the field. Princeton made a touchdown and Jim Haxall converted the goal. Princeton protested heatedly when referee Bob Watson, 1880 Yale captain, awarded Harvard the game.

Walter Camp again came to the rescue as he did with his idea of a scrimmage line and a first down. He proposed the modern scoring system in 1883: A goal from the field, or field goal, was worth five points, and the goal after touchdown was worth four points. A touchdown was valued at only two

1

Walter Camp of Yale, the father of American football.

points, and a safety, or downing the ball behind your goal, counted one point. Any team which downed the ball behind its goal was no longer in safe territory but had to pay for it in the score. Each team was also provided with an umpire, but the decision of the referee was final.

Until the end of the century "The Game" was Princeton-Yale, not Harvard-Yale. During this time Yale won nine, Princeton won six, and two were ties. Yale or Princeton was usually the champion, except for an occasional interim reign by Harvard.

This year's wide-open Yale attack featured a fake pitchout by quarterback Henry "Deacon" Twombley to halfback Wyllys Terry going wide, then a long lateral to either Howard Knapp or Arthur Farwell at end on the opposite flank. Its movement against the flow of action often fooled opponents and spectators alike, and was usually good for a long gain. Other plays which delighted the crowd were an end-around or fake end-around, reverses, and the handoffs or multiple laterals between the various backs.

Most of Yale's games were only warmups for the contest with Princeton. Led by center Louis Hull and safety Benjamin Bacon's knees-in-the-chest tackle, the Elis took an early lead when Frank Peters scored the game's only touchdown, two points, on a return of an Alex Moffat punt. The goal after, four points, was kicked by halfback Gene Richards for a final score of 6–0 for Yale.

Captain Ray Tompkins, after whom the Ray Tompkins House at Yale is named, suffered a sprained ankle against Princeton. It was doubtful if he would be ready for Harvard in five days, but his ankle was treated with hot pads all week. On game day it was taped so tightly it would hardly bend, but he played the entire game at guard and helped in the win. By beating both Princeton and Harvard, Yale won the Big Three title and was national champ.

It was also in this early period that Alex Moffat, Princeton's great kicker, put a new twist into punting. Most punters kicked the bloated rugby ball in an end-over-end rolling style called tumblers. Moffat departed from this accepted method by sending the oval-shaped ball skyward in a spiral punt, thereby changing the science of punting and punt coverage forever.

Moffat was unique in more ways than one. Not only did he punt with either foot, but he drop-kicked field goals with both feet as well. Of the 26 points which Princeton scored against Harvard that year, 20 of them were on four field goals by Moffat in the second half. He broke the game open with two left-footed kicks of 46 yards and 40 yards, and then added two more with his right foot from 43 yards and 36 yards. No cheap shots, these!

1884

Yale (8-0-1)			Princeton (9-0-1)		
31	Wesleyan	0	23	Rutgers	5
96	Stevens	0	4	Stevens	0
63	Wesleyan	0	22	Wesleyan	2
76	Rutgers	10	35	Rutgers	0
113	Dartmouth	0	31	Penn	0
46	Wesleyan	0	140	Lafayette	0
18	Alumni	0	56	Stevens	0
48	Harvard	0	57	Johns Hopkins	0
0	Princeton	0	36	Harvard	6
			0	Yale	0
491		10	404		13

As football began to wean itself away from rugby, the scoring was changed again this year. The points for a touchdown and goal after touchdown, or conversion, underwent a mutual exchange, for a touchdown was now four points and a goal after touchdown became two points. A field goal still counted five points, but a safety was now valued at two points. With a field goal still worth five points, the kicking game remained foremost. Up to now, the main value of a touchdown was that it gave an opportunity to kick the goal after it. This year they were placed in proper perspective, for the struggle to score a touchdown was viewed as more important than the points after it. The value put on crossing an opponent's goal, therefore, was one more step on the road that football was taking as it separated itself from its rugby origins.

Yale and Princeton both had outstanding teams and unbeaten seasons in 1884. Both scored over 100 points in a single game, as Yale gave a fledgling Dartmouth team the worst beating in its history, and Princeton had even less mercy in burying Lafayette. In the Dartmouth game, Yale's 290-pound guard, Alex Coxe, scored four times and was the "Refrigerator" of his day, since linemen often doubled as ball carriers. At the half it was 41-0, but Dartmouth considered the beating a valuable lesson from the champs.

Yale opened its season by downing Wesleyan in the first game ever played at Yale Field. Eleven days after the Dartmouth game, history was made in the third Wesleyan game, November 5, 1884, which was also played at Yale Field. Wyllys Terry joined the immortals with a 115-yard touchdown run, a record which will no doubt last forever, unless the playing field is lengthened again.

Terry took the ball five yards behind his goal and bulled his way through the first wave of tacklers. Then he headed for the right sideline and turned it on. At midfield, the 55-yard line, he got a step on his pursuers by cutting over to the left side of the field. When he crossed the goal at the end of his remarkable feat his thickset legs ached from exhaustion, but he gave the New Haven fans a thrill they had never seen before, a touchdown run from one end of the field to the other.

In the Penn game, Princeton introduced a new formation, the Princeton V. It was a mass-momentum play where the ball carrier ran inside a V-shaped line which tried to pierce the defense like a human plow. Princeton's captain, Clinton Bird, decided to let quarterback Richard Hodge use it in the second half after things hadn't worked out well for the Tigers in the early going.

The V-formation was a potent weapon because each man in the wedge held on to the player ahead of him. Breaking it up meant a defensive player had to throw himself at the point of the V, while his teammates hurled themselves at its sides and tried to cave it in. It was not a task for the faint-hearted. The Princeton V took them down the field for a score, but it was considered a makeshift which had served its purpose and was not used often. The V did not surface again until four years later when it was called a flying wedge.

Interference (blocking) was not widely used since the rule against it was vague, but one complained because it aided rather than hindered the game. It was looked upon as part of the new game, and the first blockers ran beside the ball carrier to keep him from being tackled. It added, however, one more aspect to football which separated it from rugby, for it provided the

American game with its unique contribution of blocking, backbone of the offense.

The national championship came down to the last game of the season between Princeton and Yale. An innovation in the rules affected the outcome of the game, for the new rule abolished the two umpires in favor of a single referee. There would be less arguments, it was hoped, with one official instead of three.

Many prolonged arguments over the rules delayed the game. When darkness fell Yale was leading, 6–4, with 18 minutes still left to play. Since the rule stated that a game was two halves of 45 minutes each, Princeton interpreted the rule to mean that the game wasn't finished, darkness or not. Randolph Appleton, last year's Harvard captain, finally terminated the dispute by declaring it "no game." Neither side was satisfied, and cries of "Wait till next year" were heard from New Haven to New Jersey.

1885

Princeton	(9-0-0)		Yale	(7-1-0)	
94	Stevens	0	55	Stevens	0
76	Stevens	0	18	Wesleyan	0
76	Penn	10	71	Wesleyan	0
80	Penn	10	51	MIT	0
64	Columbia Law School	0	52	Crescent Athletic Club	0
108	Johns Hopkins	0	53	Penn	5
76	Wesleyan	0	5	Princeton	6
6	Yale	5	61	Wesleyan	0
57	Penn	0			
637		25	366		11

The passing of a year had not diminished the strong feeling that Princeton and Yale fans both felt when their teams met for the national title. In the veteran Princeton line were captain Charles DeCamp at right end, tackles Bull Irvine and Bill Cook, Jim Adams at center, and guards Tracy Harris and Hector Cowan, a divinity student whose strongest oath, "Oh, sugar," always got a laugh from his teammates. In the backfield were fullback Henry Savage, right half Tilly Lamar, and quarterback Richard Hodge.

On the Yale team were captain Frank Peters at center, quarterback Harry Beecher, grandson of Henry Ward Beecher, end Bob Corwin, and two freshmen halfbacks, George Watkinson and Billy Bull, both good kickers. Other talented freshmen on the squad were Fred "Kid" Wallace at end, tackle Charley Gill, and George Woodruff, who came to practice wearing a straw hat and full beard. Just before the MIT game he shaved it off, and when Peters next saw Woodruff he didn't recognize him; it gradually dawned on Peters that the naked face in front of him was his star guard.

"Gad, Woodruff!" he said, "So that's what you look like."

Both teams were unhappy with the referee's decision of the previous year, and another long dispute followed until Princeton magnanimously selected Walter Camp of Yale as the sole official of the game. Camp's fairness was put to the test more than once during the contest. In the first half, Harry Beecher of Yale ran back a Princeton punt 45 yards for a touchdown, but Camp nullified the score when he ruled that Beecher had stepped out-of-bounds. After George Watkinson failed his third field goal attempt, he finally kicked one from 25 yards away for a 5-0 Yale lead. One of Yale's best plays was a reverse by Harry Beecher, but since the quarterback could not run with the ball until another player had touched it, the ball was handed back to Beecher by a guard.

Yale controlled the ball throughout the second half, but now they found themselves short of first-down yardage. With only six minutes to go, captain Peters, an early exponent of ball control whose motto was "Get the ball and keep it," decided to punt. It was a youthful mistake which was to cost them the game.

Watkinson boomed a long spiral punt downfield to safety men Savage, Lamar, and Henry Toler. Toler tried to field it on the short hop, but it bounced off his chest. Lamar came in from the right, grabbed the ball in midair at the 25, and headed for the left sideline. Lamar was famous for his bent-over running style and stiff-arm with which he vaulted around tacklers, but he had no need of that now. He cut sharply to avoid the Yale defenders converging on Toler and turned upfield.

Lamar raced toward the Yale goal 85 yards away. Following close behind him, Camp watched his flying feet as he tightroped down the sideline. At the 5-yard line, Peters dived at Lamar but missed. The Yale fans sat stunned at the sudden turn of events.

The Princeton crowd cascaded from the stands to congratulate their latest Saturday hero. They ripped Lamar's jersey from his back and gave the orange and black shreds to their ladies. When captain Peters pointed to the spot where he claimed Lamar stepped out-of-bounds, the New Haven faithful swarmed onto the field like angry bees. In the middle of the melee was Walter Camp, who once again ruled against his alma mater. During the chaotic scramble, Richard Hodge practiced kicking the goal after touchdown.

It took quite a while to get the crowd off the field. Yale could still win if Hodge missed the kick, but it was not to be. Hodge split the uprights and Yale was humbled, 6-5. It was the first defeat for the Blue in 48 games.

Just a game? Just a few college boys having some fun on an autumn afternoon? Frank Peters rolled on the ground in agony at the thought that he had cost Yale the game and the championship. At Princeton, Lamar was the hero of the hour and his run was retold many times around many hot stoves during the long winter.

Harvard had no team this year because it felt there were too many fights in football. Because of its stand, the rule on slugging was changed. Instead of being warned three times for use of fists, a player was put out of the game immediately for fighting. This season also saw a five-yard penalty for offside, the first time yardage was assessed for an infraction.

1886

Yale	(9-0-1)		Princeton	(7-0-1)	
75	Wesleyan	0	58	Stevens	0
62	Wesleyan	0	61	Stevens	6
96	MIT	0	30	Penn	0
54	Stevens	0	55	Penn	9
76	Williams	0	28	Penn	6
136	Wesleyan	0	12	Harvard	0
84	Crescent Athletic Club	0	76	Wesleyan	6
75	Penn	0	0	Yale	0
29	Harvard	4			
0	Princeton	0			
687		4	320		27

Harvard resumed play this season because new rules were instituted to make the game better. One rule said that all players on a college team must be regularly enrolled students. Another factor which brought the return of the Cantabrigians from Cambridge was that the last Princeton-Yale game was played in New Haven, and this year it was scheduled for the Princeton campus. This attracted the ladies in large numbers and made it a social event, complete with a box lunch and beverage, something the games at the Polo Grounds in New York hadn't been able to do in five tries.

Camp's integrity in last year's Princeton-Yale game had not gone unnoticed by Yale's opponents. Harvard's captain, William Brooks, selected Camp to be the referee, still the sole official, in this year's Harvard-Yale game. It didn't help much as Harvard went down to defeat, although Al Holden scored the only touchdown Yale gave up all season. The Crimson rolled up 765 points this year, the most ever made by a college team in a single campaign.

Harvard returned to the grid wars with a vengeance. In the Yale game, George Woodruff came back from Cambridge with a broken nose, and guard George Carter had a cut over his eye which needed eight stitches. Tackle Eddie Burke had both eyes closed and his lips cut to pieces. It had been his misfortune to play opposite Frank Remington, Harvard's heavyweight boxing champ.

Most of last year's Princeton and Yale veterans were back. Princeton captain Henry Savage had Hector Cowan at tackle, and a flashy newcomer in the backfield, Knowlton "Snake" Ames. Captain Bob Corwin had Yale's talented freshmen back from last year, plus two new men, halfback Ben Morison and Bill Wurtenberg at quarterback. Riding the bench was a baseball pitcher named Amos Alonzo Stagg, who got in briefly in the Penn game.

Earlier that year, Stagg hurled Yale to a baseball championship, and would make it five in a row before he devoted himself wholly to football.

The eastern championship and national title again was the last game of the year between Princeton and Yale. For the third time in three years, the contest was marked by lengthy disputes. They began when the game was delayed for two hours before a suitable referee could be found. The discord flared up again after Henry Savage deflected a field goal attempt by George Watkinson and Kid Wallace of Yale fell on it for a touchdown. The long argument over this play kept the game from being concluded. Even worse, a heavy rain fell throughout the day. George Watkinson played from start to finish with a fever and died as a result.

When darkness prevented further play, Yale was ahead, 4–0, with 20 minutes left. Referee Tracy Harris called the game, and a score of 0–0 was entered in the official records. In the last three years a single point separated the two teams, as Princeton made good on its goal after touchdown the previous year.

The goal after touchdown was also borrowed from rugby, for the ball was brought out from where it crossed the goal and put down as far back as the kicker wanted. If a touchdown was made near the sideline, the angle on the goal post could be very difficult. The team that scored had the option of a short puntout by one of their own men in order to get better position in front of the goal post. The team scored upon lined up on their goal and watched the scoring team make a free punt from behind the goal. The team that scored stood on the five-yard line and tried to keep the other team from interfering with the catch. A fair catch had to be made, and if the ball was dropped the conversion ended at that point. If the fair catch was made, the team that scored attempted a free kick from the spot where the catch was made.

Over the past few years the names for the positions of the players had taken shape. The man who charged from the outside was called an "end rush" and later simply end. The second man from the end was called "next to end" at first, but since many plays slanted over his position and he made most of the tackles, it was not long before he was called "tackler," and then tackle. In the middle of the line was the snapperback, or center, and the men who guarded him as he kicked the ball back were called guards. The name of the fullback, who played furthest back, was carried over from rugby. The quarterback played closest to the line, and the halfbacks played halfway back.

1887

Yale remained at the top in the annual battle for football supremacy, but this year the challenger was Harvard, not Princeton. The Crimson ruffled Princeton and Yale with lateral passes from quarterback Vic Harding to Joe Sears at fullback, between halfbacks Roland Boyden and Allie Porter, or from Porter to end Art Butler and back to Wilder Bancroft on the other end. Princeton lost both games to Harvard and Yale by the same score and found itself at the bottom of the Big Three for the first time.

Yale	(9-0-0)		Harvard	(10-1-0)	
38	Wesleyan	0	86	Tufts	0
106	Wesleyan	0	68	Exeter	0
74	Williams	0	62	MIT	0
50	Penn	0	52	Williams	6
74	Rutgers	0	98	Amherst	0
68	Crescent Athletic Club	0	68	Tufts	0
76	Wesleyan	4	54	Exeter	0
12	Princeton	0	110	Wesleyan	0
17	Harvard	8	12	Princeton	0
			42	Penn	0
			8	Yale	17
515		12	660		23

Football games were truly a battle at this time. There was no line charge to speak of, for players stood upright and shoved each other as they jockeyed for position or slugged it out with their fists. It was the heyday of the school boxing champ, and anyone who was ring-worthy was recruited for the football team. In one game, Yale tackle Sam Cross had arms which were black and blue from shoulder to wrist. There was no neutral zone between the opposing linemen, just an imaginary line separating them as they stood toe to toe, jaw to jaw, and eyeball to eyeball.

The lack of a neutral zone caused most of the arguments and fights. Lengthy discussions followed almost every decision by the referee, and players argued so much that one hardly knew who was captain. Most arguments were over someone supposedly being offside. There was so much accusation and pointing of fingers that it often took the quarterback a full minute just to get the ball snapped. Since there were no line sticks to keep track of the ball, the referee put down a handkerchief to mark its progress. A favorite diversion was to engage the referee in a mock discussion of the rules, while a teammate surreptitiously tried to move the handkerchief. Two officials, therefore, were used this year, a referee and an umpire. The referee's job was to handle decisions concerning the ball, while the umpire kept his eye on the players, usually to watch for slugging.

Most teams practiced every afternoon as they do now, often till dark. With no forward pass to concern them, an hour a day was devoted to scrimmage, which meant stopping a running play. The tackling was live body contact without a tackling dummy or a lineman's sled to push against. A great amount of time was spent on wind sprints and in racing downfield to cover a punt return. With this rigorous conditioning, the good teams simply wore down their opponents or outlasted them.

Games were usually played on Wednesdays and Saturdays. The kickoff didn't have to go at least ten yards, so the kick wasn't necessarily to the other team. Often the kicker nudged the ball with an "inch kick," and then tossed it to one of his backs who ran with the ball. The game was two halves of 45 minutes each, and once a player left the game he could not return. Injuries had to be serious before a player would leave the game, and the few substitutes each team had seldom got in the game.

In order to put the ball in play, signals were called at the line of scrimmage, usually by the quarterback. At first, the signals were key sentences, phrases, or words. Talking to various players in sequence or saying a few words about certain parts of the body were a clue to the play. Since there was no huddle, arm and foot movements were tried for a while. These did not work too well for the linemen, for they had to watch the quarterback instead of the man opposite them.

Equipment developed slowly, like the rest of the game. The uniform consisted of a jersey or a sweater, knee pants made of canvas, and shoes with leather strips across the soles to serve as cleats. A canvas jacket or vest tightly laced up the front was worn over the jersey. These canvas uniforms, invented by Ledou Smock, were called "smocks" after their inventor, while the players themselves were called canvasbacks. The snug fit of these canvas suits made them difficult to grab hold of during a game. Most players disdained protection of any kind, except for soft padding on the shoulders and elbows under the jersey.

Players let their hair grow long as football season neared. It was the only protection for the head other than a deep-fitting skull cap which came down to the ears. Caps, stockings, and jerseys were usually the same color as the school they represented.

1888

Yale (13-0-0)			Princeton (11-1-0)		
76	Wesleyan	0	65	Lehigh	0
65	Rutgers	0	31	Crescent Athletic Club	0
34	Penn	0	63	Penn	0
46	Wesleyan	0	80	Stevens	0
39	Amherst	0	80	Rutgers	0
30	Williams	0	38	Penn	0
68	MIT	0	82	Rutgers	0
69	Stevens	0	104	Johns Hopkins	0
58	Penn	0	44	Wesleyan	0
28	Crescent Athletic Club	0	4	Penn	0
70	Amherst	0	18	Harvard	6
105	Wesleyan	0	0	Yale	10
10	Princeton	0			
698		0	609		16

The Yale championship team of 1888. Back Row: Amos Alonzo Stagg, Billy Rhodes, George Woodruff, Pudge Heffelfinger, Charley Gill, Fred Wallace, Billy Bull. Front Row: Lee McClung, Bill Wurtenberg, Pa Corbin, Billy Graves.

Yale was the premier team of 1888. A main reason was Pudge Heffelfinger, who caught the eye of Pa Corbin while carrying the ball in freshman practice. Since Yale needed linemen more than they needed backs, captain Corbin tried him out at guard. They roughed him up by rubbing their canvas jackets across his face and kicking him in the shins. A gentle giant at 6'3" and almost 200 pounds, Pudge had to be told to get physical if he wanted to keep the job for good. He threw himself into the game and his opponents so well that he held the job for the next four years.

Other personnel on this championship squad were ends Fred Wallace and 157-pound Amos Alonzo Stagg, destined to become one of the game's greatest coaches. Another future coach who played on this team was guard George Woodruff. The tackles were Billy Rhodes and Charley Gill, with Pa Corbin at center. At quarterback was Bill Wurtenberg, the halfbacks were Lee "Bum" McClung and Billy Graves, with Billy Bull at fullback.

Pa Corbin got his name because he had reached the advanced age of 24 years, and his handlebar moustache gave him a cavalier authority his younger teammates could relate to. In those days, the captain had as much authority as the coach, especially on the field. Between classes, Corbin practiced snapping the ball with his foot to Bill Wurtenberg, and in the game he called plays from his center position. A tug on the belt meant a run over guard, touching his shoe laces indicated an end run, and a pull on the visor of his cap signaled a kick. First-year coach Walter Camp couldn't attend practice because of his job, so his wife, Allie, roamed up and down the sideline taking notes. Then the team met a few nights each week at the Camp home to discuss strategy.

Yale won 13 games and was unbeaten, untied, and unscored on. They scored 126 touchdowns, and had a two-year winning streak of 22 straight games. In nine of the 13 games, no substitutes were used. The Penn game early in the season was followed by a game with Wesleyan three days later, and the games with Amherst and Williams were played on successive days. MIT, Stevens, and the second Penn game were all played within ten days.

In the title game with Yale, Princeton used its V-formation which it had tried off-and-on for over four years. Yale met the wedge by hitting the lead man of the V in the jaw with the heel of their hands. When Heffelfinger jumped on the V in a flying leap with his knees doubled up, it collapsed and fell apart.

"Hey you, you big moose," shouted Hector Cowan, Princeton's all–American tackle, "you're going to kill somebody!"

"I'll quit," Pudge yelled, "if you stop using that V wedge!" Neither side stopped, so they continued to batter each other.

The Tigers countered by holding their hands aloft to cushion Pudge's airborne body. No touchdowns were made in the lusty game which followed, but Billy Bull's accurate left toe was good on a pair of drop-kick field goals for a win and the championship for Yale.

In addition to the moleskin pants, a mouse-colored cotton fabric that replaced canvas pants this year, two rules appeared that changed the game for the next few years. One rule allowed tackling below the waist as far as the knees, and the other rule, intended to stop slugging, made offensive linemen keep their arms at their sides. Both rules had the same result. Teams which had lined up in a spread formation across the field in rugby fashion now bunched together in close formation. The wide-open game of long lateral passes to the halfbacks disappeared, and so did the defensive ends who played wide in order to turn the play toward the middle. The close formation of the linemen also made it more difficult for the center to snap the ball with his foot.

Backfield men also lined up in a tight T-formation. Since it was easier to bring down a ball carrier by tackling him below the waist, long gains in the open field were greatly curtailed. Mass formation plays intended to bludgeon the defense with heavy blocking in front of the ball carrier took center stage for the next decade. George Woodruff tried to focus power at the point of attack even further. He pulled out of the line to run interference for the ball carrier and became the first pulling guard.

1889

Princeton	(10-0-0)		Yale	(15-1-0)	
16	Lehigh	0	38	Wesleyan	0
16	Lehigh	4	63	Wesleyan	5
49	Stevens	0	36	Williams	0
72	Penn	4	60	Cornell	6
98	Wesleyan	0	42	Amherst	0
71	Columbia	0	64	Trinity	0
41	Harvard	15	62	Columbia	0
54	Orange Athletic Club	6	22	Penn	10
10	Yale	0	30	Stevens	0
57	Washington, DC All-Stars	0	18	Crescent Athletic Club	0
			70	Cornell	0
			32	Amherst	0
			70	Cornell	0
			32	Amherst	0
			70	Williams	0
			52	Wesleyan	0
			6	Harvard	0
			0	Princeton	10
484		29	665		31

After eliminating Harvard on a last-half win in which Snake Ames scored on punt returns of 70 and 50 yards and set up another on a 105-yard runback, Princeton took on Yale for the title. The game was played on a neutral site, usually the old Polo Grounds at 110th Street and Fifth Avenue in New York City. Because the Polo Grounds were not available, the game was moved to Berkeley Oval across the Harlem River in the Bronx, a short distance away.

A heavy rain during the night turned the field into a swamp. By the time the Penn-Wesleyan game was finished, which was played there that morning, the muck was ankle deep. The hastily built bleachers, constructed to seat 15,000, were not used because they had not been approved by the building inspector, and the 1,000 hardy souls who bought tickets had to stand along the sidelines.

A sea of mud outside the narrow entrance permitted only two people at a time to enter, and in trying to navigate the ooze the spectators overturned two ticket booths. As game-time drew near the gates were jammed, and latecomers had to climb over the fence. In the confusion, women were knocked down and hats and umbrellas were stepped on and mashed. The goal posts at each end of the field, which stood on the goal line in those days, emerged from a few inches of water like marking buoys in the bay. Some spectators kept their shoes and billfolds dry by sitting in nearby trees.

After the kickoff Princeton tried to use its V-formation, but they bogged down in the wet field. The game became a punting duel between Herb McBride of Yale and Snake Ames of Princeton, who kept Yale backed up with his end-over-end punts. The Tigers also showed Yale a fake punt in the first half, the first seen anywhere. After Ames dropped back to punt, the ball was handed to Bob Channing, who started through Charley Gill's tackle slot. Gill tackled Channing as he went by, but when Gill held up on his charge after that, it allowed Ames to get away his punts.

Edgar Allan Poe, Princeton's 150-pound quarterback and a grand-nephew of the poet, knocked Bum McClung out of the game on a block-buster collision. After a 45-yard run by Ames, he missed a drop-kick field goal, and the first half ended scoreless.

In the second half Ames made another long run, but he was tackled on the 15-yard line by Lon Stagg. Yale held, then failed to move the ball, and punted out of danger. Ames snaked his way to the goal on the return, but fumbled as he was hit. Three Elis failed to collar the ball in the mud, and Princeton end Ralph Warren, who replaced Elwood Wagenhurst when he became ineligible, recovered it for a touchdown. Yale halfback Perry Harvey tried the middle behind center Bert Hanson and guard Ashbel Newell, but could not gain any yardage. Princeton scored once more to win the game and the title, and another Yale win streak was over at 37 games. It was not a good day for Handsome Dan, the bulldog, who became Yale's mascot that year.

Joining quarterback Poe and fullback Ames on the Princeton championship team was halfback Bob Channing, all three of them all–American this year. The other halfback for the Tigers was Jerry Black. In the line were two more all–Americans, gorilla-armed, granite-jawed tackle Hector Cowan and mustachioed center Bill George. The guards were Hugh "House" Janeway and captain Jesse Riggs, who played Heffelfinger even up at Berkeley Oval. At the other tackle was Walter "Monte" Cash, who brought a deck of cards from his Wyoming ranch. On the ends were Ralph Warren and Ben "Sport" Donnelly, a trickster who threw mud in an opponent's eyes and then hollered, "Referee!" The official turned just in time to see Donnelly take a punch from his victim, who was usually ejected from the game. This was the fate of fiery Billy Rhodes of Yale, who took Donnelly's bait in the game and was asked to leave the premises, a turning point in the contest.

"After the game in the early days," Richard Harding Davis later reported in *Harper's Weekly,* "all the students massed in Koster and Bial's Music Hall, then in Twenty-third Street, and packed it so that after nine o'clock a man who wished to leave had to be passed over the heads of the crowd, and this the crowd would do for him with cheerful alacrity."

An All-America college football team was selected for the first time this year. It was the brainchild of Caspar Whitney, a sportswriter for a New York magazine called *The Week's Sport.* Whitney shared his idea with Walter Camp, and Camp's selections from then on became the final word. The first All-America team appeared, then as now, at the end of the year. All the players were from the Big Three. Harvard and Yale each had three men on the team, while Princeton had five. Players from the Big Three dominated the All-America team for the next decade. Of the 121 players chosen from 1889 to 1899, 97 were from Harvard, Princeton, and Yale, and 21 from Penn.

The others were from Cornell, Chicago, and Carlisle, each with one man.

Numerical signals also began to replace word signals and hand signals this year. They are still being used to this day, with variations. Each play was assigned a certain number. For example, a run by the left halfback around right end might be play number 12. To keep the other team from understanding the signals being called, play 12 could be 3-3-6, 3-4-5, or 2-8-2. A player had to be on his toes and add quickly, but as long as the numbers totaled 12, it was left halfback around right end. A separate number told the team when the ball would be snapped, and rhythm quickly developed so that each player could feel the cadence and move at the same time. Some teams even held signal drills at night in order to perfect their timing and execution. As signals became more complex, rival clubs spent much time and effort trying to break the other team's code.

1890

Harvard (11-0-0)			Yale (13-1-0)		
41	Exeter	0	8	Wesleyan	0
43	Dartmouth	0	18	Crescent Athletic Club	6
74	Amherst	6	34	Wesleyan	0
38	Williams	0	26	Lehigh	0
64	Dartmouth	0	40	Trinity	0
54	Bowdoin	0	16	Orange Athletic Club	0
55	Wesleyan	0	36	Williams	0
77	Cornell	0	12	Amherst	0
33	Orange Athletic Club	0	76	Wesleyan	0
64	Amherst	0	52	Crescent Athletic Club	0
12	Yale	6	70	Rutgers	0
			60	Penn	0
			6	Harvard	12
			32	Princeton	0
555		12	486		18

A new champion was crowned this year as Harvard was the top team of the Big Three. The driving force behind the team was captain Arthur Cumnock, who was determined to beat Yale. He kept his players in shape with calisthenics all year long, and started new ideas such as spring practice and a tackling dummy. Cumnock also designed the first nose guard, which Edgar Allan Poe wore in the Princeton-Yale game later in the year. Like the Princeton-Yale games played in New York, the games between Harvard and Yale were also played on a neutral site, usually at Hampden Park in Springfield, Massachusetts, halfway between Cambridge and New Haven.

The Cantabs put together a powerful team, many of them all–Americans. The backfield had halfbacks John Corbett and Everett Lake, with lettermen Dudley Dean at quarterback, halfback Jimmy Lee, and fullback Bernie Trafford, who drop-kicked a record-five field goals against Cornell. The mowing-machine line was equally tough on offense or defense. In addition to Cumnock, who played guard and end, there were center John Cranston, guards Perry Trafford and Jim Finlay, tackles Joshua Upton and Jim Alward, end Frank Hallowell, and everyone's all–American, Marshall "Ma" Newell.

Newell was the first of only four men to make all–American four times. He played tackle at 166 pounds, but he had a long torso and short legs, which gave him a strong leg drive. With his short limbs, Newell was cat-quick off the line and used his hands in short jabs to neutralize opposing linemen, after which he dropped the ball carrier with a sure-handed tackle. Off the field Newell was a pussycat, for he got his nickname "Ma" by counseling lonely freshmen away from home for the first time.

During the first half, the Elis had an edge over Harvard, but as the game progressed the superlative Crimson line began to wear down the Blues. Ma Newell tore through the line time after time to tackle the Yale backs before they got under way. Near the end of the half Yale drove down to the Harvard goal, but they were stopped again. Captain Cumnock shut the door on a sure touchdown for the Elis when he crashed into Heffelfinger and then nailed the man with the ball, Bum McClung.

Two long runs on two miscues won the game for Harvard in the second half. On the first turnover, Jimmy Lee picked up a Yale fumble and dashed 40 yards to a touchdown. Moments later, Dudley Dean knocked the ball loose from the Yale quarterback at midfield, scooped it up and ran for a touchdown. In a matter of minutes, this tooth-and-nail contest turned into a 12-0 Harvard lead.

Yale got going on a 60-yard march to get back in the ball game, with McClung scoring on a 10-yard burst to make it 12–6. Soon after, Ben Morison was racing for the tying touchdown on a 40-yard sprint around end. Heffelfinger was out in front leading interference as Trafford and Dean moved up to tackle Morison. Pudge could only block one of them. With just a split second in which to react, he took out Dean while Trafford brought Morison down. It was the last gasp of the Elis, and Harvard won it all, 12–6.

It was only the third game Yale had lost in the last eight years, twice to Princeton in 1885 and 1889, and now to Harvard. Yale captain Billy Rhodes was so heartbroken that he never saw another Harvard-Yale game as long as he lived. Years later, he would pace the lobby of the Massasoit House in Springfield with a ticket in his pocket while the game was going on.

Heffelfinger added a new dimension to the game this year. George Woodruff, who had played in the line with Pudge, showed him the benefits of a pulling guard as a blocker. Heffelfinger took it one step further and became the first pulling guard to cut back through tackle on the other side of the center. Bum McClung, who followed Pudge through the hole, became the first ball carrier to fake an end run and then cut back over tackle. It was Heffelfinger's downfield interference for Morison which almost tied the score in the final minutes of the Harvard game.

Another change took place as close line play made it difficult for the center to snap the ball with his foot. It now became legal for him to roll it to the quarterback with his hand instead of snapping it with his toe, as everyone did up to that point.

As blocking and tackling became more refined, Stagg, who was now coaching football at the YMCA in Springfield, Massachusetts, invented the ends back formation. He had both of his ends drop back in a double wing formation, but instead of blocking on the defensive tackle, the ends blocked for the ball carrier on mass interference plays. The end was also used as a ball carrier on the end-around, or gave it to a halfback on a reverse, or as it was called in those days, a crisscross. Another Stagg invention this year was the 7-2-2 defense, also called a seven-box defense. Stagg had two defensive men, or linebackers, play behind the line in order to back it up on running plays.

It was also in 1890 that cadet Dennis Michie approached his father about a challenge he had received. His father was Peter Michie, professor of Natural and Experimental Philosophy at the United States Military Academy in West Point, New York. As the senior professor, he was Dean of the Academic Board and chairman of its meetings. The challenge was not an ordinary one, for the Naval Academy had challenged West Point to a football game.

Professor Michie, who was killed in the battle of San Juan Hill, had all he could do to get the approval of the board and Academy superintendent, Colonel John W. Wilson, but it was done. The real struggle was ahead, however, for Army did not have a football team and had never played a game with another school, while Navy had played four years. Under these circumstances the outcome was predictable and Army lost, 24–0. But a return match was scheduled next year, and the great Army-Navy series was born.

1891

Yale was back at the top this year with its best team to date. From end to end the Yale line was a row of smoking volcanoes weighing an average of 176 pounds. Over center was George Sanford, Pudge Heffelfinger and Stan Morison on each side of him as guards, Ham Wallis and Wallie Winter at the tackles, with Frank Hinkey and John Hartwell at the terminals. At quarterback was Frank Barbour (148 pounds), a soft-spoken leader whose constant jokes kept a lid on his fire-breathing forwards. The fullback was Vance McCormick (159 pounds), and the halfbacks were Laurie Bliss (150 pounds) and captain Bum McClung (155 pounds).

Yale was unbeaten, untied, and unscored on in 13 games this year. Beginning with the last game of 1890 in which Princeton was beaten, 32–0, Yale now had a string of 14 consecutive shutouts. With four good running backs, and guard Stan Morison who often dropped back to carry the ball, the Blue also had a good offense. Much of their yardage was gained by Laurie Bliss, who ran behind Heffelfinger's bull-like blasts. Pushing and pulling the runners were permitted, so Bliss held on to the ring attached to Pudge's belt and was hauled through the line.

Yale	(13-0-0)		Harvard	(13-1-0)	
28	Wesleyan	0	16	Dartmouth	0
26	Crescent Athletic Club	0	17	Exeter	0
36	Trinity	0	18	Amherst	0
46	Williams	0	26	MIT	0
28	Springfield YMCA	0	26	Williams	0
36	Orange Athletic Club	0	76	Andover	0
38	Lehigh	0	39	Amherst	0
70	Crescent Athletic Club	0	79	Bowdoin	0
76	Wesleyan	0	34	Springfield YMCA	0
27	Amherst	0	124	Wesleyan	0
48	Penn	0	44	Springfield YMCA	4
10	Harvard	0	38	Trinity	0
19	Princeton	0	51	Boston Athletic Association	12
			0	Yale	10
488		0	588		26

One good reason for Yale's goose-egg defense was a freshman end named Frank Hinkey, in the first of his four years as all–American. At 5'9" and 150 pounds, Hinkey was an anemic-looking individual who wouldn't catch your eye on the street, but old-timers were in unanimous agreement that on the field, pound-for-pound, he was the greatest of them all. Off the field he was sullen, reserved, and even gruff, but in a game he released his repressions like an avenging angel.

Instead of fighting off the blockers, Hinkey had a way of sifting through the interference, as Walter Camp said, "like a disembodied spirit." He would squat low in front of a play so that the interference slipped over him. Then he would grab the runner's knees, turn him in midair, and throw him to the grass with a thud that rattled his teeth. Even his teammates avoided his end in practice, and in a game many runners made a deal with Hinkey not to finish his whiplike tackle when they cried down. He had the defensive lineman's ability to smell out a play and was rarely fooled, and his tackles were as sure as the grip of the Yale bulldog on the sideline.

Penn had a man on the All-America team for the first time, center John Adams. Harvard and Princeton both had strong teams, and Princeton was not scored on until they played Yale. Both of them lost to Yale, and the Elis were champion once more.

Amos Alonzo Stagg was back to coach the Springfield YMCA again this year. Since the rules stated that only one man had to be on the line of scrimmage, Stagg took his ends' back play one step further. He moved the entire line into the backfield in a turtleback formation except for the center. When the ball was snapped to a ball carrier inside the oval-shaped backfield, it moved ahead in a mass or around the end. The interference peeled off one at a time as they met the defense, and the ball carrier finally emerged for a short gain. It was the ultimate in mass football play and football at its worst.

A variation of the turtleback play called for one of the men who peeled off to remain on the ground with the ball until the turtleback had moved across the field. Then the downed man would get up and run with the ball since it was allowed by the rules. Down in those days meant held down. Since Stagg was a Christian who took his religious experience seriously and led his team in prayer before each game, this hidden ball play on the ground brought forth a barrage of uncomplimentary remarks by Stagg's opponents, who thought it beneath him.

Due to the cold weather in December, Stagg's Springfield team played in one of the first indoor football games at Madison Square Garden in New York the previous year. Ever the innovator, his team returned in 1891 to play in the first night football game there. After football season was over, another worker in the Springfield YMCA, James Naismith, nailed up some peach baskets in the gym and invented basketball.

1892

Yale	(13-0-0)		Harvard	(10-1-0)	
6	Wesleyan	0	48	Dartmouth	0
28	Crescent Athletic Club	0	62	Exeter	0
32	Williams	0	26	Amherst	0
22	Manhattan Athletic Club	0	55	Williams	0
29	Amherst	0	40	Boston Athletic Association	0
58	Orange Athletic Club	0	32	Chicago Athletic Club	0
50	Springfield YMCA	0	34	MIT	0
44	Tufts	0	32	Amherst	10
72	Wesleyan	0	20	Cornell	14
48	New York Athletic Club	0	16	Boston Athletic Association	12
28	Penn	0	0	Yale	6
6	Harvard	0			
12	Princeton	0			
435		0	365		42

After a slow start against Wesleyan, coached by former Yale fullback, Billy Bull, the Elis were again unbeaten, untied, and unscored on. For the second year in a row, Yale won all 13 of its games, and stretched its winning and unscored on string to 27 straight. Phil Stillman was now at center, the guards were Jim McCrea and William "Wild Bill" Hickok, Wallie Winter and Ham Wallis were still the tackles, and on the ends were John Greenway and the incomparable Frank Hinkey. Captain Vance McCormick was now quarterback, at fullback was Frank Butterworth, and the halfbacks were Laurie Bliss and his brother, Cliff.

In the line on captain Bernie Trafford's Harvard team were all–Americans at almost every position. At guard was Bert Waters, Marshall Newell was back at tackle, Frank Hallowell was at end, and at center was William Henry Lewis, the first black to be honored as an all–American. The backfield also boasted an all–American of its own, halfback Charley Brewer.

Harvard was unbeaten in ten straight games when it met Yale for the championship. The highlight of the game was Harvard's flying wedge, an outgrowth of the Princeton V-formation. It was invented by Lorin Deland, who never played football but enjoyed the game for its technical aspects. The flying wedge added momentum to the mass-formation play.

Harvard saved its flying wedge for the start of the second half against Yale. Bernie Trafford, the Harvard captain, stood with the ball in the middle of the field to form the apex of the V. Nearest Trafford were the slowest men in the V, positioned 15 yards away and about halfway to the sideline on both sides. The fastest men were near the two ends of the V about 25 yards away. When Trafford waved his hand, both sides of the V moved obliquely forward toward Trafford at the apex.

At the precise moment, Trafford inch-kicked the ball and tossed it to Charley Brewer, the runner inside the V-formation. The flying wedge bowled over the Yale men until Brewer was dragged down at the 15-yard line. Yale held near its goal, mainly because the living flame, Frank Hinkey, made tackles everywhere.

The Crimson didn't score, but the flying wedge became the accepted way of kicking off during the next year. Laurie Bliss skirted end for the game's only score in a 6–0 win when injuries forced Harvard's right tackle, Joshua Upton, and right end, Bob Emmons, from the game. Both of them were carried off the field after they had been given a pop by Frank Hinkey.

The surprise team of the year was Penn, now coached by ex–Yale guard George Woodruff. They won 15 games, beat Princeton for the first time, 6–4, and lost only to Yale. Led by captain Charles Schoff at end, the Quakers had a man on the All-America team for the second year in a row, fullback Harry Thayer.

One of Woodruff's surprises was the quick kick, sometimes called the quarterback kick or onside punt. It was a legitimate play if the backfield was behind the quarterback when he punted the ball, for then they could recover it downfield and maintain possession. The play was really a forward pass with the foot, and some punters were so good at it that the backs could run a dozen yards downfield and catch the ball before it touched the ground. Try that on your granddad's double-bell euphonium! It was first used by Bucky Vail against Lafayette in November, and later in the month against Wesleyan on Thanksgiving Day.

As the game spread west across the country, many ex-college players went with it. One young man who went west was ex–Yale star Alonzo Stagg, who became coach at the newly-opened University of Chicago. Another

man who went west was ex–Yale quarterback Frank Barbour, who helped
upgrade an already growing program at Michigan. John Heisman took over
at Oberlin, where his team won six of seven starts. At Purdue, ex–Princeton
fullback Snake Ames found the quickest success. His 1891 team beat four
opponents easily and was unscored on. This year's squad won all eight
games, surrendered only 24 points while scoring 320, most of them by halfback Bill Finney and fullback Jimmy Studebaker.

1893

Princeton	(11-0-0)			Yale	(10-1-0)	
20	Lafayette	0		18	Brown	0
12	Lehigh	0		16	Crescent Athletic Club	0
26	Crescent Athletic Club	0		28	Dartmouth	0
8	Lawrenceville	4		52	Amherst	0
46	Cornell	0		50	Orange Athletic Club	0
28	Lehigh	6		82	Williams	0
76	Wesleyan	0		28	Army	0
4	Penn	0		42	New York Athletic Club	0
8	Orange Athletic Club	0		14	Penn	6
36	Army	4		6	Harvard	0
6	Yale	0		0	Princeton	6
270		14		336		12

Yale's string of unscored on games reached 35 straight, the longest
on record. All the linemen in this tight-fisted defense were back except the
tackles, where Fred Murphy and Anson Beard now knocked heads. At quarterback was George Adee, and halfback Brinck Thorne added power to the
running attack. Frank Hinkey was still at defensive left end where most of
the traffic was. He was also captain, and his flaming spirit put brimstone into
the backbone of his men.

Shutout number 34 was over the Military Academy in a game at West
Point, Yale's first meeting with the Cadets. Army end Butler Ames replied
in like manner to Hinkey's aggressive style of play, and they exchanged
punches on several occasions. The academy superintendent saw the fisticuffs
and ordered the bugler to sound recall. Everyone in the military snapped to
attention, including the players on the field.

"Mr. Ames!" bellowed the commandant. "Mr. Ames, if you hit that
man again, sir, I'll put you in the guardhouse!"

Then he directed his gaze at Hinkey. "And you man, you man, if you
hit Mr. Ames again, sir, I'll put you off the Post."

The bugler blew again and play resumed.

It was not until the ninth game of the year that a surging Penn team,
behind 10–0, scored the first points Yale had allowed in almost three years.
As Mitchell Rosengarten and Charles Upton protected the flanks, Penn

switched to its flying wedge formation and made the touchdown against Yale's miserly defense look easy. Win Osgood, Art Knipe, and captain Harry Mackey ripped off huge chunks of yardage to narrow it to 10–6. After Brinck Thorne was injured, Hinkey moved to halfback and scored again for the win. The casualties numbered five for Penn and 12 for Yale, including Frank Butterworth, who had teethmarks on his back.

Princeton had its best team so far. Lining up for them were captain Tom "Doggie" Trenchard at end, halfbacks Frank Morse and Bill Ward, tackle Augustus Holly, guard Knox Taylor, and its trio of three-time all–Americans, 5'7", 190-pound Phil King at quarter, tackle Langdon "Biff" Lea, and guard Arthur "Beef" Wheeler. Led by this herculean host, Princeton met Yale for the championship.

The Princeton-Yale title game was played at Hamilton Park, later the new Polo Grounds under Coogan's Bluff in New York. It was the game of the century, and the seats around the field were packed with those infected by the autumn madness. It was also standing room only on the switchback path up Deadhead Hill, as the Bluff was called. Hundreds stood on every level spot up the Bluff, and a few watched from the Victorian houses at the top.

Princeton made good use of Stagg's ends back formation, as they ground out one first down after another with their massed interference. The contest was so rough that Hinkey was carried from the field after a collision with Jim Blake, the Princeton fullback. It was the only time Hinkey was ever helped off the field, although he later returned with a bandaged head.

Since they couldn't turn Hinkey's end with their ends back play, the Tigers used a charade. As Phil King gave Biff Lea an apparent tongue lashing, Hinkey stood entranced. On the sideline, Frank Morse was tying his shoe. In a flash, Dave Balliet centered the ball. King quickly threw a lateral to Morse, and the sleeper play was born. Morse caught the lateral and raced 50 yards downfield before he was overtaken by Frank Butterworth. It was one of the two times in Hinkey's career that anyone ever made a yard around his end. The Tigers later scored to win the game, and Princeton was the 1893 champion. It was the first and only time that Hinkey was to know defeat on a Yale team, and the loss also ended another Yale winning streak at 37 games.

As a result of the Princeton V, ends back, turtleback, and the flying wedge, 1893 was the roughest year in college football to date. Mass-momentum plays, especially on the kickoff, degenerated the game to resemble a streamroller moving in a cloud of dust. The Penn-Yale game was so rough that it was not renewed until 1925, and the Army-Navy game was cancelled for five years. To protect themselves in these savage games, many players began to wear ear muffs and shin guards for the first time.

1894

Yale	(16-0-0)		Pennsylvania	(12-0-0)	
42	Trinity	0	34	Franklin & Marshall	0
28	Brown	0	66	Swarthmore	0
10	Crescent Athletic Club	0	22	Crescent Athletic Club	0
23	Williams	4	46	Georgetown	0
34	Lehigh	0	30	Lehigh	0
34	Dartmouth	0	18	Crescent Athletic Club	10
24	Orange Athletic Club	0	14	Virginia	6
23	Boston Athletic Association	0	12	Navy	0
12	Army	5	26	Lafayette	0
42	Volunteer Athletic Club	0	12	Princeton	0
12	Brown	0	6	Cornell	0
67	Tufts	0	18	Harvard	4
50	Lehigh	0			
48	Chicago Athletic Club	0			
12	Harvard	4			
24	Princeton	0			
485		13	304		20

Because of the brutality in college football, Harvard, Yale, Princeton, and Penn met at the end of the 1893 season to revise the rules. The result outlawed the flying wedge and V-formation, and a kickoff had to travel ten yards unless touched by an opponent. Playing time was also shortened from two 45-minute halves to equal halves of 35 minutes each. A linesman was added to keep track of the time, while the referee marked the progress of the ball, and the umpire watched the players.

The new rules had done away with mass-momentum formations, so inventive coaches now filled their playbooks with mass-interference plays. Foremost of these was the guards-back formation of George Woodruff at Penn. He used a five-man line with both guards lined up behind one end and behind each other in a right angle to the line. The right or left end formed the point of the angle, and it moved like a plow no matter which way the play went. In this alignment, the backs were in a T-formation. When the backfield lined up in a wishbone formation, the guards were put in front of the halfbacks. Either way, it was a ferocious alignment which had five backs to block for the ball carrier.

The guards-back offense was used for the first time against Princeton at the Trenton Fair Grounds, and the guards who made it go were Buck Wharton and Wiley Woodruff. When they were in front of halfbacks Win Osgood and Art Knipe, their attack was a terror. At quarterback was Carl Williams, a master of the onside punt.

Woodruff was also the first to have the defensive end play close to the tackle. Most ends still spread wide in rugby style to turn the play in. Woodruff had them play tight, take on the blockers, and let a halfback turn the play in or get the runner.

Another coach with a mass-interference play was Alonzo Stagg of Chicago, who employed it in the Michigan game on Thanksgiving Day. Stagg

Left: Chicago's first all–American, Clarence Herschberger. Right: Yale's four-time all–American, Frank Hinkey.

also used a five-man line, but he pulled his tackles back instead of the guards. Each tackle lined up behind a guard for added blocking, especially on power plays through the line.

The Chicago-Michigan game this year also saw the use of an onside kickoff, or dribble kick, for the first time. In Stagg's play, Chicago captain Charles "Warhorse" Allen ran,at the ball as if to kick it deep, but then kicked it gently. First-year man Clarence Herschberger fielded it near the sideline after it went ten yards and carried it to the Michigan 22 before he was downed.

Lon Stagg was also the first to have his quarterback, Frank Hering, take the ball from center in a standing position instead of a low squat. Hering, whose big hands allowed him to grip the ball, was the first to use a sleeper play on the kickoff, a play in which a lateral is thrown across the field to gain more yards.

Stagg took his bride of three months to the coast in December where his team beat Stanford in the first intersectional game, 24–4. Two of Stagg's pioneer squad played, lineman Andy Wyant who never missed a minute in three years, and backfield man Henry Gale.

Back for their final year at Yale were all–Americans Frank Butterworth at fullback, Wild Bill Hickok at guard, center Phil Stillman, and captain Frank Hinkey at end. Yale had one of its best years, winning all 16 contests, an all-time record, and was national champion. Penn was also undefeated, winning 12 times in 12 starts, and was regarded by many as the titleholder.

The Harvard-Yale game was the most brutal in the roughest year in college football. Harvard tackle Bob Hallowell's nose was broken, and halfback Edgar Wrightington had a broken collarbone. Frank Butterworth of Yale received a severe eye injury, and tackle Fred Murphy was out cold for five hours in a Springfield hospital after being taken from the field unconscious. In this game, known as the Hampden Park bloodbath, both teams had four regulars hurt, and the game was cancelled for two years.

In the South, Dr. William L. Dudley of Vanderbilt organized the Southern Intercollegiate Athletic Conference, and was its first president for 20 years. Forerunner of the Southern and Southeastern conferences, its charter members were Alabama, Georgia, Georgia Tech, North Carolina, Sewanee, and Vanderbilt.

1895

Pennsylvania (14-0-0)			Yale (13-0-2)		
40	Swarthmore	0	8	Trinity	0
40	Bucknell	0	4	Brown	0
42	Franklin & Marshall	0	26	Union	0
32	Crescent Athletic Club	0	36	Amherst	0
54	Lehigh	0	8	Crescent Athletic Club	2
36	Carlisle	0	26	Dartmouth	0
54	Virginia	0	24	Orange Athletic Club	12
30	Duquesne Athletic Club	0	54	Williams	0
30	Lafayette	0	0	Boston Athletic Club	0
12	Brown	0	32	Dartmouth	0
12	Chicago Athletic Club	4	28	Army	8
35	Penn State	4	18	Carlisle	0
17	Harvard	14	6	Brown	6
46	Cornell	2	26	Orange Athletic Club	0
			20	Princeton	10
480		24	316		38

In the spring of the year, Princeton and Yale invited Harvard and Penn to join in taking the barbarity of mass plays out of the game. The four schools could not agree. Harvard and Penn wanted to keep mass formations, especially Penn, which was having so much success with its guards-back formation, but Princeton and Yale wanted to abolish them. Two sets of rules prevailed, one followed by Harvard and Penn, and the other adhered to by Yale, Princeton, and Cornell, which sided with the latter two.

There was also concern about the game's ferocity in the Midwest, especially since the leaders in the East were divided among themselves. Seven schools — Chicago, Illinois, Lake Forest, Minnesota, Northwestern, Purdue, and Wisconsin — met and adopted rules to clean up the game. Disagreement also prevailed at this meeting, for the rules were not accepted by all. Nothing was done, and football limped into another season.

Penn continued to win under George Woodruff. Led by its two all-Americans, center Al Bull and end Charley Gelbert, famous for his blond moustache and long hair, Penn was unbeaten and untied in 14 games. Woodruff was the first to use the delayed buck this year, a play in which the quarterback faked to one back going by, then gave the ball to a second back running into the line.

The closest game Penn had this year was with Harvard. The Crimson scored three touchdowns to Penn's two, but on the kick after touchdown, Harvard was able to convert only one of three tries. George Brooke converted after both of Penn's touchdowns and added a field goal to provide the winning margin, 17–14.

George Brooke was a chief reason for Penn's success. Last year's Cornell punter, Billy Ohl, said Brooke was "adept at the ordinary end-over-end punt." Brooke coined the phrase, "coffin corner," for with his tumbling punts he consistently rolled the ball out-of-bounds at the corner of the goal near the sideline. Playing in the shadow of their own goal posts, Penn's opponents were shut out 19 times in two years.

At the end of the year, Penn had a 26-game winning streak. Many considered last year's Quaker team to be national champs, but this year there was no doubt they were numero uno.

Yale was also unbeaten but tied twice, once by Brown, 6–6, and once by the Boston Athletic Club, 0–0. The scoreless match was the first time that Yale had ever failed to score at home.

Cornell was the first team outside the Big Four to place a man on the All-America team, as quarterback Clint Wyckoff made it this year. Two men who later became great coaches took their expertise south this same year. Wyckoff's teammate and captain at Cornell, Glenn S. Warner, called "Pop" because he was older than the rest of the team, began at Georgia. John Heisman, who played at Penn in 1890 and 1891, became head coach at Auburn.

Heisman was already applying his fertile mind to the game. In his first coaching job at Oberlin in 1892, he used the quarterback at safety on defense, the first to do so. At Akron the next year, he had the center toss the ball to the quarterback on the snap instead of rolling it to him as many teams did the past few years. One of Heisman's plays at Auburn this year was a variation of Stagg's hidden ball play. Instead of the runner lying on the ground as Stagg had him do, Walker Tichenor, the quarterback, hid the ball under his jersey at the start of a mass-formation play. When the massed interference moved away, Tichenor, who was tying his shoe, ran for a score.

One play which impressed Heisman this year was an illegal forward pass in the Georgia-North Carolina game. The Carolina punter couldn't get the kick away, so he threw the ball forward to get rid of it. A teammate caught it and ran for the game's only score, which was allowed because the referee had not seen the ball thrown. Heisman, however, saw that the forward pass was the play needed to end the rut brought by mass interference.

At the end of the season, the seven members of the Western Conference again met to draw up rules. Lake Forest dropped out, and Michigan replaced them in next year's first scheduled games.

1896

Princeton	(10-0-1)		Lafayette	(11-0-1)	
44	Rutgers	0	44	Volunteer Athletic Club	0
0	Lafayette	0	0	Princeton	0
16	Lehigh	0	18	Virginia	0
22	Carlisle	6	6	Virginia	0
11	Army	0	34	Virginia	0
48	Virginia	0	6	Penn	4
39	Penn State	0	18	Dickinson	0
46	Lawrenceville	0	17	Bloomsburg	0
37	Cornell	0	23	Wyoming Seminary	0
12	Harvard	0	38	Franklin & Marshall	0
24	Yale	6	18	Wesleyan	0
			18	Navy	6
299		12	240		10

In the summer of 1896, the Big Four in the East met again and came to an agreement on the rules. The heart of the reform tried to eliminate mass-formation plays. One new rule stated that five men had to be on the line of scrimmage, and another said that no player on offense could take more than one step without coming to a full stop before the ball was put in play. These rules did not end mass-formation plays, but they slowed them down and were a big step in the right direction.

The power in the Big Four this year was Princeton. Harvard, Yale, and Princeton still used the system in which the team was coached by the alumni. This year's coach was Phil King, who used a variation of the ends back formation which had taken Princeton to the title when he was quarterback in 1893. It was called the revolving tandem, an alignment which used the blocking power of the ends back with the turtleback added to it. In King's tandem formation, the right end played back and blocked inside the right tackle. The left tackle pulled out of the line and teamed with the right end to create a hole for the runner. It not only used the mass interference of the ends back formation, but the quick-moving turtleback made it difficult to know who had the ball.

Some say the Princeton team of 1896 was the greatest ever to wear the orange and black. The line was as rough as a bear with a bad tooth. At center was a 245-pound man mountain named Bob Gailey. On either side of him were a pair of frisky guards who liked it rowdy, Eddie Crowdis and Houston "Sport" Armstrong. Tackles Doc Hillebrand and Bill Church were as knotty as any Ol' Nassau ever had. Doc Hillebrand was one of those individuals made tougher by pain, while Church's favorite ploy was a punch to an opponent's jaw. Captain Garry Cochran held down one end of the line, while Howard Brokaw was the stopper on the other.

The backs played up to the level of the line. Quarterback Fred Smith directed the team, and halfback Billy Bannard gave them speed around the ends. A pair of all–Americans completed the backfield. Fullback Johnny Baird handled the kicking, and halfback Add Kelly ripped off tackle like a human buzz saw.

Princeton won all its games except for an early-season tie with Lafayette. Until Yale, the only score against them was a 100-yard touchdown run by Artie Miller of the Carlisle Indians, coached by ex–Yale guard Wild Bill Hickok. After the win over Army, big defeats were hung on Virginia, Penn State, and Cornell.

Other than Lafayette, the toughest game was with Harvard, whose huge line held Princeton to a scoreless struggle at half-time. Near the end of the half, Johnny Poe, assisting King on the coaching staff, gave each man the most famous one-liner in Princeton football history, "If you won't be beat, you can't be beat." The words kindled the team after the half, and they went out front on Billy Bannard's 40-yard touchdown gallop. Another score followed after Bill Church tore through to smother a punt which rolled around the end zone before Howard Brokaw landed it.

In the last game of the year, Princeton demolished a good Yale team which had won all 13 games. After Yale led briefly on a blocked punt covered in the end zone by Lyman Bass, Princeton tallied five touchdowns to win, 24–6, the first time anyone ever scored over 20 points on a Yale team. The Princeton line pushed the Blues around so much that they ran plays at game's end without calling signals. It was the last Princeton-Yale game to be played in New York, as future games returned to the campus.

Penn was unbeaten in over two years, and they continued to win until they met Lafayette at Franklin Field in Philadelphia. After years of running up big scores on small schools, many of them in three figures, Lafayette evened it for all of them when they became the first small college to beat one of the Big Four. Parke Davis coached them to victories over everyone except for the scoreless deadlock with Princeton, while surrendering only two touchdowns all year. Missing from the schedule was traditional rival, Lehigh, which objected to Lafayette's George Barclay, who was accused of playing semipro baseball. It proved to be the only break in over a century of games which began in 1884, when captain Jake Robeson used the V-formation at Lehigh.

Early in the Penn game, Lafayette tackle Fielding Yost was carried off the field with a broken leg. Penn scored first but missed the goal after and led at halftime, 4–0. In the second half, a Quaker punt was blocked by Lafayette's right tackle, Gus Wiedenmayer, and recovered by left end Bill Worthington. Moving behind guard Babe Rinehart, left half George Barclay went around end to the five-yard line. With Rinehart again clearing the way, Barclay went over standing up and added the goal after for a 6–4 lead. At the end of the game, Lafayette was driving to another score. Penn's 34-game winning streak was over, while Lafayette fans kept the pubs on Broad Street busy far into the night. In addition to scoring all the points which toppled Penn, Barclay made the game notable by being the first player to wear a football helmet. It protected his head as well as his ears, and was made by a local harness maker, who called it a head harness.

Penn's guards-back formation had met its match. It was the guards-back offense which caused linemen to crouch and take the brunt of the Penn attack on their shoulders, but today Penn was beaten by a line which took them head on and walked away winner. In the Lafayette line from left to right were Bill Worthington, Harry Gates, P.G. "Stop" Rowland, Martin Jones, Charlie Rinehart, Gus Wiedenmayer, and Tom Speer. At halfback with Barclay was captain George Walbridge, the fullback was Ed "Kidney" Bray, who did the punting, with Charles Best at quarterback.

It was only a short step from George Woodruff's quarterback kick, or quick kick, at Penn in 1892 to a direct pass from center to punter. Stagg used it at Chicago this year when he had his punter, Clarence Herschberger, drop back from his left half spot and take the snap directly from center, a legal move as long as the punter was five yards behind the scrimmage line. In having a halfback do the punting, Stagg eliminated the quarterback from handling the ball and being the kicker. He also had his center, Phil Allen, pass the ball back underhanded with a spiral motion. At one end the same time, therefore, Stagg originated the short punt formation and the spiral pass from center.

Yet another Stagg invention this year was the indoor huddle. In the last game of the season with Michigan on Thanksgiving Day, Chicago used a huddle for the first time in a game played inside the Chicago Coliseum. Because of the crowd noise, Stagg had his men huddle before each play in order to get the signals. It was the outgrowth of his experience with cheering crowds at Madison Square Garden in 1890 and 1891. The use of an outside huddle did not come until many years later, when crowd noise again forced a team to get the signals in a huddle. Chicago won the game, 7–6, on a safety and a 40-yard drop-kick field goal by Herschberger.

At the end of the year, the shape of the ball was changed for the first time. Another step away from rugby was taken, as the ball lost its round shape and was given elongated ends which formed a prolate spheroid, but with no fixed measurements. Its shape was still designed for kicking and not throwing, and the short circumference remained only an inch or two shorter than the distance around the ends.

1897

Pennsylvania	(15-0-0)		Yale	(9-0-2)	
17	Bucknell	0	10	Trinity	0
33	Franklin & Marshall	0	30	Wesleyan	0
18	Washington & Jefferson	4	18	Amherst	0
46	Lafayette	0	32	Williams	0
33	Bucknell	0	10	Newtowne Athletic Club	0
57	Gettysburg	0	18	Brown	14
58	Lehigh	0	24	Carlisle	9
42	Virginia	0	6	Army	6
34	Dartmouth	0	16	Chicago	6
24	Penn State	0	0	Harvard	0
40	Brown	0	6	Princeton	0
20	Carlisle	10			
22	Wesleyan	0			
15	Harvard	6			
4	Cornell	0			
463		20	170		35

The Quakers were on top again with maybe their greatest team ever. Gone were the tandem steam-hammer guards, Buck Wharton and Wiley Woodruff, who led the guards back offense during the past three years, but coach George Woodruff found more than adequate replacements in Truxton Hare and Josiah McCracken. Hare played every minute of every one of the 54 games he started at Penn in the next four years, and no one ever put him on his back. The ends this season were two of Penn's best, Byron Dickson and Sam Boyle. At center was Pete Overfield with Sam Goodman at tackle.

Two other Penn players joined Hare on the All-America team this year, tackle Jack Outland and fullback Jack Minds. Penn suffered from inexperience at first, but they quickly matured and won all 15 games and held their opponents to 20 points for the year. Washington and Jefferson scored one touchdown, and Harvard scored the other and converted the goal after.

The other ten points scored against Penn were made on two field goals by Frank Hudson, the Carlisle Indians' drop-kicker. Carlisle coach Billy Bull, ex–Yale kicker, had Hudson practice all year until he was second to none. In the off-season, Hudson used the parallel bars in the gym as goal posts and became adept at kicking with either foot. This year Carlisle also became the first team to have every player wear a football helmet in a game.

Against Harvard, a place-kick field goal from a center snap was made for the first time. The Penn team didn't think it could be done because of the timing involved in placing the ball down for a kick. The goal after touchdown was a place-kick on almost every attempt, but that was a free kick with the holder stretched out on the ground and no onrushing linemen to block it. A field goal from placement was also used on the free kick after a fair catch, such as Jim Haxall's 65-yarder in 1882 out of Tom Baker's hold. The Quakers thought a play could be run from a fake place-kick, however, so they let some newsmen see it in practice. With Harvard looking for a fake kick and Bill Morice holding the ball, Jack Minds kicked it through the goal posts all the way to the gym at the west end of Franklin Field. Behind 6–0 at halftime, Penn shut out the Crimson in the second half for a 15–6 win.

On Thanksgiving Day after the Harvard contest, Cornell almost upset the Penn juggernaut in the last game. Twice Cornell came down the field and twice they were halted, once on the 10-yard line and again at the 6. Penn's front wall of Hare, Overfield, McCracken, and Outland was immovable. Then they scored the game's only points at the final whistle and were the champs.

On this same Thanksgiving Day in the Chicago Coliseum, which stood on 63rd Street across the Midway south of the Chicago campus, Clarence Herschberger duplicated the first place-kick field goal scored by Jack Minds five days before. With Gordon Clarke holding the ball, his three field goals helped Chicago overcome Michigan, 21–12. The Herschberger and Clarke place-kicking combination went on to become the most famous one of the day.

Yale was also unbeaten with nine wins, but was tied twice. Princeton allowed no points in ten wins, but lost to Yale on a Charlie Dudley score and George Cadwalader's conversion. Baird and Kelly were back, but Cochran and Hillebrand could not stop the Elis. The Yalemen had quarterback Charlie DeSaulles, halfback Ham Benjamin, ends John Hall and Joe Hazen, guard Charles Chadwick, and tackles Burr Chamberlin and captain Jim Rodgers.

Beginning this season, two men appeared on the All-America team for the next four years. One was Truxton Hare of Penn and the other was Gordon Brown of Yale, and they joined Harvard's Ma Newell and Frank Hinkey of Yale as the only players to make all–American four times. With the selection of Hare and Brown, no other guards had a chance for all–American honors during this time. Perhaps this is the reason why Babe Rinehart, Lafayette's 6'3", 225-pound guard, was relegated to second team All-America. Truxton Hare said Rinehart was the best lineman he ever faced, and none other than Pudge Heffelfinger said Rinehart was one of the two greatest players who ever lived.

1898

The scoring system was changed again for the coming season. This year a touchdown would be valued at five points instead of four, making it the first time that a touchdown was equal to a field goal. The points after a touchdown were also cut from two to one. A touchdown and conversion were still worth six points, but more value was put on the touchdown than the goal after.

In his second year as coach, Cameron Forbes developed one of Harvard's greatest teams. Captain Ben Dibblee's eleven ended Penn's 31-game winning streak, and beat Yale for the second time under modern scoring rules. In the middle of the line was Percy Jaffray, its 225-pound center, with a pair of strapping guards, Bill Burden and Walter Boal, on each side of him. At one tackle was Malcolm Donald and at the other was Percy Haughton, who also did the punting, and went on to even greater fame in coaching. In the backfield was another player who found fame as a coach, quarterback Charley Daly. At halfback was mercury-footed Ben Dibblee, with line-buster Bill Reid at fullback.

Harvard (11-0-0)			Michigan (11-0-0)	
11	Williams	0	21 Michigan Normal	0
28	Bowdoin	6	29 Kenyon	0
21	Dartmouth	0	39 Michigan State	0
53	Amherst	2	18 Western Reserve	0
28	Army	0	23 Case	5
22	Newtowne Athletic Club	0	23 Notre Dame	0
39	Chicago Athletic Club	0	11 Alumni	2
11	Carlisle	5	6 Northwestern	5
10	Penn	0	12 Illinois	5
17	Brown	6	22 Beloit	0
17	Yale	0	12 Chicago	11
257		19	216	28

Penn was turned back, 10-0, for only its second setback in five years. Penn's all–Americans, center Pete Overfield, tackle Jack Outland, and guards Josiah McCracken and steely-eyed Truxton Hare gave their best, but could not prevail against the Crimson line. Frank Burnett's 43-yard place-kick field goal put Harvard in front, 5-0. When the Crimson made a second score, it was more than enough to give the Quakers their first loss of the season.

Harvard's final game of the year was played against the Elis at Yale Field in a driving rainstorm. Percy Haughton's punts out-distanced the Yale kicker's and picked up ground on every exchange. Ben Dibblee swivel-hipped around the ends on runs of 50 and 40 yards and scored once against the Blues. When Yale spread out to protect its flanks, Bill Reid banged straight ahead for two touchdowns, the first man to score twice against Yale in one game. Charley Daly was not only a superb field general but a bearcat on defense, preserving a shutout for the Crimson with a touchdown-saving tackle to lead them to the national title.

Michigan was also unbeaten as they won all 11 games. Two narrow wins over Northwestern and Chicago gave them their first Western Conference title. In Michigan's line-up were halfbacks Bill Caley and John McLean, Bill Cunningham holding down center, and tackles Allen Steckle and Chuck Mc-Donald. Princeton blanked 11 teams, but tied Army, 5-5. Pop Warner, coach at Cornell for the past two years, had ten wins but lost to Princeton, 6-0, and Penn, 12-6. Starring for Cornell were tackles Ed Sweetland and Dan Reed, Tar Young at quarter, and fullback Bucky Starbuck.

Wisconsin's legendary kicker, Pat O'Dea, a native of Australia.

Yale started off well as they won their first nine games, seven by shut-outs, and allowed 11 points. Then disaster struck in the first half of the Princeton game. Yale was on the march to a score when Doc Hillebrand drove into Al "Dusty" Durston and piled up the play on the 15-yard stripe. In on the stop was the Tigers' 5'6", 147-pound end, Arthur Poe. As Durston twisted, Poe stripped the ball from his hands and raced 95 yards to the only score of the game. Abe Ayres converted for a 6–0 final.

In the Midwest, Clarence Herschberger of Chicago became the first man to make all–American who was not from an eastern team. Four years ago, due to Stagg's inventive spark, Herschberger had participated in the first onside kick when he recovered the ball on the kickoff after it had gone ten yards. Next season, he was not in school due to an injury to his hand while hunting.

In 1896, Herschberger returned to become the first punter to take a di-rect pass from center. His punting style was truly unique. He raised the ball high over his head, and then placed it down on his foot as he brought his leg up. His fluid punts had so much flair that they were called a "Herschberger" in the Midwest, not a spiral. This year, he added another first when he faked a punt in the Michigan game, and then gave the ball to Walter Kennedy, who came around behind him and ran for 35 yards. Against Penn, Herschberger worked the onside kick again on the kickoff, only this time he recovered the ball after he had done the kicking. Sitting in the stands was Walter Camp, who saw it and put Herschberger on his All-America team.

Another player from the Midwest famous for his kicking was Australia's gift to Wisconsin, Pat O'Dea. Known as the "Kangaroo Kicker" because of his origin and great leg power, he may be the best long-distance kicker of them all. His running-style rugby kicks were unrivaled, and in 1896 and 1897 he helped the Badgers win the first two Western Conference titles.

In a game with Carlisle played inside the Chicago Coliseum in 1896, O'Dea kicked an onside punt so high that it was lost in the rafters by the safety man and recovered by Wisconsin's Ike Carroll for a score. In 1897, O'Dea drop-kicked a 57-yard field goal against Chicago and two against Minnesota, one of 55 yards and another a 40-yarder while on the run. Trainer Dad Moulton, watching on the sideline, dropped his water bucket in amazement.

In the Northwestern game this season, coach Phil King said he'd buy his players all the champagne they could drink if they scored in the first two minutes. After the kickoff Northwestern had to punt, and O'Dea made a fair catch on his 45. He quickly stepped back and drop-kicked a field goal (65 yards in Big Ten records, 62 according to Wisconsin) to beat the two-minute deadline. In this same contest, O'Dea also got off a gigantic punt which was measured at 87 yards, 10 inches.

At Chicago this year, Stagg used a man-in-motion, or as he called it, a flier. He had his right half, Ralph Hamill, angle out and away from the other backs and take a lateral pass from the quarterback. At Auburn another first took place, as a vocal "hike" was used by John Heisman in order to put the ball in play.

1899

Most of Harvard's 1898 champions were back, and this year they held everyone scoreless except for ten points given up to Carlisle. Against Yale, Harvard had three chances to score but failed each time. Frank Burnett and Jack Hallowell both missed on field goal attempts. The Cantabs also marched to the 1-yard line, but lost the ball on downs when fullback Tub Ellis rammed into the goal post at the goal. The game ended without a score, but Harvard was champion for the second straight year.

Sewanee won all its games in spite of a nightmare schedule. It opened in Atlanta with two wins in three days. Two days after leaving Tennessee, they downed Texas and celebrated the win at a dance in Austin. One day later they beat Texas A&M in Houston and then rode the night train to New Orleans. The next day they trimmed Tulane. Sunday was a day of sightseeing, but on Monday they routed Louisiana State in Baton Rouge. On the next day in Memphis they tamed Mississippi. Auburn, in its last year under John Heisman, got the only points Sewanee gave up all season.

Harvard	(10-0-1)		Sewanee	(12-0-0)	
29	Williams	0	12	Georgia	0
13	Bowdoin	0	32	Georgia Tech	0
20	Wesleyan	0	46	Tennessee	0
41	Amherst	0	54	Southwestern	0
18	Army	0	12	Texas	0
29	Bates	0	10	Texas A&M	0
11	Brown	0	23	Tulane	0
22	Carlisle	10	34	Louisiana State	0
16	Penn	0	12	Mississippi	0
11	Dartmouth	0	71	Cumberland	0
0	Yale	0	11	Auburn	10
			5	North Carolina	0
210		10	327		10

The high point of the year again occurred in the Princeton-Yale game. In a Frank Merriwell script not even Hollywood would believe, Arthur Poe had an encore to equal his game-winning performance which beat the Elis last year. The game was only seven minutes old when Bosey Reiter's long run put the Tigers ahead by 6–0. Bert Wheeler's end-zone punt was blocked by tackle George Stillman, and fullback Malcolm McBride recovered it for a score. Gordon Brown missed the conversion, and Yale still trailed by a point. As intermission drew near, Al Sharpe's 45-yard drop-kick field goal sent the Elis to the locker room with a 10–6 lead.

Yale's flimsy advantage stood up until the end of the game. By this time, eight Princeton starters were gone with injuries, including center Walter Booth, guard Marshall Mills, tackle Doc Hillebrand, and halfback Herb McCord. Only captain Bill Edwards at guard, tackle Williamson Pell, and Poe were still in. With victory a few minutes away Yale fumbled at midfield, and Bill Roper, in for Lew Palmer at end, fell on it for Princeton.

The Tigers moved to the 25-yard stripe where Edwards agreed to let Poe try a field goal. He took his place nine yards back, but since Princeton kickers Wheeler and Ralph Hutchinson weren't in, Yale thought it was a fake. With a minute remaining, Poe's soccer-style drop-kick field goal curved a yard inside the pole for an 11–10 win. The reporters, who were putting the finishing touches on the story of Yale's triumph, quickly rewrote the last lines. For the first time ever the Tigers vanquished Yale two years running, and Arthur Poe had enough glory for a lifetime.

This year Glenn "Pop" Warner became coach of the Carlisle Indians, a team which was already flexing its football muscles. Like many early state

The 1899 Sewanee team. Top row: Ralph Black, Bill Claiborne, manager Luke Lea, coach Herman Suter, Joseph Kirby-Smith, Dan Hull. Middle row: Ringland Kilpatrick, Bill Poole, Henry Keyes, John Jones, Rich Bolling, Ormand Simkins. Bottom row: Hugh Pearce, Quint Gray, Henry Seibels, William Wilson, Bart Sims.

colleges, Carlisle was an agricultural and mechanical school which taught its students a practical skill in these areas and in the industrial and stenographic arts as well. It had been opened 20 years before by Lieutenant Richard Pratt in the Carlisle Barracks, an old army post in southern Pennsylvania.

  · Carlisle's first students had arrived robed in blankets just three years after the Custer massacre, and they needed their own school because of the harsh feeling against them. Now they were showing the country how to play the game of football. Always a road team, they barnstormed across the land playing the nation's best. In Philadelphia this year, where Seidel's Woodland Avenue Restaurant was offering a full meal for 15 cents, they beat Penn, 16–5. In New York they thrashed Columbia, 45–0, and in San Francisco they stopped California, 2–0, on the only points Cal ceded all year. Isaac Seneca was halfback on the All-America team.

    It was in the Columbia game this year that Carlisle halted Harold "The Hurdler" Weekes. The specialty of Harold Weekes was a play in which he stepped on the backs of his closely-bunched linemen, vaulted over the defense, and came down running on the other side. The Indians slowed him down by jamming the heel of their hands into his face and gut. This game was also the first in which the line used a three-point stance like trackmen, as Pop Warner had his players use a crouching start when the ball was snapped. Warner also employed a shift in this game for the first time. The Carlisle linemen moved right or left for one or two or three steps. Then the ball would be put in play by a guard or tackle or end, according to how many steps were taken.

Pat O'Dea continued to drop-kick field goals for Wisconsin from midfield this year. Before the Yale game in New Haven, a murmur went through the crowd as he stood in the middle of the field and put one ball after another over the crossbar. In the game which was played mostly in Badger territory, he had one try which Yale blocked at its 20-yard line. Howard Richards later turned left end for 65 yards to give the Elis a 6-0 verdict.

His field goal from placement in the Illinois game was in a class by itself. After a fair catch, O'Dea prepared to kick into the 20-mile an hour wind.

"What are you doing?" asked the referee.

"What do you think?" replied O'Dea.

"I think you're nuts," the referee said, "if you're trying to score against this wind."

Bill Juneau held the ball. O'Dea aimed at the right-hand corner of the field and put his foot into it. The crowd held its breath as the ball fought its way upward, wobbling a little as it struggled against the wind. With a mighty whoosh, the wind caught it like a jet stream and bent it back through the goal post, an almost impossible kick of 57 yards.

In the Minnesota game, O'Dea eluded Gil Dobie after taking a punt, and then drop-kicked a field goal of 60 yards with one swish of his leg. Against Michigan, he drop-kicked a 35-yard field goal, and then had to leave the contest because a piece of broken bone was sticking out of his hand.

"We could have won," said Michigan center Bill Cunningham after the game, "if we had gotten O'Dea out sooner."

Wisconsin and Chicago met for the conference championship in the last game of the year. Special trains from Chicago took fans by the thousands north to Madison for its biggest crowd up to that time. Stagg devised a rush which put pressure on O'Dea all afternoon, and the closest he could get was an attempt from 55 yards away. Chicago won, 17-0, their first touchdown coming on a split buck, a play in which the quarterback faked the ball to one back running into the line, and then gave it to a second back going into the line on the other side of center.

With linemen Herb Ahlswede, Fred Feil, and John Webb, ends Jimmy Sheldon and Billy Eldridge, and halfbacks Frank Slaker and Jimmy Henry, Chicago won 12 and had 5-5 ties with Iowa and Penn. In the Penn game, Chicago had the ball near the goal but made the mistake of trying to go through the line where McCracken, Hare, Outland, and Overfield reigned, and were turned away empty-handed.

Yale surrendered just one touchdown until the game with Princeton, with Columbia getting the score. Bill Morley and Harold Weekes carried the attack to the Elis, with Weekes scoring on a 45-yard run for a 5–0 win. Iowa and Indiana joined the seven members of the Western Conference to make it almost the Big Ten. Iowa was unbeaten and unscored on except for the tie with Chicago, while Kansas, under Fielding H. Yost, was victorious in all ten games. Yost was well on the way to his lifetime record of 196 wins, 36 losses, and 12 ties for a .828 average and seventh-place rank among college coaches.

II. The Turning Point

1900

Yale	(12-0-0)		Harvard	(10-1-0)	
22	Trinity	0	24	Wesleyan	0
27	Amherst	0	12	Williams	0
30	Tufts	0	12	Bowdoin	0
50	Bates	0	18	Amherst	0
17	Dartmouth	0	24	Columbia	0
30	Bowdoin	0	41	Bates	0
38	Wesleyan	0	29	Army	0
12	Columbia	5	17	Carlisle	5
18	Army	0	17	Penn	5
35	Carlisle	0	11	Brown	6
29	Princeton	5	0	Yale	28
28	Harvard	0			
336		10	205		44

It was in 1900 that Dr. Henry Williams began his long and successful career at Minnesota. While he was at the University of Pennsylvania as an instructor in gynecology, Dr. Williams had been impressed with the guards back formation of George Woodruff. Williams devised a tackle back formation in which one tackle was lined up behind the other. This gave enough power on an end run with an extra man in front of the ball carrier for interference, but it also kept six men in the line for enough power forward. Williams brought this formation to Yale in 1899, and Walter Camp liked it so much that he built this year's Yale team around it.

Williams turned down Stagg's offer to be his assistant at Chicago, but later, upon Stagg's recommendation, Williams took the head coach's job offered to him at Minnesota. Immediately, Minnesota swept everything before it, going through the season unbeaten except for two ties and winning the conference title.

Yale was the class of the country and placed seven of its players on the All-America team. With Dick Sheldon and four-time all-American Gordon Brown at the guard positions, and Beau Olcott at center, the Elis were more than adequate in the middle. When this fearsome front was flanked by tackles Jim Bloomer and George Stillman, and ends Sherman Coy and Chuck Gould, it was well-nigh impassable. The backfield of this elite outfit included fullback Perry Hale, play-caller Bill Fincke, and halfbacks George Chadwick and Al Sharpe, who also did the kicking.

In addition to the caliber of its players, especially the linemen, another reason for Yale's success was the brute power of Henry Williams' tackle back formation. Speed and efficiency were also mainstays of this formation, for five plays were run off in three separate sequences before the defense could get set. Another feature of the Yale attack was a mousetrap play designed by Walter Camp. He taught the guards and tackles to deflect an opponent off to the side on an apparent missed block, so that the ball carrier could run through the hole left vacant by the hard-charging defensive lineman.

Yale held its opponents scoreless in the first seven games. The eighth game was with Columbia, and Yale prepared to stop the hurdling of Harold Weekes, who had beaten them the year before with a 45-yard touchdown run. When the Yale team arrived at the Polo Grounds where the game was to be played, they found another surprise awaiting them. The local firemen, loyal supporters of the Lions, had flooded the field to look like a low-lying inlet at high tide. The Lion team had also put wooden cleats on their shoes to get better traction in the muck, while Yale's cleats, designed for use on a hard field, were almost useless. Not to be outdone, Malcolm McBride, the Yale coach, bought some shoes at the nearest store and took them to a carpenter to have the regular cleats replaced with wooden ones.

With Harold Weekes and Bill Morley moving behind guard Jack Wright, Weekes scored on a 50-yard run to give Columbia a 5-0 halftime lead. Luckily, the carpenter was not a Lion fan like the firemen, and the wood-cleated shoes arrived at intermission. Columbia was blanked in the last half while Yale scored twice to win, 12-5.

Princeton was beaten easily by the powerful Yale team, but Harvard had won ten games, seven of them by shutouts. With its pair of all-American ends, Jack Hallowell and Dave Campbell, the Crimson team was considered to be one of its best, second only to the champions of 1898. The middle of the Harvard line, however, was no match for Yale's interior linemen. They halted the Harvard offense before it could get under way and forced them to cough up the ball twice on fumbles. One fumble on the Harvard 26-yard line led to a Yale touchdown soon after. The second fumble was seized by Sherman Coy and returned for a score, as the Elis sang "Boola, Boola" for the first time and were national champions once again.

Harvard's coach, Ben Dibblee, later remarked, "Such a line as that of the Yale team of 1900 has hardly ever been seen on a gridiron." With this game, Princeton was replaced by Harvard as the last game of the year on Yale's schedule, and ever since the turn of the century, Harvard-Yale has been The Game.

1901

With the coming of Fielding H. Yost to Michigan in 1901 as head coach, the Wolverines built a dynasty. For continued excellence against top teams over a five-year span, no team has approached Michigan's record. In the next 56 games, they were undefeated and tied once while amassing 2,821 points to 40 for their opponents. Only six touchdowns were scored against them, four by fumbles and two on sustained drives.

Michigan	(11-0-0)		Harvard	(12-0-0)	
50	Albion	0	16	Williams	0
57	Case	0	12	Bowdoin	0
33	Indiana	0	16	Bates	6
29	Northwestern	0	11	Amherst	0
128	Buffalo	0	18	Columbia	0
22	Carlisle	0	16	Wesleyan	0
21	Ohio State	0	6	Army	0
22	Chicago	0	29	Carlisle	0
89	Beloit	0	48	Brown	0
50	Iowa	0	33	Penn	6
49	Stanford (Rose Bowl)	0	27	Dartmouth	12
			22	Yale	0
550		0	254		24

Included in this year's 11 wins was a Rose Bowl victory over Stanford. A crowd of 8,500, more than half the people in Pasadena, paid $2.00 for a reserved seat and 50 cents for a general admission ticket to see the game. Neil Snow scored five touchdowns, still a record. The loss embarrassed tournament officials so much that chariot racing was substituted for the next decade. No one, including Stanford, made a running play of more than 15 yards against the Wolverines all year, and four of the teams that played Michigan never got past midfield. Michigan led 17-0 at the half, and Stanford's best efforts were two field goal tries from 40 and 45 yards out by tackle Bill Traeger. Michigan's two substitutes, Art Redner and Herb Graver, never got in the game.

Yost lived and breathed football. If he met a member of the team on campus, he would pause to demonstrate a fine point of the game, and before long coach and player were surrounded by onlookers. Like last year's Yale team, Yost stressed speed of execution, and one play followed another in rapid succession. Over and over in practice, Yost could be heard telling his team to hurry up. In the game, the quarterback called the signals for the next play while the team was still getting up from the last one, and many yards were gained against teams who weren't ready when the ball was snapped.

Speed was the essence of five-yard football, and it was not uncommon for a team to run a hundred plays in each half. This speed was intended to wear down the opposition, and the team in the best physical condition often won in the last half.

Harvard was undefeated and untied in 12 games and was the best team in the East, if not the country. Five of its players made first-team All-America, and the whole left side of the line, its killer "B's," Ed Bowditch, Blagden, and Barnard, were on the second team. Right end Dave "Soup"

Campbell was captain, and his 29 years of age gave the team leadership stability. At the tackles were Crawford Blagden and Oliver Cutts, who was one year younger than Campbell but preferred mayhem to diplomacy. Yale protested to Harvard for using Cutts because he had taught math at Haverford, allegedly for pay. The guard spots were manned by Bill Lee and Charley Barnard, with Elbridge Greene at center. The backfield included quarterback Carl Marshall, halfbacks Bob Kernan and Al Ristine, and fullback Tom Graydon.

Army placed two men on the All-America team for the first time. One was Charley Daly, ex–Harvard quarterback, now playing for the cadets at West Point. Army gave Harvard its toughest game. At the end of the hard-fought battle, Bob Kernan sprinted 60 yards in the final seconds for the only score of the contest. Charley Daly, who seldom missed a tackle, failed to bring down Kernan and got a stiff-arm in the face for his trouble. Army lost only to Harvard, 6–0, and tied Princeton and Yale.

Much of Harvard's success was due to the tackle back formation which it borrowed from Yale. With it, they rolled over the Carlisle Indians, a light team which was rebuilding under Pop Warner and outweighed 25 pounds per man. The Crimson also crushed Penn, 33–6, as Tom Graydon scored all six touchdowns.

In the final game of the season at Soldiers Field in Cambridge, Harvard gave Yale its worst beating up to that time. It was only the second time any team scored over 20 points on Yale, and the 22-point difference was the most suffered by a Yale team so far. Three-time all–American end Dave Campbell set a pattern of line play which was copied for years, as he broke through to stop the Yale backs behind the line. Two days before the game, Blagden had an appendicitis attack. He was fitted with a brace, played on Saturday, and had an operation on Sunday. All 11 men, including Blagden, played the full 70 minutes.

1902

Michigan	(11-0-0)		Yale	(11-0-1)	
88	Albion	0	40	Trinity	0
48	Case	6	34	Tufts	6
119	Michigan State	0	23	Amherst	0
60	Indiana	0	35	Wesleyan	0
23	Notre Dame	0	10	Brown	0
86	Ohio State	0	32	Vermont	0
6	Wisconsin	0	11	Penn State	0
107	Iowa	0	24	Syracuse	0
21	Chicago	0	6	Army	6
63	Oberlin	0	36	Bucknell	5
23	Minnesota	6	12	Princeton	5
			23	Harvard	0
644		12	286		22

The Michigan giant strode through a second straight perfect year and was again national champion. The Wolverines erupted for 644 points, but permitted a pair of touchdowns this season. They maintained their point-a-minute role with a whopping average of 58.5 points per game, second highest for a major team. Michigan State was annihilated, and so was Ohio State. Member schools in the Western Conference were treated like small-town colleges, as Iowa and Indiana were both inundated by tidal-wave scores.

Many of the players from last year's victorious Rose Bowl team were back. The captain and quarterback was Harrison "Boss" Weeks. Paul Jones replaced Neil Snow at fullback, and the halfbacks were Willie Heston and Al Herrnstein. On the flanks were Curtis Redden and Everett Sweeley. Last year's captain, tackle Hugh White, was replaced by Joe Maddock, but Bruce Shorts still held the other tackle spot. George Gregory was back at center, with veteran guard Dan McGugin on one side and newcomer Charles "Babe" Carter, who took Ebin Wilson's place, on the other.

This was the year of the famed Irish line at Yale. Frank Hinkey called it "the best ever seen on any field." From end to end, their names sounded like a roll call in the halls of Tara. The ends were Chuck "Riff" Rafferty and Tom Shevlin, who was an all–American as a freshman, and the tackles were sophomore Ralph Kinney and senior Jim Hogan, who used his ham-sized hands like clubs. The guards were George Goss and Ned Glass, an easy-going Samson good enough to be mentioned with Heffelfinger as one of Yale's all-time guards, and at center was Henry C. Holt, as tall and sturdy as a pine tree. At quarterback was Foster Rockwell, whose 140 pounds could hardly be seen behind the massive Yale line. The fullback was Morgan Bowman, who also did the kicking, and leading the iron-jawed Bulldogs were halfbacks Harold Metcalf and captain George Chadwick.

Yale placed seven men on the All-America team this year, including Hogan and Kinney, among the best pair of tackles the Blue ever had. Also included was Tom Shevlin, who boasted that no one ever made a yard around his end. It was a boast backed up with deeds, for many of Shevlin's opponents considered the game a success if they could turn his end for a few yards. In the minds of many, this year's team was thought to be as good, if not better than, the champs of two years ago. The only flaw was a 6–6 tie with Army, which cost them the national title.

Army continued its winning ways this year, losing only to Harvard. Although the Cadets were outgained, they managed to tie Yale, the best team in the East. The game had two halves of 20 minutes each, since the Army players had to pass inspection before being dismissed. Tackle Pot Graves slammed in to block a punt which end Joe McAndrew captured at the 2-yard line, and in two plays it was tied. Linemen were captain King Boyers at center, guard Napoleon Riley, tackle Tom Doe, and end Ed Farnsworth. Paul Bunker was the only Army player to make all–American at two different positions: tackle in 1901 and halfback in 1902.

John DeWitt's drop-kicks began to make his presence felt by Princeton's opponents. He kicked one of 55 yards and another of 45 yards to score

Left: Fielding H. "Hurry Up" Yost led his beloved "Meeshegan" to a 55-1-1 record over five years. Right: All-American halfback Willie Heston of Michigan.

all the points which beat Cornell, 10–0. He also kicked a 50-yarder in the Yale game and a 45-yarder against Columbia. Princeton defensed the hurdling of Harold Weekes with a hurdle of their own. When Weekes catapulted himself over the line with one of his famous leaps, he was met at the pass by a human projectile from the Princeton side, Dana Kafer. Both of them had to be carried from the field.

In the Midwest, Nebraska was unbeaten, untied, and unscored on in ten games, while scoring 187 points themselves. They beat Minnesota, 6–0, Colorado, 10–0, Kansas, 16–0, and had 12–0 wins over Missouri and Northwestern. It was also in the Midwest that an unbalanced line was used for the first time. Stagg tried it at Chicago when he moved a tackle from one side of the line and put him next to a tackle on the other side.

The canvas jackets which had been popular for over a decade were now being replaced by jerseys. A new rule said the offense must have seven men on the scrimmage line when the ball was between the 25-yard lines.

1903

When Princeton and Yale met for the national title, both had won each of their ten games. Princeton captain John DeWitt continued his stellar role as kicker, for he already had a 50-yard field goal against Cornell. Beside him in his position at right guard were tackle Charles Reed and center Harold Short, with Howard Henry at end. On the left side of the Tiger line were guard Herb Dillon, tackle Jim Cooney, and end Ralph Davis. In the backfield were quarterback Roy Vetterlein, halfbacks Dana Kafer and Henry Hart, and Sumner Rulon-Miller at fullback.

Three-time all–American end Tom Shevlin of Yale.

DeWitt saved his best performance for the last game of his career against Yale at New Haven. Yale scored the only points Princeton gave up all year, as Jim Hogan went over on a tackle-back play and Ledyard Mitchell converted for a 6–0 lead. After DeWitt failed to make a 65-yard field goal try, the Blues came down the field again, but the Tigers held at their 26-yard line. Yale attempted a field goal, but the left side of the Princeton line poured through to block it. DeWitt scooped up the ball and headed upfield escorted by his two ends, Davis and Henry. They peeled back to knock off two pursuers, and DeWitt raced 70 yards to a touchdown, then tied it with the point after.

The score stayed at 6–6 until the game drew to a close. In the last minute, Princeton had the ball near midfield. DeWitt lined up for a place-kick field goal from the 53-yard line. The ball climbed end-over-end in an arc as graceful to the football eye as any female curve and split the uprights for an 11–6 Princeton win. DeWitt ended his career in a blaze of glory by scoring all his team's points and kicking them to the title.

Michigan allowed only one touchdown all year and posted an 11-0-1 record. Leading the point-a-minute team was all–American halfback Willie Heston. His running mate at right half was Herb Graver, with Tom Hammond at full and Fred Norcross at quarter. Out in front of the Wolverine attack were captain Curtis Redden at left end, left tackle Joe Curtis, left guard Henry Schulte, veteran Rose Bowl center George Gregory, Cecil

Gooding at right guard, right tackle Joe Maddock, and right end Frank Longman.

Princeton	(11-0-0)		Michigan	(11-0-1)	
34	Swarthmore	0	31	Case	0
5	Georgetown	0	79	Beloit	0
68	Gettysburg	0	65	Ohio Northern	0
29	Brown	0	51	Indiana	0
12	Lehigh	0	88	Ferris Institute	0
11	Carlisle	0	47	Drake	0
17	Bucknell	0	76	Albion	0
17	Dartmouth	0	6	Minnesota	6
44	Cornell	0	36	Ohio State	0
11	Lafayette	0	16	Wisconsin	0
11	Yale	6	42	Oberlin	0
			28	Chicago	0
259		6	565		6

The lone touchdown Michigan surrendered cost them a third straight national title. It was scored by Minnesota and ended their 29-game winning streak, Michigan's longest. Coach Henry Williams took the suggestion of his old teammate at Yale, Pudge Heffelfinger, and varied the Minnesota defense to stop Heston's lightning blasts through the line. Since there was no forward pass to concern them, most teams used a nine-man line with the fullback as a linebacker and the quarterback at safety. Fullback Earl Current and quarterback Sid Harris lined up as usual, but halfbacks Hunky Davies and Jim Irsfield were placed behind tackles Fred Schacht and George Webster. The line also had Mose Strathern at center, guards Walt Thorp and "Big Dan" Smith, and Usher Burdick, Bobby Marshall, and captain Ed Rogers at the ends.

Minnesota's seven-man line held Michigan to just two first downs. Heston scored on a short plunge in the second half, and Tom Hammond added the conversion. Fullback Egil Boeckmann later went over behind Big Smith at guard, and Rogers tied it with the point after. Minnesota equipment man Oscar Munson picked up the water jug left behind by the Wolverines, and the Little Brown Jug has gone to the winner of the Michigan-Minnesota game ever since.

The talk of the 1903 season was the hidden-ball trick which Pop Warner used in the Carlisle-Harvard game. It was a simple fooleroo tried by many sandlot teams when the light is starting to fade. Referee Mike Thompson had been told about it two weeks before in the game between Carlisle and Princeton. In the first half, Harvard scored a touchdown and led at intermission, 6–0.

At the start of the second half, the Harvard kickoff came down inside the 5-yard line. The Carlisle quarterback, Jimmy Johnson, caught the ball, and the Indians quickly retreated to form a wedge. Charlie Dillon, who was inside the wedge, faced the goal, and Johnson put the ball on Dillon's back under his jersey. The Harvard team tore into the wedge which fell apart man by man. The Crimson players tackled the man who supposedly had the ball, but all he had under his arm was his helmet.

In the meantime, Dillon slowly withdrew from the crumbling wedge, and when he was in the clear, sprinted for a touchdown. The Harvard team never knew who had the ball until it was too late, but the crowd, seeing the hump on Dillon's back as he ran by, screamed and pointed wildly. On the ground over the goal, Dillon rolled around trying to get the ball from his back, as he kept asking the referee, "Down, Mike? Down, Mike?"

At that moment, Johnson raced up and pulled the ball from Dillon's jersey and touched it down. The tailor at the Indian school, Mose Blumenthal, did a job which was almost too good, for he had sewn elastic inside the jersey to make sure the ball wouldn't come out while Dillon was running. The Indians later added a 25-yard field goal by captain Johnson, but the Cantabs scored another touchdown for a 12-11 victory in the last game ever played at Harvard's Soldiers Field.

A small school in the wilds of Indiana called Notre Dame was unbeaten and unscored on this year. Only a scoreless romp with Northwestern kept them from a perfect season. A 40-yard scoring run was negated when Irish captain, Lou "Red" Salmon, was caught holding. Salmon scored 250 career points at Notre Dame, a record which stood for over 80 years.

In order to reduce mass-formation plays, a new rule took over when the ball was between the 25-yard lines. Until now, a quarterback could not run with the ball until another player touched it, but now he or any back who first handled the ball could run forward as long as he was five yards from the center.

1904

Pennsylvania (12-0-0)		Michigan (10-0-0)	
6 Penn State	0	33 Case	0
6 Swarthmore	4	48 Ohio Northern	0
24 Virginia	0	95 Kalamazoo	0
34 Franklin & Marshall	0	72 Physicians & Surgeons	0
24 Lehigh	0	31 Ohio State	6
21 Gettysburg	0	72 American M&S	0
6 Brown	0	130 West Virginia	0
16 Columbia	0	28 Wisconsin	0
11 Harvard	0	36 Drake	4
22 Lafayette	0	22 Chicago	12
18 Carlisle	0		
34 Cornell	0		
222	4	567	22

Football took another step away from rugby by changing the value of a field goal again. It was reduced from five points to four, and for the first time a touchdown was worth more than a field goal. Another rule change this year required at least six men to be on the offensive scrimmage line. If only six men were on the line of scrimmage, one player had to line up outside the end a step out and a step back. In addition, the checkerboard which first appeared the previous year between the 25-yard lines now covered the entire field with five-yard squares, as the first man who handled the ball had to be five yards from the center before he could run forward.

Penn's all-conquering eleven were national champs this year. The Red and Blue won all 12 games, never had its goal crossed, and gave up only four points on a field goal by Swarthmore quarterback Wilmer Crowell. Penn was coached by Dr. Carl Williams, 1895 Quaker captain, who took over from George Woodruff in 1902.

One reason for Penn's rugged defense was its all–American center, captain Bob Torrey. The volcanic Torrey roamed back and forth behind the impenetrable Quaker line, and became the first roving center on defense. Penn's front wall was a collection of flint-edged competitors in itself. The guard positions were held by Frank Piekarski, the "Terrible Pole," and by Gus Ziegler, the "German Oak." At the tackles were Tom Butkiewicz and Otis Lamson, with Wharton Sinkler and Garfield Weede on the ends.

The Quaker backfield was as rough as the men up front. At fullback was the workhorse of the squad, Andy Smith, later coach of California's "wonder teams" in the early 1920s. The halfbacks were Ed Greene and Marshall Reynolds. The quarterback slot had another All-American, Vince Stevenson. Besides his ability as a signal caller, Stevenson was a clever runner. He did not skip over the line like Columbia's Harold Weekes, but using a stiffarm as solid as the Penn line, he vaulted around a tackler like Princeton's Tilly Lamar. His talent as a runner wasn't obvious, for he could get an angle on a tackler as he dashed toward him. When the defender finally committed himself he was leaning the wrong way, and with the half-step Stevenson gained he was gone.

Michigan's point-a-minute team was again the class of the West, scoring 567 points in ten games for a 56.7-point average, third best ever. A big gainer in the Michigan arsenal was the old 83 play, which was run from short punt formation. It was a fake end-around with a second fake into the line by one back, then a give to the halfback going around end. The quarterback faked the ball to an end coming around behind the line, then faked it to a back going into the line, and finally gave it to the halfback going around end. It was a play which had opened the end zone to left half Willie Heston again and again.

Willie Heston was all–American for the second season in a row. Playing his last year at Michigan, he continued to be the team sparkplug. At 5'8" and 185 pounds, he was built for power. Like many great runners, he was not fast, but quick. In just two steps he was moving at top speed, and for 40 yards he as as fast as anyone. More than once when a play started, he took the ball from the quarterback, who was attempting to give it to another back. At the end of the year he had 93 touchdowns, an all-time record.

In addition to Heston, who was captain this year, the backfield had Tom Hammond at right half, quarterback Fred Norcross, and Frank Longman at fullback. At right end was Harry Hammond, with Ted Stuart on the left. The middle of the line was a no-thoroughfare crew with 245-pound center Adolf "Germany" Schulz, 265-pound Babe Carter at right guard, 195-pound Henry Schulte at left guard, 245-pound right tackle Walter "Octopus" Graham, and 210-pound left tackle Joe Curtis.

Michigan's toughest game of the year was its last one with Chicago. Led by its all–American quarterback, Walter Eckersall, end Fred Speik, and its rotund guard, Robert "Tiny" Maxwell, the Maroons won all their games except for a 6-6 tie with Illinois. They had mammoth shutout wins over Indiana, 56-0, Purdue, 20-0, Iowa, 39-0, Northwestern, 32-0, and Texas, 68-0, and coach Fielding H. Yost was more than a little concerned about the outcome.

Yost came up with a special play for the game in which Babe Carter carried the ball when Michigan neared the Chicago goal. On Thursday and Friday before the game, spectators were barred from practice, but the play was leaked to the press on purpose. It was a decoy, for Carter was never intended to carry the ball. During the game the Wolverines advanced to the Chicago goal, and Carter was pulled from the line and put in the backfield. When the ball was snapped, the quarterback faked to Carter who drove into the line. Every Maroon player met him like piranhas after blood, while Heston scored untouched around end to give Chicago its only loss of the year.

Yost had outfoxed the old fox himself, Amos Alonzo Stagg. Always thinking, it was this year that Stagg used a lineman's charging sled in practice for the first time. It was also at Chicago this year that a backfield shift was used by Stagg for the first time anywhere.

Another powerful team in the West this year was Minnesota. Under its coach, Dr. Henry Williams, Minnesota won all 13 games and outscored their opponents 725 to 12. They had 12 shutouts, and all 12 points against them came in a 16-12 win over Nebraska. At the end of the season, the Gophers had a two-year unbeaten streak with only last year's tie with Michigan to tarnish their record.

In the South, two new coaches brought quality football to their schools immediately. Dan McGugin, left guard for Yost on Michigan's point-a-minute Rose Bowl team, took over at Vanderbilt and began its glory years. In his first season, McGugin started with huge wins over Mississippi State, 61-0, Georgetown (Ky.), 66-0, and Mississippi, 69-0. By season's end, Vanderbilt scored 474 points while winning all nine games and holding opponents to one field goal. On his stay in Nashville for McGugin's wedding, Yost met the bride's sister, married her soon after, and the two coaches became brothers-in-law.

At Auburn, Mike Donahue made Tiger football respectable. This ex-Yale athlete made the name of Auburn synonymous with defense, as they gave up only two touchdowns this year and won all five games. His memorial today is the street Auburn's stadium stands on, Donahue Drive.

After a 63–0 beating from John Heisman's Auburn team, and a 73–0 defeat while he coached at Clemson, Georgia Tech decided to hire him, and in 1904 the Heisman dynasty began at Georgia Tech.

Nebraska's winning streak of 27 games came to an end. After being unscored on in 1902 and adding another ten wins last year, they were finally halted by Colorado, 6–0. Helping to build the longest win span in Husker history were Maurice Benedict at end, center Charles Borg, and fullback John Bender. Nebraska's coach was Walter Booth, center on the 1899 Princeton team when Arthur Poe's field goal in the final minute defeated Yale, 11–10.

Yale had nine shutouts and ten wins, but was beaten by Army for the first time, 11–6, on a 100-yard touchdown dash by Henry Torney in the closing minutes. Pitt also had nine shutouts and ten wins, but gave up a touchdown in the 22–5 victory over Penn State in their last game. Dartmouth, coached by Fred Folsom, was unbeaten in eight games, but had a scoreless fracas with Harvard.

1905

Chicago	(10-0-0)		Yale	(10-0-0)	
33	Lawrence	0	27	Wesleyan	0
15	Wabash	0	16	Syracuse	0
38	Beloit	0	24	Springfield	0
42	Iowa	0	30	Holy Cross	0
16	Indiana	5	12	Penn State	0
4	Wisconsin	0	20	Army	0
32	Northwestern	0	53	Columbia	0
19	Purdue	0	11	Brown	0
44	Illinois	0	23	Princeton	4
2	Michigan	0	6	Harvard	0
245		5	222		4

Michigan's point-a-minute dynasty was in its fifth year. The Wolverines scored 495 points in 12 games and held opponents scoreless. From tackle to tackle the line still had its 200-pounders: Octopus Graham, Harry Hammond, Germany Schulz, Henry Schulte, and Joe Curtis. At the ends were Ted Stuart and John Garrels. The backfield was also a veteran outfit with captain Fred Norcross at quarterback, halfbacks Tom Hammond and Denny Clark, and fullback Frank Longman. Only Willie Heston and Babe Carter were missing, but it was Yost's best team since the Rose Bowl champs.

With his special touch of turning straw into gold, Stagg also had a great team at Chicago, including a battle-hardened line which averaged 193 pounds. At the ends were captain Mark Catlin and Ed Parry, with Art Badenoch and Bubbles Hill at the tackles. Clarence Russell and Babe Meigs were the guards, and Burt Gale was at center. Walter Eckersall returned at

All-American quarterback Walter Eckersall of Chicago.

quarterback, and so did his understudy, Jesse Harper. Fred Walker and lynx-legged Leo DeTray ran at left half, and W.J. "Dan" Boone and Carl Hitchcock were at right half. Back for his last year was fullback Hugo Bezdek.

Another Stagg touch seen for the first time in the Wisconsin game was the quarterback keeper. In it Eckersall faked a handoff into the line, and then ran around end with the ball on his hip, a play he worked three times with success against the Badgers.

There was little love lost between Stagg and Yost. Although neither drank, smoked, or used profanity, and both followed Christian teachings, they were fierce competitors and liked to win. At a track meet earlier in the spring they got into an argument, and Yost promised Stagg another beating in the fall like the ones he'd been giving him for the last four seasons. Just before the game for all the hurrahs, Stagg told his players, "Don't let him cram this game down my throat!"

The game took place at Marshall Field, later named Stagg Field, on Thanksgiving Day, November 30. The eager crowd of 25,791 was the largest in the Midwest up to that time. It attracted none other than Walter Camp and Caspar Whitney, proof that good football was no longer played just in the East.

In the first half, Michigan barely crossed the midfield stripe only once, while Chicago moved into Wolverine territory three times. The game became a kicking duel between Eckersall of Chicago, who punted 12 times, and John Garrels of Michigan, who punted 10 times. A 41-yard field goal from placement was attempted by Michigan's Tom Hammond, but it failed.

The second half was hardly under way when Garrels punted to the 15-yard line, and Chicago incurred a penalty for half the distance to its goal. With their backs to the wall, Eckersall retreated to punt. As he dodged the Michigan linemen trying to block it, the crowd jumped to its feet. Running to his right, they cheered his every step as he dashed between the goal posts and out to the 22-yard line before he was chased out-of-bounds.

Eckersall's daring maneuver gave the Maroons new life, and three first downs took them to midfield. From there, Eckersall lofted a punt which Denny Clark caught behind the goal and tried to run out as Eckersall had done. Racing behind the goal posts, Art Badenoch hit him low as he moved across the goal line. At the same moment, Mark Catlin hit him high and downed him behind the goal for a two-point safety. The Maroon fans screamed with joy, while Clark looked for some place to hide.

The game continued to be played at midfield as Michigan punted nine times and Chicago ten. Eckersall, who kicked five field goals in the previous game against Illinois, attempted a drop-kick of 37 yards, but it was partially blocked. Chicago moved into Michigan territory six times, but could not score. The two points were the ball game and the national title, and the Chicago fans tore down the fence in their giddy delight.

"Clark 2, Michigan 0," was the cruel headline which glared back at Clark from the newspaper. People treated him like a leper on the Michigan campus. By the end of the week, he left school. He withdrew to Michigan's northwoods, where the trees didn't hurt back. There he lived a hermit's life, refusing to see his family and friends. It was years before he got out of the woods and back into the ball game again.

Yale was unbeaten and untied in ten games, their goal line was not crossed, and they gave up only one field goal all year. In the lineup for the Blues were ends Jack Cates, Howard Jones, and captain Tom Shevlin, Bob Forbes and Horatio "Ray" Biglow at the tackles, guards Art Erwin and Roswell Tripp, and centers Phil Smith and Carl Flanders. Tad Jones was at quarter, Jim Quill at fullback, and the halfbacks were Sammy Morse and Paul Veeder.

At midseason, Penn State's stubborn line, stoked by William "Mother" Dunn at center, played the Elis to a standstill before the Lions lost on a pair of touchdowns late in the game. Against Army, Tad Jones ran 40 yards for a score, and Shevlin added two points when he dropped Army back George Beavers behind his goal.

An injury to Tad Jones kept him out of the Princeton game, and Guy Hutchinson took over at quarterback. Forbes ran eight yards for the first score, and Hutchinson's 25-yard punt return led to a second touchdown by Rex Flinn. Another dazzling punt return of 65 yards by Hutchinson set up a third score by Forbes. The last score came on Howard Roome's 5-yard run, and Hutchinson added his third conversion of the day. Princeton's Norm Tooker kicked a field goal for the only points made against the Elis.

A crowd of 43,000, the largest up to that time, showed up for the Harvard game on the Saturday before Thanksgiving. They saw a barroom brawl right from the start. Morse punched Crimson fullback Jack Wendell for continually holding his jersey and was put out of the game. Later, Shevlin and Quill smacked Harvard's Hooks Burr after he signaled for a fair catch, but neither drew a penalty even though Quill hit Burr in the face and broke his nose. Quill contended that Crimson tackle Karl Brill had bitten him on the hand and showed the teethmarks as proof.

The score remained tied until Yale recovered a fumbled punt on the Harvard 30-yard line late in the game. A fresh fullback, Dutch LeVine, was sent in. He and Forbes cut through the tiring Cantabs until Forbes ran over behind LeVine's lead block. Lydig Hoyt converted, and Yale was again the best team in the East.

The main reason for Yale's success was Tom Shevlin, its cocky three-time all–American end. There was no question that Shevlin could peel off the interference and eat the ball carrier like a steam shovel. He kept asking the Yale trainer, Mike Murphy, if Frank Hinkey was as good as they said he was. In answer to his constant questions about size and speed and strength, Mike told Shevlin that Hinkey wasn't as big or as fast or as strong as he was. Shevlin finally got to the bottom line one day and asked Mike to tell him if Hinkey was as good an end as he was.

The trainer looked Shevlin in the eye. With the finality of a broken egg, he spelled it out for him: "Tom, if you and Frank were playing at opposite ends of the same Yale team, his playing would make you look like a sleep walker."

Shevlin was not without his supporters. None other than Howard Jones, a young sophomore end for Yale, but later a great coach at Yale, Iowa, and Southern California, gave Shevlin his vote as the best football player he ever saw. Apparently, Mike Murphy, father of movie star George Murphy, didn't agree.

This year also saw Pop Warner's invention of shoulder and thigh pads. After using a shoehorn made of fiber, he wrote the company and ordered some of the fiber, which he shaped into pads for shoulder and thigh protection. Felt was attached to the inside in order to cushion the blows the players would receive. The shoulder pads were held in place by a strap under the armpit, while the thigh pads were put in a pocket inside the pants.

The year 1905 was a fateful one for American football. In moving away from rugby, football developed into a game of mass interference which leveled the defense. Line play deteriorated to brute force where linemen slugged one another and the ball carrier was pulled and pushed into this mass of humanity.

During October, President Theodore Roosevelt invited a few representatives from the Big Three to the White House and told them to save football by removing its savagery and foul play. By the end of the year, the *Chicago Tribune* reported 18 deaths and 159 serious injuries. Columbia quit the game from 1906 to 1914, California and Stanford replaced it with rugby for these nine years, Northwestern did away with it for two seasons, and Western Conference schools cut their schedules in half.

On December 9, Chancellor Henry M. McCracken of New York University called a conference of 13 schools to reform the game. When they met again on December 28, 62 schools sent representatives. They formed the Intercollegiate Athletic Association of the United States, and appointed a Football Rules Committee headed by Captain Palmer E. Pierce of West Point.

1906

Yale	(9-0-1)		Princeton	(9-0-1)	
21	Wesleyan	0	24	Villanova	0
51	Syracuse	0	22	Stevens	0
12	Springfield	0	6	Washington & Jefferson	0
17	Holy Cross	0	52	Lehigh	0
10	Penn State	0	5	Navy	0
12	Amherst	0	32	Bucknell	4
10	Army	6	14	Cornell	5
5	Brown	0	42	Dartmouth	0
0	Princeton	0	8	Army	0
6	Harvard	0	0	Yale	0
144		6	205		9

On the 12th of January in New York, the new Football Rules Committee of Captain Pierce sat down with the old Football Rules Committee of Walter Camp and formed the American Intercollegiate Football Rules Committee. Four years later the name was changed to the National Collegiate Athletic Association (NCAA).

The biggest single change since the implementation of the scrimmage line and a system of downs was to make the forward pass legal this season. It did not change the game immediately, but opened it up a great deal. John Heisman had campaigned for it ever since he first saw it a decade earlier, although it had been used illegally. Football took a giant step away from rugby when it added the thrill of the pass to the power of the run and the skill of the toe.

A second rule providing a neutral zone between the two opposing lines was equally momentous. Up to now linemen squared off cheek to jowl and tried to get the jump on each other. This close proximity invited plenty of scuffling before the ball was put in play. Games were often delayed five or ten minutes while the locked linemen were pried apart. A neutral zone the length of the ball in which no encroachment was permitted made linemen back off from each other until the ball was snapped.

The game was also shortened to equal halves of 30 minutes, hurdling was forbidden, and ten yards instead of five was needed for a first down. To reduce mass formations, interior offensive linemen could not drop behind the line of scrimmage unless they retreated five yards. Stagg added a safety measure of his own at Chicago by padding the goal posts for the first time.

At first, the forward pass developed slowly because of the restrictions imposed on it. The man who took the snapback had to run five yards left or right of center before he could throw the ball. If an incomplete pass went out-of-bounds on last down, the ball went to the other team at the point where it went out, and for a few years a long sideline pass on last down was as good as a punt. The ball also went to the other team if an offensive interior lineman touched it or if the ball hit the ground before it was caught, and if a pass was touched but not caught it was a free ball. A receiver was lucky to catch a pass since a defender could knock him down before he caught it. With such rules, just to throw the ball was a risk which required great skill, and it is no wonder that the forward pass was not used more at first.

At Chicago, Stagg, ever trying to improve the game, used a play-action fake to a back running into the line followed by a pass from the quarterback to an end, or a pitch to a halfback who then threw a pass, or a rollout pass to an end or halfback, or a forward pass to an end in tight or a flanker split wide.

It was not Stagg, however, but Eddie Cochems, ex-teammate of Pat O'Dea at Wisconsin, who first made extensive use of the forward pass. Cochems, who took over at St. Louis this season, was unbeaten in 11 games with the new offensive weapon. During the summer, he developed the first passing combination of Brad Robinson to Jack Schneider. Robinson completed the first legal forward pass early in September against Carroll College. With Robinson throwing eight to ten passes each game, the opposition was always off balance trying to defend against them. A month later on October 3, Sam Moore of Wesleyan completed an 18-yard pass to Irv Van Tassell in the Yale game.

Chicago's 5'7", 145-pound quarterback, Walter Eckersall, was all-American this year for the third time. In the last game of the year against Nebraska, he drop-kicked five field goals for the second time in his career, the only player to perform this feat twice. At halftime, the students and faculty presented a diamond-studded watch to Eckersall bought with donations limited to 25 cents. At the top in place of noon was a picture of coach Stagg, and at the bottom was Eckersall's picture. The remaining numbers, five on each side, were replaced with pictures of the Chicago starting lineup.

With Tad Jones at quarterback, Yale won nine games and gave up only one touchdown all season. In the backfield were captain Sammy Morse at fullback, and halfbacks Howard Roome, Billy Knox, and Paul Veeder. At the ends were Bob Forbes, Clarence Alcott, and Howard Jones. The interior linemen from right to left were Horatio Biglow, Art Erwin, Clarence Hockenberger, Arthur "Butch" Brides, and Ray Paige, the intercollegiate wrestling champ.

Yale had thrown a few passes during the season, but Walter Camp put in some new ones for use against Princeton and Harvard. One was a deep pass to Alcott, who was surrounded by Yale players to protect him. Since the opposing line was on the passer before Alcott was downfield, he had Veeder throw from punt formation or a fake end run. Another version was a tackle-eligible pass in which Forbes dropped off the line, making Paige a pass receiver.

Under its new coach, Bill Roper, Princeton won nine games and gave up only a touchdown and a field goal. They played Yale in the tenth game and battled to a 0–0 tie. Near the end of the first half, Yale drove to the Princeton 25. The tackle-eligible pass was completed at the seven-yard line but disallowed because the official did not see Forbes drop back. Cap Wister scored for the Tigers on a 33-yard run, but it was negated by a holding penalty.

Against unbeaten Harvard, Camp's new play was tried again. After each team blocked a field goal, Veeder faked an end run at the Harvard 25 and tossed to Alcott on the four-yard line. Roome punched it in two plays later for the only score, and Princeton and Yale divided the championship.

Members of this championship Princeton team were quarterback Eddie Dillon, halfbacks Eddie Harlan and Sumner Rulon-Miller, and fullback Jim McCormick. In the line were center Walt Phillips, guards Ed Stanard and captain Herb Dillon, tackles Jim Cooney and Don Herring, and ends Caspar Wister and Amos Hoagland.

1907

With Tad Jones returning at quarterback, Yale was unbeaten for the second year in a row. The Bulldogs won nine games, and the only hurt was another scoreless battle, this time with Army. Tackle Ray Biglow was captain this year, and beside him at right end was Clarence Alcott. On the other end were Bob Burch, who shared the job with Howard Jones, and tackle Graham Foster. The guards were sophomores Carroll Cooney and William "Dutch" Goebel, with Ed Congdon at center. The halfbacks were Steve Philbin and Art Brides, who was switched from guard this year. At fullback was another sensational sophomore, Ted Coy.

Other than Army, the game which caused most concern was with Princeton. Yale fell behind early as Tiger center Walt Phillips and tackle Al

Booth blocked an outside punt. Booth scooped up the bounding ball and ran 70 yards for a score. The fired-up Tigers then drove to Yale's eight-yard line, where Ed Harlan went to the bar for a field goal to give Princeton a 10–0 halftime lead.

Yale (9-0-1)			Carlisle (10-1-0)		
25	Wesleyan	0	40	Lebanon Valley	0
11	Syracuse	0	10	Villanova	0
17	Springfield	0	91	Susquehanna	0
52	Holy Cross	0	18	Penn State	5
0	Army	0	14	Syracuse	6
44	Villanova	0	15	Bucknell	0
11	Washington & Jefferson	0	26	Penn	6
22	Brown	0	0	Princeton	16
12	Princeton	10	23	Harvard	15
12	Harvard	0	12	Minnesota	10
			18	Chicago	4
206		10	267		62

Hardly anyone spoke in the Yale dressing room during intermission. George Sanford, center for the 1891 Blues who watched line play from his seat behind the north goal eight rows up, was called in. Walter Camp offered a few comments. Ted Coy paced up and down like a caged tiger. Tad Jones fought to hold back the tears. Ray Biglow sat wrapped in a blanket, praying.

In the second half, it was the Elis who were fired up. Tad Jones returned a Princeton punt 40 yards to the Tiger 32. Three plays picked up ten yards. Then Coy banged ahead to the four-yard line and scored two plays later. Biglow's PAT made it 10–6.

On their next possession, Coy ran like a tornado through a greenhouse for five yards, ten yards, five yards. Finally, he was over the goal, but a penalty cancelled the score. Jones put down the ball on a fake field goal, then tossed a 15-yard pass to Alcott at the 10-yard line. From there, Coy blasted into the end zone, and another Biglow conversion gave them a 12–10 victory.

Yale Field could not contain the delirious crowd. It overflowed onto Derby Avenue and east to the campus. The names of Coy and Jones and Biglow were on everyone's lips at the school rally the following week. A generation later, Coy's name was still voiced with reverence by old Blues.

On the next Saturday in Cambridge, the fervor of the Yale and Harvard fans lasted the entire game. In the first two minutes, Harvard tried a field goal but failed. Two minutes later, Coy missed a field goal for Yale. After Coy ran back a punt to the Crimson 45, he led a drive to the goal and finally scored. Coy scored again in the second half and became a living legend, as the Bulldogs were national champs. Near the end of the game, Jack Wendell was stopped at the one-yard line to keep intact Yale's record of not being scored on through the line this year.

After a three-year stint at Cornell, Pop Warner returned to Carlisle.

With an enrollment of only 250 boys of college age, he built the Indians into one of the best teams in the country. As usual, they played a few warmup games at home against local schools. Then with a handful of subs, they traveled the nation taking on top teams everywhere and beating most of them. Pride of race and a chance to compete with the white man as equals gave them a determination which usually made their few subs unnecessary. Their enthusiasm for sports and good hand, eye, and foot coordination made them adept at the game, but their weakness was a cavalier attitude. The game following a decisive victory was a letdown they often lost. Never did they have a perfect season, and 1907 was no exception.

After Stagg, Warner was the most inventive of coaches. He was not the first to use the forward pass, but he was the first to use it extensively in the East. Warner did not invent pulling linemen, but his plays often had guards and tackles preceding the runner as blockers. For the past few years, the rules required a man outside and behind an end if six men were on the scrimmage line. Warner took the "boxing the tackle" maneuver, in which an offensive end blocked the tackle and a halfback sealed off the defensive end, and made it a power formation which had more backs to block for the ball carrier. Without using mass interference, Warner came as close as he could while staying within the rules.

It was the Carlisle Indians who opened the eyes of the East to the forward pass. Because Warner had a pair of halfbacks who were no bigger than schoolboys, Frank Mt. Pleasant (134 pounds) and Fritz Hendricks (143 pounds), he mixed in the passing game. Since the ball could not be thrown unless it was five yards from the center, Warner had his left half take the snapback, and with this fast-paced attack they ran the opposition ragged.

Last year's fifth-place Carlisle team used the forward pass from the opening gun. All of Carlisle's points in the Villanova game came as a result of the forward pass. Fullback Pete Hauser scored a touchdown after Mt. Pleasant completed a 30-yard pass to Albert Exendine. Another Mt. Pleasant pass from his spot at left half set up Hauser's 25-yard field goal. Seven days later, after a midweek warmup in which Susquehanna was buried, Exendine scored against Penn State on a pass from Mt. Pleasant. In the Bucknell game, Jim Thorpe, in his first year as a sub for Hendricks, ran a kickoff back but fumbled. The ball was taken on the bounce by Owl, who ran it in for a touchdown.

One week later, Penn was humiliated with the forward pass. The Penn players threw the ball end-over-end, while the Indians riddled the Quaker secondary with spiralled bullet passes. Hendricks helped the Indian cause with a 100-yard touchdown run. As usual after a great victory, Carlisle suffered a letdown, as they lost their only game of the year to Princeton.

On the following Saturday against Harvard, the Indians came out throwing. In the opening minutes, Mt. Pleasant's completions of 25 yards and 20 yards put the ball on Harvard's five-yard line, where Hauser plunged over. In Carlisle's second scoring drive, Mt. Pleasant connected on a 31-yarder, and again Hauser crashed over. Mt. Pleasant also scored on a 75-yard touchdown dash as the Indians beat the Crimson for the first time, 23–15.

Next week found Carlisle in Minneapolis against Minnesota. On the fourth play of the game, the Gophers went ahead on George Capron's 35-yard field goal. Not long after, the Indians passed their way to Minnesota's 5-yard line. From a fake field goal, captain Antonio Lubo scored on a short pass. Then end William Gardner scored on a 35-yard touchdown pass to give the Indians a 12–4 halftime lead. In the last half, a Carlisle fumble at the goal line was returned the length of the field for a Minnesota touchdown by end Ed Chestnut to make the final score 12–10.

In the last game of the year against Chicago, the Indians held Wally Steffen to a single field goal. Hauser place-kicked three field goals for Carlisle and threw to Exendine at end for the game's only touchdown as the Maroons were downed, 18–4.

Harvard never recovered from the Carlisle defeat and lost its last two games. Princeton lost to both Cornell and Yale. In the Midwest, the Missouri Valley Conference was formed, and Michigan left the Western Conference for ten years because of a dispute over control of athletics. Carlisle's ten wins and one loss was the best so far for the Indians, and made them runner-up nationally.

1908

Pennsylvania	(11-0-1)		Harvard	(9-0-1)	
6	West Virginia	0	5	Bowdoin	0
30	Ursinus	0	16	Maine	0
16	Bucknell	0	18	Bates	0
11	Villanova	0	10	Williams	0
6	Penn State	0	44	Springfield	0
23	Gettysburg	4	6	Navy	6
12	Brown	0	6	Brown	2
6	Carlisle	6	17	Carlisle	0
25	Carnegie Tech	0	6	Dartmouth	0
34	Lafayette	4	4	Yale	0
29	Michigan	0			
17	Cornell	0			
215		14	132		8

Penn won 11 games this year but was tied by Carlisle, 6–6. Other than this lone touchdown, which was scored by Jim Thorpe on a 60-yard run, the Quakers yielded only two field goals all year. Thorpe and captain Bill Hollenback, Penn's all-American fullback, were so beat up from pounding each other all afternoon that both of them spent most of the next week recuperating in a hospital. Penn destroyed a good Michigan team that included

Harvard's 1908 champions. Front row: Charles Crowley, Perry Smith, Fred Ver Wiebe. Second row: John Cutler, Charles Dunlap, Hooks Burr, Hamilton Fish, Joe Nourse, Gil Browne. Third row: Ham Corbett, Henry Sprague, Bob McKay, Bob White, Vic Kennard, Howard Leslie. Back row: coach Percy Haughton, Sam Hoar, Paul Withington, George West, manager Rich Eggleston.

guard Al Benbrook and center Germany Schulz. The Quaker line triple-teamed Schulz so often that he left the game with a hip injury. Yost, the Michigan coach, made many Crimson faces turn redder when he said that Penn was a better team than Harvard.

Penn's head coach was Sol Metzger, captain and end on the 1903 Quakers. In addition to Hollenback, end Hunter Scarlett was also chosen on Walter Camp's first team All-America. Other members of this Penn eleven included center Bill Marks, guards George Dietrich and Bob Lamberton, tackles Fred Gaston and Dexter Draper, and Harry Braddock at end. The ball carriers were halfbacks Jack Means and John Manier, and Penn had a pair of alternating quarterbacks, Al Miller and Chuck Keinath.

Metzger had a lot of help from great Quaker players of the past. The defense was handled by Dr. Buck Wharton, guard on the first guards-back formation, and also by Dr. John Hedges, an end on the 1897 champions. The offensive strategy was outlined by Dr. Carl Williams, quarterback and captain of the 1895 Quakers. Dr. Williams used his specialty, the onside punt, and the split and delayed bucks which were effective the year he was captain.

This year began the regime of Percy Haughton as head coach at Harvard. With Haughton's arrival, Harvard began its golden age of football, and for the next dozen years eclipsed Yale as the perennial power in the East and the country. Haughton brought to Harvard a discipline and expertise never seen before on the Cambridge campus. He was the first to hire a full-time coaching staff, one for linemen, one for ends, one for backs, and one for scouting opponents. Using dominoes to demonstrate, the coaches pooled their ideas like generals in a military campaign, and the result was a well-conceived operation to which everyone had contributed.

Haughton's Harvard teams were rough cut, and anyone on their schedule knew they were in for a struggle when they played the Crimson. In the first month of the season, Haughton drove his players in practice and lashed them with his tongue. This six-week period of discipline and training produced a team which was capable of competing physically with anyone at anytime. During this grueling session, the resentment built against Haughton until they developed the confidence that breeds champions; then the attitude of coach and team welded together and built an unshakeable loyalty.

As an ex-punter, Haughton emphasized all facets of the kicking game. The punt was used as an offensive weapon to gain field position, and much of the time Harvard punted on first or second down when the ball was in Crimson territory. Downfield coverage of punts was stressed in order to recover a punt which the enemy had fumbled. Downfield tackling was also stressed to prevent the runback of a punt. Pressure was put on the other team's punter in order to block the kick or cause a poor one. Half of Haughton's plays were run from punt formation, and the Crimson put on an offensive charge only when they were within scoring distance.

Like any intelligent person, Haughton took what was good in other systems and discarded the rest. He used the fundamentals of Yale's superior line play, Warner's deception at Carlisle, the power of Penn's guards-back formation, the discipline of the Army team, and made them his own. To that end, he hired Charley Daly to coach the backs, and for line coach he hired ex–Army tackle Ernest "Pot" Graves, who was familiar with Yale's line play. If Haughton had a system it was superb conditioning, play for the breaks, and wear down an opponent to win in the final quarter.

Haughton was the first to use defensive signals, given by both sign and number, so that everyone knew his assignment. He was also the first to have the defensive end charge the play in order to stop it before it got started, instead of letting him follow the play as a safety man. He used a metronome to teach his quarterbacks the right cadence with which to call signals.

Haughton's play-callers were known for their smooth handling of the ball as they fed it to different backs. These fakes, trick plays, pivots, and mouse-traps were called "psychologicals," for their purpose was to lure the defense into making a mistake.

The Harvard team was a tightly knit outfit led by its 6'4", 200-pound tackle, Hamilton Fish. Since an end was permitted to drop off the line into the backfield, the tackle became an end and a pass receiver. With his strength and height, Fish won as much fame for catching passes as he did for blocking. In those days, a defensive back could hit a pass receiver before he even touched the ball. On a pass against Dartmouth, Fish was belted to earth at the 5-yard line. Without taking his eyes off the ball he caught it on his knees, a play which led to the game's only score by halfback Howard Leslie.

Others on the team were quarterback John Cutler, halfbacks Ham Corbett and Bob White, fullback Fred "Dutchy" Ver Wiebe, center Joe Nourse, guards Sam Hoar and Paul Withington, tackle Bob McKay, and end Gil Browne.

Jim Thorpe and the Carlisle Indians gave Harvard a little concern because of their win the previous year. Always seeking to bend the rules, Pop Warner, the Carlisle coach, came up with a new wrinkle. In the Carlisle-Syracuse game one month earlier, Warner had sewn football-shaped pads on the jerseys which were worn by backs and ends. The Syracuse coach, Howard Jones, told Haughton about it. When Carlisle arrived in Cambridge, Haughton asked Warner about the sewn-on footballs and was told there was nothing in the rules against it. On game day, Haughton had the game ball painted crimson like the Harvard jerseys.

"You can't do that!" Warner protested.

"Glenn, there's nothing in the rules against it," Haughton replied.

Both coaches agreed to a regulation ball, while Warner had the Carlisle team change jerseys. The Indians couldn't dent the Harvard defense and were shut out, 17–0. A pass took them to the 10-yard line, but here they stalled. Thorpe also broke loose on a 65-yard run, but was pulled down by Cutler on the four-yard line.

Harvard and Yale both came down to the last game unbeaten, but each had a tie. Vic Kennard of Harvard had practiced drop-kicks all summer with all–American center Joe Nourse. Instead of waiting for the signals to be called, they worked out a play in which Nourse centered the ball when Kennard raised his right toe. With a storybook finish, Harvard moved the ball 65 yards to the 15-yard line where Yale stiffened.

"Send me in, coach," Kennard pleaded.

"All right, all right. Give it a try," was the answer.

While both teams waited for the signals which never came, the toe was raised, and Nourse snapped the ball. Everyone was caught off guard, including Haughton. Kennard left-footed the ball over the crossbar for a 4–0 win and the championship. The Harvards were ecstatic that day, but Kennard and Nourse laughed all the way to the locker room because they had put one over on the Old Drillmaster himself, Percy Haughton.

At Carlisle, Warner used a cross-body block for the first time. Instead of just using the shoulder to block, the Indians threw their bodies across an opponent's legs, and for the next few years this method was known as the Indian block.

Behind all–American Wally Steffen, Eckersall's successor at Chicago, the Maroons won the Western Conference championship for the second year in a row. A pair of honey-fingered ends in the line-up, Pat Page and John Schommer, made it possible for Steffen to retreat on a fake pass and then dash through center or around end, the first quarterback to run the ball in this manner.

Steffen worked this play to perfection in the Cornell game. Fading back as if to pass, he faked a run to the right and gave the ball to right end Page on a reverse. Page then ran 30 yards to the Cornell 15-yard line. Two plays later, Steffen employed a variation of this fake pass and reverse. He dropped back as if to pass, faked another run right and handed the ball to Page going left. Page stopped after a step or two and left-handed a scoring pass to Schommer in the end zone for a 6-6 tie. Steffen added to his laurels with a 100-yard touchdown run against Wisconsin and a 75-yard scoring run against Minnesota.

Elsewhere in the country, tackle Cap Gandy, guard Babe Noblet, and Doc Fenton at quarter helped Louisiana State win all ten games while holding opponents to a touchdown, field goal, and safety. Gil Dobie became coach at Washington and was unbeaten in the next nine years, an all-time record. Kansas won all nine games, and Washington and Jefferson wore numbers on football jerseys for the first time.

1909

Yale (10-0-0)		Harvard (8-1-0)	
11 Wesleyan	0	11 Bates	0
15 Syracuse	0	17 Bowdoin	0
12 Holy Cross	0	8 Williams	6
36 Springfield	0	17 Maine	0
17 Army	0	11 Brown	0
36 Colgate	0	9 Army	0
34 Amherst	0	18 Cornell	0
23 Brown	0	12 Dartmouth	3
17 Princeton	0	0 Yale	8
8 Harvard	0		
209	0	103	17

Yale was unbeaten, untied, and unscored on in ten games and was national champion. Six members of the squad made first team All-America, including the whole right side of the line from center to end, plus Ted Coy at fullback and halfback Steve Philbin. The left guard, left tackle, and quarterback were second team all–American. So many Yale linemen were on the All-America team that Bill Goebel, who was first string all–American guard in 1908, was placed on the second team this year.

From tackle to tackle, Yale's interior line averaged over 209 pounds. At center was 232-pound Carroll Cooney, as fast as he was big. The left guard was Ham Andrus, and at left tackle was Henry "Heine" Hobbs, both 208 pounds. The right tackle was 188-pound Ted Lilley, and the right guard was 210-pound Dutch Goebel, the eastern intercollegiate wrestling champion. On the left end of the line was 190-pound John Kilpatrick, whose knee operation the previous year for cartilage damage was one of the first. Right end was shared by Ed Savage, a 184-pounder, John Field, and Henry Vaughan, a lightweight at 165 pounds.

Ted Coy at 195 pounds was the line-busting fullback on this stellar team, and Art Howe was at quarterback. Captain Coy was famous for his towering punts and field goals, although he drop-kicked with his instep instead of his toe. His blond wavy hair, white headband, and boyish good looks belied the piston-legged knees he gave to tacklers, and sometimes to the backs of his own men if they did not open a hole. At left half was 177-pound Steve Philbin, who provided the breakaway thrills, with Fred Daly and Fred Murphy, both 170-pounders, alternating at right half.

Two weeks before the season opened, Coy had his appendix removed and missed the first four games. Forced to cut down on carrying the ball, he concentrated in other areas. Against Army, he threw a 30-yard pass to Henry Vaughan, who sidestepped the remaining 15 yards to a touchdown. In the next game with Colgate, Coy kicked two field goals and added another against Princeton. Hobbs also blocked a Tiger punt for a safety, and Cooney blocked another one which Lilley picked up and ran in for a touchdown.

The Yale team was so tenacious on defense that no one seriously threatened their goal all year, and the closest anyone got was the 28-yard line. Completed passes were rare, and all year long Yale fans were treated to the greatest thrill of them all, the quarterback sack, as these battle-tempered forwards broke up passes in the enemy's backfield before they were able to set up. On offense, Art Howe seldom needed to pass, for the Yale backs gained consistently behind a line which cleared out the opposition with relentless efficiency.

The Yale team was the personification of talent and training. The training was provided by Howard Jones, an end on the 1907 squad just two years earlier. As a coach, Jones devoted over half of his practice time to the fundamentals of blocking and tackling. He watched everything with an eagle eye, often demonstrating to his players how he wanted it done. Then he would follow a play on the run in order to check the progress and iron out miscues. Jones spent much of his days and a part of his nights thinking football, often forgetting his appointments and misplacing his keys. He was so preoccupied that he frequently took a wrong turn going home, and questions had to be asked a second and third time before he looked up.

Jones taught line play in very simple terms: "You have a spot about a yard or two either side of you to see that nobody gets through. No matter who winds up with the ball, they won't go anywhere if you guard your own small territory and don't get faked out, trying to find where the ball is."

In his second year as coach of the Crimson, Percy Haughton had improved Harvard's interior line and it is doubtful if two better lines ever faced each other up to this time. In the middle were the Withington brothers, Lothrop at center and Paul at guard, both 190-pounders, with 193-pound Bob Fisher at the other guard. The tackles were 208-pound Bob McKay and their 200-pound captain, Hamilton Fish, with Perry "Bud" Smith and Gil Browne at the ends. In the backfield were halfbacks Howard Leslie and Ham Corbett, fullback Wayland Minot, and Dan O'Flaherty at quarter.

Harvard and Yale were both unbeaten when they met for the championship at the end of the year. Ted Lilley of Yale, who scored on a blocked punt against Princeton, was knocked out on the kickoff. Neither team could gain consistently, and Yale never got within 25 yards of a touchdown. Carroll Cooney poured through to block a Harvard punt by Wayland Minot in the end zone for a safety and two points. Yale was held to a pair of first downs in the game, so they usually punted on first down in order to get better field position. The strategy paid off, for Harvard fumbles of Coy's skyscraper punts turned the tide. Coy drop-kicked two field goals after these fumbles, one at the end of each half. With a safety and two field goals, which were now worth three points this year, Yale had an 8–0 victory.

Haughton also used a mousetrap play in this Harvard-Yale game, although backfield coach Charley Daly didn't think much of letting a lineman cross the line of scrimmage unmolested. Haughton's version of the mousetrap went through right tackle, where Henry G. Holt was playing in place of injured Ted Lilley. Holt darted across the line of scrimmage and then was smacked from the side by a Harvard back or the right end coming across. Harvard halfback Ham Corbett delayed, and then ran through the open spot for good yardage. The mousetrap was finally stopped by John Kilpatrick, who came across from his left end position to support Holt at tackle. Kilpatrick did yeoman work against the Crimson, for he not only backed up Holt but sped downfield all afternoon to cover Coy's booming punts.

Behind its all–American quarterback, 5'5", 145-pound Johnny McGovern, Minnesota won the Western Conference title. Against Chicago, McGovern drop-kicked three field goals and scored once on a touchdown. The touchdown was the result of a dipsy-doodle play which went from Rosenwald to Pettijohn to McGovern. Right half John Rosenwald took the snap from Earl Farnam at center and tossed a lateral out to Lyle Pettijohn, who had dropped back from his right end spot. Pettijohn then threw to McGovern at the line of scrimmage, and he ran 50 yards to the score. The right side of the line that bought the time to make it work were tackle Jimmy Walker and guard Harry Powers. This play has since come to be known as a flea flicker. It started as a sleeper play in which one player takes a long lateral in order to make a gain, but it ended in a forward pass to another player.

In the last game of the season with nonconference Michigan, the unbeaten Northmen lost the Little Brown Jug to the Wolverines, 15-6.

Earlier in the month, Michigan was handed its only loss of the year by Notre Dame, 11-3. After a field goal by Michigan's Dave Allerdice early in the game, Harry "Red" Miller carried the ball ten straight times to the Michigan goal, where Pete Vaughan took it over. The 5-3 Irish lead was never in danger until they fumbled late in the last quarter, but a Michigan field goal try was blocked, and Notre Dame's Billy Ryan later went 30 yards to the score that wrapped it up. It gave the Irish their first win over the Wolverines, and "The Notre Dame Victory March," introduced this year, began to be heard across the land.

In its second season under coach Hugo Bezdek, Arkansas won all seven of its games, mainly on quarterback Steve Creekmore's tosses to halfback Clint Milford. Beaten last year by St. Louis, 24-0, Bezdek turned to his former coach, Lonnie Stagg, for help. Stagg showed up in Fayetteville with Walter Eckersall, Bezdek's old teammate. Eckersall worked with Creekmore and taught him to throw a football effectively, a weapon that blitzed other teams for better than 26 points each game. Included were consecutive wins over Oklahoma, 21-6, and Louisiana State, 16-0.

Another Midwest team with an unbeaten record was Missouri. Coached by ex-Princeton end Bill Roper, Missouri had seven wins and tied Iowa State, 6-6. Led by captain Carl Ristine at center, they bested Kansas State, 3-0, Iowa, 13-12, and Kansas, 12-6.

Coach Bill Hollenback took Penn State to five wins and tied Carlisle, 8-8, and Penn, 3-3. In the Carlisle game, the Indians broke the ice on Pete Hauser's 38-yard scoring run as the second half started. Penn State struck back with a touchdown but still trailed, 6-5, when the conversion try by Larry Vorhis rebounded from the crossbar. Vorhis kicked the Lions into the lead with a 30-yard field goal, but later touched the ball down for a safety in the end zone when he thought it was a touchback.

Navy quarterback Earl Wilson and Army tackle Eugene Byrne were among the dozen gridiron fatalities which occurred this year. Byrne died after an injury in the Harvard game, and Army cancelled the rest of its schedule. His injury was aggravated by a rule which kept a player from returning to a game once he had left it; although Byrne departed after his injury, he had prolonged his stay in a game despite the terrific punishment he was taking.

III. Football Comes of Age

1910

Harvard (8-0-1)			Illinois (7-0-0)	
22 Bates	0		13 Millikin	0
32 Bowdoin	0		29 Drake	0
21 Williams	0		3 Chicago	0
17 Amherst	0		11 Purdue	0
12 Brown	0		3 Indiana	0
6 Army	0		27 Northwestern	0
27 Cornell	5		3 Syracuse	0
18 Dartmouth	0			
0 Yale	0			
155	5		89	0

The rules took another drastic change because of last year's deaths and injuries, especially at tackle. With halfbacks playing deeper to defend against forward passes, the tackle position was unsupported and became vulnerable to mass interference. In order to reduce injuries from mass interference plays, all interlocking interference was forbidden, no lineman could line up in the offensive backfield, and seven men had to be on the line of scrimmage when the ball was snapped.

In addition, the first man who handled the snapback could run anywhere without moving five yards left or right of center before he ran forward. The game was still one hour, but it was divided into four quarters, thanks to the work of John Heisman. Pushing and pulling the runner were forbidden, and any player who left the game could return at the start of the next period.

Another step in the right direction eased the restrictions on the forward pass. For the first time, a forward pass could be thrown across the scrimmage line at any point, but the passer still had to be five yards behind the line of scrimmage. Since the ball could cross the scrimmage line by a run or pass at any spot, the chalk lines parallel to the sideline disappeared, and the field changed from a checkerboard back to a gridiron again. After four years of getting battered by defensive backs, it was forbidden to make contact with a pass receiver until he touched the ball. To keep the foot in football, a forward pass could not exceed 20 yards, and the officials got a workout trying to change the 20-yard marking sticks on every play.

At Chicago, Stagg was among the first to take advantage of the new rule

Dr. Henry Williams, coach at the University of Minnesota, was an early innovator of the game.

which allowed the first man who took the ball from center to run anywhere. The result was Stagg's version of the first quarterback spinner. He had his quarterback, Norm Paine, spin and fake to a halfback or fullback, keep the ball himself, then complete the spin and dash straight ahead into the line.

In order to counter the loss of offensive punch due to no mass interference, Henry Williams devised the Minnesota shift. In this formation, one tackle lined up behind each guard, and both jumped into the spot between the guard and end just before the ball was centered. The backs shifted to line up behind the tackles, and each paused only long enough to meet the requirement that all must come to a complete stop. Then the ball was snapped, and everyone converged on a single spot. It was mass interference within the rule of seven men on the line of scrimmage. Its success lay in the inability of the defense to shift quickly to the point of attack, whether center, tackle, or end.

Glenn Warner's answer to no mass interference and seven men on the line of scrimmage was the Z-formation. It grew out of the rule requiring six men on the scrimmage line and one man outside the end a yard out and a yard back. He had already used it in a simple form at Carlisle with Frank Mt. Pleasant throwing passes from his position at left halfback. With the rule requiring seven players on the line of scrimmage, Warner moved a halfback outside the end one step out and one step back, and he placed one tackle beside the other to form a strong side line. The quarterback lined up behind the tackles, one halfback was out and behind an end as a wingback, and the fullback and other halfback were four yards to the rear in the shape of a Z with a truncated base. The extra tackle, quarterback, wingback, and fullback gave added power on a running play to the strong side as well as additional protection for the halfback on a pass play.

At Georgia Tech, John Heisman invented the Heisman shift in order to utilize backfield blocking behind a seven-man line. The team stood in back of the center and then shifted into position, usually with a balanced line. The backfield lined up behind the line in an I-formation, but sometimes shifted to the T with the ball going directly to the tailback. Just before the ball was snapped, everyone jumped into position and came to a brief stop. Like the Minnesota shift, Heisman's jump shift depended on the inability of the defense to react quickly enough to contain it. When both guards pulled and led the whole team to one side or the other, it was like trying to stop a runaway locomotive.

Harvard won all its games except for a scoreless fight with Yale and was national champion. They yielded only one touchdown all year, mainly because of their gold-plated defensive linemen, tackles Bob McKay and captain Lothrop Withington, and guards Bob Fisher and Wayland Minot. At the ends were Larry Smith and Dick Lewis, with Jim Perkins at center. In the backfield were Rich Wigglesworth at quarter, halfbacks Ham Corbett and Sam Felton, and a "vest-pocket Hercules" at fullback, Percy Wendell. At 5'5" and 175 pounds, it was like tackling a barrel when he burrowed through the line. Once in the clear, he caromed off players or sidestepped them with equal dexterity. The Cantabs escaped the ax in the last moments of the last game as captain Fred Daly of Yale drop-kicked a 45-yard field goal, which missed by inches.

For the first time, Illinois was a serious contender for the national title. The Illini were unbeaten, untied, and unscored on in seven games. The games with Chicago, Indiana, and Syracuse were won by identical 3–0 scores on field goals by halfback Otto Seiler. The one against Indiana came in the last minute of play to preserve a perfect year. Center John "Heavy" Twist anchored a steel-ribbed line which no one dented all season. Beside him at guard were captain Glen Butzer and Chet Davis, with tackles Red Springe and Jake Lanum, who took over when Charlie Wham was injured, and ends Tom Lyons and Ollie Oliver. The backfield had Henry Belting and John Merriman at quarter, halfbacks Lou Bernstein and Chet Dillon, and fullback William "Wooly" Woolston.

Two other teams were also unscored on this year. Pitt went through all nine of its games unbeaten, untied, and unscored on. Navy was unbeaten and unscored on, but met Rutgers in a scoreless conflict. Against Army, a gusting wind frustrated six field goal tries by Jack Dalton, but the seventh was good for a 3–0 victory.

With a line which averaged 234 pounds from tackle to tackle, Minnesota was unbeaten and unscored on until they met Michigan in their last game. The Wolverines were also unbeaten, but had three ties. In Michigan's line were its two all-Americans, 6'5", 265-pound captain Al Benbrook at guard and Stan Wells at end.

Yost, of Michigan, slowed down the Minnesota shift by having his linemen tear into the play before it took shape, and the contest became a titanic struggle between two huge behemoths. The Gophers fell on a blocked punt for a score early on, but it was voided because the ball had touched umpire Frank Hinkey and ruled dead.

Michigan went to its passing attack in the closing minutes. Wells moved to the backfield and hit on a pair of passes to end Stan Borleske at the 3-yard line. One crack at the Gopher line gained nothing. In the huddle, Benbrook told quarterback Neil "Shorty" McMillan, "Run this play over me." Behind Benbrook's earth-moving block, Wells surged over for the only score of the game, and Ann Arbor's Ferry Field was bedlam.

With its all-American quarterback, Earl Sprackling, kicking three field goals and completing five of six passes, Brown beat Yale for the first time, 21-0. One year before, 5'9", 150-pound Sprackling returned a kickoff 105 yards for a touchdown against Carlisle, which was minus Jim Thorpe for two years.

1911

Princeton	(8-0-2)		Navy	(6-0-3)	
37	Stevens	0	27	Johns Hopkins	5
37	Rutgers	0	21	St. John's	0
31	Villanova	0	16	Washington & Jefferson	0
6	Lehigh	6	0	Princeton	0
31	Colgate	0	0	Western Reserve	0
0	Navy	0	17	North Carolina State	6
20	Holy Cross	0	32	West Virginia	0
8	Harvard	6	0	Penn State	0
3	Dartmouth	0	3	Army	0
6	Yale	3			
179		15	116		11

Coach Bill Roper made Princeton the best team in the nation this year. Roper put together a defensive unit which had three linemen on the All-America team: end Sam White, guard Joe Duff, and tackle Eddie Hart. Offense was not to Roper's liking, for he had no system and devised no new plays. Most of his offense consisted of plays which had already worked for someone else, so he took what he liked and made it work for him. He had his assistants drill the squad in practice and master the details of coaching a team. His strength was in preparing a team emotionally for the struggle ahead. To Roper, football was 90 percent fight, and everything else was 10 percent. As a locker-room orator, Roper had few equals. He even told his players that anyone who wore the orange and black already had the other team licked.

In the Princeton-Harvard game, resumed for the first time since 1896, the Tigers put an all-out rush on a field goal try. Charles Dunlap swept in from his end position to block it. As Sam White picked up the ball, quarterback Tal Pendleton wiped out the last Crimson defender and White ran 90 yards to a score. Later, as Harvard kick return man Henry Gardner fielded a punt, White drove him back into the end zone for the winning safety.

Against Dartmouth, Roper's opportunism had a little help. On fullback Wally DeWitt's 45-yard field goal attempt, the ball hit the ground in front of safety man Frank Llewellyn and hopped over the crossbar for the only points of the contest.

In the season-ender with Yale, Sam White was the hero once more. After he ran 68 yards to score on a bad snap by Yale center Henry Ketcham, halfback Hobey Baker kicked the extra point for a 6-3 victory. The Tigers didn't make one first down, but the defense held on to win and take the title. Other members of this championship eleven were center Art Bluthenthal, guard Tom Wilson, tackle George Phillips, and halfback Bob Vaughan.

Last year's unscored on Navy team was unbeaten again, but they gave up 11 points and were tied three times. Babe Brown, sophomore guard, starred in the line. Captain Jack Dalton beat Army with another field goal to down the Cadets two years in a row by the same score, 3-0. As K.P. Gilchrist held the ball, this year's instant replay from the 23-yard line earned him the nickname of "Three-to-Nothing" Jack Dalton and a berth at fullback on the All-America team. The Midshipmen's scoreless brush with Princeton gave them a share of the national title.

With Jim Thorpe back after a two-year absence, Carlisle was again near the top nationally. The highlight of the season was with heavily favored Harvard, at Cambridge. The Crimson started its second team, a unit which was better than the first team of most schools. Thorpe, who sat out the previous week's Penn game with an injury, played with his right leg bandaged from ankle to knee.

Harvard roared to a quick touchdown by Ken Reynolds and led, 6-0. Thorpe cut the lead in half with a first-period field goal of 13 yards, and tied it by intermission on a 43-yarder. In the second half Haughton sent in his first squad and Harvard pushed ahead, 15-9, as Bob Storer scored for the Crimson and Thorpe's 37-yard field goal offset one by Paul Hollister of the Cantabs. With Thorpe carrying the ball on almost every play, the Indians took it to the Harvard front wall and shoved them back 70 yards on a sustained drive, even trying the wingback reverse Warner had designed for them. The line play and slugging were brutal, and Thorpe was knocked out and carried off unconscious. Possum Powell lunged over with a touchdown to tie the score.

Thorpe sat on the bench most of the last quarter. Only a few minutes were left in the game when he limped out and kicked a 48-yard field goal for an 18-15 victory. With right half Alex Arcasa holding each time, Thorpe's three-pointer in every quarter put him on the All-America team at half-back.

At quarterback for the Indians was Gus Welch. In the line from right to left were captain Sam Burd, Lone Star Dietz, Elmer Busch, Joe Bergie, Peter Jordan, Newashe, and Henry Roberts.

Six days later on a muddy field, the comatose Indians lost to Syracuse, 12–11. Thorpe's missed conversion would have tied the score and given them the best record of the year. As it was, their one-point loss and 11 wins were not far off the mark.

1912

Harvard	(9-0-0)		Wisconsin	(7-0-0)	
7	Maine	0	13	Lawrence	0
19	Holy Cross	0	56	Northwestern	0
26	Williams	3	41	Purdue	0
46	Amherst	0	30	Chicago	12
30	Brown	10	64	Arkansas	7
16	Princeton	6	14	Minnesota	0
9	Vanderbilt	3	28	Iowa	10
3	Dartmouth	0			
20	Yale	0			
176		22	246		29

This year brought rule changes which made the game familiar to modern eyes. The rule limiting a forward pass to 20 yards was abolished, and so were the 20-yard marking sticks which officials had to change continually. The field was shortened to 100 yards, an end zone of ten yards was added at each end of the field, and a forward pass caught in the end zone by an offensive team now became a touchdown instead of a touchback. A touchdown was now worth six points, a fourth down in which to gain ten yards was added, and a field goal which hit the ground before it bounced over the crossbar did not count. Harvard captain Percy Wendell invented a rubber nose guard which was held in place by gripping it with the back teeth. It was a marked improvement in that it had a hole in it to breathe through.

The zenith of Harvard football arrived this year. For over two seasons, the Cantabs were victorious in every game, as they rolled to 22 straight wins. Beginning with the last two games in 1911, Harvard won 30 times and was held to three ties in its next 33 games, the longest unbeaten streak in Harvard football.

Harvard won all nine games and was national champion. The 1912 Crimson edition possessed a remarkable mixture of lettermen and sophomores. In addition to left-footed punter Sam Felton at end and quarterback Henry Gardner, juniors Bob Storer and Harvey Hitchcock were back at tackle. Among the gifted sophomores were guard Stan Pennock, halfback

Huntington "Tack" Hardwick (so good that Percy Wendell was moved to fullback) and Charley Brickley, a drop-kicker without equal under 40 yards.

It was in the stretch drive that Brickley's masterful toe proved most devastating. Against Princeton, he drop-kicked two field goals and place-kicked one of 47 yards. In the Dartmouth game, he missed two field goals before making good on his third attempt from the 7-yard line. In the final game against Yale, he drop-kicked a field goal of 33 yards in the first half and another of 17 yards in the second half. In between, he ran 18 yards to a score after picking up a fumble. His 13 field goals, nine touchdowns, and one conversion gave him 94 points, a one-year Crimson record. To blink was to miss Brinkley's accomplished toe, for his kicks were known for their quickness and accuracy.

In his first year at his alma mater, coach Bill Juneau's Wisconsin team won all seven of its games and was Western Conference champion. Nine members of the team were placed on the All-Conference squad by the *Chicago Tribune,* including tackle Bob Butler, Wisconsin's first all-American lineman. The other eight members were tackle Ed Samp, guards Max Gelein and Ray Keeler, ends Ed Hoeffel and Hod Ofstie, fullback Al Tanberg, halfback John Van Riper, and Eddie Gillette at quarterback. The only player in the Wisconsin line not to make the All-Conference team was its center, Walter Powell.

Being number one is always important when you're at the top, and a game between Harvard and Wisconsin for the national title was proposed, but it was voted down by the Wisconsin faculty and never got off the ground.

For the past two years, coach Bill Hollenback's Penn State team was unbeaten in 17 games. Each year they won eight times, but in 1911 Navy held them to a scoreless tie. This year's team allowed only one touchdown while scoring 285 points themselves. During the off-season, Hollenback studied Pop Warner's methods at Carlisle, and the result was an attack which was unstoppable all year. One of the assistant coaches was a tackle on the 1911 Penn State team, Dick Harlow. At quarterback for the 1912 Lions was 5'5", 140-pound Shorty Miller, with pile-driving Pete Mauthe at fullback. The tailback was Punk Berryman, with Dan Welty at wingback. The line from left to right had Al Wilson, Dad Engle, Red Bebout, John Clark, Al Hansen, Levi Lamb, and Dexter Very.

Another good team was Vanderbilt. In the past three years, they won eight games each year, lost twice and were tied twice. The only game to slow them in 1910 was a scoreless skirmish with Yale. Led by quarterback Ray Morrison, guard Frog Metzger, and tackle Ewing "Big Un" Freeland, they gave up nine points in 1911 on a 9–8 loss to Michigan. This year's team, with center Buddy Morgan, tackle Tom Brown, end Enoch Brown, and Lewie Hardage at halfback, lost only to Harvard and played Auburn to a 7–7 tie.

At Carlisle, Pop Warner gave the Indians a new formation to use against their opponents. It was the single wing, an outgrowth of the Z-formation. Like its forerunner, the single wing had an unbalanced line and a wingback, both of them on the strong side. This strength to one side was

The Carlisle Indians of 1912. Top row: Charles Williams, Gus Welch, Jim Thorpe, coach Pop Warner, Robert Hill, William Garlow. Middle row: Pete Calac, Joe Bergie, Joel Wheelock, Stancil Powell, Joe Guyon, Elmer Busch. Front row: George Vetternack, Roy Large, Alex Arcasa. (Courtesy Cumberland County Historical Society.)

Warner's answer to greater use of backfield blocking, as all the backs were in a power alignment, especially the wingback, with hardly any shifting. In the single wing formation, called by Walter Camp the Carlisle formation, the halfback became a triple-threat tailback who could run, pass, or punt. It was an alignment which was tailor-made for versatile players like Jim Thorpe, who could do all three with equal skill.

Warner unveiled his single wing formation on November 9 at West Point. With Army tackles Leland Devore and Walter Wynne cut down by the wingback and end, the Indian backs raced around the open ends with ease. After Warner convinced Thorpe that a run off-tackle was as easy as running the ends, Thorpe ran inside while Army tried to protect its flanks. Reverses between Thorpe and Alex Arcasa bewildered the Cadets further. Carlisle lost the ball four times near the Army goal, or the score could have been higher. By the end of the contest a good Army team, including Charley Benedict and Dwight Eisenhower as linebackers, whose job was to shadow Thorpe, had been badly beaten, 27–6.

In their usual way, the Indians lost after a great win and had a 12-1-1 record. Their 504 points were high for the season, and so was Thorpe's 25 touchdowns and 198 points, a mark second only to the 210 points of Jim Leech at VMI in 1920.

1913

Harvard	(9-0-0)		Chicago	(7-0-0)	
34	Maine	0	21	Indiana	7
14	Bates	0	23	Iowa	6
23	Williams	3	6	Purdue	0
47	Holy Cross	7	28	Illinois	7
29	Penn State	0	14	Northwestern	0
23	Cornell	6	13	Minnesota	7
3	Princeton	0	19	Wisconsin	0
37	Brown	0			
15	Yale	5			
225		21	124		27

Harvard won its nine games for the second year in a row and repeated as national champion. Gone was the Crimson's great line smasher Percy Wendell, but his ability to slip tackles was taken by Eddie Mahan, in the first of his three years as all–American halfback. Charley Brickley was now fullback, with Fred Bradlee at halfback, and Mal Logan running the team at quarterback.

The hardboiled Harvard line was without weakness. At one flank was Frank O'Brien and at the other was Tack Hardwick, a fierce competitor who would rather block and tackle than carry the ball. At the tackles were Harvey Hitchcock and captain Bob Storer. The guard slots were held by Joe Gilman and two-time all–American Stan Pennock, with Wally Trumbull at center.

Charley Brickley continued to adorn his reputation as one of the greatest field goal kickers of all time. In the Princeton game, after captain Storer blocked a punt and recovered it, Brickley drop-kicked a 19-yard field goal in the mud to nip the Tigers, 3–0. It was the first time Harvard had ever beaten the striped knights in their bailiwick at University Field.

In the last game of the year against Yale, Haughton tried to psych the Elis before it began. He placed footballs on the field every ten yards, and then had Brickley punch them through the uprights one after the other. In the game, before a crowd of 42,000, Brickley was just as convincing. The Crimson gained ground on every exchange of Packy Mahan's cloud-scraping punts, and moved the ball into Yale territory. Brickley dropped back, and with his patented fluid motion drop-kicked a 35-yard field goal to put Harvard ahead, 3–0. Yale chose to kickoff, but the ball bounced off the crossbar and back on to the playing field. Harvard end O'Brien picked it up and touched it down behind the goal for what he thought was a touchback. The official promptly awarded the Blues a safety, which slimmed the score to 3–2.

After another punt exchange Logan held the ball for Brickley, and he kicked one from 40 yards out. Then the Yale safety man, Alex Wilson, erased an Eddie Mahan punt with a beautiful runback of 35 yards, and the half ended soon after.

Early in the second half, after a 30-yard run by Brickley, he drop-kicked his third field goal from the 38-yard line. Not long after, he boomed his fourth one through from 32 yards away. After Brickley intercepted a pass, the Cantabs worked the ball to the Yale 15. Brickley stepped back to the 24-yard line and drop-kicked his fifth field goal. His wrecking-ball right foot scored all Harvard's points in a 15-5 win, as Otis Guernsey of Yale kicked a 38-yard field goal in the last frame. Brickley's 11 field goals during the season pushed his career total to 24.

For the first time ever, Harvard had beaten Yale two years in a row and given the Crimson its first win over Yale at Harvard Stadium in six tries. The fans rushed onto the field and pounded Brickley on the back and clutched his uniform. In a few minutes, his jersey was in shreds and he ran for the locker room. In his absence, Percy Haughton was momentarily raised aloft in triumph. Then they began a snake dance around the classic Roman coliseum which lasted long after the game was over. Along the curve of the Charles River the revelry filled the evening air — even the old grads paraded noisily in the Yard that night.

Brickley's remarkable feat spread across the country like ripples in a pond. People everywhere felt the vicarious thrill of what he had done. In the streets and paths they talked about him in the same breath with the weather. In the shops his name was on everyone's lips like that of a personal friend. Schoolboys were bitten by the drop-kick mania, for they put down their hoops and sticks and tried to emulate their new hero by plunking footballs over every available fence and shed.

In the Midwest Stagg had another winner at Chicago, as his team won all seven games and was Western Conference champ. Led by all-American center Paul des Jardien, and a pair of horny-handed guards in Art Scanlon and Harvey Harris, and two ramrod tackles, Harold Goettler and Spike Shull, Chicago had a tough, aggressive line which nobody kicked sand on. At the ends were two shifty receivers, Stan Baumgartner and Earl Huntington, who made Stagg's passing game go, and gave the Maroons a good claim on the national title since all seven wins were over conference rivals, with no warmups against small schools.

Stagg helped himself to the title with the Statue of Liberty play, a variation of a fake which had been around for years. The principle of the Statue of Liberty went all the way back to 1898 when Clarence Herschberger handed the ball back to Walter Kennedy on a fake punt. After the forward pass had been legalized, Stagg modified this play for use against Cornell in 1908. He had Wally Steffen run back as if to pass, then give the ball to Pat Page, an end running behind him. In neither case did Herschberger or Steffen raise their hand as if to pass.

The Statue of Liberty play with the ball held aloft in an upraised arm appeared in the Minnesota game this year, only it was called the "cherry picker" at the time. It took place when the Minnesota safety man fumbled a punt which Chicago recovered on the Gopher 30-yard line. Chicago struck quickly, as captain Nels Norgren faked a pass. Pete Russell ran behind him and took the ball from his uplifted arm and almost ran it in for a score. He was pulled down near the goal, but fullback Snitz Pierce went over on the next carry. Fast-stepping Dolly Gray completed one of the best backfields Stagg ever had.

Ever since 1894, Stagg had not lost to Purdue. Year after year, "Stagg fears Purdue" headlined the sports page, but this year it was no joke. Coached by Andy Smith, Purdue had a good team with Elmer Oliphant its star running back. Early in the contest, Norgren zapped Oliphant with a tackle which flip-flopped him in midair. He came down running and raced ten yards the wrong way before he was downed for good. Quarterback Pete Russell later won it on a pair of field goals for Chicago. It was also this year that Ohio State was admitted to the Western Conference with John W. Wilce as its coach.

Another Midwest team making history this year was Notre Dame, only the Irish made news against Army by using the forward pass, not faking it. The pass had been used by Midwest teams as far back as 1906, when it became legal, but the East still put a premium on line play, a strong ground game, and punting. Coach Jesse Harper's Irish gave eastern teams a lesson at West Point that first day of November as the forward pass came of age.

Like Robinson and Schneider at St. Louis before them, Gus Dorais and Knute Rockne worked out during the summer to perfect their throwing and receiving skills. Notre Dame won its first three games of the season with a volley of passes each outing, so they were ready for the Cadets come game time. The Notre Dame victory over a strong Army team was no fluke.

The first quarter of the game was played at midfield, as both teams probed for a weakness. Army's all–American end, Lou Merillat, almost broke free on an end-around, but Rockne felled him with a slashing tackle. Merillat got up slowly, and Army knew the Fighting Irish had come to play. The heavier Army line shut down the Irish running attack, so Notre Dame took to the air. Short passes to Joe Pliska and smashes over center by fullback Ray Eichenlaub gained three first downs. When left end Rockne lulled an Army defensive back to sleep with a fake limp, Dorais threw a 35-yard strike to Rockne, whose limp underwent an instant recovery. Captain Rockne caught the ball in full stride on the five-yard line and stepped into immortality.

The Cadets struck back with plays they had practiced on by running into a pile of sandbags. The Army line inched the Irish back, and then a Vern Prichard to John Jouett pass moved them to the Notre Dame 15. Army's battlewagon backs, Leland Hobbs and Paul Hodgson, steamed ahead until Hodgson scored to tie it, 7–7.

Using the same punishing ground game, Army marched down the field again. Another pass from Prichard to Jouett put the ball on the five-yard line. The Irish called time out and dug in lower. Three smashes into the line and the ball was near the goal. An Irish holding penalty gave Army a first down. Three more blasts and they were over, with Prichard going in behind John McEwan after a fake pitch. Captain Ben Hoge's missed point-after kept it 13-7.

Now it was Notre Dame's turn. Starting on their 15, a pass from Dorais to Rockne took them to midfield. Then Dorais threw to Pliska on the Army 17 and hit Sam Finegan for a dozen more. Pliska went over tackle for the tying touchdown down from five yards out. The Irish had zipped 85 yards in just four plays. Dorais added the extra point, and Notre Dame led at the half, 14-13.

Charley Daly, Army coach, made some defensive adjustments at intermission. When he beefed up his porous defensive backfield, his weakened line became vulnerable to the Irish running game. Army's offensive whammo had not diminished, however, as Hodgson, Hobbs, and Frank Milburn carried the ball to the Notre Dame two-yard line. But Dorais intercepted a pass to Merillat in the end zone, which took the steam out of the West Point attack.

Notre Dame now opened up the Army's defense. After the ball sailed to Rockne and right end Fred Gushurst, Eichenlaub ran over to put Notre Dame ahead, 21-13. On the next drive the Irish filled the air with more passes, and right half Pliska caught the last one to make it 28-13. Notre Dame came right back with another pass to left half Finegan on the Army 30-yard line, and Eichenlaub carried it in for a 35-13 Irish victory. Notre Dame connected on 14 of 17 passes for 243 yards, and Goliath learned again what a missile can do in the hands of David.

. Paced by sophomore tackle Earl Abell, and their first all-American, quarterback Ellery Huntington, Colgate had a good team this season. After a scoreless bout with Cornell in the opener, they won five games, including a win over Yale, 16-6, and lost only to Army by a single point, 7-6. The winning score came on a 75-yard touchdown run by Vern Prichard in the closing seconds.

Mike Donahue's Auburn squad was the best one in the South, as they won all eight games and gave up only 13 points. After losing to Georgia and Bob McWhorter at the end of the previous season, the Tigers won 22 of their next 23 games, 21 by shutouts. Outstanding on the team, which used the cheer "War Eagle" for the first time, were end Henry Robinson, tackles Bill Louisell and Monroe Esslinger, halfbacks Kirk Newell and Rich Kearley, fullbacks Red Harris and Bedie Bidez, and Ted Arnold at quarter.

1914

With all-American John McEwan at center, Army was unbeaten in all nine of its games. It was their first all-winning season and their first national championship. Aided by Pot Graves, who helped build top-rated lines at Harvard for Percy Haughton, coach Charley Daly made the Army forward wall as good as any turned out at the Point. Alex "Babe" Weyand at tackle and Laurence "Cowboy" Meacham at guard were both all-American caliber. Bill "Bruiser" Butler and Joe O'Hare held down the other tackle and guard spots, respectively. With Bob Neyland at one end and Lou Merillat back at the other, the brawling Army defense held opponents to three touchdowns all year. Offensively, captain Vern Prichard ran the team at quarterback, with veteran Paul Hodgson providing enough punch to beat everyone by two touchdowns except Springfield. In the backfield with them were Charley Benedict, James Van Fleet, and Bill Coffin. Other team members who saw action were linemen Omar Bradley, John Goodman, Tom Larkin, and Charles Herrick.

Army	(9-0-0)		Illinois	(7-0-0)	
49	Stevens	0	37	Christian Brothers	0
13	Rutgers	0	51	Indiana	0
21	Colgate	7	37	Ohio State	0
14	Holy Cross	0	33	Northwestern	0
41	Villanova	0	21	Minnesota	6
20	Notre Dame	7	21	Chicago	7
28	Maine	0	24	Wisconsin	9
13	Springfield	6			
20	Navy	0			
219		20	224		22

In his second year at Illinois, coach Bob Zuppke had one of his better teams. He used an I-formation in which the quarterback was behind the center, and the rest of the backs lined up in a single file behind him. The quarterback turned and handed the ball to one of the backs running past on the right or left, and this swift-striking attack held the defense momentarily as they tried to figure which back had the ball on which side. With all-American guard Ralph Chapman to open holes, and a spirited foursome of George "Potsy" Clark at quarter, Gene Schobinger at full, and Harold Pogue and Bart Macomber as halfbacks, the Illini were undefeated in seven games. The linemen on this championship team were center Jack Watson, guard Frank Stewart, tackles Lennox Armstrong and Manley Petty, and ends Perry Graves and George Squier.

Zuppke stayed at Illinois for 29 years, a tenure at the same school surpassed only by a few other coaches. He was the first to have his guards drop back to protect the passer, for up to this time it was considered unmanly to give an inch on the line of scrimmage. He was also a master at preparing his squad emotionally for a game, especially if they were underdogs. When the material was thin, he employed the razzle-dazzle and flying trapeze, plays in which the ball was lateraled a number of times to confuse the opposition. His most enduring plays were the hook-and-lateral (a forward pass with a quick lateral to a trailing back), and a screen pass to a receiver who had a bevy of blockers in front of him. Zuppke's personality and wit were second only to Knute Rockne of Notre Dame.

Frank Hinkey, the Yale immortal, was signed to a three-year contract to coach his alma mater. He had always been a part of the Yale graduate coaching system in which the alumni assisted the captain of the previous year. Hinkey lasted two years. He had the qualities of a leader, but he assumed that everyone in a football suit could block and tackle like he used to do. He did not school his players in these fundamentals, and he was undone by the truism that football games are won by defense, for a poor defense will give up more points than the offense can score.

Hinkey's contribution as a coach was the lateral pass formation. He placed two men behind the quarterback in a V-alignment which allowed them to throw the ball backward to each other or forward to someone else. Notre Dame, still feeling its oats after stomping Army the year before, came into New Haven on the crest of a 27-game unbeaten streak. The Irish were demolished, 28-0. On the long train ride back to South Bend, Jesse Harper and his new assistant, Knute Rockne, overhauled the Notre Dame offense. In practice the following Monday, Harper installed the backfield shift he had learned at Chicago under Lon Stagg. He also added Rockne's idea of spacing the ends one step away from the tackles and shifting them in or out with the backfield.

Harvard was loaded this year with all-Americans Tack Hardwick at end, halfback Fred Bradlee, and versatile Wally Trumbull at tackle. Back at guard was three-time all-American Stan Pennock, and in his second year as all-American halfback was Eddie Mahan. Mahan could run as well as he could punt and drop-kick, and Hardwick loved nothing better than to put a shoulder into a ball carrier and hear him grunt. Dependable men were found at every position, including end Jeff Coolidge, tackle Ken Parson, guard Mel Weston, center Don Wallace, fullback Hugo Francke, and Mal Logan, the slickest of Haughton's faking quarterbacks. On the bench were a fistful of top-flight subs such as linemen Bill Underwood, Henry Atkinson, Al Weatherhead, Chuck Coolidge, Henry Smith, Fred Withington, and backs Richard King and Ernie Swigert.

Captain Charley Brickley missed most of the season because of an appendicitis operation, and it showed on the scoreboard. The Crimson got by Washington and Jefferson 10-9, but only on a touchdown in the final minutes of play. Against Penn State, Harvard was able to keep its unbeaten streak alive with another last-minute save. The Lions took a 10-0 lead and led 13-6 late in the game. Many of the fans were heading for the exits when Harvard fell on a fumbled punt by Penn State. Westmore Wilcox was sent into the game to run the buck lateral 99 play, a fake into the line with a lateral past the fast-charging Penn State end. Wilcox raced 60 yards for the score and crossed the goal at the corner of the end zone. Instead of a puntout for better position on the conversion, Fred Withington kicked it from the difficult angle to knot the score at 13-13, and give those who were left the last-minute thrill of escape from certain defeat.

Harvard's punchless offense beat Michigan 7–0 in its next game, but not before Michigan's 5'7", 153-pound Johnny Maulbetsch gained more yards than the whole Crimson backfield. Maulbetsch was placed on the All-America team, and for his heroic effort an award was named for him at Michigan. It is given to the freshman showing the greatest character, leadership, and spirit.

Although they fumbled continually, Harvard lived up to its potential against Princeton. The Crimson line was so inflexible that the Tigers never crossed midfield until late in the game. Eddie Mahan filled in beautifully for Brickley with two drop-kick field goals in a 20–0 win. In the next game with Brown, it was a different story. The Cantabs had to settle for a scoreless contest, as their field goal attempts failed time after time.

It was in the last outing against Yale that Harvard played its best game. Two long marches gave them a 12–0 lead, but Yale came back with a drive to the four-yard line, only to fumble. Jeff Coolidge picked up the ball and ran 96 yards to a score, breaking open the game. Charley Brickley, who had not been in the lineup since his operation six weeks before, stepped onto the field late in the game amid wild cheering. Harvard used a five-man line and spread its defensive backs to cut down the middle man in Hinkey's lateral pass attack. The 36–0 beating, the worst for Yale up to that time, dampened the inaugural of the Yale Bowl. As the Sunday sports page put it, "Yale had the Bowl, but Harvard had the punch." Harvard's two ties gave them a 7–0–2 record, but Haughton's greatest team did not finish at the top.

With Clyde Littlefield throwing to ends Charles Turner and Pete Edmond, Texas scored 358 points in winning its eight games. Wins included Rice, 41–0, Baylor, 57–0, Mississippi, 66–7, and Oklahoma, 32–7. Len Barrell's 121 points are still a one-year Longhorn mark. Linemen were tackles K.L. Berry and Alva Carlton, guards Lou Jordan and Jim Goodman, and center Pig Dittmar.

1915

Cornell (9-0-0)			Pittsburgh (8-0-0)		
13	Gettysburg	0	32	Westminster	0
34	Oberlin	7	47	Navy	12
46	Williams	6	45	Carlisle	0
41	Bucknell	0	14	Penn	7
10	Harvard	0	42	Allegheny	0
45	Virginia Tech	0	19	Washington & Jefferson	0
34	Michigan	7	28	Carnegie Tech	0
40	Washington & Lee	21	20	Penn State	0
24	Penn	9			
287		50	247		19

In Ithaca, New York, far above Cayuga's waters, Cornell had its first perfect season. They won all nine of their games, including two hard-fought victories over Harvard and Penn, and were national champions. The team was coached by ex–Yale halfback Al Sharpe, and led by all–American quarterback and captain Charley Barrett. Other members of the backfield included Fritz Shiverick, Carlton Collins, and Hans Mueller. In the line were all–American center William Cameron "Gib" Cool and end Murray Shelton. The tackles were Fred Gillies and Rex Jewett, Paul Eckley was the other end, and the guards were Ed Anderson, Pete Miller, and Herb Snyder.

Harvard boasted a stout line and its three-time all–American halfback, captain Eddie Mahan when they met Cornell in midseason. Both had won four games, and the eastern championship was at stake, so it was beat Harvard and take it all. Any game with a Haughton-coached team was a near brawl, and this one was no different. In the early minutes, the ball was chopped loose from Eddie Mahan on his own 25 and Cornell took over. Six plays later, Barrett went over for the only touchdown of the game and kicked the extra point. Not long after, Barrett and Mahan met head on, and Barrett was carried off the field unconscious. He awoke at halftime, but did not see any more action.

Mahan and Shiverick, who took over the kicking chores, then engaged in a fabulous kicking duel. One Mahan punt rolled dead on the three-yard line, and Shiverick put one out on the Harvard 13. Mahan's end sweeps were shut off by the Cornell outposts Shelton and Eckley, and the Crimson spent the last part of the game in their end of the field. In the third period, Shiverick iced the game with a 38-yard field goal, and Harvard's 33 games in a row without defeat ended in a 10–0 goose egg.

In the Penn game at Franklin Field, halfback Ben Derr and fullback Bill Quigley helped the Red and Blue to a 9–0 lead, but Barrett cut it to 9–7 with a touchdown. Led by Dave Hopkins and Heine Miller on the ends, tackle Neilson Matthews, guard Chuck Henning, and center Lud Wray, the resolute Quaker line held its thin margin until the final period began. Then Barrett pulled out all the stops. He dashed 40 yards around end for a touchdown to put Cornell ahead for the first time. Moments later, he scored another touchdown on a 25-yard sprint. He also kicked a field goal to score all of Cornell's points in a 24–9 victory.

Those who played that day and felt the electricity of Barrett's performance did not forget him. Years later, after a premature death due to an injury suffered in World War I, a memorial was erected in his honor at the entrance to Schoellkopf Hall on the Cornell campus. The inscription reads as follows:

IN MEMORY OF
CHARLES BARRETT – '16

Who died May 21, 1924, as a result of illness contracted in an explosion on the USS Brooklyn in Yokohama Harbor, Japan, during the World War.

As a tribute to his splendid loyalty and leadership and as homage to a most worthy gridiron adversary, we respectfully dedicate this tablet to Cornell University.

His Team Mates and Friends
and
The 1915 Pennsylvania Football Team

Late in February, Pop Warner and his wife were given a farewell dinner at Carlisle. Congressional investigations had disrupted practice the year before, and Warner must have seen it was the end of the trail for the Indians. The reforms and programs were not to his liking, and neither was the 5-9-1 record of 1914, his worst ever at Carlisle. In the 10–3 loss to Pitt, Warner was no doubt impressed by the excellent material he saw, especially center Bob Peck, whose outrageous yells in the game filled Forbes Field more than the Indian yells of the Indians themselves.

In any event, Warner found himself in the head coach's job at Pitt this year. The first day of practice passed without any incident, considering the stories which had preceded Warner from Carlisle. After three days there were still no rough workouts. By the end of the week, the Pitt squad was won over by Warner's humanity and know-how. A close-knit relationship formed between them that only respect and trust can build. They never lost for over three years, while forging a string of 31 consecutive wins. Only World War I stopped them.

At Pitt, Warner found good material indeed, and very well coached by Joe Duff, all–American guard on Princeton's defense-drilled 1911 national champs. Defense was also the name of the game this year for the Panthers. The team surrendered only 522 total yards all year, 300 by rushing and 222 by passing, for an average of just over 65 yards per game, all still Pitt records. In addition to Peck, the penurious defense included two future coaches, Claude "Tiny" Thornhill at tackle and John Bain "Jock" Sutherland, who was moved to guard this season.

Besides senior captain Guy Williamson at quarterback, the Pitt offense was fueled by not one, not two, but three fine running backs: freshman George McLaren at fullback, and sophomore halfbacks Andy Hastings and Jimmy DeHart. Against Navy, DeHart had a 105-yard scoring run, and in the Washington and Jefferson game he ran 60 yards to a score. Football historian Parke Davis rated Pitt number one, but they would be even better next year.

Led by coach Ewald "Jumbo" Stiehm, the Nebraska Cornhuskers won all eight of their games for the second time in three years, and only a scoreless go last season kept their three-year slate from being perfect. Since Stiehm took over in 1911, his Huskers won 35 games, lost 2 (both to Minnesota in the first two years), and tied 3. They also won the Missouri Valley Conference crown six straight times, including one title before Stiehm's arrival.

Guy Chamberlain, the big cannon in the Nebraska armory, was named the most valuable player in the Missouri Valley Conference for the past two

All-American Fritz Pollard of Brown.

seasons. As a halfback the previous year, he scored on a 95-yard run against Michigan State, and on an 80-yard jaunt in the Kansas State game. Against Kansas, he scored twice on runs of 70 and 58 yards. This year he was shifted to end, and scored 96 points on 16 touchdowns. Five of his touchdowns were against Iowa when he returned to halfback for the game.

It was in the Notre Dame game that Champ Chamberlain brought Husker football national attention. Playing halfback in another game, he tossed a pass 37 yards to end Ted Riddell, and hustled around end to score on the next play. The Irish came alive after they blocked a punt and cruised to a 13-7 lead. In the second half, Nebraska again went to its passing game as Joe Caley hit Chamberlain for 20 yards and Chamberlain passed to Caley for 19 more. The Champ then tore around end for his second touchdown to even the count at 13 points each. The score remained knotted until late in the game when Nebraska drove goalward once more. Chamberlain threw 17 yards to Herb Reese and 35 yards to Riddell, and the Huskers forged ahead 20-13. Notre Dame stormed back as Arthur "Dutch" Bergman scored again, but the extra point fluttered to the side and the Cornhuskers had a one-point win.

Members of the 1915 Nebraska team included Chamberlain and Riddell on the flanks, tackles Edson Shaw and Ed Corey, guards Paul Shields and Earl Abbott, with Ellsworth Moser at center. Joe Caley was at quarterback, the halfbacks were Jimmy Gardner and Dick Rutherford, and at fullback was Hugo Otoupalik.

The midlands also spawned another great team this year, as Oklahoma became the first team to use the forward pass as their main offensive weapon. Due to the weakness of its running game, coach Benny Owen continued the aerial circus started the previous year by Texas coach Dave Allerdice. Even though opponents geared up for Oklahoma's passing game, the Sooners still scored 25 touchdowns through the air. OU completed passes for over 1700 yards, and in many games the passing yardage exceeded the yards gained by running. Oklahoma won all ten of its games, and in half of these contests the passing attack gave them a come-from-behind win. Opponents usually rushed Sooner halfback Forest "Spot" Geyer (so named because of his pin-point passing), but he still managed to get the ball away to right end Homer Montgomery, who was double-teamed most of the time. Geyer averaged 30 passes each game, and in the celebrated shoot-out with Clyde Little-field of Texas, this air-express duo put the ball in the air no less than 71 times.

A favorite weapon in the OU attack was the option pass or run. If the defensive back came up to stop a run, the ball was thrown over his head. If he played back for a pass, OU ran the end. It never worked better than in the Missouri game, which Oklahoma won 24-0. On OU's second touch-down, Rayburn Foster completed a 20-yard toss to Monty "Hap" Johnson. On the next play, Foster faked a pass to keep the defensive man back, and then ran for a touchdown behind a convoy of blockers.

To the north, Minnesota and Illinois were the powers in the Big Ten. Led by captain Bernie Bierman at halfback and end Bert Baston, Minnesota had six wins and a 6-6 tie with Illinois. The Illini had five wins and were again undefeated but had two ties, one with Minnesota and a 3-3 decision with Ohio State. Returning with captain Jack Watson at center were end George Squier, quarterback Potsy Clark, and halfbacks Bart Macomber and Harold Pogue.

In Texas, eight schools met and formed the Southwest Conference. Its first members were Arkansas, Baylor, Louisiana State, Oklahoma, Okla-homa A&M, Southwestern, Texas, and Texas A&M. At the end of the year, Southern Methodist replaced Oklahoma, and Rice took Louisiana State's place. After two years, Southwestern dropped out, and in 1923 Texas Chris-tian replaced Oklahoma A&M.

In California, the Rose Bowl game was renewed at the end of the year, with Brown chosen to play Washington State. Among the 60-minute players for the Cougars were linemen Silas Stites and Asa Clark, and halfback Ben-ton Bangs. At right guard for Brown was Wallace Wade, who would return to the Rose Bowl as a coach. At halfback was their great black all–American, 5'8", 150-pound Fritz Pollard, whose hunched-over running style made tacklers slide over him. Before 7,000 spectators who ignored the rain, Pollard gained only 46 yards in the mud. A pair of last-half touchdowns by Ralph Boone and Carl Dietz won it for the Cougars, 14-0.

Numbers on the backs of jerseys became standard this year. At first, some teams changed a player's number each week in order to confuse the op-position. The field judge, who was used sporadically, as numbered jerseys were, since 1908, became a permanent position. His main duty was to keep time, and from his position deep behind the defensive secondary, he also aided the referee on any downfield decisions concerning the ball.

1916

Pittsburgh (8-0-0)		Army (9-0-0)	
57 Westminster	0	3 Lebanon Valley	0
20 Navy	19	14 Washington & Lee	7
30 Syracuse	0	17 Holy Cross	0
20 Penn	0	53 Trinity	0
14 Carnegie Tech	6	69 Villanova	7
46 Allegheny	0	30 Notre Dame	10
37 Washington & Jefferson	0	17 Maine	3
31 Penn State	0	17 Springfield	2
		15 Navy	7
255	25	235	36

Pop Warner knew what he was doing when he became head man at Pitt, for he rated the 1916 Panthers as the best team he ever coached. Back at center was vocal Bob Peck, along with tackle Tiny Thornhill and guard Jock Sutherland. Back were the stableful of stallions in the backfield named Hastings, McLaren, and DeHart, with Foxy Miller at quarterback. The remainder of this wrecking crew were tackles Len Hilty and Pud Seidel, guard Dale Sies, and ends James Patrick Herron and Clifford "Red" Carlson.

With this outfit, Pitt won all eight games again and was national champion. DeHart and Hastings made big gains around Navy's ends but could only earn a one-point win. The Panthers then proceeded to beat everyone by 20 points, except for their inter-city neighbor a mile down the road, Carnegie Tech. The winning touchdown against Carnegie was made by quarterback Foxy Miller on an 88-yard dash. Jimmy DeHart gained 786 yards overland this season, and George "Tank" McLaren built a reputation by never being stopped without making a gain. After the game with Penn, Quaker coach Bob Folwell stated most emphatically, "Pop Warner has the best team that ever played football. Man for man no team in the country can compare with Pitt."

With this formidable line up, the single wing formation and its unbalanced line gave Pitt all the power it needed. In the last few seasons, however, opposing defenses learned to minimize the power of the Z-formation and the single wing by spreading out to stop the strong side of the offensive line. In order to counter this strung-out defense, Warner had used a reverse to the weak, or short side, at Carlisle. The reverse to the short side was, in turn, stopped by the defensive tackle.

To neutralize the effectiveness of the defensive tackle on a short-side reverse, and to give all his grade-A backs a chance to carry the ball, Warner experimented with the double wing, or A-formation this year. In the double wing, a halfback, or wingback, was put outside and back of each end to block a defensive tackle on one side or the other. The quarterback still lined up behind a tackle, and the fullback was the lone back in the rear.

Fakes and reverses abounded in the double wing, as a play was run to either side with equal facility. The fullback gave the ball to a wingback, who in turn kept it or handed it to the other wingback going the opposite way. The fullback could also run into the line, give the ball to a tackle on a buck lateral, and the tackle could then hand it to a wingback coming across behind the line. The double wing also made the passing game effective, as the two wingbacks spread the defense. It worked best with a fullback who could throw accurately to both sides.

This year's Army team was even better than the national champions of 1914. Only three men remained from that championship eleven, captain John McEwan at center, Cowboy Meacham at guard, and Bruiser Butler at tackle. Filling out the rest of the squad were O'Farrell Knight at guard, Lawrence "Biff" Jones at tackle, and ends Ed Shrader and Ed House. In the backfield were quarterback Charley Gerhardt, halfbacks Elmer Oliphant and Royal Place, and fullback Gene Vidal.

Army was victorious in all nine games, giving Notre Dame its worst beating in their series until World War II. Gene Vidal caught three touchdown passes and drop-kicked a 52-yard field goal against the Irish. Vidal was an Olympic-class high jumper with great body control. He pulled in many passes by simply outjumping the coverage, and then with a twist of his body would snatch the ball from the defender's outstretched hands.

All-American Elmer Oliphant, Army's 5'7", 174-pound halfback, scored six touchdowns and 45 points against Villanova, both West Point records. In the Navy game, he had a hand in all of Army's 15 points. On the first play of the game, he sped 85 yards to the five-yard line, from which he scored three plays later. Then he kicked a 21-yard field goal for a 9–0 first period lead. Not long after in the second quarter, he faked a field goal and threw a 16-yard touchdown pass to Gene Vidal. No wonder the orders of the day at Annapolis were as follows: "6 a.m.—rise. Stop Oliphant. 7 a.m.— breakfast. Stop Oliphant. 8 a.m.—go to class. Stop Oliphant."

Led by its two-time all–American end, captain Bert Baston, Minnesota had a powerful team this year. In seven games they amassed 348 points, an average of almost 50 each game. Their only defeat was a midseason loss to Illinois, as Bob Zuppke's team derailed the Gophers at Minneapolis. A special box was built for Walter Camp to watch the Minnesota machine. Coach Zuppke needled his players by telling them that they'd all be on crutches after the game, but the Illini were needled even more by the 20-1 odds on Minnesota which were offered by the bellhops in the hotel where the team was staying.

Zuppke did his homework well. Minnesota always opened a game by giving the ball to Joe Sprafka, Arnold Wyman, and Hal Hansen on its first three plays, and Zuppke told his squad to tackle the Gopher backs in that order.

"But coach," piped up someone from the rear, "what if the ball goes back to someone else?"

"Then I'll tackle him myself," Zuppke hollered.

Minnesota took the kickoff and gave the ball to its three backs just like Zuppke said they would. The Illini downed them each time, and after three

Coach Bob Zuppke of Illinois was also a noted philosopher, wit, and oil painter.

plays the Gophers hadn't gained an inch. At midfield after a punt, Illinois lined up in a single file across the field in a spread formation, and Bart Macomber tossed a 25-yard pass to Eddie Sternaman. Running plays worked the ball to the five-yard stripe, where an offside penalty on the jumpy Gophers put the ball a yard from the goal. From there Macomber squeezed it over. After the kickoff Minnesota moved the ball to midfield, but a pass to Baston was intercepted by Ren Kraft and returned 50 yards for another Illinois score.

The Gophers charged back in the last half, but the defense Zuppke devised for the Minnesota shift held them to nine points. In the Minnesota shift, the tackles lined up behind the guards and jumped into the line when the ball was snapped. Zuppke had his tackles slide out to cover the Minnesota players when they shifted wide. He also had his center and guards line up as far from the line as the Minnesota tackles did, and when the Gopher tackles shifted into the line, Zuppke's three middle men jumped into the line at the same time to check the Minnesota momentum. Illinois got half the points scored against Minnesota all year in a 14–9 win, and Zuppke had one of his biggest upsets.

Under its new coach Tad Jones (Howard's younger brother), Yale won all its games except for the one with Brown. It was Brown's second straight win over Yale, as Fritz Pollard scored three second-half touchdowns to overtake the Elis 21–6.

Although he had a paid coaching staff, Jones invited some of the old grads to help out. One old-timer who showed up was Pudge Heffelfinger, now 48 years old. On the Wednesday before the Harvard game, Pudge was giving Clint "Cupe" Black and Mac Baldridge some lessons in the finer points of line play, when they decided to hit him high and low. Pudge flipped over and landed on Baldridge, breaking two of his ribs. Jones stepped in and ended the pleasantries, and on Saturday against Harvard Baldridge played 60 minutes with his ribs taped up.

Before the game, Jones gave the most famous pep talk in Yale history: "You are now going out to play football against Harvard. Never again in your whole life will you do anything so important." A touchdown by Joe Neville outpointed Bill Robinson's field goal, and Yale beat Harvard for the first time in seven years, 6–3.

This year Ohio State won all its games for the first time. The Buckeyes also had their first all–American, 5'9", 165-pound halfback Charles "Chic" Harley. Early in the season, he led a 75-yard march to upend Illinois on a muddy field. On last down, he faked a pass from the 15-yard line and outran the defenders to the corner of the goal for the game's only touchdown. After the puntout for better position on the conversion was caught on the 24-yard line, Harley coolly kicked the point after touchdown for a 7–6 win. Against Wisconsin, he ran back a punt for a touchdown and kicked both extra points to trip the Badgers 14–13, and Columbus had its first genuine hero.

In Atlanta on October 7, Georgia Tech crushed Cumberland, 222–0, the highest score on record. Neither team made a first down, as Georgia Tech scored each time they had the ball. In the first quarter the Yellow Jackets scored nine times and led 63–0. They had nine more touchdowns by halftime, and the margin doubled to 126–0. Even tackle Canty Alexander dropped back to carry one over. Jim Preas hit all 18 conversions, an all-time mark. The Yellow Jackets lost their sting in the third period as the score only mounted to 180–0. Nine fumbles by Cumberland attended their demise. Georgia Tech did not throw any passes, while Cumberland completed two of 11 tosses for 14 yards. The Tech team gained 527 yards rushing, while Cumberland had minus 45.

This was the first season of the Pacific Coast Conference, composed of California, Oregon, Oregon State, and Washington. Stanford and Washington State joined the next year, Idaho and Southern California in 1922, Montana in 1924, and UCLA in 1929.

Oregon met Penn in the Rose Bowl. In the Penn lineup were quarterback Bert Bell, later commissioner of the National Football League, end Heinie Miller, future president of the National Boxing Association, and tackle Lou Little, who later became Columbia's football coach. Also back were linemen Neilson Matthews, Chuck Henning, Lud Wray, and backfield men Bill Quigley and Ben Derr.

Penn coach Bob Folwell invited Oregon coach Hugo Bezdek to practice one day. Bezdek was enchanted by a forward pass thrown from a fake reverse. The game itself was a slow-motion contest in the first half. Everyone was rudely awaked in the third quarter, however, when end Lloyd Tegert scored for Oregon on a pass thrown from a fake reverse by Shy Huntington. The Ducks scored again in the last period when Johnny Parsons ran 42 yards to the one-yard line, where Huntington went over on the next play. Tackle John Beckett, rated by Bezdek as one of his best players ever, was voted player of the game.

On the Notre Dame freshman squad was a free spirit named George Gipp. Not willing to settle for a tie with Kalamazoo, Gipp eschewed a punt in the closing minutes and drop-kicked a 62-yard field goal to win the game for the frosh, 10–7.

1917

Georgia Tech	(9-0-0)		Pittsburgh	(9-0-0)	
33	Wake Forest	0	14	West Virginia	9
25	Furman	0	40	Bethany	0
41	Penn	0	41	Lehigh	0
32	Davidson	10	28	Syracuse	0
63	Washington & Lee	0	14	Penn	6
83	Vanderbilt	0	25	Westminster	0
48	Tulane	0	13	Washington & Jefferson	0
98	Carlisle	0	27	Carnegie Tech	0
68	Auburn	7	28	Penn State	6
491		17	230		21

For the past two seasons Georgia Tech was unbeaten, but had been tied once each year. There were no ties this year to stain their season, and John Heisman's Yellow Jackets were the number-one team. Except for fullback Tommy Spence, guard Bob Lang, and end Jim Senter, most of the team which had obliterated Cumberland were back, and they continued to ramble on all cylinders. In the last five games they scored better than a point a minute, as they tallied 360 points for an average of exactly 72 points per game.

Early in the season the Rambling Wreck buried last year's Rose Bowl entry, the Penn Quakers. On the game's first play, Ev Strupper sped past Hobey Light and Howard Berry and ran 68 yards to a score. It was that way

John Heisman's inventive mind took him to a .711 mark with 185 wins, 70 losses and 17 ties.

all year as Heisman's jump shift, with its horde of blockers, steamrollered the opposition. Only Buck Flowers, in a Davidson uniform, gave them any alarm. Near the end of the season, the Golden Tornado devastated Carlisle and closed the doors of the Indian school forever. In the last game they beat Auburn by over 60 points. One game before, Auburn had held unbeaten Ohio State, led by Chic Harley, to a no-score tie.

Heisman was fascinated by southern boys with their devil-may-care whoops and hollers in a game, and this year's veteran team lined up with some of the greatest players ever developed south of the Mason-Dixon line. Beside George "Pup" Phillips at center were guards Ham Dowling and Dan Welchel, the tackles were Bill Fincher and captain Walker "Big Six" Carpenter, and ends Si Bell and Ray Ulrich. The halfbacks were Ev Strupper and

Charles "Chic" Harley, the first of many all-Americans at Ohio State.

Carlisle transfer Joe Guyon, Al Hill at quarter, with Judy Harlan at full. Reserves were lineman Babe Higgins and ball carrier Shorty Guill.

Pitt would have been the number-one team this year except for Heisman's Georgia Tech colossus. There was still a lot of claw left in the Panther, but not enough to be king of the forest. With Bob Peck and Tiny Thornhill gone from the line, the Pitt defense were not the hatchet men they had been for the last two years. The absence of Hastings and DeHart in the backfield took away the smooth execution of their sparkling reverses, and the double wing trickery was put on the back burner for a while.

The Pitt offense became a bang-up-the-gut attack with Tank McLaren doing most of the banging. Occasional flashes of last year's brilliant ground game were turned in by McLaren, who went 91 yards to a score against

Syracuse, and by Foxy Miller, whose 59-yard scoring run clinched the bitter Washington and Jefferson game. Penn State coach Dick Harlow showed Pitt some fakery with a pass thrown off a double lateral. After center Paul Griffiths snapped the ball to Red Gross, it went from Gross to Harry Robb to Charley Way, who threw it forward to right end Larry Conover.

Ohio State, with its triple-threat back Chic Harley, won the Western Conference for the second year in a row. They went through the season undefeated, but battled Auburn to a 0–0 tie. The Buckeyes have known many Saturday heroes, but none greater than their first one, Chic Harley. More than anyone else, Harley set the pattern for greatness at Ohio State. He could block and tackle with authority, and defense the run or pass from his halfback spot like a crazed bulldog. His accurate passes kept defensive backs on their toes, and his punts kept the Buckeyes in game after game. A hush spread over the crowd when Harley set himself for a field goal, and he brought them to their feet when he ran the ball. If anyone was Frank Merriwell come to life, it was Chic Harley. He could do it all, for his presence in a game gave the Scarlet and Gray a lift that was contagious to players and fans alike. Many years later, when Red Grange was asked to pose for a picture with Harley, the Redhead responded humbly, "I would consider it an honor."

Elmer Oliphant was cast from the same mold as Chic Harley. At Purdue (where he starred before coming to West Point) Ollie won 17 letters, most of them in football, basketball, baseball, and track. On the trophy-room wall at Purdue hang four life-size portraits of Oliphant, dressed in the uniform for each of these sports. At the Military Academy he was a four-sport man again, adding boxing, swimming, and hockey to the list of letters he won. A thickset boy with hardly any neck, Ollie was built like a stump and just as tough to deal with. His compact torso helped him avoid injury, and his dedication to the routine of practice helped him keep in shape. He scored 125 points this season, still a West Point record.

After working with A&M's freshmen in 1916, Dana X. Bible took over as head coach at Texas A&M this year. While he was coaching the freshmen, Louisiana State fired its coach in midyear and asked the Aggies to lend them Coach Bible so they could finish the season. With Bible at the helm, LSU won two games and tied two. At the start of the year Bible had two job offers, LSU and Texas A&M, but he felt a commitment to the Aggies and returned to College Station. Apparently, he made the right choice, for Texas A&M not only defeated Louisiana State 27–0, but was unbeaten, untied, and unscored on in eight games.

On A&M's team were ends Tim Griesenbeck and Bryan Gouger, tackles Danny McMurrey and captain Marvin "Ox" Ford, 230-pound J.B. McKnight and 220-pound Gene Wilson as guards, and center George Anderson. At quarterback was Kyle "Slippery" Elam, the fullback was Jack Mahan, and the halfbacks were Roswell Higginbotham and Rip Collins, whose twisting punts were legendary.

With the god of war setting up military camps throughout the land,

Rose Bowl officials invited two service teams to the New Year's Day game. The Fort Lewis Army team from Tacoma, Washington, played the Mare Island Marines from Vallejo, California. Back for his second year in a row was Hugo Bezdek, who coached the victorious Marines to a 19–7 victory. With Bezdek were three of his Oregon players, among them Hollis Huntington, the player of the game.

1918

Pittsburgh (4-1-0)			Michigan (5-0-0)		
34	Washington & Jefferson	0	33	Case	0
37	Penn	0	13	Chicago	0
32	Georgia Tech	0	15	Syracuse	0
28	Penn State	6	21	Michigan State	6
9	Cleveland Naval Reserve	10	14	Ohio State	0
140		16	96		6

With the nation geared for war, many schools did not field a team, or they played an abbreviated schedule. In the Ivy League, Cornell and Yale had no team at all. The Army-Navy game was cancelled, and Army's lone game was a 20–0 win over Mitchell Field. In the South, Alabama, Georgia, Louisiana State, North Carolina, Tennessee, and Virginia did not have teams. No crown was awarded in the Southwest or Pacific Coast conferences because most games were played with questionable freshmen or military personnel.

Pop Warner had Pitt back on top once more. The demand for a postseason game between last year's best teams resulted in a game this season, but the long-awaited playoff was a bummer. Although Georgia Tech averaged 66 points per game, the all-time mark, Pitt sent the Engineers back to the drawing board. Nifty runners Joe Guyon and Buck Flowers got nowhere against the huge Panther line.

Pitt met the Cleveland Naval Reserve in a postseason game. Pitt scored in just six minutes, but the Reserve team bullied the officials so much that penalties were overlooked. The half ended a minute early when the Panthers reached the goal, and six minutes were added to the last period. During this extra time Pitt fell on a fumble, but the Reserves would not give up the ball. After Warner said "Play it out," a Reserve pass to Pete Stinchcomb from Moon Ducote won it, and Pitt's four-year win streak was fini.

Captain Tank McLaren completed his fabulous career at Pitt with a total of 30 touchdowns and 1,920 yards rushing. His 183 yards passing reveals that he threw a few times from the double wing formation as a fullback, but not often. Beside him in the single wing alignment Warner used this year was another all-time great, halfback Tom Davies, all–American in his freshman year.

George Gipp was elected a charter member of the National College Football Hall of Fame in 1951.

In the Georgia Tech match-up, Davies raced 50 yards to one touchdown, returned one punt 50 yards for a touchdown, ran back a second punt 60 yards for another score, and threw for two more touchdowns to halfback Katy Easterday. Providing the blocking in the Pitt line were center Herb Stein, guards Vance Allshouse and Jake Stahl, tackles Len Hilty and Lou

Mervis, ends Harry McCarter and Bill Harrington, with Roscoe Gougler at quarter.

Captain Tad Wieman did not play because of military duty, but his Michigan team had five wins, including one over Syracuse and their all-American guard, Joe Alexander. The remaining games were cancelled due to a flu epidemic sweeping the land in early fall.

Freshmen were allowed to play this year because of wartime conditions. Four freshmen were on the Michigan varsity: center Ernie Vick, right tackle Frank Czysz, left end Bob Dunne, and all-American fullback Frank Stekete. Other personnel on this wartime team were left guard Bill Fortune and right guard Paul Freeman, left tackle Angus Goetz, right end Ted Boville, halfbacks Abe Cohn and Art Karpus, and quarterback Ken Knode.

Navy had a good team under Gil Dobie, in his second year as coach. For the past two seasons Navy ran up big scores, beating Villanova 80-3 the previous year, and Ursinus 127-0 this year, their highest score ever. Halfback Bill Ingram closed out his career with 263 points, a Naval Academy record. Their only defeat this season was by the Great Lakes Sailors on a highly disputed play.

Navy was out front 6-0 and driving for another score when Ingram fumbled deep in Sailor territory. Harry Eielson picked it up for Great Lakes and set sail for the Navy goal 90 yards away. As he sprinted past midfield, tackle Bill Saunders bolted from the Navy bench and brought Eielson to earth in front of the dazed crowd. At first, Eielson's teammates tried to help him up so he could continue his run. Then the officials decided to give the ball to Great Lakes and penalize Navy half the distance to the goal. Finally, they awarded Great Lakes a touchdown, and Hugo Blacklock added the extra point for a 7-6 Great Lakes win.

At Notre Dame, George Gipp was playing while Knute Rockne was still an assistant to Jesse Harper. In this first year last season, he had out-Ollied the great Oliphant himself in the 7-2 win over Army. Gipp could punt and drop-kick a ton and was one of the best long-distance passers of his day. At six feet and 180 pounds, he had power to go between the tackles and enough speed to run the ends. He had a tendency to skip practice and loaf when he did show up, but his talents were so great that he was ready to go after a few warmups. Although he wasn't always easy to handle, Rockne loved him because Gipp had the ingenuity which took over where the coaching left off. Gipp often improvised in a game to win it, for he had the brains and emotional spark which Rockne looked for in selecting his players. It was a quality Rockne himself possessed, such as the fake limp he used against Army and the buttonhook passes he made up while playing. As a boy, Walter Eckersall had turned Rockne to football, and Rockne wanted to inspire Gipp as Eckersall had inspired him.

Rockne took over as head coach at Notre Dame this season. More than any other coach, he made college football popular on a nationwide basis. Rockne's Ramblers met the best teams from coast-to-coast, and Notre Dame's victory march became the first college fight song most youngsters learned. Its fervent rhythm infected young and old alike, and people everywhere from actor to zoo keeper supported the Irish as subway alumni.

One reason for Notre Dame's success was that Rockne changed the way football was played. He took the game out of the "score and hang on to win" category and made it a wide-open game which had fan appeal. The Irish usually scored in double figures, and their games were sellouts wherever they played. Football became big business, and immense stadiums were built to accommodate the crowds who flocked to these new meccas of concrete and steel.

Like any great coach, Rockne was a father-confessor to his players. He made it a point to know their problems and what made them tick. He was a master psychologist, knowing which player to praise and which one to needle. After his stirring locker-room talks, which he delivered in the staccato style of a Gatling gun, unwary visitors standing outside the door were sometimes knocked down by his team on their way to the field.

Rockne was a warm, genuine person whose humanity appealed to his players, but he was also a dedicated disciplinarian who inspired his men to give their best. Like Warner, Rockne would not tolerate dirty football. "Dirty play," he told his players, "is only an honest admission that your opponent is a better man than you." From the moment he said "Everybody up" at a quarter to four each afternoon, he gave to the Fighting Irish a spirit during practice which made them feel like supermen in a game.

Like an old navy chief, Rockne had an endless supply of remarks and stories, but his comebacks were usually delivered with style and charity. He was the heart and soul of the gridiron camaraderie which makes football the grandest game of them all, and he symbolized the American dream that a poor boy can have a dream and make it come true. It was a dream won by sacrifice, for his credo was "Work, work hard, prepare yourself, then go!"

Rockne was trained for a profession like many fine coaches, and a few short years ago he was a chemistry professor and research assistant to the man whose discoveries led to synthetic rubber. Rockne also knew enough classical literature to know a Latin misquote when he heard it. Where are the snows of yesteryear who can quote the ancients in their own tongue?

Was Rockne the greatest football coach? His won-lost mark says he was. Without doubt, his wit made him one of the greatest speakers in the locker room or before an audience, and his enthusiasm inspired his players as no coach has done before or since. Year after year, he sent coaches throughout the land who had his dedication and competence. In 1969, almost four decades after his death, he was voted the number one coach in the first one hundred years of college football.

The Rose Bowl game was almost cancelled because of the flu epidemic in the fall, but by Armistice Day it vanished as quickly as it came. The Rose Bowl officials again invited two military teams to play on New Year's Day, Great Lakes and the Mare Island Marines. Great Lakes was loaded with ex-college players who had been together all year, while Mare Island was in a playoff game as late as Christmas Day. In the lineup for Great Lakes were Notre Dame guards Emmett Keefe and Jerry Jones, and center Charley

Bachman, who went on to coach Michigan State. The team also included George Halas, who founded and coached the Chicago Bears to the first pro title in 1921, and Jimmy Conzelman, who would bring the Chicago (later St. Louis) Cardinals a championship.

In the first quarter, Northwestern's Paddy Driscoll drop-kicked a 30-yard field goal for a 3-0 Great Lakes lead. In the next period, he caught a pass which set up the first six-pointer by the Sailors' 6'2", 215-pound fullback Andrew Reeves. After the half, Driscoll and Halas connected on a 32-yard scoring pass to wind it up at 17-0. Halas almost added another touchdown in the final quarter when he intercepted a pass and returned it 72 yards to the Mare Island three-yard stripe where Jim Blewett caught him from behind. Halas was named player of the game.

1919

Harvard	(9-0-1)		Texas A&M	(10-0-0)	
53	Bates	0	77	Sam Houston	0
17	Boston College	0	28	San Marcos	0
35	Colby	0	16	Southern Methodist	0
7	Brown	0	12	Howard Payne	0
47	Virginia	0	42	Trinity	0
20	Springfield	0	28	Oklahoma A&M	0
10	Princeton	10	10	Baylor	0
23	Tufts	0	48	Texas Christian	0
10	Yale	3	7	Southwestern	0
7	Oregon (Rose Bowl)	6	7	Texas	0
229		19	275		0

World War I was over, and the veterans returned from places in France they could hardly pronounce. After two years of empty stadiums and short schedules, campuses were engulfed by a flood of manpower, and most teams rebuilt with returning servicemen.

Harvard was one team that rebuilt with these men home from the war. With Percy Haughton pursuing a business career, Bob Fisher, ex-Crimson guard and captain of the 1911 team, was the new head coach. His team began a 25-game unbeaten streak this year and edged Oregon in the Rose Bowl, as the Ducks were held to a pair of field goals. Fred Church scored on a 13-yard run, and Arnie Horween added the extra point for the win. Harvard's number-one rating paled a bit when Oregon barely missed a game-winning field goal in the last quarter. For Hollis Huntington, it was his third 60-minute Rose Bowl game, having gone all the way for Oregon in 1917 and the Mare Island Marines in 1918.

Fisher rebuilt with veteran backs and ends from Haughton's last team, quarterback and captain Bill Murray, halfback Eddie Casey, fullback Ralph Horween, and ends George Batchelder and Morris Phinney. Up from the prewar freshmen team was Babe Felton, with Rich Humphrey completing the backfield. In the line from left to right were John Desmond, Bob Sedgwick, Tom Woods, Chuck Havemeyer, Chuck Clark, Rich Kane, and Percy Steele.

One team which didn't need to do very much rebuilding was the Texas Aggies. Many players of the 1917 squad served in the military in 1918, including its coach Dana X. Bible, who was a flight instructor and pilot in France. In 1919, after the war, most of the Texas A&M team were reunited, and they were again unbeaten, untied, and unscored on. By the end of the season, Bible's 1917 and 1919 teams had not been scored on in 18 games, an enviable record any time and any place.

Bible's Aggie team was well schooled in the fundamentals of blocking and tackling. As the record shows, he believed in a dogged defense and a good punting game to keep the other team from the Aggie goal. On offense, his plays were run from the Bible shift. The guards lined up beside the center, with the tackles behind the guards. The ends were beside the tackles, but spaced out a step, with the backfield lined up behind the tackles. Just before the ball was snapped, everyone shifted into position, usually a single wing or short punt formation.

The men who secured this dead-end defense were halfbacks Heine Weir and Roswell Higginbotham, the team's punter, quarterback Art Knickerbocker, and three-time Southwest Conference fullback Jack Mahan. On the ends were Jewel Davis and Scott Alexander, the tackles were C.R. Drake and R.L. Carruthers, at the guards were Cap Murrah and captain Gene "Woodrow" Wilson, with Art Vandervoort at center.

At Dartmouth, Clarence "Doc" Spears fashioned his worldly-wise veterans into a roughhouse crew. A 5'7", 235-pound guard at Dartmouth in 1915, Spears was a furious competitor and just as grim in practice. He had to be in order to handle his mix-it-up foursome of guard Swede Youngstrom, center Wild Bill Cunningham, and tackles Gus Sonnenberg and Cuddy Murphy. Sonnenberg had the playful habit of tearing hotel radiators from the floor, a trick which cost the Dartmouth Athletic Association a bundle, but prepared Gus for the pro heavyweight wrestling title he later won.

Spears usually gave two pep talks — one for the wild bunch, and one for the rest of the squad. After letting the good guys go with a "do-or-die" speech, he called in the quartet of mayhem-makers and told them he'd kick their butts if they loafed in the game. The rest of the team spared the last speech were ends Eddie Lynch and Guy Cogswell, guard Norman Crisp, captain Jack Cannell at quarterback, fullback Zack Jordan, and halfbacks Jim Robertson and Pat Holbrook.

The Colgate team was also a group of hardened ex-military men. They were led by all–American tackle captain Belf West, with Roy Wooster at the other tackle. The center was George Woodman, flanked by guards Mason Barton and Bob Martin. John Cottrell and Lew Harris were the ends. In the backfield were quarterback Oscar C. "Oc" Anderson, fullback Hank Gillo, with Jim Laird and Ray Watkins as halfbacks.

When these two veteran outfits butted heads in midseason, it was trench warfare in France all over again. Each team was undefeated, although both of them later lost their final game. It rained for three days in Hanover, and the field was a swamp. Colgate coach Larry Bankart could not go against his alma mater, so he sat out the game a few miles away in White River Junction.

In the first period, Hank Gillo took a short over-the-line pass from quarterback Oc Anderson to put Colgate in front, 7–0. Both teams sloshed back and forth in the mud until the closing moments. With only two minutes left, Swede Youngstrom blocked a Colgate punt on the 20-yard line, found the handle on it at the five and thick-stepped over for a score. But the excitement wasn't over yet. The point after touchdown was attempted from a difficult angle. With Jack Cannell putting the ball down as if it were a fresh egg, Jim Robertson's conversion hit the upright, fell to the crossbar, and slipped over to tie it, 7–7. The men of Dartmouth forgot their cosmopolitan sophistication and slapped each other on the back like schoolboys.

The other tackle on this year's All-America team was Wilbur "Fats" Henry of Washington and Jefferson. At 5′10″ and 230 pounds he looked like a cherub, and the player most likely to be out of breath after the kickoff. His chubby appearance and the perpetual smile on his face were deceiving, however, for he was usually the first one downfield to make the tackle after a kick. He got his compact bulk moving so quickly that he often carried the ball on a tackle-around play. He had strength and agility as well as speed, but he won his reputation by faking out opponents and then blocking their punts. On one occasion he broke through and took a punt off the kicker's foot and ran 45 yards to a touchdown. Before he graduated, he was credited with blocking more punts than any man in a football suit.

With George Gipp playing up to form, Knute Rockne had his first perfect season at Notre Dame. Gipp was the top runner in the Irish backfield with 729 yards on 106 carries, an average of 6.8 yards each time he ran with the ball. Gipp was also the best passer, connecting on 41 of 72 tosses for 727 yards for a 56 percent completion rate. He also averaged 20.8 yards on returning kickoffs and led the team in scoring with 49 points.

Gipp's greatest talent surfaced in the Army contest. The Cadets were leading 9–0 with halftime approaching. A flurry of passes by Gipp took the ball to the one-yard line. Out of the corner of his eye, Gipp saw the head linesman raise his horn to signal the end of the half. Quick as a wink, he had the center hike the ball to him. As he dived over for the touchdown, the horn blew to end the half. Notre Dame still trailed 9–6, but Gipp's quick thinking had kept his team in the ball game. The Irish scored once more in the second half for a 12–6 win.

Gipp's supporting cast included some of the greatest names to walk under the Golden Dome. At the ends were Eddie Anderson and Bernie Kirk, the tackles were Frank Coughlin and Lawrence "Buck" Shaw, the guards were Clipper Smith and Heartley "Hunk" Anderson, with centers George Trafton and Slip Madigan. In the backfield were halfbacks Arthur "Dutch"

Bergman, fullback Fritz Slackford, and captain Pete Bahan at quarterback.

After a year in the Army, the glorious career of Chic Harley at Ohio State came to an end. In his three varsity seasons, he led the Buckeyes to a 21-1-1 record. The defeat came in the last game against Illinois. With Ohio State leading 7-6 and only five minutes left, the Illini intercepted a Harley pass on their own 20. Laurie Walquist threw to Chuck Carney on almost every play, and Illinois marched to the Buckeyes' 22-yard line. Only eight seconds showed on the clock when Bob Fletcher place-kicked a field goal to win the game, 9-7. A lump arose in the throats of the stricken Ohio State fans, and on the field tears streaked the faces of Chic Harley and his teammates as they wept openly. It was the first and only time they had tasted defeat together, and Camelot in Columbus was over for Chic Harley and his Scarlet and Gray knights.

In its second year under Hugo Bezdek, Penn State won seven of eight games. The only loss was to Dartmouth, 19-13, a game in which quarterback Charley Way ran back the opening kickoff 90 yards for one score, and later pirated a fumble and returned it 85 yards for State's second score. In the last game with Pitt, Harold Hess tossed a pass from punt formation in the end zone to end Bob Higgins, who ran 75 yards to a touchdown in a 20-0 win. After the loss to Dartmouth, Penn State began a 30-game unbeaten streak, the longest in Lion history. They won 25 games and tied five before losing to Navy, 14-0, deep in the 1922 season.

IV. The Golden Decade

1920

California	(9-0-0)		Notre Dame	(9-0-0)	
21	Olympic Club	0	39	Kalamazoo	0
88	Mare Island Marines	0	42	Western Michigan	0
127	St. Mary's	0	16	Nebraska	7
79	Nevada	7	28	Valparaiso	3
63	Utah	0	27	Army	17
17	Oregon State	7	28	Purdue	0
49	Washington State	0	13	Indiana	10
38	Stanford	0	33	Northwestern	7
28	Ohio State (Rose Bowl)	0	25	Michigan State	0
510		14	251		44

The 1920s were America's golden decade. People were full of optimism that the world would be made safe for democracy. There were giants in those days like Charles Lindbergh, who made us feel that nothing was impossible. It was an age of sports heroes such as Knute Rockne and Red Grange, Babe Ruth and Jack Dempsey. It was also an age of innocence where people thought that drinking would end by outlawing it, and in which everyone thought they could have endless prosperity and credit without having to pay for it.

Football was slowly becoming the American game. Gone was the game of their grandfather's in which linemen slugged each other from a standing position, and the whole team turned into a human tank. It was now a wide-open game of forward passing and razzle-dazzle, played in the bright colors, crisp air, and long shadows of autumn. It had become an extravagant festival of weekend gladiators, acrobatic cheerleaders, marching bands, young men in fur coats, and cheering crowds in the stands.

Beginning this year, coach Andy Smith started a dynasty at California which stands with the best in college football. During the next five years his wonder teams were unbeaten, as they won 46 of 50 games and tied four. It is a record that compares with Yale in the early years, George Woodruff's Penn teams in the gay nineties, Yost's Michigan squads a decade later, and Haughton's Harvard regime before World War I. Cal's average of 56.6 points per game this year ranks fourth best among major schools.

California was the first team from the Far West to win the national title. The Bears were led by all–American end Harold "Brick" Muller, who could throw a football like others threw a baseball. Like most championship teams, the Cal line was solid from end to end. At center was George "Fat" Latham, skirted by guards Lee Cranmer and captain Olin "Cort" Majors. The tackles were Dan McMillan and Stan Barnes (later an assistant attorney general of the United States), with Bob Berkey at the other end. In the backfield were quarterback Charley Erb, halfbacks Pesky Sprott and Crip Toomey, and a buffalo-shouldered pair at fullback — Duke Morrison, the team's top scorer, and Archie Nisbet, whose high, ice-gathering punts usually ended in a fair catch.

In addition to the ability in the Berkeley lineup, they possessed the optimism of youth and a confidence in each other which made them feel they could beat anyone. It was a combination which gave the squad a feeling of all-for-one and one-for-all. When Andy Smith prepared the team by telling them what to expect in a game, the Golden Bears held all the trump cards.

The Cal team was relatively unknown until they played Ohio State in the Rose Bowl. Jack Wilce's Buckeyes won the Western Conference title with seven wins this season. The left side of their line had two standouts in guard Johnny "Tarzan" Taylor and captain Iolas Huffman at tackle, and a great passing combination of Harry Workman to Pete Stinchcomb, OSU's all-American halfback this year. It was Workman's 40-yard touchdown pass to Stinchcomb in the last 20 seconds which had overcome Wisconsin, 13-7, and the Bucks were 8-5 favorites to beat the Bears in the Rose Bowl.

Pasadena's 88-degree temperature on New Year's Day helped undo the Buckeyes. The Bears led 7-0 in the second quarter when the roof fell in on Ohio State. After a plunge by Nisbet to the Ohio State 37-yard line, he got up and said something to one of the Cal players along the line of scrimmage. The Cal backs waited for the huddle, while Muller stood off to the left.

Suddenly, Nisbet snatched the ball and flipped it back to Sprott, who faked a run. Sprott then lateraled to Muller, who was moving to his right. Muller retreated to his own 47-yard line and let go. The ball took off on a clothes line and hit end Brodie Stephens on the goal for a touchdown. As he whizzed past Buckeye safety man Stinchcomb, he yelled at Brodie, "Where do you think you're going?" It became a greeting that Brodie heard for years to come whenever people passed him in the street. It is estimated that Muller's toss traveled over 60 yards through the air, since it was thrown diagonally. For his gargantuan pass, Muller was named player of the game.

After many trials, George Gipp was back to lead Notre Dame to its second straight unbeaten season under Knute Rockne. Army was trying to recruit him and so was Michigan, but when Rockne offered him a job as assistant coach after graduation, Gipp came back to Notre Dame. In the meantime, Gipp had to take a makeup exam in order to pass last year's classes. School life boxed him in, so he took a room in the Oliver Hotel in downtown South Bend. He quickly returned to his former life of playing cards, shooting pool, and frequenting speakeasies. He was readmitted to school just four days before the season started.

The dissolute life he was living began to show on him. His sallow complexion paled to chalky white. He became so emaciated that his ribs stuck out in the shower. All season long, he had an attack of nausea before each game. He was also betting $500 a week on every game in which he played.

The Army game was the high-water mark of Gipp's career. He gained 124 yards rushing although he was used as a decoy most of the time. While Gipp was carrying out a fake to the right, Johnny Mohardt scored twice on plays to the left and Chet Wynne squirted straight ahead for the third touchdown. He also passed for 96 yards and ran back kicks for 112 more. After completing a pass to Roger Kiley for a touchdown, Gipp was exhausted. He was taken out late in the game, as the Irish won 27–17. This time all the Notre Dame players bet on themselves and shared in the winnings, except for Wynne who was broke. Gipp put $10 in a hat and passed it around, and everyone had pocket money.

Gipp was hurt in the first period of the Indiana game, and his dislocated shoulder was taped from neck to wrist. He sat on the bench while Indiana built a 10–0 lead. After a drive to the Hoosier goal with ten minutes left, Gipp came in and helped Notre Dame to score. Indiana took the kickoff but had to punt. Gipp passed the Irish to Indiana's 15-yard line, where it was fourth down and four to go. Instead of a field goal to tie the score, Gipp completed a pass to Eddie Anderson on the one-yard line. As the Hoosiers ganged up on Gipp driving into the line on a fake, Joe Brandy sneaked over for a 13–10 Notre Dame victory.

Gipp didn't get off the train that night in South Bend but went on to Chicago for a weekend drunk with a friend. When he got back to the campus, he was coughing. By the middle of the week, he had a sore throat. Against Northwestern, he completed a 45-yard pass to Norm Barry for a touchdown, but the career of number 66 ended that day in Evanston. While the Irish were in East Lansing for the last game of the year with Michigan State, Gipp was on the critical list in St. Joseph's Hospital in South Bend. As he lay dying of a strep throat infection, a telegram arrived from Walter Camp saying that Gipp had been put on the All-America team at fullback this season.

Just before he died in the early evening of December 14, he turned to Rockne and whispered, "Sometime, Rock," the words came out with a struggle, "when the team's up against it, when things are wrong and the breaks are beating the boys, tell them to give it all they've got and win one just for the Gipper."

In his last year, Gipp gained 827 yards on 102 carries for an 8.1 average, a Notre Dame record, and his 9.37 yards total offense per attempt is also a single-season Irish mark. Gipp's greatest contribution to the Notre Dame attack was his career total offense records, which stood for over 40 years. His 86.7 yards rushing per game, total offense of 7.39 yards per carry, 4,833 yards total offense, and 113.5 yards each game in all-purpose running (rushing, pass receiving, kick returns) are still good enough for second-place records at Notre Dame. Most of these marks were only recently eclipsed by quarterbacks who got the bulk of their yards by passing. Gipp's achievements are even more remarkable because he got most of his yards by running.

Dana X. Bible's Texas Aggies were finally scored on this year. The string of unscored on games included eight in 1917, ten in 1919, and the first seven games this year. It ended on Thanksgiving Day before 20,000 people in the annual battle with Texas at Clark Field in Austin. A&M had a 3-0 lead on a Bugs Morris field goal when Texas moved to the Aggie 11-yard line.

On the crucial play late in the game, left half Francisco Domingues ran to his right and gave the ball to right half Jack Barry running left. At the end of this reverse was a tackle-eligible pass. The right end lined up in the backfield making Tom Dennis, the right tackle, an end. Dennis went diagonally downfield to his left and hauled in Barry's pass at the four-yard line. From there, Domingues plowed over, captain Maxey Hart added the extra point, and A&M's goal was sullied, 7-3.

1921

Cornell (8-0-0)			Iowa (7-0-0)		
41	St. Bonaventure	0	52	Knox	14
55	Rochester	0	10	Notre Dame	7
110	Western Reserve	0	14	Illinois	2
31	Colgate	7	13	Purdue	6
59	Dartmouth	7	41	Minnesota	7
41	Columbia	7	41	Indiana	0
14	Springfield	0	14	Northwestern	0
41	Penn	0			
392		21	185		36

In his second year at Cornell, Gil Dobie made the Big Red the best in the land. Fresh from a successful three-year stay at the Naval Academy, and an even more impressive 58-0-3 record at Washington from 1908 to 1916, Dobie continued to be a winner. His 39 wins in a row at Washington is the second longest win streak in college football, and the unbeaten string of 63 games (one game before and after Dobie) for the Huskies is a national record.

Dobie was known as "Gloomy Gil" because of his profoundly negative outlook. To him, his championship teams were never great, and his great players were only good. After a resounding win, he was known to have his team take a few laps around the track because of their poor performance. There was method in his pessimistic pronouncements, for if he won with mediocre material, then he made himself look even better. No coach was mentally tougher than Dobie, for he was loathe to halt practice even in winds of hurricane proportions. He meanmouthed and insulted his players and every now and then one of the them wanted to punch him out, yet many of them showed up years later at a reunion to see their old coach.

For the next three years Dobie's teams were unbeaten, as they won eight games each season, and their win streak reached to 26 games, the longest in Cornell history. The secret of Dobie's teams was their power and timing. His runners were taught to gain three yards, and anything more was only frosting on the cake. Whole afternoons were spent on a single play in order to perfect its timing. The blockers took so many steps, the guard pulled at the right moment, the ball was centered to the exact spot, and the runner hit the hole with the power of a Wagnerian opera. As a drillmaster in preparing a team, Dobie was without equal, and his off-tackle play was so letter perfect that its precision has seldon been equaled.

Under the tutelage of Howard Jones, Iowa had a perfect year for the first time. Almost everyone was a 60-minute player, and all of them were Iowa born and bred. Jones used a single wing formation in which two backs blocked and the other two carried the ball. Other than Aubrey Devine and Gordon Locke, no one handled the ball all season except as a pass receiver. Behind Duke Slater's rhinolike charge at right tackle, Iowa was able to grind out three or four yards on sweeps and tackle slants. Slater and right guard Leo Kriz wore no helmets, yet neither of them lost a minute due to injury. Freedom from injury is the inscrutable equation which can make or break a team, but it smiled on the Hawks all year. No one was removed from any game except Gordon Locke, who was out on his feet trying to crack the Notre Dame line.

After a bruising battle early in the season, Iowa stopped Notre Dame's 20-game, two-year winning streak with a 38-yard field goal by Aubrey Devine. The midseason contest with Purdue was played in ankle-deep water, but Devine kept the Hawks in the game with a touchdown pass to Les Belding. Late in the final period, Purdue was fighting to maintain a slim 7–6 lead. They punted from their own end zone, but the waterlogged ball rose in the air like a pregnant quail trying to fly. Devine gathered in the slippery oval on the 30-yard line and began to wade through the ooze as tacklers slipped off his legs into the puddles. Hampered by the mud, his teammates couldn't make many blocks, but a few moments later he splashed over the goal for the winning touchdown.

In Minneapolis, Devine gained 162 yards from scrimmage and passed for another 122. He completed touchdown passes of 43 and 25 yards to Les Belding and returned kicks and intercepted passes for 182 yards. He also drop-kicked five extra points, and his 29-point effort that day was a Big Ten single-game record. When he was taken out of the game in the last period, the Minnesota fans gave him a standing ovation.

A week later, Devine continued his crowd-pleasing heroics against Indiana. This time he scored four touchdowns, kicked four extra points, ran for 183 yards and passed for 102 more. By the end of the year he had 895 yards rushing, and a three-year career total of 1961 yards gained overland. Walter Camp put him on his All-America team at quarterback.

Members of this iron-man brigade who usually played without relief were left end Max Kadesky, left tackle George Thompson, left guard Paul

Minick, center John Heldt, right guard Leo Kriz, right tackle Duke Slater, and right end Les Belding. At quarterback was captain Aubrey Devine, the two halfbacks who were used as blockers were Craven Shuttleworth and Aubrey's brother, Glenn Devine, with Gordon Locke at fullback. Two reserves who saw action were lineman Chet Mead and halfback Glenn Miller.

One small school which stepped for a brief moment into the winner's circle was tiny Centre College of Danville, Kentucky, enrollment 254. They got their nickname of "Praying Colonels" two years before when the team knelt in prayer at intermission. In 1920 they attracted national attention when they held Harvard to a halftime tie before their line collapsed at the end of the game. Coach Charley Moran hired ex–Pitt tackle Tiny Thornhill to strengthen the front wall. The result was that Centre gave up only one touchdown in its first ten games this year.

Included in the list of shutouts was mighty Harvard, still unbeaten in 25 games. Five railroad cars of Danville faithful almost emptied the town for the game at Cambridge, but the team was too intent on beating Harvard to join in the merrymaking on the train. Just before the game, the team knelt to pray in the locker room. As they headed for the field, sobbing and drying their eyes, quarterback Bo McMillan spoke to the referee.

"Mistuh," he said with emotion, "pay attention, cuz youah Yankee eyes are gonna see somethin' today!"

In the first half Harvard marched down the field, but they were stopped at the 11-yard line by the fired-up Kentucky Colonels. Right end Red Roberts smothered a drop-kick field goal, bringing a groan to the crowd of 43,000. Another missed field goal by Charley Buell of Harvard made the crowd cry in disgust.

The second half was hardly under way before Centre returned a punt to the Crimson 47. A Harvard penalty for piling on put the ball on the 32-yard line. In the huddle, McMillan exhorted his men. "Here is the break we've been waiting for, boys. Block a little better than you know how, and I'll take her home."

Center Ed Kubale fed McMillan the ball, and he slanted off right tackle. Guards George Jones and Bill Shadoan and tackle Minos Gordy took the man opposite them. Backfield men Tom Bartlett, Norris Armstrong, and Terry Snoddy blocked on the right. As he cleared the line, his number 11 darted into the open with only the defensive backs ahead. He cut left behind right tackle Ben Cregor, who blocked the linebacker, while left end Bill James took the other. Bo outran the rest and took her home.

Centre controlled the ball most of the second half to preserve their tenuous lead. Once Harvard got as far as the three-yard line on a pass, but they were offside, and the ball was brought back to the 37. When the final whistle blew, the ecstatic Danville fans cascaded onto the field and carried McMillan to the locker room on their shoulders. Then they took off their hats and sang "My Old Kentucky Home" almost reverently. The victory party at the Lenox Hotel lasted long into the night.

When the homeward-bound train left Cincinnati and crossed the Ohio

River into the promised land, Bo McMillan climbed into the cab of the engine and took over the throttle. Red Roberts handled the fireman's job and shoveled coal while everyone sang "Casey Jones." At the station in Danville, the team was swept off the train onto a fire truck and paraded up the main street. There was dancing in the streets and victory bonfires throughout the week. All over town the symbol of victory, C-6, H-0, was painted on sidewalks, store fronts, mail boxes, and the local water tower. It was even painted on cows which were sent bawling and pop-eyed through the downtown area.

At the end of the year, Centre again chose to play a postseason game during the holidays. Last year they had a 63-7 win over Texas Christian in Fort Worth's Panther Park. Ten Centre players were from the Dallas–Fort Worth area, so they chose to play in their home town instead of the Rose Bowl against California. The game between Centre and Texas A&M at Fair Park later gave birth to the Cotton Bowl game in Dallas. As a final touch, Bo McMillan was married on the very morning of the game.

It was in the Texas A&M–Centre game that the tradition of the Aggies' Twelfth Man was born. During the fiercely contested game A&M suffered a great many injuries, and the reserves on the bench grew thin. Coach Bible sent word to the Aggie spotter in the press box, King Gill, to put on a uniform and be ready if needed. At halftime under the stands, Gill put on the uniform of an injured player and sat on the bench during the last half.

Gill was never needed, as Texas A&M gave Centre its only loss of the season, 22-14. That is the reason the Aggie Cadet Corps stands throughout the game, to be "ready if needed."

Washington and Jefferson accepted the invitation to play in the Rose Bowl against California. Cal's wonder teams had won 18 games in two years and were heavy favorites. Although they had all–American tackle Russ Stein and end Herb Kopf, few westerners had ever heard of Washington and Jefferson and its coach, Earle "Greasy" Neale. The Bears ran aground on their own self-confidence and were lucky to get away with a no-score tie. One W&J touchdown was called back, and Cal made only two first downs all day. Brick Muller tried to intimidate the Presidents with his 60-yard tosses before the game, but they upstaged him by wiping their hands on his clean uniform when he later entered the game.

At Penn State, Hugo Bezdek added a new play to his attack, the tailback spinner. It began by accident two years ago when the wingback did not take the ball from quarterback Harry Robb as he made a pivot. This was nothing new, for Stagg had used a quarterback spinner a decade earlier at Chicago. When Bezdek's team shifted from a T-formation into a single wing, quarterback Glenn Killinger ran the spinner from the rear of the backfield. Killinger and halfback Harry "Lighthorse" Wilson, who lit a fire under the Lions with a 56-yard run against Harvard to salvage a 21-21 tie, ran to fame on big gainers off the deep spinner. Pop Warner saw it in the Pitt-Penn State game this year, and later worked it into his single and double wing formations.

Another small school which enjoyed a brief hour in the sun this season was Lafayette. They won all nine games, including wins over Pitt, 6–0, Fordham, 28–7, and Penn, 38–6. Coach Jock Sutherland used the single wing formation he had learned under Pop Warner at Pitt. Lafayette's ham and eggs play was the off-tackle smash, run with razor sharpness by end Charley Berry and tackle Art Deible. Guards Frank Schwab and John Budd, tackle Joe Williams, and Milt O'Connell at end also made the wingback reverses and power sweeps work for halfbacks Mike Gazella and Bots Brunner. Lafayette's attack was such a meat grinder that they hardly threw half-a-dozen passes all year.

At Boston College, Frank Cavanaugh's 13-game winning streak came to an end. Known as the "Iron Major," he won acclaim after his teams beat Yale two years in a row. In 1920, his BC Eagles were undefeated and untied. A major who earned his commission and had half his face shot away in World War I, he was as tough on the football field as he was on the battlefield.

Frank Cavanaugh coached at Dartmouth before the war, where he taught his star guard, Doc Spears, that football was a game of conditioning and contact. Nobody ever beat a Cavanaugh team in the last quarter by being in better physical condition. He invented his own set of calisthenics called the grass drill, a torturous exercise which consisted of running in place, dropping to the ground flat on the belly, up and running in place, down again, up, down, up, down, up. It is still the heart of conditioning drills on many practice fields to this day.

1922

Cornell (8-0-0)			Iowa (7-0-0)		
55	St. Bonaventure	6	61	Knox	0
66	Niagara	0	6	Yale	0
68	New Hampshire	7	8	Illinois	7
14	Colgate	0	56	Purdue	0
56	Columbia	0	28	Minnesota	14
23	Dartmouth	0	12	Ohio State	9
48	Albright	14	37	Northwestern	3
9	Penn	0			
339		27	208		33

Cornell's Big Red machine was unbeaten again and repeated as national champion. They were victorious eight times and extended their win streak to 16 games. This year's squad was even better than last year's dynamo because of its experience and maturity. Dobie had so much good material on Schoellkopf Field that the top players from last season were hardly missed.

Dobie's teams were known for their meticulous execution and ability, the twin columns on which any great team is built. To this must be added the cohesiveness of the offensive team that comes only from working together as a unit. After the three-week survival scrimmage in which he picked his starting eleven, Dobie alone worked with them to perfect their timing, adjusting their skills to function like a finely tuned mechanism.

This year's backfield was one of the best ever seen on the Cornell campus. Quarterback George Pfann, halfback Floyd Ramsey, and fullback Charley Cassidy were all juniors by now with a year of varsity technique and savvy under their belts. Captain Eddie Kaw was a senior. Kaw was a clever runner in the open field who got by tacklers with a stutter-step, a move which helped him run for five touchdowns in the mire and mist at Franklin Field the previous year against Penn. George Pfann was a brainy quarterback and a thick-legged power runner with a quick start. His lower body strength and fast acceleration enabled him to break a tackler's grasp or go around him. These two men gave Cornell's ten-gauge gun a double-barreled blast which not many teams survived.

It is always the men up front who make the machine go, and it was no different at Cornell. Gone was last year's captain, 6'5", 220-pound Wilson Dodge at tackle, but his place was ably filled by Frank "Sunny" Sundstrom. Field-goal kicker Leonard "Swede" Hanson was at the other tackle spot. Departed guards Brayman and Jones were replaced by Flynn, Ebersole, and Rollo, with Bart Richards at center in place of Charley Brayton. On the ends Gouinlock, Buckley, and Henderson took over for Munns and Cassidy, who was now in the backfield.

Iowa finished behind Cornell for the second year in a row. The Hawkeyes again won all seven games and stretched their win streak to 17 straight. They lost four starters through graduation, but it was basically the same team as last season except for its standouts, Aubrey Devine and Duke Slater.

With Devine gone, Gordon Locke came into his own. Twice during the year he scored four touchdowns in one game, once in the opener and again in the final game. He scored three times against Minnesota, and twice more for all of Iowa's 12 points against Ohio State. His 72 points in five conference games stood for over 20 years.

Bill Roper's Princeton Tigers won all eight of their games. They were called the "Team of Destiny" because they refused to lose. Week after week they were underdogs, yet they continued to win. Virginia was beaten 5-0 on a field goal and safety, Colgate was stopped 10-0 by a touchdown and field goal, Harvard lost by a touchdown, 10-3, and Yale went down 3-0 on Ken Smith's 18-yard field goal. In one of the greatest games ever played, Chicago was nipped 21-18, the result of three missed extra points.

The 1922 battle between Princeton and Chicago ranks with the top dozen football games of all time. It was Princeton's first venture into the Midwest, and Tiger grads flocked to the Windy City to cheer their team on. Behind its enormous bone-crunching line, Chicago moved down the field for a quick touchdown. An omen of things to come occurred in the second period when Princeton scored a touchdown to lead by a point, 7-6. The

Gilmour Dobie had a career coaching record of 180-45-15 for a .781 winning average.

Maroon-jersied giants marched relentlessly down the field again for a score and led at halftime, 12-7.

Chicago scored again after the intermission, and it looked like they had the game locked up at the end of the third quarter with the score 18-7. Three minutes into the final period Princeton found itself backed up to its own two-yard line. With the Chicago fans yelling "Block that kick," Princeton lined up to punt. On a play quickly made up in the huddle, John Cleaves, deep in his end zone, faked a punt and threw a long sideline pass which John Gorman caught and ran out to midfield. It was no kiss Gorman got on the tackle, for he was carried off the field.

It was the prelude to the disaster. Chicago center Rolph King was hurt, and his replacement centered the ball high to Willie Zorn. It bounced off his shoulder into the hands of Howdy Gray, who ran 43 yards to score. It was 18-14 with six minutes left.

Not long after, a Princeton pass and a Chicago penalty put the ball on the Maroon 15. A four-yard foray and another Chicago penalty moved the ball to the six. Three plays gained only three yards. On fourth down and goal to go, Harry Crum squirmed in and Princeton led 21-18. There were two minutes remaining.

"It's not over," shouted the Staggmen. Behind the blocking of guards Harold Lewis and Joe Pondelik, and tackles Frank Gowdy and Harold

Iowa tackle Duke Slater was later to become a Superior Court judge in Chicago.

Fletcher, they swept like a whirlwind to the Tiger six. The stadium was a near riot as two bulldozer jolts took the ball to the one-yard line. The Princeton quarterback ran back and forth slapping his men on the rear. There were ten seconds to play.

Bill Roper turned away. Lonny Stagg shook his head. The two lines dug in for the final charge. John Thomas bulled his way forward but was stopped short of the goal. No one heard the final whistle. No one left until the shock of the last moments drained away. Then Stagg turned and began the long walk to the dressing room, his Christianity sorely tested by the defeat.

The words of assistant coach Fritz Crisler kept ringing in his ears. "Send in your son with orders to pass," Crisler had pleaded, a tactic which was contrary to the rules. "With Princeton massed to stop Thomas, the end zone is wide open. Your son will be the hero of the game."

"No," replied Stagg. "I have to live with my conscience. Let the kids work it out by themselves."

In 30 years, Dan McGugin compiled a 197-55-19 record at Vanderbilt.

Members of the Princeton squad were ends Saxby Tillson and Howard Gray, tackles Harlan "Pink" Baker and all–American Herb Treat, guards Barr Snively and captain Melville Dickenson, and center Oliver Alford. At quarter was Johnny Gorman, halfbacks were Charlie Caldwell and Harry Crum, with Jack Cleaves at full.

At Vanderbilt, Dan McGugin continued to turn out near perfect seasons. His record in 1921 was seven wins and a 7–7 tie against Georgia. This year Vanderbilt erected the first stadium in the South used only for football. An airplane flew over the field and dropped the inaugural-day game ball, which bounced into McGugin's outstretched hands. Michigan was chosen as the opponent for the inaugural game, and on one occasion the Wolverines got to the two-yard line. Thousands of cheering Vanderbilt fans inspired the surge of center Alf Sharp, guard Gus Morrow, tackle Tex Bradford and end Lynn Bomar, who stopped Michigan cold in four attempts. Neither team could score in McGugin's best effort against his alma mater, but he still won eight of nine games.

In the next game, Michigan was asked by Ohio State to help dedicate its new stadium in Columbus. After end Paul Goebel blocked a punt, Michigan kicked a field goal. Then Harry Kipke began to dedicate the stadium in earnest with a 34-yard scoring run on a shovel pass. After the intermission, he intercepted a pass and returned it 45 yards for a touchdown. After intercepting still another toss, he drop-kicked a field goal from the 37. It took him two punts to get the range, but then he rolled nine straight punts out-of-bounds inside the Buckeye eight-yard line. Walter Camp was in the stands and placed Kipke on his All-America team. The game ended 19–0, with the Vanderbilt tie Michigan's only minus.

The puntout on the point after touchdown was abolished this year. Instead of kicking the conversion from the spot where the puntout was caught, the ball was put in front of the goal posts for the attempt. A scrimmage play followed, and the team that scored had the option of running or passing the ball over the goal line, or kicking it through the goal posts as before.

The Southern Intercollegiate Athletic Conference had been in existence since the turn of the century, but it was replaced this year by the Southern Conference. It was an unwieldly mass of 20 schools stretching from Virginia to Louisiana. Included were 11 state universities, six state colleges, and three private schools. Its very size precluded any clear-cut title, for many of the member schools never played each other for years.

The winner of the Indiana-Purdue game was awarded the Old Oaken Bucket this year. A link in the shape of a "P" or "I" is added each year, depending on the victor, who keeps the trophy until the next game. A tie is represented by both letters.

Hugo Bezdek's Penn State team, led by guard Joe Bedenk and Harry Wilson, met Southern California in the first game played in the new Rose Bowl. State stayed too long at the parade and was late for the game. Bezdek and USC coach Elmer Henderson almost fought, but a 14–3 Trojan win settled it, Bezdek's first Pasadena loss.

1923

At Illinois, the word got around the previous year that Bob Zuppke had a real stallion in his freshmen corral. Now a sophomore, it didn't take long for Harold "Red" Grange to start rewriting the record books. In the next three seasons, he gained 3,637 yards from scrimmage and kick returns for an average of 1,212 yards each year, more than anyone up to that time. He surpassed the great ones like Heston and Thorpe, and did for football what Dempsey did for boxing and Ruth did for baseball. On the radio and in the magazines and newspapers, Grange had more time and space devoted to him than any player of his time.

Illinois	(8-0-0)		Yale	(8-0-0)	
24	Nebraska	7	53	North Carolina	0
21	Butler	7	40	Georgia	0
9	Iowa	6	29	Bucknell	14
29	Northwestern	0	21	Brown	0
7	Chicago	0	31	Army	10
10	Wisconsin	0	16	Maryland	14
27	Mississippi State	0	27	Princeton	0
9	Ohio State	0	13	Harvard	0
136		20	230		38

Like Heston, Grange had a quick start and blinding speed. He also had the great runner's attributes of peripheral vision, balance, an exquisite sense of timing, and the smooth footwork which allowed him to change directions as if he had never slowed down. At 5'10" and 170 pounds, he kept in trim by delivering ice during the summer in his hometown of Wheaton, Illinois. "Grainche," as Zuppke called him, was like a deer bounding along while others strained to keep up. To the rest of the world, he would soon be known as "The Galloping Ghost."

Grange was in high gear right from the start. In his first game against Nebraska, he went 38 yards around end for a touchdown in the first quarter. In the second period, he returned a punt 66 yards for another touchdown. After the half, he scored again on a short run. He was an instant headliner.

In the next game against Butler he scored twice, the second time on an end sweep of 22 yards. In the third game with Iowa, he scored the only touchdown of the game, as Illinois ended the Hawkeyes' 20-game winning streak with the help of Earl Britton's 55-yard place-kick field goal. In the Northwestern game, Grange intercepted a pass and ran it back 91 yards for the first of his three touchdowns that day. Against Chicago, he scored the only touchdown of the game to beat the Maroons, 7-0. He also scored the only touchdown of the game against Wisconsin, as he dashed 26 yards around end. In the last game of the year against Ohio State, he again scored the game's only touchdown on a 34-yard cannon shot through the line.

Grange scored 12 touchdowns and led the nation with 1,260 yards gained. He was the hottest thing in a football suit, and the Illini were national champions. Grange always gave credit to his blockers — end Frank Rokusek, halfback Wally McIlwain, and 6'3", 240-pound fullback Earl Britton — for springing him loose on his patented play, the end run.

Other starters on the Illini squad were center Lenny Umnus, guards Lou Slimmer and captain Jim McMillen, tackles Bunny Oakes and Dick Hall, end Stub Muhl, and quarterback Harry Hall.

At Yale, Tad Jones fielded one of his greatest teams. Two good freshmen squads produced a team deep in talent, with capable men on the bench ready to replace the first unit. Wingback Bill Mallory and tackle Century Milstead (born January 1, 1900) were first team All-America, and on the second team were center Win Lovejoy, quarterback Lyle Richeson, and halfback Mal Stevens.

It was not a collection of stars, however, that graced the Yale campus, but an assembly of brothers who played together as family. Alertness was their stock in trade, for they recovered 23 of 27 fumbles during the year. Captain Mallory was the inspirational leader. Although he was as talented as anyone in the backfield, his willingness to block and tackle lifted the team and exacted from them the same selfless spirit.

Yale scalped everyone with three touchdowns in the first four games. In game five, 80,000 people packed the Yale Bowl for the Army set-to. Ed Garbisch drew first blood for the Cadets with a 15-yard field goal. Shortly afterward, tackle Ted "Shark" Blair fell on an Army fumble behind their goal to put Yale ahead. The Cadets traded touchdowns with a 75-yard punt runback by George Smythe to lead at halftime, 10-7. In the last half, Yale intercepted five passes and took Army into camp, 31-10.

Maryland came closest to derailing the Blue express. Yale was behind 14-0 before they settled down. Then halfback Widdy Neale, Greasy's younger brother, scored a touchdown and Mallory kicked a field goal to stay in the ball game. Yale pulled the game out when Mal Stevens caught a punt near midfield and ran it down to the two-yard line. On the next play, he scored to put Yale ahead for the first time, 16-14. In the last quarter, the Terrapins got close enough to attempt a field goal, but the kick by quarterback John Groves just missed, and Yale was home free.

Before 78,000 at New Haven, Yale shut out Princeton 27-0, as the Tigers got their worst beating from the Elis since 1890.

Although it rained half the night and turned the Cambridge turf into a quagmire, 55,000 showed up to see The Game. In the first quarter, Raymond Pond collared a punt which was dropped by Harvard safety Marion Cheek, and plodded with glued feet down the sideline 68 yards to a score. The Elis were agog at this second touchdown made on the Crimson in 14 games, and the man who waddled through the mud was known forever as "Ducky." In the third period, Mallory added a field goal from the 24 to make it 10-0. Then Harvard fumbled away another punt on its 29, and Mallory was good on his second field goal of the quarter. By the end of the contest it was difficult to tell red jersey from blue, as Harvard fumbled 14 times and Yale 11, with each side covering ten of its miscues. Now it was Yale's turn to snake dance around the field, singing and stumbling and skating in the ooze.

Other Yale men were halfback Newell "Flash" Neidlinger, Russ Murphy at quarter, guards Dick Eckart and Tex Diller, tackle Les Miller, and ends Tony Hulman, Dick Luman, and Shep Bingham.

Captain George Pfann took Cornell to its third straight unbeaten year and shared the eastern title with Yale. Led by captain Harry Kipke, all-American center Jack Blott, Irwin Uteritz at quarter, and guard Ed Slaughter, Michigan won all nine games and divided the Western Conference crown with Illinois.

This year saw the development of the aerial circus in the Southwest. Under coach Ray Morrison at Southern Methodist, the Mustangs won all nine games and their first conference championship. With a diminutive squad averaging only 166 pounds, SMU turned to the forward pass as an equalizer. Using a short punt formation, the guards dropped back to protect the passer, Stolly Stollenwerck. James Stewart and Blinky Bedford were the ends, but sometimes all the backs fanned out as pass receivers. With the defense held in check by the threat of a pass, lots of yards were gained by halfbacks Mule Dickinson and Wally Walling.

Because of an injury to his knee, captain Wilton Daniels had each player sign a pledge to give 110 percent. They fulfilled it by giving up only nine points all season. One side of the line was known as "The Stone Wall," and the other side called themselves "They Shall Not Pass." Behind them as linebackers were center Buddy King and fullback Smack Reisor. Texas Christian, with its new coach, Matty Bell, was unceremoniously welcomed into the Southwest Conference with a 40-0 shellacking.

The last feature of rugby, the onside punt, was abolished this year. Up to now, anyone behind the kicker could down the ball and maintain possession for the kicking team. Today, the quick kick can only be used for better field position. Once a ball is punted, it is surrendered to the other team, and it is not a free ball unless first touched by the receiving team.

1924

Notre Dame	(10-0-0)		California	(8-0-2)	
40	Lombard	0	13	Santa Clara	7
34	Wabash	0	17	St. Mary's	7
13	Army	7	28	Pomona	0
12	Princeton	0	9	Olympic Club	3
34	Georgia Tech	3	20	Washington State	7
38	Wisconsin	3	7	Southern California	0
34	Nebraska	6	7	Washington	7
13	Northwestern	6	27	Nevada	0
40	Carnegie Tech	19	20	Stanford	20
27	Stanford (Rose Bowl)	10	14	Penn	0
285		54	162		51

On October 18, Red Grange helped dedicate the new Illinois stadium against Michigan. Bob Zuppke had pointed to this game by writing letters to his squad all summer long. Fielding Yost, on the other hand, told his players to beware of tricks when he saw Illinois without any knee-length socks. What the Wolverines were about to see was not trickery but talent.

Grange took the opening kickoff on the five and started to his left behind Wally McIlwain and Earl Britton, who blocked the first two Michigan men. Then he reversed his field to the right side and cut back a second time to the left. He was in the clear as he crossed midfield and went all the way to score standing up.

Red Grange of Illinois.

Grange gained ten yards on the following kickoff before he was downed. The next time he touched the ball was on an end run at the Illinois 33. He moved to his right, and when he got past the defensive end, he veered back in the sweeping S-curve Zuppke had taught him and raced 67 yards to a touchdown.

The fourth time Grange touched the ball was on another run around right end. Instead of heading upfield immediately, he again cut back to the left, found no one in front of him, and swept 56 yards to a touchdown, his number 77 flashing in front of the crowd like a runaway rocket. As he put the ball on the turf and patted it gently he was mobbed by his teammates, while in the stands people slapped each other in their frenzy.

Grange scored a fourth time on the same play to the right. Again the defensive end was turned in by the quarterback, Harry "Swede" Hall, and when Grange cut back to the left he found the defense still drifting right. He bounded past them like a deer out of a thicket and sped 44 yards for yet one more touchdown.

The Four Horsemen of Notre Dame: Don Miller, Elmer Layden, Jim Crowley, Harry Stuhldreher.

Red Grange did what no football player has done before or since. He ran the ball eight times and scored four touchdowns, all in the first 12 minutes of the contest. As he came out of the game for a rest, 66,609 Illini fans stood on their feet to cheer the incredible performance of the Galloping Ghost.

Grange came back in the third quarter and scored a fifth touchdown on a 15-yard scurry, and in the last period he threw an 18-yard scoring pass to Marion Leonard for a 39–14 Illinois win. His four long scoring runs on eight tries were a once-in-a-lifetime achievement, his five touchdowns a Big Ten record and enough to give any fan something to talk about for years.

After the game, a Michigan newspaper nominated itself for the odious editorial of the year award with the comment, "All Grange can do is run." "Yeah," snorted Bob Zuppke, who could have handled that sour grapes remark while sleepwalking, "and all Galli-Curci can do is sing."

Grange's four long runs made radio sales increase because fans couldn't wait to read about him on Sunday morning. He also made the football huddle popular. Due to the cheering of the crowd, the Illini could not hear their own signals. Long before, at the turn of the century, Stagg had used a huddle indoors to combat crowd noise. Bob Zuppke became the first to use it outdoors in 1921, but the rules committee threatened to abolish it. Zuppke revived it last year when Grange brought the crowd to life with his remarkable

Knute Rockne

running. After the crowd noise this year in the Michigan game, the huddle was here to stay.

On the very afternoon that Red Grange stepped into football Valhalla, another legend was born at the Polo Grounds, a neutral site where Notre Dame and Army were playing each other for the first time. After watching the rhythm of the Notre Dame shift, George Strickler, the Irish publicity director, commented in the press box that the Notre Dame backfield reminded him of Rudolph Valentino's latest movie, *The Four Horsemen of the Apocalypse.*

Grantland Rice picked it up and wrote the greatest opening line in sports the next day in his column: "Outlined against the blue-gray October sky, the Four Horsemen rode again. In dramatic lore they were known as famine, pestilence, destruction, and death. These are only aliases. Their real names are Stuhldreher, Miller, Crowley, and Layden." After reading it, Strickler phoned his dad in South Bend and told him to get four horses ready. On Monday, a picture was taken of the four backs mounted on horses and developed into a legend.

The photo of the Four Horsemen is the most famous one in football,

Babe Horrell, center on the last of Cal's wonder teams.

and they became the most famous backfield in gridiron history. The legend has not diminished to this day, for they did as a unit what Grange did as an individual. Usually, the Four Horsemen sat on the bench at the start of the first and third quarters. After the heavier players, acting as shock troops, had softened up the opposition, the Four Horsemen came in to dazzle the other teams with their fast-breaking speed. Along with the Notre Dame line, they made the Irish the best team of the year and national champions. They also made Notre Dame synonymous with football and Rockne the epitome of coaching. The mantle which Yale had worn so long was passed to Notre Dame.

The success of the Four Horsemen and the Irish was built on the Notre Dame system. In his system, Rockne used speed of execution to get the ball carrier to the hole quickly with as many blockers in front of him as possible. Most teams utilized their blockers to get the runner past the scrimmage line, after which he relied on his own ability in the open field. In contrast, Rockne's system used smaller, speedier players who could get downfield in a hurry to block a defensive back. The downfield blocking helped make long runs more frequent, and Notre Dame became the most exciting team in football to watch.

At the heart of Rockne's system was the Notre Dame shift. From a T-alignment, the backfield shifted into a box formation. The spacing in the Notre Dame box was similar to a single wing, except that the fullback was a few steps away from the halfback in order to form a box. With a hop, skip, and a step the backs paused momentarily, and then they were off to the races. Before the defense could get set, the fullback knifed through the line or a halfback sped around end. The precision of the Notre Dame shift was as beautiful to watch as the flight of a punt turning over in the sky, for it had crowd appeal just like the wide-open game which the Irish played.

The last of California's wonder teams was still undefeated after five years, but had two ties this season. The second tie was with unbeaten Stanford, now coached by Pop Warner. A crowd of 76,000 in Berkeley watched the game which determined the West Coast representative in the Rose Bowl. Another 24,000 saw the game from "Tightwad Hill," a vantage point on the east side of the stadium opposite San Francisco Bay. Cal was led by captain Babe Horrell, its all–American center. Horrell blocked a punt last year and fell on it in the end zone for the first touchdown ever scored in Cal's newly dedicated Memorial Stadium.

Stanford led at the half on a pair of second-quarter field goals by Murray Cuddeback, the last one a 43-yarder. Cal took a 7–6 lead in the third quarter on Bert Griffin's thrust which capped an 81-yard blitz in five plays. The score went to 14–6 on a halfback-to-halfback pass from Jim Dixon to Tut Imlay. A second score by Griffin early in the last period made it 20–6.

There were ten minutes to go when Fred Solomon returned a punt to the Cal 35. Then Stanford took to the air and trimmed it to 20–13 on a pass from Ed Walker to sophomore end Ted Shipkey. In a rip-roaring finish, Stanford now tore 81 yards to a touchdown. Cliff Hey reeled off 32 yards on a fake reverse and picked up ten more on a full spinner. Cuddeback went over with two seconds left, then calmly kicked the game into a 20–20 tie.

With a 3-0-1 conference record, Stanford went on to play Notre Dame in the Rose Bowl, while California's 2-0-2 mark was second best. The Bears invited eastern champion Penn, 9-0-1 on the year, to play them in Berkeley on New Year's Day. Cal scored early and late in the game to beat the Quakers, 14-0.

New Year's Day found Notre Dame in Pasadena, and the fame of the Four Horsemen brought a glamour to the Rose Bowl that it has never lost. With the Four Horsemen were the Seven Mules, better known as the Notre Dame line. Rockne was known to let the Four Horsemen run behind a second-string line from time to time, just so they would know who was up in front opening holes for them. From right to left the Seven Mules were Ed Hunsinger, Edgar "Rip" Miller, Noble Kizer, captain Adam Walsh at center, Johnny Weibel, Joe Bach, and Chuck Collins.

Stanford earned the right to play Notre Dame in the Rose Bowl by a last-second tie in the Big Game with California, and it was Warner against Rockne. Warner had a surprise for Rockne, for it was in the Rose Bowl game this year that Warner used the double wing formation as his main offense for the first time. After working out the wingback reverses at Pitt and polishing the halfback spinners he learned from Hugo Bezdek in the Penn State games, Warner now added a passing fullback to his double wing. With a healthy Ernie Nevers (who was out most of the year from injuries) now faking and passing from fullback, Warner unmasked the offensive machine he had tinkered with for years.

Notre Dame's shock troops started in the Rose Bowl. On the first series by the Four Horsemen they fumbled, and Stanford had a 17-yard field goal by Murray Cuddeback. The next Irish drive died on the 10-yard line, but they got a break when a Stanford punt tailed out-of-bounds on the 32. Notre Dame took advantage of its good fortune, and Elmer Layden ran in for a 6–3 lead.

Another break came Notre Dame's way after an exchange of punts. Using its whirling reverses and fakes, Stanford marched to the Irish 31. On fourth and six, a sideline pass by Nevers was intercepted by Layden, who returned it 80 yards for a score. Nevers spearheaded a drive to the Irish 10-yard line, but the ball was fumbled away on a reverse, and the half ended 13–3.

In the third period, another Stanford fumble on a punt was picked up by Ed Hunsinger and run in for a 20–3 bulge. Nevers, who ran the ball most of the time and made most of the tackles, intercepted an errant Notre Dame toss on the Irish 29. With end Jim Lawson, the Stanford captain, running the ball on reverses and Nevers stabbing up the middle, the Cardinals marched toward the Notre Dame goal. The Irish braced themselves for another run, but halfback Ed Walker got the ball on a reverse and threw a short scoring pass to Ted Shipkey to close the gap to 20–10.

In the final period, another Notre Dame pass was stolen by Stanford center George Baker on the Irish 31. A reverse by end Ted Skipkey gained five yards. On four straight carries, Nevers picked up 20 yards to the Notre Dame six, and then spurted to the one-yard line. On the next two ram-headed lunges by both sides, the Seven Mules held Nevers to half-a-yard each time. The Irish took over on their one-foot line and punted out of danger.

Again Stanford fought back with Nevers running the ends and hitting the center. At the 30-yard line, the Nevers-to-Layden tandem clicked once more, as Layden bagged another sideline pass and ran it back 70 yards to a touchdown to make the final 27–10.

Pop Warner was a tough loser. His high-powered double wing formation made ten more first downs than the Irish, completed 12 of 17 passes, and outgained the Four Horsemen 298 yards to 179. Ernie Nevers carried the ball for 114 of those yards. Even in defeat, his great effort could not be overlooked. Along with Elmer Layden, he was voted the player of the game.

Army's captain, Ed Garbisch, won immortality in the Army-Navy game. After missing three drop-kick field goal attempts due to swirling winds in Baltimore's new Municipal Stadium, he put one through in the second quarter from 27 yards away. In the third period, he booted one of 42 yards and another of 20 yards. In the final quarter, he added his fourth one from 28 yards out for a 12–0 Cadet victory. Garbisch was also famous for his pregame prayers. Just before each game, coaches and subs left the locker room and Garbisch led the team in prayer: "Dear God, help us to acquit ourselves like men and to play the game within the rules to the best of our abilities."

1925

Dartmouth	(8-0-0)		Alabama	(10-0-0)	
59	Norwich	0	53	Union	0
34	Hobart	0	50	Birmingham Southern	7
50	Vermont	0	42	Louisiana State	0
56	Maine	0	27	Sewanee	0
32	Harvard	9	7	Georgia Tech	0
14	Brown	0	6	Mississippi State	0
62	Cornell	13	31	Kentucky	0
33	Chicago	7	34	Florida	0
			27	Georgia	0
			20	Washington (Rose Bowl)	19
340		29	297		26

Dartmouth won all its games in 1924 except for a 14–14 tie with Yale, and only a mix-up in the backfield on the one-foot line late in the contest spoiled their perfect season. This year the Big Green got it right and went all the way to a national title. In spite of Eddie Dooley's miscue, these teams had it above the shoulders, for every starter in both years was a Phi Beta Kappa.

Andrew "Swede" Oberlander was pulled out of the line this season and moved into the backfield. With his strong right arm, he led the Big Green passing attack. From his position at right half in the single wing, he faked an end run to the left, then stopped and pivoted to throw a pass. As he set up to throw, he timed his passes by repeating to himself, "Ten thousand Swedes jumped out of the weeds at the battle of Copenhagen." Then he unleashed his bombs to a spot where he knew his receiver would be, usually ends George Tully and Heine Sage or halfback Myles Lane. Behind the blocking of fullback Hooker Horton and quarterback Bob MacPhail, it was a perfect counter play for the end sweeps and tackle slants which coach Jess Hawley's team ran so effectively. The men up front who protected Oberlander and gave him time to throw were centers Josh Davis and Willard Sprague, guards Carl "Dutch" Diehl, Herb Rubin, and George Champion, and tackles Jack Holleran and captain Nate Parker.

Except for Brown, Dartmouth never made less than five touchdowns a game. They helped the Bruins dedicate their new stadium in Providence and won on two blocked punts. In the Chicago game, Oberlander threw four touchdown passes to bury the Maroons, 33–7.

Cornell matched Dartmouth score for score, and at the end of the first quarter only a point separated them, 14–13. Dartmouth pulled back on the throttle in the next period, including a toss of 50 yards from Oberlander to Lane, and led at halftime, 42–13.

In the second half, Oberlander scored on a 50-yard run and Dartmouth breezed to a win. Another player who hit paydirt was Charles Starrett, who intercepted a pass on the Cornell 25-yard line and scored as "The Durango Kid" in cowboy westerns.

In his third year at Alabama, Wallace Wade brought southern football into national prominence. The Tide had nine victories during the season and gave up only one touchdown. After Tulane turned down an invitation to play in the Rose Bowl and Alabama accepted, the Crimson Tide has been a fixture in bowl games ever since. Alabama was led by Pooley Hubert at quarterback and had a stellar halfback named Johnny Mack Brown. In his two years on the team, Brown had nine long touchdown runs to his credit, all upwards of 43 yards, including a 55-yard punt return this year against Georgia Tech for the only score of the game.

Coached by Enoch Bagshaw and paced by all-American halfback George Wilson, Washington was the host team in Pasadena's Arroyo Seco. In the first quarter, Wilson abducted a Bama pass on the Husky 15 and returned it to midfield. Then he picked up most of the remaining yards, with Harold Patton going in for a 6-0 lead.

In the next period, Wilson shook loose for 36 yards to the Tide 20. From there he hit Johnny Cole on a scoring toss, and UW was ahead, 12-0. Just before intermission, Wilson was hit by three Alabama players and carried off the field unconscious.

While Wilson sat out the third quarter, the Crimson Tide struck quickly. In less than seven minutes, they scored three touchdowns. From the Washington 41, Pooley Hubert ran 26 yards to the 15. Then on four straight carries Hubert scooted over, and it was 12-7. No sooner did Alabama get the ball when Grant Gillis completed a 59-yard pass play to Johnny Mack Brown, and Bama led for the first time, 14-12. The Huskies cooperated by fumbling at midfield. Hubert then threw a 30-yard touchdown pass to Brown, and the Tide was cresting on a 20-12 margin.

In the final period, Wilson came back to direct an 88-yard scoring drive, capping it with a toss to George Guttormsen, but they went under, 20-19. Johnny Mack Brown was voted the game's most valuable player, and two years later he was making movies in Hollywood. Another Rose Bowler from this game who stayed in Tinseltown was Washington tackle Herman Brix, a.k.a. Bruce Bennett, who played the title role in Tarzan flicks.

In addition to halfbacks Brown and Gillis and quarterback Hubert, the fullback on Alabama's first Pasadena team was Emile "Red" Barnes. Other members on this victorious squad were ends Hoyt Winslett and Tolbert Brown, tackles Claude Perry and Fred Pickhard, Bill Buckler and captain Bruce Jones as guards, with Gordon "Sherlock" Holmes at center. The reserves were lineman Ben Enis and backfield man, Herschel "Rosy" Caldwell.

Like many teams before and after, Michigan missed being the national champion by just one point. They avenged themselves on Illinois by forcing Grange to run inside, where he was held to 64 yards rushing. Yost savored the sweet moment with the comment, "Grange didn't gain enough ground to bury him in, y'know. Even if they'd a buried him head daown!" Michigan's stingy defense blanked seven teams, including Illinois, 3-0, and allowed only one field goal all year. Their potent passing attack of Benny Friedman to Benny Oosterbaan scored big on most teams they met, including a 54–0 drubbing of Navy, the Midshipmen's worst to date.

Michigan was undone by the field goal in the Northwestern game and by a pregame storm in Chicago. This was the first year that Soldier Field was in use, and the field had neither grass nor proper drainage. It rained for five days before the game, and both teams faced each other in ankle-deep muck. As kickoff time approached, a 55-mile per hour gale blew in from Lake Michigan. Friedman fumbled Northwestern's first punt, and the Wildcats recovered on Michigan's one-yard line. Three cracks at the goal proved futile, so Leland Lewis found a firm spot in the bog and booted an 18-yard field goal.

The Friedman to Oosterbaan passing combination was negated by the terrible weather conditions. No one could get downfield in the soggy turf, and any ball thrown into the air was caught by the wind and carried to the next county. Near the end of the third quarter, Northwestern was backed up to its own goal line. Instead of punting into the teeth of the gale, captain Tim Lowry had Lewis fall on the ball in the end zone for a safety. With the wind behind them in the final period, the Wildcats hung on for a 3–2 win. Michigan gained 35 yards and Northwestern 28, and the game saw only one first down and one attempted pass.

Yost always felt the 1925 team was his best one, even better than the point-a-minute squads at the turn of the century. Like the Dartmouth team this year, they were alert and brainy and seldom made a mistake. Their quarterback and captain was Benny Friedman, who threw five touchdown passes in the Indiana game. The halfbacks were Bruce Gregory, Lou Gilbert, and Wally Weber, with John "Bo" Molenda at fullback. The ends were all-American Benny Oosterbaan and Bill Flor, who scored the quickest touchdown on record by taking the ball off a Navy punter's foot in the end zone for an immediate touchdown. The interior line included tackles Tom Edwards and Harry Hawkins, guards Ray Baer and John Lovette, and center Bob Brown.

On the last day of October, Illinois went east to play Penn in Philadelphia. A day of intermittent rain and snow before the game turned the field to mush. The fire department took up where nature left off and poured water on the field in order to cancel Red Grange's running ability. It didn't even slow him down. On his first attempt he bumped off tackle, headed for the sideline, cut back downfield, and outdistanced everyone 56 yards to score standing up. Franklin Field was a madhouse of 65,000, and eastern fans became believers on the spot.

The Philadelphia crowd was still buzzing in the next period when Grange ripped loose on a 55-yard run and scored soon after. Shortly after halftime, he had his third tally on a 20-yard hook-and-lateral to Charlie Kassell, the right end. Kassell caught a pass, then tossed it back to Grange who took it on the short side and ran over at the corner of the end zone. His day's work was 363 yards on 36 carries, and Illinois had a 24–2 win.

This year saw the origin of naming the number one college football team for the season. An economics teacher at Illinois named Frank G. Dickinson was a football buff who enjoyed rating the teams according to his own mathematical formula. One day he mentioned this in class, and a student who was sports editor of the college paper wrote a story about it. The article came to the attention of Jack Rissman, a Chicago clothing manufacturer.

Rissman decided to use Dickinson's ratings in awarding a trophy to the best team in the Western Conference. When Knute Rockne heard of it, he invited Dickinson and Rissman to lunch in South Bend and asked them to make it a national trophy so Notre Dame could share in it. He also suggested the idea of making it retroactive so his 1924 Rose Bowl team could be named the first national champion, and so the race to number one was born.

1926

Stanford (10-0-1)			Navy (9-0-1)		
44	Fresno State	7	17	Purdue	13
13	Cal Tech	6	24	Drake	7
19	Occidental	0	26	Richmond	0
7	Olympic Club	3	27	Princeton	13
33	Nevada	9	13	Colgate	7
29	Oregon	12	10	Michigan	0
13	Southern California	12	53	West Virginia Wesleyan	7
33	Santa Clara	14	10	Georgetown	7
29	Washington	10	35	Loyola	13
41	California	6	21	Army	21
7	Alabama (Rose Bowl)	7			
268		86	236		88

Pop Warner had enough top players at Stanford for two good teams. Gone was Andy Kerr, who had taken over for Warner in 1922 and 1923 while Pop was at Pitt fulfilling the last two years of his contract. Warner's team swept through ten regular season games before being tied by Alabama in the Rose Bowl. It was the best football squad in Stanford history to date, for Warner had put spirit into the Stanford Red.

Stanford was deep in talent at every position. Tackles Leo Harris and Ward Poulson were backed up by junior Chris Freeman and sophomore Tiny Sellman. Hal McCreery and Stan Natcher were the centers. In addition to captain Fred Swan and Nate Symonds at guard, there was sophomore Don Robesky. At the ends were Ted Shipkey, Ed Walker, and sophomore Ted Harder. The quarterbacks were Eli Post and sophomore Laurence "Spud" Lewis. Behind fullback Biff Hoffman were Ernie Patchett and Sam Joseph. Halfbacks Frank Wilton, Don Hill, Mike Murphy, and Bob Sims all tried to share time with starters Dick Hyland and George Bogue.

The season got under way with a doubleheader against Fresno State and Cal Tech, an innovation that let Warner view the 51 members of his squad in action. Against Fresno State George Bogue scored in the first two minutes and by halftime Stanford had 32 points, but Cal Tech tied up the score before losing. The doubleheader also marked the first appearance of sophomore Biff Hoffman, who won the job of passing fullback in Warner's double wing formation.

Occidental went down to defeat 19-0 as Warner looked at 31 more players, but against the Olympic Club he had to use his best men in order to beat the ex-collegians. A second quarter field goal by the Olympic Club stood up until the last two minutes before Bob Sims scored from five yards out for a 7-3 win.

Warner emptied the bench against Nevada, but Stanford still ran up 33 points. In the Oregon game, George Bogue dropped the ball on a 35-yard run, but it bounced back into his hands like a yo-yo, and Bogue scored without losing stride. In the papers Pop was accused of trickery with his new "dribble play."

Southern Cal gave Stanford its first big test. The Trojans scored twice in the second quarter, the last on a fumble that was plucked out of the air and returned 48 yards to a touchdown. Don Hill took the kickoff and ran it back to midfield. A pass of 20 yards from Hoffman to Shipkey, and a 16-yard run by Bogue, moved the Cardinals downfield. Hoffman scored on last down from two yards out, but the Trojans still led at the half, 12-6. In the third quarter, Hoffman heaved a 45-yard toss to Hyland who caught it on the 15 and took it in for the tying score. Bogue added that extra point, and that was the ball game, 13-12.

Stanford finished with three convincing wins. On their way to five touchdowns against Santa Clara, they scored twice in the first period, once on a double reverse and again after a blocked punt. In the Washington game, it was tied at ten apiece late in the third quarter, but three touchdowns in the last few minutes won it big. On the first play against Cal in the Big Game, Dick Hyland took a reverse and raced 48 yards to a touchdown, and by halftime it was 27-0. The Bears' touchdown came after a blocked punt, but Stanford had its biggest win yet over Cal, 41-6.

The Rose Bowl game, with Graham McNamee announcing for NBC, was the first radio hookup aired nationally. Alabama was back for the second year in a row, but the game couldn't compare with the previous year's thriller. Warner's zone defense against passes also couldn't compare with the Stanford uniforms: They were clad in silk pants, but instead of missed tackles they brought only cute remarks such as "Take if off" and "Shall we dance?" After Stanford scored early on a 20-yard pass play from Bogue to Walker, the two teams danced the game away. In the second period, Dick Hyland almost gave Warner and the crowd of 57,000 a heart attack when he took a punt on his five-yard line, retreated into his end zone as a Tide defender ran into the goal post and knocked himself out, and made it back to the 20 before he was tackled.

With only a few minutes left, Alabama blocked a punt deep in Stanford territory and moved to a quick score. On the point after touchdown, the signals were started and then checked. As the Cardinals relaxed, Gordon Holmes centered the ball and Rosy Caldwell kicked the game into a 7–7 finish. Coach Wallace Wade had flimflammed Warner out of a perfect season.

Under its new head coach, Bill Ingram, Navy experienced its first unbeaten season in 15 years. Ingram liked to score whenever possible, and the Middies often came away with a field goal if they couldn't get a touchdown. Most of the seniors were dedicated to make their last season a success. Linemen on this Navy team included ends Henry Hardwick and Russ Lloyd, tackles Tom Eddy and captain Frank Wickhorst, guards Art Born and Johnny Cross, and center Herb Hoerner. In the backfield were quarterback Ed Hannegan, fullbacks Howard Caldwell and Howard Ransford, and halfbacks Tom Hamilton, Alan Shapley, and Jim Schuber.

Navy won its first nine games and tied the last one. The final game was a tie against Army at Soldier Field in Chicago. It was the first time that the two military schools played each other away from the East Coast. On hand were 110,000 people, the largest crowd to watch a football game so far, while thousands more milled around in the snowstorm outside.

Army coach Biff Jones started his second squad as shock troops, and Navy quickly went to town. A 38-yard pass from Tom Hamilton to Hank Hardwick put the ball on Army's one-yard stripe, where Caldwell slammed over. On the next march, the Middies faced fourth-and-one four times but made a first down each time. Behind the blocking of Wickhorst on the Army tackle and Hardwick who took the end by himself, Schuber scored to expand the Navy lead. Tom Hamilton drop-kicked the point after both times.

Down 14–0, Army's first team went in. The Cadets surged to life as Harry "Lighthorse" Wilson carried to the Navy 40. Chris Cagle picked up 20 more, and Wilson took it all the way on a run of 17 yards. Moments later, Skip Harbold scooped up a punt fumbled by Navy on their own 25 and ran in to tie the score, 14–14.

After the intermission Chris Cagle started around end, then doubled back on one of his patented reverses and outran everyone 44 yards to put Army in front for the first time. Wilson place-kicked his third conversion to make it 21–14.

Army led until late in the contest. With only four minutes left, Shapley intercepted a pass on the Navy 35. Captain Wickhorst called time and rallied his team to a now-or-never effort. As dusk enveloped the stadium, Navy slowly ground away toward the Army goal. With fourth-and-four on the eight-yard line and a minute to go, Navy went into a double wing formation. Wickhorst led the play, and Ransford hit off right tackle. As the Army line piled into Wickhorst, Ransford handed the ball to wingback Shapley, who ran around Army's left end to score standing up. Tom Hamilton drop-kicked his third PAT, and one of the greatest games ever ended in a 21–21 tie.

While Knute Rockne was in the press box watching the Army-Navy classic, Carnegie Tech gave Notre Dame its only loss of the year, 19–0.

Thousands of fans asked why Rockne wasn't with his team, but his fame was so great he was almost beyond criticism.

With the coming of Bob Neyland to Tennessee, southern football took a great leap forward. A West Point graduate, Neyland played end on Army's 1914 national champion football team, had a 35 and 5 record as a pitcher on the baseball team, and was heavyweight boxing champion at the Military Academy. As a coach, his influence is surpassed only by Rockne, Stagg, and Warner.

Neyland's main job was to beat Tennessee's intrastate rival, Vanderbilt. Under Dan McGugin, Vanderbilt had an imposing 12-2-1 record against the Vols. Neyland reversed this situation with a 16-3-2 record against Vanderbilt, and ended Dan McGugin's reign as the premier coach of southern football.

Neyland's record against Vanderbilt was just the beginning. He believed that football games were won with hard tackling and hard blocking. It was a concept he learned from Pot Graves, his line coach at Army. Neyland used a book written by Graves called *The Lineman's Bible,* and Tennessee teams soon became famous for their defense. He also agreed with Yost that football games were lost and not won, so Neyland put emphasis on the kicking game and pass defense. Hour after hour was devoted to covering punts and punt returns, with more hours assigned to returning kickoffs and covering them. Pass defense received as much time as punts and kickoffs, so that only 25 percent of practice was spent on the single wing offense Tennessee used.

If genius is defined as attention to detail, then Neyland is at the top of the list. With his military mind and training, he gave to the game a toughness and thoroughness it has seldom seen, and Rockne called Bob Neyland "football's greatest coach." Tennessee teams soon surpassed Notre Dame for the best record in football, and Neyland-trained coaches began appearing across the nation as much as Rockne-schooled men. Neyland's maxims adorned the locker room walls, and he repeated them before every game:

> Gang tackle. Protect and cover.
> Play for and make the breaks.
> The team that makes fewer mistakes WINS.

Eddie Robinson had coached Brown since the turn of the century, but he turned in his playbook one year too soon. The new coach, Tuss McLaughry, immediately gave Brown its only unbeaten season. They won nine games, shutting out Yale 7-0, Dartmouth 10-0, and Harvard 21-0, all within a month, and tied Colgate in the last one, 10-10. The starters went all the way against Yale and Dartmouth and were called the "Iron Men." They were also in the Harvard contest until the last few minutes and used only one sub against Colgate. Linemen from left to right were Hal Broda, Ed Kevorkian, Lou Farber, Charlie Considine, Orland Smith, Paul Hodge, and Thurston Towle. Halfbacks were Ed Lawrence and Dave Mishel, Roy "Red" Randall at quarter, and Al Cornsweet at full.

Herb McCracken's Lafayette team had a perfect slate of nine wins. Senior quarterback Rabe Marsh, halfback Frank Kirkleski, tackles Bill Highberger and Harold Cothran, and end Frank Grube took them to a third straight win over Pitt. Other team members who stuck Washington and Jefferson with its only setback, 16–10, were junior end Bill Atkinson, sophomore linemen John Thompson, Dave Warren, John Kressler, and backs Mike Wilson and Dick Guest.

1927

Illinois (7-0-1)			Minnesota (6-0-2)		
19	Bradley	0	57	North Dakota	10
58	Butler	0	40	Oklahoma A&M	0
12	Iowa State	12	14	Indiana	14
7	Northwestern	6	38	Iowa	0
14	Michigan	0	13	Wisconsin	7
14	Iowa	0	7	Notre Dame	7
15	Chicago	6	27	Drake	6
13	Ohio State	0	13	Michigan	7
152		24	209		51

Four major rule changes occurred this year. The point after touchdown had become routine in the past five years, so the goal posts were moved back ten yards from the goal line to the rear of the end zone. To encourage punt runbacks, a fumbled punt could not be advanced beyond the point where it was recovered by the kicking team. To prevent stalling, a play had to start within 30 seconds after the ball was put in play by the referee. In order to keep the offense from taking advantage of the defense, a complete stop of one second was imposed on any backfield shift.

Illinois won the national title with a 7-0-1 record. Except for an early-season tie with nonconference Iowa State and a narrow win over Northwestern, Illinois finished this year with relative ease. They were called "the nobodies from nowhere" because the team was not considered one of Zuppke's best at first. But Zuppke had an ideal blend of experienced seniors, eager juniors, and ambitious sophomores who worked hard because they didn't know how good they really were. When confidence came to this go-get-'em line and speedy backfield, the Illini showed everyone they weren't nobodies at all, but for real.

One nobody on the Illinois team who could not be overlooked was its matchless center, captain Bob Reitsch. To his left and right were two flint-faced guards, Bill McClure and Russ Crane, all–American this year as a sophomore. At the tackles were Butch Nowack and Lou "Step-and-a-half" Muegge, a nickname he answered to because a childhood ailment gave him an irregular gait. Zuppke carried players like Muegge on his squad because their cheerful outlook kept everyone loose, but Muegge soon won the tackle position on his ability. Other linemen who saw action were Ernie Schultz, Leroy Weitz, and Lou Gordon. The ends were Arnie Wolgast, Walt Jolley, Bob Hickman, and Gardie Grange, Red's younger brother.

Zuppke was a survivor because he tailored his attack to the available material. With a line deep in talent and reserves and a backfield gifted with speed, Zuppke had no need of trick plays this year. He simply outhustled other teams with rapier thrusts through the line and sweeps around the ends. The pony backfield was led by a pair of sophomores, halfback Jud Timm (164 pounds) and fullback Fritz Humbert (166 pounds). The other whirlaway backs were Blair French and Doug Mills (both 148 pounds), Frank Walker (154 pounds), and Dwight Stuessy (156 pounds).

At Minnesota, Doc Spears continued to teach that football was a game of conditioning and contact, a philosophy he learned under Frank Cavanaugh and which he taught before at Dartmouth. The 1927 Gophers were unbeaten but tied twice. On this squad were some of the greatest to wear the maroon and gold: guards George Gibson and Harold Hanson, quarterback Fred Hovde (later president of Purdue University), and captain Herb Joesting, the first of Minnesota's power-pack fullbacks. An all-American two years in a row, Joesting hung up his cleats after gaining 2,018 yards rushing for an average of 4.53 yards per carry.

At right tackle was another rawboned bruiser from the north woods, Bronko Nagurski. At 6'2" and 200 pounds, Nagurski was Paul Bunyan come to life. He was tried at end, but the Gophers owned the best pair of ends in the league—Ken Haycraft and Bob Tanner—each of whom pulled in a second-half touchdown pass to overcome Michigan, 13–7. Nagurski was equally at home at fullback, but with Joesting already there, Nagurski ended up at tackle where he was needed most. With his brute strength, Nagurski was not known for his finesse. He took a bead on the man in front of him and decked him whether he was at tackle or running with the ball. While he was in the lineup during the next three years, Minnesota lost four games by a total of only five points.

With Spears at the helm, the Gophers developed a reputation for physical football which left their opponents battered after each game. Last year, Michigan played Minnesota twice because other Big Ten teams did not want to schedule the Gophers. Ohio State coach Jack Wilce said it best: "You may beat Minnesota, but the next week you can't beat anybody."

The Gophers invaded South Bend to play Notre Dame but were met by an early November blizzard. Rockne had so much respect for the unbeaten Northmen that he did not open with his second squad. On their first series, quarterback Fred Hovde fumbled the ball. The Irish had it deep in Minnesota terrain, and within a minute halfback Christy Flanagan ran the end for a touchdown.

Seven points were all Notre Dame could get that afternoon. Late in the fourth quarter, Nagurski smashed through to block an Irish punt by fullback Elmer Wynne. Both benches jumped to life as they unpeeled the players one at a time. At the bottom of the pile with the ball was Nagurski. Behind his duck-or-die charge Minnesota scored in three plays on Joesting's pass to Len Walsh. The game ended in a 7–7 knot, and Nagurski quickly became a household word in Minneapolis.

One week later Army handed Notre Dame its only loss of the year, 18–0. Dana X. Bible's Texas Aggies were the Southwest Conference champs. Led by Joel Hunt, Texas A&M was 8-0-1 and missed being national champion by one yard. Captain Hunt was a one-man team. He kicked off, called signals, did the passing and punting, and carried the ball half the time. His 128 points were a SWC scoring mark and high for the country this year. "He ain't so fast, but you couldn't catch him in a telephone booth," said an observer.

Hunt's nemesis was TCU's Ray "Rags" Matthews, all-time end on the Southwest Conference team. Matthews earned his nickname because his jersey was always hanging in shreds. A cocky fellow like Yale's Tom Shevlin, he challenged ball carriers to try his end, and in the Texas A&M-Texas Christian game, he threw down the gauntlet to Hunt. Texas A&M's bread-and-butter play was an option pass or run, depending on what the defensive end did. Matthews didn't take the bait, and opted to take Hunt instead.

The door to the national crown closed on the Texas Aggies when Joel Hunt was brought down a yard from the TCU goal after a long gain. Hunt wanted his teammates to share in the scoring, so he called their play. Three A&M backs tried to perforate the Texas Christian goal line, but they were hurled back to the 10-yard stripe. On fourth down, Hunt called his own play. He got back nine yards, but the ball went over to the Froggies on the one-yard line where it began, and the game ended scoreless.

Another team which came close to getting the gold ring was Pitt. Paced by tackle Bill Kern and all–American halfback, Gib Welch, Jock Sutherland's Panthers had eight wins and a nothing-to-nothing tie with Washington and Jefferson before their loss to Stanford in the Rose Bowl, 7–6. Welch had touchdown runs of 105 yards against West Virginia and a 98-yard kick-off return in the Nebraska game. He ended his career with 1,880 yards rushing, but was held to 18 yards in the Rose Bowl, thanks to Stanford's interior line of tackles Tiny Sellman and Chris Freeman, guards Don Robesky and Dynamite Post, and center Hal McCreery.

Pitt moved out front in the third quarter when Jimmy Hagan pocketed a Stanford fumble and went 17 yards to score, but the point after was blocked by Walt Heinecke, subbing for injured Chris Freeman. Stanford took the kickoff and drove to the Pitt two-yard line, Richard Worden getting 31 yards on a pass. Again the Cardinals fumbled, but halfback Frank Wilton picked up the ball and ran in to tie it. Biff Hoffman added the extra point, and one of the hardest-hitting Rose Bowl games was history.

1928

Southern California	(9-0-1)		Georgia Tech	(10-0-0)	
40	Utah State	12	13	VMI	0
19	Oregon State	0	12	Tulane	0
19	St. Mary's	6	13	Notre Dame	0
0	California	0	20	North Carolina	7
19	Occidental	0	32	Oglethorpe	7
10	Stanford	0	19	Vanderbilt	7
78	Arizona	7	33	Alabama	13
27	Washington State	13	51	Auburn	0
28	Idaho	7	20	Georgia	6
27	Notre Dame	14	8	California (Rose Bowl)	7
267		59	221		47

The Army-Navy game was cancelled for two years because of eligibility rules. Navy insisted that Army not use any players who had more than three years of college football experience. The problem went all the way to the White House where President Hoover reinstated the game but changed nothing.

Pop Warner's Stanford team replaced Navy as the final game of the year on Army's schedule. The game was played in the Polo Grounds, and it was the last brilliant chapter in Warner's long and illustrious career. Warner gave eastern fans a look-see at his double wing formation, although he had used it extensively on the West Coast after the Rose Bowl game with Notre Dame.

Army won eight games this year, but it was not prepared for the trickery of Warner's double wing assault. The fake double reverse consistently decoyed the Army linemen out of position. When the Cadets tried to shore up their weak flanks, Biff Hoffman and Herb Fleishhacker ran inside the tackles for big gains. When Army plugged the center of its line, Stanford swept around the ends almost untouched. Even when Chuck Smalling took over for Fleishhacker at quarterback and Bill Simkins replaced Hoffman at fullback, it made no difference. The fakery of the spins and hand-offs confused Army completely, and everyone spent the afternoon wondering who had the ball in the 26-0 Stanford win.

The eastern coaches watching in the stands could not help but be impressed. With Rockne losing four games in his worst season at Notre Dame, they thought Warner's double wing was the ultimate formation. At a coaches' convention in New Orleans a month later, they gave Warner the attention they had previously given Rockne. Like devotees around a guru, they consulted Warner about his system, and he spoke at length on it. The result was that a dozen top coaches in the East climbed on the Warner bandwagon, and his double wing formation, or Warner A, and his single wing, or Warner B, with variations, became the fashion.

One coach who did not embrace the Warner system was Howard Jones of Southern California. A wizard in his own right, Jones had built championship teams at both Yale and Iowa. This year he humbled Notre Dame

Southern Cal tackle Marion Morrison, before he became a movie star known as John Wayne.

and turned back Warner's Stanford team, 10-0. The win over Stanford was a remarkable achievement, for the Cardinals still had many players from their national championship team two years earlier. It was the beginning of the end for the double wing formation in the West, as supremacy on the coast passed from Pop Warner to Howard Jones.

Jones defensed Warner's double wing formation by using a six-man line with the seventh man as an extra linebacker. The linebacker's job was to handle the fullback when he ran through the line after the fakes. He also had his ends play in close so they could charge the wingbacks and break up the play before it got started. His final tactic was to have his linemen hold back and not charge the play, an idea he had used at Yale two decades earlier. Instead, Jones had them hold their position until the slow-forming wingback plays developed. They could then tackle the ball carrier without being fooled by the fakes.

Jones added a superb offense to his well-conceived defense. He used a single wing formation with the tailback carrying the ball most of the time. He mixed in some spinners and ran a few plays to the short side to keep the defense honest. Most of the plays were to the strong side of an unbalanced line, often with four blockers in front of the ball carrier. This interference was so overpowering that it was known as the "thundering herd," and the defense often could not stop a play even when they knew it was coming. The Trojans were coast and national champions, but due to a disagreement with Tournament of Roses authorities, California was invited to play in the Rose Bowl instead.

USC's all–Americans, quarterback Morley Drury and halfback Mort Kaer, were gone, and so was tackle Marion Morrison, who would soon be known to moviegoers as John Wayne. The Trojan camp still showed plenty of horsepower, especially at tackle and guard. The starting tackles were Frank Anthony and captain Jesse Hibbs, who kicked a field goal in the Stanford game. The reserve tackles were Bill Seitz and Ward Bond, whom John Wayne would soon introduce to movie director John Ford. The guards were Chuck Boren, Bob Gowder, and Clark Galloway, Nate Barrager was at center, with Lowry McCaslin and Frank Tappaan at the ends. In the backfield were blocker Harry Edelson at right half, fullback Russ Saunders, who scored the touchdown against Stanford, tailback Lloyd Thomas, and quarterbacks Don Williams and Marshall Duffield.

John "Chick" Meehan had winning teams at New York University during the past three years. He had been hired to bring big-time football to the Big Apple. He gave the big city a show by firing a cannon every time NYU scored a touchdown. He also caught their eye with his military huddle, a stratagem on which long hours of practice were spent. When the squad broke the huddle, everyone pivoted on their left foot. Then they advanced to the scrimmage line in a 1-2-3 cadence and took their place ready for the play. They formed an unbalanced line by having either the center or a guard line up over the ball to snap it. Often, the defense was not set in trying to shift right or left with the NYU alignment.

NYU's star this year was Ken Strong, its all–American fullback. He gave the cannon a workout by scoring 22 touchdowns and 28 conversions for a total of 160 points, high for the country.

Against Carnegie Tech, with its all–American quarterback, Howard Harpster, Strong put on a sizzling performance in a 27-13 win. He threw for two touchdowns and ran for the other two, one on a 40-yard dash. Carnegie's coach, Wally Steffen, later said Strong was "the greatest football player I have ever seen, and that includes Willie Heston and Walter Eckersall. He ran over my team, and we were good enough to beat Notre Dame, 27-7."

The Big Apple saw plenty of action this year, especially in the Army-Notre Dame game at Yankee Stadium on Armistice Day weekend. The game was a cruncher, and at the half neither team had a score. Having lost to Wisconsin 22-6, and to Rose Bowl-bound Georgia Tech, Rockne didn't want any more losses.

In the locker room at halftime, Rockne told the Notre Dame squad about the deathbed wish of George Gipp. He bent over the rubbing table and carried on a dialogue in a quiet voice. It was as if Gipp were on the table telling the team to win one for him when the game wasn't going right. Then Rockne straightened up. He looked at the tear-streaked faces choking back a lump in each throat. "Boys, let's go get 'em," he said. "This is that game."

As Chris Cagle's number 12 ate up the turf before 78,000 in Yankee Stadium, Army began to move. Cagle raced 20 yards almost to midfield, and then completed a 40-yard pass to the Irish 15. With a first down on Notre Dame's three, Army scored and led, 6–0.

After an exchange of punts, the Irish had the ball on the Army 36. Fred Collins made four yards through the middle, and then eight more around right end. Jack Chevigny popped through the center for 14 yards where Cagle brought him down on the 10. Slowly but surely the Irish chewed up the yards until Chevigny went over to tie it up. As he got to his feet in the end zone he said, "That's one for the Gipper."

Like many Notre Dame touchdowns, the winning one was the result of Rockne's personal touch on the bench. With the ball on the Army 45, Chevigny circled right end for 15 yards. Then Chevigny fumbled and was replaced by Bill Dew. Rockne also sent Johnny O'Brien into the game for a cameo appearance at left end. Notre Dame lined up in a box left at the Army 32. Dew ran left and then handed the ball to Johnny Niemiec going right. Niemiec stopped and arched a pass to Johnny "One Play" O'Brien, who took it at the goal and stepped in for a 12–6 Notre Dame lead.

The thunderous roar of the crowd continued during the last two minutes. The kickoff went to Cagle, who returned it 55 yards before he was downed. Then he sped around end for 20 more, and the Cadets were on the one-yard line when the final whistle blew.

The turnaround for Tennessee football came in the Alabama game. With two Rose Bowl appearances under its belt, the Tide was unaware of the welcome that upstart Tennessee had for them. Gene McEver took the opening kickoff two yards in front of the goal and started upfield. The crisscross blocking which Bob Neyland taught took out nine men. The last two defenders met McEver at midfield, but he tore through them and ran in to make it 7–0 for the Vols.

Alabama scored four plays later. The conversion failed, and Tennessee still led 7–6. Their lead went to 9–6 as Hobo Thayer chased a Tide fumble out of the end zone. Bobby Dodd's touchdown pass made it 15–6, but Alabama replied with a score by Tony Holm before intermission to draw within two. The scoring ended there, as Bama threw two interceptions and lost four last-half fumbles.

Kentucky's 0–0 tie slowed the Vols, but UT stopped Florida, 13–12. Florida had won its first eight on Carl Brumbaugh's running and quarterback Clyde Crabtree's tosses to Dale Vansickle at end.

Bronko Nagurski continued his larger-than-life escapades. On the last Saturday in November, Minnesota met its traditional rival, Wisconsin, in the season finale. The Badgers had already beaten Notre Dame early in the year, and had shut out Michigan, Alabama, Chicago, and Iowa on successive weekends.

It was Viking weather that day in Madison, and the blocking and

Bronco Nagurski of Minnesota set the standard for hard-hitting football.

tackling were as crisp as the turf. There was no score in the second quarter, when Wisconsin fumbled on their 18-yard line and Nagurski recovered for Minnesota. Bronko got the ball five times on straight ahead plays. Two pneumatic-drill jabs brought a first down on the seven. Two more jabs took it to the one. On the fifth time he was in for the only score of the game.

Nagurski also made his presence felt that day on defense. In addition to his fumble recovery which set up the Minnesota touchdown, he kept Wisconsin from scoring on a touchdown-saving tackle at the 10-yard line. On another occasion he batted down a pass on the goal line, and on the final play of the game he intercepted a pass to turn the Badgers away once more.

Cal met Georgia Tech in the Rose Bowl. Led by their all–American center, captain Peter Pund, coach Bill Alexander's Yellow Jackets were victorious in nine games. Cal had a 6-1-2 record, but ties with Stanford and USC made the Bears a respectable host team.

The Cal–Georgia Tech game featured the most unforgettable play in

Rose Bowl history. It was just one of many plays which kept Cal from winning that day. In the first period, Benny Lom threw a 40-yard strike to Stan Barr all alone on the Tech goal, but it trickled through his fingers like water through a broken pot. In the next quarter, Lom whisked up a Tech fumble and scurried 60 yards to a score on a play that was already blown dead.

Then it happened. Stumpy Thomason started from his 25 and ran off tackle for a few yards. Irv Phillips, Cal captain and end, gave Thomason a good hit and the ball squirted loose. Cal center Roy Riegels caught it on the bounce and side-stepped two Tech defenders. In twisting away he reversed his field at the 34 and headed for the wrong goal 66 yards away.

The crowd leaped to its feet in disbelief, pointing to the streaking Riegels. As the yard lines melted away beneath him, Benny Lom slowly gained ground on Riegels. At the 10-yard line, Lom grabbed Riegels and dragged him to a stop just short of the goal. Then both of them were buried by the Tech infantry.

Riegels was downed near the sideline, and that's where Cal took over. As Lom tried to punt, Tech tackle Vance Maree broke through on the short side and blocked it. The ball rolled back out of the end zone for a safety and Tech led at halftime, 2-0.

Georgia Tech blocked another punt on the nine-yard line after the half. The Bears stopped them at the goal and Lom punted to the 45. The Yellow Jackets scored in two plays. Warner Mizell tore off 30 yards around end, and then Thomason sliced off tackle, cut back and ran 15 yards to a score. Cal was now behind, 8-0.

Cal continued to self-destruct. Cal's quarterback fumbled the ball away in the third period. A receiver deep in the Tech secondary fell down as he was about to catch the ball. Another pass was later dropped. Still one more pass was caught but lost on a fumble. Riegels then blocked a punt, but it tumbled out-of-bounds before he could capture it. Finally, when Lom attempted a punt, the ball popped and fluttered to the ground.

With less than two minutes left, Cal began from its 20-yard line and scored, mostly on long passes from Lom to Phillips and Lee Eisan, but Nibs Price's men came up a point short. Riegels was never allowed to forget his mistake, and for the rest of his life he was known as "Wrong-Way" Riegels. Because of his error, a rule was put into the book saying that a recovered fumble could not be advanced but was dead at the point of recovery.

In the line with Pund and Maree on the Georgia Tech eleven, which was voted number one by the Helms Athletic Foundation, were tackles Ken Thrash and Frank Speer, who stayed out due to injury, guards Raleigh Drennon and Joe Westwood, and ends Tom Jones and Frank Waddey. Backfield men with Thomason and Mizell were fullback Roy Lumpkin, and Bob Durant and Izzy Shulman at quarter.

Two small eastern schools — Detroit and Boston College — won all nine games. At Detroit, Gus Dorais' team blanked seven opponents and had a pair of sterling halfbacks, Lloyd Brazil and Tom Connell, the nation's second highest scorer with 126 points. He had 18 touchdowns and 18 conversions, including all 19 points against Fordham. Boston College head coach Joe McKenney was one of the youngest coaches any time and any place. Two years previously he was BC's quarterback, and last year he was only 22 years old when he was an assistant coach for the Eagles.

1929

Notre Dame (9-0-0)		Purdue (8-0-0)	
14 Indiana	0	26 Kansas State	14
14 Navy	7	30 Michigan	16
19 Wisconsin	0	26 DePauw	7
7 Carnegie Tech	0	26 Chicago	0
26 Georgia Tech	6	13 Wisconsin	0
19 Drake	7	27 Mississippi	7
13 Southern California	12	7 Iowa	0
26 Northwestern	6	32 Indiana	0
7 Army	0		
145	38	187	44

In spite of losing four games the year before, including two in a row for the only time in his career, Knute Rockne rebuilt Notre Dame into national champs this year. The job was made difficult because Notre Dame Stadium was under construction, and all games were played on the road. Even more important was the phlebitis, or blood clot, in Rockne's leg.

After the first game of the year, Rockne was forced off his feet. He directed practice from his wheelchair with a bullhorn. In the away games, the team was led by his first assistant, Tom Lieb, but Rockne called long distance to talk with Lieb and the starters before each game.

Two days after the stock market crash, Notre Dame played Carnegie Tech at Pittsburgh in the fourth game of the year. Rockne was so enfeebled that Tom Lieb carried him into the locker room at halftime. Rockne used everything to win, and the infection in his leg was no exception. Although the excitement could loosen the clot, Rockne still pleaded with his players.

His words were straight from the shoulder: "Why do you think I'm taking a chance like this? To see you lose? Are you going to let that happen? Go out there and crack'em, crack'em, crack'em. Fight to win. Fight to live. Fight to win."

Corny? Maudlin? Not if you were there. Like outstanding players from the past who would be great today, Rockne's oratory would also be just as effective. Carnegie got nowhere after the half, but Joe Savoldi pushed over a score for a 7-0 Irish win.

Rockne was also at the game in Chicago's Soldier Field where Notre Dame edged USC 13-12 before 112,000 people. Russ "Racehorse" Saunders

Purdue's first all–American, Elmer "Red" Sleight.

scored on a 95-yard kickoff return, but Rockne countered with a touchdown pass by speedster Jack Elder. On the last Saturday in November, 79,000 showed up in Yankee Stadium to see the Army-Notre Dame game. It was a month and a week after the start of the Great Depression, and the field was as frigid as the economy. In the second period, Elder purloined an Army pass and skipped 96 yards down the sideline for the only score of the game. It was a perfect ending to a perfect season.

Besides backfield men Savoldi and Elder on this championship team there were Frank Carideo, Larry "Moon" Mullins, and Marty Brill. On the flanks were John Colrick and Tom Conley, backed up by Johnny O'Brien, Eddie Collins, Manny Vezie, and Tom Murphy. At the tackles were Ted Twomey and Dick Donoghue. The guards were captain John Law and Jack Cannon, who played without a helmet, and Tim Moynihan at center. Reserve linemen were Al Culver, Joe Nash, Bert Metzger, Tom Kassis, and Frank Leahy. Gifted sophomores were Tommy Yarr and Marchy Schwartz.

Purdue won the Big Ten title for the first time. At right tackle was the

Tennessee guard Herman Hickman.

Boilermaker's first all–American lineman, Elmer "Red" Sleight, a hard-bitten head banger who asked no quarter. At the other tackle was George Van Bibber. Center Ookie Miller and guards Horace Buttner and George Stears formed the rest of the interior line. The Purdue backfield also had an all–American, Ralph "Pest" Welch, a real triple-threater. At fullback was Alex Yunevich, a rough customer who liked contact as a ball carrier or blocker. John White was quarterback, and the right half was Glenn Harmison. The well-oiled machine of coach Jimmy Phelan, ex–Notre Dame captain and quarterback, ran so smoothly that the backs averaged 4.5 yards per carry during the season.

The turning point for the Boilermakers was against Michigan early in the year. At the end of three periods, the Wolverines led 16–6. Then Welch broke free for a pair of scores, one on a 35-yard run. Purdue added two more touchdowns while holding the Wolverines scoreless and won going away, 30–16. The only other team to give Purdue any trouble was Iowa, but the Boilermakers again showed they could win in the clutch. In the last period,

Albie Booth of Yale.

Harmison hit Bill Woerner on an 18-yard touchdown toss for the game's only score. Indiana was beaten in the season ender, and Purdue not only had the Old Oaken Bucket but a perfect year.

With its flaming sophomores now juniors, Tennessee finished its third unbeaten season in the last three years. Only a tie each year soiled their record, and this year's tie with Kentucky in a snowstorm kept them from a Rose Bowl invitation.

Bobby Dodd was the triple-threat back in Neyland's single wing. He was a good runner and a better passer, with an arm so accurate that Neyland let him pass from behind his own goal. Beside him at fullback was Gene Mc-Ever, who led the nation in scoring with 129 points. In the wingback position was the other half of the "Hack and Mac" duo, Buddy Hackman.

One reason for the lusty Tennessee attack was a sophomore guard in the line, Herman Hickman. Like Wilbur Henry a decade earlier, Hickman's looks were deceiving. At a round 215 pounds he looked like he still had his baby fat, but the only two men on the team who could outrun him were McEver and Hackman. When he dug in, no one ever budged him an inch. At the snap of the ball he fired off the line like a cannon ball, often scrambling the blockers and ball carrier behind the line of scrimmage.

Francis Schmidt took over at Texas Christian and promptly won the SWC title with nine wins and one tie. The first hurdle was defending champ Texas, which was unbeaten and unscored on in seven games. Texas broke in front 6–0, but Cy Leland ran the kickoff back 95 yards to put TCU ahead by a point. The Purple Gang scored again to make it 13–6. Then Texas dropped back to punt, but Dexter Shelley caught the Frogs asleep and ran in to stay close at halftime, 13–12. Later, on another Shelley punt, his foot hit the end line for a safety and a 15–12 Froggie win.

In the traditional game with Southern Methodist, TCU ran into a buzz saw. The Mustangs were no pushover, for they had played Texas to a scoreless draw. In the second half against TCU, Bobby Gilbert launched a missile from his 35. Speedy Mason tipped it, then clutched it and ran the last 35 yards to score.

TCU had its own aerial artist in Howard Grubbs, the first of many great Froggie throwers. Behind the protection of guard Mike Brumbelow and center Noble Adkins, Grubbs chipped away at SMU with his passes, then scored from the one-yard line himself. The 7–7 tie left the Purple unbeaten at the top of the heap.

At Arkansas, Wear Schoonover became the Razorbacks' first all-American. He played 60 minutes of every game and had enough credits for two men. Against Texas A&M, he intercepted five passes and blocked the PAT for a 14–13 Arkansas win. He caught 14 passes in the Baylor game. He had 33 catches for the year, seven for scores, and added 13 conversions for good measure.

In New Haven, a 5′6″, 144-pound sophomore quarterback named Albie Booth gave luster to Yale's fading glory. Before 80,000 people in the Yale Bowl, he put on a one-man performance which ranks with Grange's effort against Michigan five years before.

Army scored in each of the first two quarters to move out front, 13–0. Chris Cagle, Army's three-time all–American halfback, snared a Yale aerial and ran it back 45 yards to a touchdown. Then John Murrell sliced through tackle 27 yards for the second touchdown. There was no joy in Yalesville as it looked like a runaway for the powerful Army team.

Enter Albie Booth. After an Army fumble on its 32, Yale marched to the Army goal. As Booth carried the ball again and again, the momentum changed sides. Behind the Yale line, which had tackle Frank Vincent and end Herty Barres on the right side, Booth scored and added a conversion to make it 13–7 at the half.

The Yale fans could hardly settle down at halftime. They were not to be disappointed in the next period. The right side of the Army line became porous as end Dan Hickok, Don Ferris at tackle, guard Fred Linehan, and center Art Palmer cleared it out for Booth. When Yale put on another march of 35 yards and Booth ran over to tie it, the crowd erupted with a thunderous ovation. The tumult subsided just long enough for Booth to drop-kick his second point after, and Yale led for the first time, 14–13.

With his mother watching her first football game from the stands, the stage was set for the legend of "Little Boy Blue." Army took the kickoff and was forced to punt. Booth fielded it on his 35 and headed for the sideline. The Cadets converged on Booth to drive him out-of-bounds, but he cut back through them unmolested. When his number 48 broke into the open, the crowd came to its feet in a cheer. The Army safety put an arm around him at the 25, but Booth made a complete spin and ran in. Right guard Firp Greene almost pounded him to the turf with joy.

The stands were in chaos, and so was the Army team. Booth scored all the points to dismantle the Cadets, 21–13. The Army team was in such disarray that it never made a first down in the third quarter, while Yale made six. Five of Army's seven first downs were made after Booth left the game in the fourth quarter. As he walked to the sideline, the crowd stood up as one and gave him the greatest hurrah in Yale history.

V. End of an Era

1930

Notre Dame (10-0-0)		Alabama (10-0-0)	
20 Southern Methodist	14	43 Howard	0
26 Navy	2	64 Mississippi	0
21 Carnegie Tech	6	25 Sewanee	0
35 Pitt	19	18 Tennessee	6
27 Indiana	0	12 Vanderbilt	7
60 Penn	20	19 Kentucky	0
28 Drake	7	20 Florida	0
14 Northwestern	0	33 Louisiana State	0
7 Army	6	13 Georgia	0
27 Southern California	0	24 Washington State (Rose Bowl)	0
265	74	271	13

The first precept of coaching is don't get caught with your material down. Because this rule was put into effect at Northwestern, the Wildcats came within five minutes of being national champions. The team was the result of a coaching clinic held by Northwestern coach Dick Hanley. Hundreds of high school coaches attended the clinic, and they later sent Hanley 36 all-state high school players. Among these recruits were quality people such as Frank Baker and Dick Fencl at the ends, tackles Dallas Marvil and Jack Riley, guards Jim Evans and Red Woolworth (another helmetless player) and center Bob Clark. Backfield men included quarterback Lefty Leach, sophomores Pug Rentner at halfback and fullback Reb Russell, and "Hard Luck" Hank Bruder the other half. Bruder won this dubious distinction with a hip injury in 1928, a broken leg in 1929, and getting smallpox this year.

Northwestern began by handing Bernie Bierman's Tulane team its only loss of the year. In the succeeding games, the Wildcats never scored less than three touchdowns in any game during the season. In the final game against defending champion Notre Dame, the bubble burst. For 55 minutes the Wildcats outgained the Irish 350 yards to 40, but couldn't score. Twice they drove deep into Notre Dame territory, once to the four-yard line and once to the one-yard line, but both times they fumbled the ball away.

Then Notre Dame's two-time all–American Frank Carideo put his punting shoe to work. Carideo was tutored in punting by the master of coffin-corner punts, Leroy Mills. With less than five minutes left, Carideo punted on first down from midfield. The idea was to back the Wildcats to their goal, hold them, and try to block their punts. Carideo's kick rolled out-of-bounds on the one-half yard line. Two more of his first-down punts rolled out on the one-half yard line, and one went out at the one-yard marker.

On Northwestern's fourth return punt, Carideo ran the ball back to the Wildcat 28. Carideo then called for a reverse, and Marchy Schwartz ran all the way for the first score of the game. After the kickoff Northwestern was forced to punt, and the kick was returned to the 30. Another Schwartz reverse ended with a pass to Carideo who was downed on the one-yard line. From there, Notre Dame scored again to give Northwestern its only defeat.

Leroy Mills was in a class by himself as a punter. After playing on the freshmen team at Princeton, he left school to get married but spent the rest of his life teaching punters to "kick 'em where they ain't." He was unpopular with those coaches who favored high spiraling punts, for Mills was an exponent of the end-over-end style of punting. Instead of dropping the ball on his foot, he placed the ball on his instep and kicked it short for about 35 yards. Then it would hop and bounce crazily in a straight line for another 35 yards. Usually it would roll out-of-bounds and cancel any runback. Mills taught his students by putting a red flag in the corner for them to aim at.

Mills was equally adept at drop-kicking. He would stand on the goal near the sideline, then hook the ball through the goal posts with a 90-degree curve. During the winter when snow and cold forced him inside, he practiced in the gym. He kept crowds of onlookers fascinated all afternoon by drop-kicking footballs through the basketball hoop from midcourt. For his encore, he would turn around and drop-kick the footballs one after another through the basket at the other end. Believe it or not.

Rockne's last team has often been called his masterpiece, and rightly so. From end to end, the line read like a list of all–Americans, with many top replacements sitting on the bench. The backs could not only run and catch the ball, but all of them were good blockers. The caliber of this national championship squad was revealed in the Northwestern game. The Wildcats had three dozen of the best high school players in the state, but they still lost to Notre Dame.

From the moment Joe Savoldi ran back the opening kickoff for a touchdown against SMU, the Irish were off like a comet. Before 80,000 in Franklin Field, Notre Dame humiliated a good Penn team. In the first period, Marty Brill wriggled over right guard on a spinner and went 67 yards for the first of his three touchdowns.

At the start of the second quarter Joe Savoldi scored, and soon after Brill intercepted a Quaker pass. On his first play from scrimmage, Paul "Bucky" O'Connor went around right end 59 yards for a score, and the crisp downfield blocking brought the crowd to its feet as much as the run. In the third period, Brill added two more touchdowns on runs of 38 and 25 yards. The Irish totaled 557 yards to Penn's 73 in an awesome 60–20 win.

The mandatory rule this year calling for a one-second stop before the ball was snapped didn't hurt the Notre Dame shift at all. Rockne countered by adding spinners in which the halfback or fullback cut back to the short side on off-tackle plays and end runs. He also had a heavier backfield, and his 1930 version of the Four Horsemen outweighed the original by almost 18 pounds per man. Northwestern and Army tried to flag the Irish express, but Carideo's punting downed the Wildcats, and Army was beaten on a 55-yard touchdown run by Marchy Schwartz with 3:30 to go and Carideo's all-important extra point.

Even at the end of the year when Joe Savoldi was gone from school for getting married and Moon Mullins was injured, Notre Dame didn't slow down. Bucky O'Connor was installed at fullback to refresh the weakened backfield. With 74,000 watching in the Los Angeles Coliseum, the Irish beat Southern California easily. Notre Dame went in front on a pass from Schwartz to Carideo. Then on a reverse, Brill lateraled to O'Connor who went around end 80 yards for a second score. On still another lateral, this time from Schwartz, O'Connor scored again on a seven-yard run around end. Mullins, who could hardly move, was sent in for one play, and the hometown fans stood on their feet to cheer him. Marchy Schwartz led the team in rushing with 927 yards on 124 carries for a 7.5 average, second only to George Gipp.

In addition to this sparkling backfield, the line was also a collection of standouts. At the ends were captain Tom Conley and Ed Kosky. The tackles were Joe Kurth and Al Culver. At the guards were Tom Kassis and a 5'9", 149-pound stick of dynamite, Bert Metzger, with Tommy Yarr at center.

Rockne died next spring on the last day in March in an airplane crash near Bazaar, Kansas. His 105 wins, 12 losses, and 5 ties for a .881 average is still unsurpassed. But his contribution to football is more than just his record. It is even more than the Rockne Memorial on the Notre Dame campus, a sports facility for everyone who wants to engage in athletics. It is more than his shock troops, the forerunner of the platoon system, or the spacing out of an end which he designed in order to get a better angle on the defensive tackle, or the wide-open game which gave football its crowd appeal. His real contribution is that he was the genuine human being we all want to be. It is best expressed in Rockne's favorite poem:

> Lord, in the battle that goes through life
> I ask but a field that is fair,
> A chance to be equal with all in the strife
> The courage to strive and to dare.
> And if I should win let this be my code
> My courage and honor held high,
> But if I should lose let me stand by the road
> And cheer as the winners go by.

Coach Wallace Wade's last year at Alabama had all–American tackle Fred Sington and sophomore tailback Johnny "Sugar" Cain, a triple threater who could run, pass, and punt. They also had a good defense, giving up only two touchdowns all year. In the line were guards John Miller and Frank Howard (later a coach at Clemson), center Jess Eberdt, and end

Jimmy Moore. The fullback was John "Monk" Campbell, with John "Flash" Suther at wingback, fast on the reverse. Wade started his shock troops in the Rose Bowl as he did all season. When the first team entered the game in the second period, they quickly scored three times on passes, two of them to player of the game Monk Campbell. A field goal was added by J.B. "Ears" Whitworth in the third quarter.

With his best team ever, coach Babe Hollingbery's Cougars from Washington State won all nine games. Behind a line that hit like the hammer of Thor, halfback Tuffy Ellingson and Elmer Schwartz at fullback fattened their rushing average each week. Leading this hard-nosed crew was center Mel Hein, who backed up the line on defense and stacked up ball carriers like cordwood. The tackles were Turk Edwards and Harold Ahlskog, George Hurley was at guard, and at end was his brother, John Hurley. A pair of tooth-and-claw victories over USC 7–6, and Washington 3–0, put the Cougars in Pasadena. For the Rose Bowl they wore bright red suits from helmet to shoes but didn't impress Alabama, which took them to the cleaners. As one Los Angeles sportswriter put it, "The Cougars showed up looking like 11 bottles of strawberry pop—and displayed about as much fizz."

1931

Southern California	(10-1-0)		Tulane	(11-1-0)	
7	St. Mary's	13	31	Mississippi	0
30	Oregon State	0	7	Texas A&M	0
38	Washington State	6	40	Spring Hill	0
53	Oregon	0	19	Vanderbilt	0
6	California	0	33	Georgia Tech	0
19	Stanford	0	59	Mississippi State	7
69	Montana	0	27	Auburn	0
16	Notre Dame	14	20	Georgia	7
44	Washington	7	40	Sewanee	0
60	Georgia	0	34	Louisiana State	7
21	Tulane (Rose Bowl)	12	28	Washington State	14
			12	USC (Rose Bowl)	21
363		52	350		56

After the untimely death of Knute Rockne, the Notre Dame team which he built remained unbeaten until deep in the year. Another seven games ran the string to 26. Only the powerful Northwestern team slowed down the Irish by holding them to a scoreless duel on a soggy field. A Philadelphia paper suggested that Notre Dame's first and second squads play each other for the national title.

No one could ever replace Rockne as head coach, so Notre Dame named Heartley "Hunk" Anderson and Jack Chevigny to run the team.

Their job was made easier by the 300 candidates who showed up for practice, a legacy held over from Rockne's belief that anyone who wanted to throw or kick a football should have the opportunity to do so. An even greater legacy was the spirit which Rockne left the team. It has made Notre Dame a perennial winner to this day.

Notre Dame's unbeaten streak came to an end against Southern California in their next-to-last game. After getting blown out by the Irish last season, Howard Jones gave his offensive machine an overhaul. To the power of the Trojan single wing he added double wing reverses, fakes, and spinners. He also put in trick plays and multiple offensive formations which began in a 4-4-3 alignment and then shifted into an unbalanced line, often with only one man on the short side.

A preview of things to come occurred soon after the kickoff when Southern Cal marched down the field, only to fumble the ball away at the three-yard line. A few moments later, USC had to give up the ball on downs at the 11. The crowd of 52,000 then settled back to watch the Irish scuttle the Trojan horse.

Early in the second period, Notre Dame took a punt on their 40 and began a march of their own. A long pass from Schwartz to Chuck Jaskwhich carried to the Southern Cal 18. Schwartz picked up 14 yards before he was tackled at the four-yard line. Two plays later Steve Banas carried it in for a 7-0 lead.

The Irish struck again late in the third period, scoring in just four plays from their 37. Ray Brancheau ran for nine yards on a reverse, and Schwartz peeled off 14 more around end. Then Schwartz lateraled to Banas who took it to the three-yard line on a 37-yard pickup. From there, Schwartz scored to make it 14-0.

The Trojans took the kickoff and marched another 60 yards only to surrender the ball on downs at the 11-yard line. A nose injury suffered by SC fullback Jim Musick served to crystallize the men of Troy at this point. The Irish were forced to punt, and Southern Cal went to work at midfield.

Orv Mohler lateraled to Gus Shaver who tore around end for 16 yards to start the fourth quarter. Then came the play that put the skids under the Irish. As the right halfback lined up at right end, left end Ray Sparling moved into the backfield as the left wingback. Mohler took the ball and ran into the line on a fake and made a complete spin. He gave the ball to Sparling, who cut in at right tackle and carried it to the one-yard line. On the third play of the period, Gus Shaver went around end and outraced everyone to the corner for SC's first touchdown. Joe Kurth broke through to block the kick and keep the score at 14-6.

After the kickoff Notre Dame was forced to punt, and again the Trojans began at midfield. A pass interference penalty on the Irish put the ball on their 32. Three plays later, Southern Cal was on the Notre Dame 10-yard line. From there, Mohler ran into the line again, spun around, and threw a pass to Shaver on the left flank who went over to make it 14-13.

Notre Dame was again forced to punt after the kickoff, and the ball rolled out-of-bounds on the Trojan 20. With only four minutes left, Shaver faded back to his 10-yard line and launched a 50-yard bomb which nestled in the arms of Sparling on the Notre Dame 40. It was SC's first pass completion, and it sent them to their bag of tricks once more. Sparling moved from left end to left wingback as before, and the right halfback again became the right end. Left tackle Bob Hall was now at left end, and Shaver hit him on the Irish 17 for SC's second completion of the day.

An offside penalty moved the ball to the 12, but two plays gained nothing. On third down, the Trojans lined up for a field goal. The stadium was silent as a tomb. Thinking it was a fake, the Irish line did not charge. Stan Williamson gently centered the ball, Orv Mohler put it down like a piece of fine china, and guard Johnny Baker boomed it through with only a minute left.

The luck of the Irish had run out. What looked like another one-point win for Notre Dame over the Trojans for the fourth time in the last six years was now a two-point win for Southern Cal, 16–14. It was only the second Irish defeat at home since 1905. Howard Jones was so unhinged that he rushed onto the field and hugged captain Williamson, who had just hugged Baker. An Irish wit provided the epitaph, "We blocked the wrong kick."

In the Southern Cal locker room after the game, Jack Rissman presented Jones with the national championship trophy. In return Jones asked Rissman for directions to Rockne's grave. Within an hour Rissman led Jones and the Trojan squad to Highland Cemetery, where the USC coach paid his last respects by leading a memorial service for his fallen comrade.

Others on the Southern Cal team were end Garrett Arbelbide, guards Aaron Rosenberg and Larry Stevens, tackles Tay Brown and Ernie Smith, and halfbacks Erny Pinckert and Tom Mallory.

By the end of the year, most top teams dropped at least one game. Notre Dame not only lost to USC but to Army, 12–0. Pitt and all–American tackle Jess Quatse lost to Notre Dame, 25–12. Behind guard Sam Voinoff and halfback Jim Purvis, Purdue downed Northwestern 7–0 in a charity game for the poor of the Great Depression. Purdue was upset by Wisconsin, 21–14. Fordham fell to Bucknell and fullback Clark Hinkle in its last game, 14–13.

Coach Bernie Bierman gave Tulane its three best consecutive seasons. Led by halfback Bill Banker they won all nine games in 1929, and had eight victories and a loss to Northwestern in 1930. At the end of the regular season this year, Tulane was the only major undefeated and untied team in the country.

Bernie Bierman's Green Wave was solid offensively and defensively. They had a nimble-footed rushing game which ran for 176 first downs and was a yard short of gaining 3,000 yards. Out of 51 touchdowns scored this year 39 were on the ground, all Tulane rushing records. The defense was grudging against both pass and run. In blanking seven teams, they held opponents to just under 32 percent pass completions and permitted them 93.3 yards total offense per game, both Tulane defensive records.

Tulane's Rose Bowl squad lined up with quarterback Lowell "Red"

USC guard Aaron Rosenberg, a mainstay on their offensive line.

Dawson and fullback Nollie Felts, whose punting was effective all season, especially against Texas A&M. The halfbacks were Frank Payne and Don Zimmerman, the team's wheelhorse. From left to right the linemen were Vernon "Lefty" Haynes, Dick Bankston, John "Red" McCormick, Winnie Lodrigues, John Scafide, Clag "Tick" Upton, and captain Jerry Dalrymple.

In Pasadena fumbles put Tulane in the hole, and USC led 7–0 at the half. In the next quarter, Erny Pinckert scored twice on runs of 30 and 23 yards. The Green Wave lashed back with a touchdown in the third and fourth periods, one on a pass to Haynes and one on a dive by bare-headed Harry Glover, but at the end of the game Southern Cal was still high and dry with a 21–12 win.

After the Rose Bowl, Tennessee was the only major unbeaten team. The Vols usually had a tie on their record which voided a perfect season, and an undefeated team would slip past them to the top. This year was no different, except that Southern Cal lost its opening game. Kentucky was again the spoiler for Tennessee as they had been in three out of the last four games, and by the same score of two years ago, 6–6. Back after a year's layoff with a knee injury was Gene McEver, but it was sophomore star Beattie Feathers who brought the fans to their feet with his long touchdown sprints. He scored twice against Mississippi on runs of 60 and 80 yards, once against Duke on a 65-yard dash, went 70 yards for the touchdown that tied Kentucky, and finished off the year with a 65-yard scoring run against New York University.

USC coach Howard Jones compiled a 194-64-21 record with five Rose Bowl victories.

Paced by all-American guard, Herman Hickman, Neyland's rugged defense gave up only two touchdowns and a safety all season. A misguided Vanderbilt quarterback decided to pick up some yards through the "Fat Boy" at guard. Hickman bucked the interference back and piled it up into the ball carrier. On the last play of the series, the Commodores were looking at fourth-and-ten. In a postseason charity game at Yankee Stadium to aid New York City's poor, Hickman tore loose again. With a first down on Tennessee's three-yard line, the NYU quarterback decided to run a play over the "Fat Boy" for a score. On last down, a disheveled NYU team faced fourth-and-14. Hickman worked over his man so badly that the NYU tackle, Galahad Grant, was taken from the contest, and Grantland Rice quickly reworked his All-America team to put Hickman on it.

1932

Michigan coach Harry Kipke was a true disciple of Fielding H. Yost. A great punter for the Wolverines a decade earlier, he believed that if the other team couldn't score they couldn't beat you. He was an ardent supporter of Michigan's punt, pass, and prayer system. To him, punting was the name of the game, for a blocked punt was a 50-yard play. Like Neyland at

Tennessee, Kipke spent hours on blocking punts and keeping them from being blocked. It was not in vain, for none of Michigan's punts was blocked during the season. Then the defense took over, with a hope and a prayer that the other team would drop a punt or fumble the ball. This too was not in vain, for the Wolverines surrendered only a pair of touchdowns all year and were national champions.

Michigan (8-0-0)			Southern California (10-0-0)		
26	Michigan State	0	35	Utah	0
15	Northwestern	6	20	Washington State	0
14	Ohio State	0	10	Oregon State	0
32	Illinois	0	6	Loyola	0
14	Princeton	7	13	Stanford	0
7	Indiana	0	27	Calfornia	7
12	Chicago	0	33	Oregon	0
3	Minnesota	0	9	Washington	6
			13	Notre Dame	0
			35	Pitt (Rose Bowl)	0
123		13	201		13

The pass part in the Michigan system was supplied by Harry Newman, their all–American quarterback. He earned the position by tossing footballs through a hole in a canvas which Kipke hung in the gym, but he was booed off the field in the Wisconsin game the previous year after four of his first six passes were intercepted.

Newman bounced back with his eagle-eye passing better than ever this year. After captain Ivy Williamson blocked a punt and Chuck Bernard fell on it for a touchdown in the Princeton game, Newman completed an eight-yard pass for the winning score. Against Indiana, he ran for 35 yards to set up the Michigan touchdown, and then sneaked over for the only score of the game. In the Chicago game he scored both touchdowns, one on a 78-yard punt return and the other on a 26-yard run. In the last game of the year with Minnesota, he helped keep the Little Brown Jug in Ann Arbor by kicking a field goal for the only points of the game.

Another team which gave up only 13 points during the year was Southern Cal. With such an ungenerous defense, they were never behind at any time all season long. They won all ten of their games and raised their winning streak to 20 straight.

Most of the linemen from last year's championship team were back, but the backfield had some new faces. From left to right, the line included Ray Sparling, Tay Brown, Aaron Rosenberg, Curt Youel, Larry Stevens, all–American Ernie Smith, and Fred Palmer. In the new-look backfield were left half Bob McNeish, right half Bob Erskine, fullback Gordon Clark, and quarterbacks Orv Mohler, Homer Griffith, and Irvine "Cotton" Warburton.

The Trojans shut out their first five opponents, including tough wins over Oregon State, Loyola, and Stanford. In the game with Stanford, known as the Indians since 1930, Pop Warner's team lost its zip after they threw their best punch in the first period. They had a first down on the SC 15, but on last down at the six, Ernie Caddell got only half-a-yard, and the Trojans took over on their five-and-a-half-yard line. Southern Cal scored after Bill Sim punted and Mohler ran it back 24 yards to the Stanford 21. On second down, Bob McNeish took a reverse and then threw 17 yards to Fred Palmer for the touchdown. In the third quarter, Palmer was on the receiving end of a 35-yard toss from Gordon Clark and ran for six more before he was downed on the Stanford nine. Mohler picked up four yards on the first crack and scored on the second, and Warner made up his mind to leave at the end of the season.

Near the end of the year, a 5'6", 145-pound cotton top named Warburton began to steal the headlines. Against Cal, he intercepted a pass and returned it 61 yards for a score. He scored the touchdown which kept SC in the Washington game and starred against Notre Dame, but it was in the Rose Bowl that he glowed brightest. Jock Sutherland's Pitt team, led by its pair of all-Americans, halfback Warren Heller and end Joe Skladany, was unbeaten with eight victories, but had two scoreless stalemates with Ohio State and Nebraska. Pitt trailed 14-0 at the end of three quarters in the Rose Bowl, but Warburton shut the door in the final period with two touchdowns for a 35-0 Trojan win.

Tennessee was again unbeaten with its second 9-0-1 season in a row. In his first seven years at Tennessee, coach Neyland fashioned an incredible 61-2-5 record. In five of those years his teams were undefeated, and only a loss or a tie ruined their perfect year. Neyland drilled his players in proper execution, for he believed that football was a game of errors, and the team which made fewer mistakes had the best chance of winning. With his dedication to defense and kicking, he was content to let the other team have the ball until they made a mistake.

A good example of Neyland's belief that football contests are won or lost with the kicking game took place in this year's Alabama-Tennessee game. A steady rain slowed down the running and passing of both teams, so Beattie Feathers of Tennessee and Johnny Cain of Alabama battled each other with punts all afternoon. Feathers averaged 46 yards on 23 kicks, while Cain punted 19 times for a 43-yard average. As the sky grew dark late in the game, Feathers set a punt down on the Alabama one-yard line. Cain hurried his return punt because of a poor snap from center, and the ball skittered off his foot to the 12-yard line. Three plays later, Feathers scored the only touchdown for a 7-3 Tennessee win.

Another southern team with a 9-0-1 record was Chet Wynne's Auburn Tigers. Led by their first all-American, halfback Jimmy Hitchcock, Auburn was victorious until the last game of the year when South Carolina handcuffed them with a 20-20 tie.

After being an assistant to Pop Warner for almost a dozen years, Andy Kerr came into his own as a head coach this season. He took over at Colgate in 1929 and began to turn out top-flight teams immediately. He lost one game in each of his first three years: 8-1-0 in 1929, 9-1-0 in 1930, and 8-1-0 in 1931. The 1930 team was led by fullback Len Macaluso, the nation's leading scorer with 145 points. The 1932 squad was his showpiece, for it was unbeaten, untied, and unscored on. It was known as the 4-U team, for it was also uninvited to the Rose Bowl.

Kerr's double wing offense displayed wingback reverses and buck laterals in which the fullback gave the ball to a pivoting tackle who then lateraled to a wingback. His team also used the hook-and-lateral, a forward pass in which the receiver lateraled to a runner racing by. Kerr was also the first to use the downfield lateral, a play which swept the country for the next few years. He saw the possibilities of the downfield lateral as he watched the Stanford rugby team, and he resurrected the multiple laterals which had been the heart of the offense in the game's early days. He rehearsed his players hour after hour in throwing and catching a ball while running at top speed.

In the fourth game of the year, Kerr took the wraps off his double spinner. In this play, fullback Bob Rowe took the ball and made a complete spin toward quarterback Charley Soleau, who was pivoting to him. The fullback could give the ball to the quarterback, fake it and keep it himself, or hand it to one of the wingbacks, Renato Antolini, Whitey Ask, or Bob Samuel.

It was also in this fourth game against Lafayette that Kerr gave his team a futuristic look as he dressed them in bright red pants, white jerseys trimmed in red, and gleaming white helmets. Colgate's press agent, Dexter Teed, quickly dubbed them "the Red Raiders of the Chenango," and so the Colgate nickname was born.

As the season progressed, Kerr urged his team not to lose. By the sixth game, he was exhorting them not to permit a first down. At the end of the year, he was pleading with them not to let the other team score. His zeal bore fruit, for in the last game of the year with Brown, the Bruins were stopped only a few inches short of the goal as the first half ended.

The Colgate line that gave the backs time to perform their fakery included ends Winnie Anderson and Vernon Lee, Bart Ellis and Ed Prondecki at the tackles, razor-sharp pulling guards Joe Hill and captain Bob Smith, and center Glen Peters.

Francis Schmidt had another winner at Texas Christian. On their way to the SWC crown, the Froggies beat all six conference foes, the first team to perform this feat. The Purple Gang gave up only 23 points while winning ten and tying one. Much of the team's success was due to its man-eating line which placed five men on the All-SWC team: tackles Ben Boswell and Foster Howell, guards Lon Evans and Johnny Vaught (later coach at Mississippi), and center J.W. Townsend. The only blemish on their year was a tie with Louisiana State on a field goal apiece.

While at TCU, Schmidt added to his reputation for erratic behavior, even surpassing Howard Jones in concentration and forgetfulness. One day while his car was on a hoist being greased, Schmidt was in the seat diagramming plays. He was so engrossed in his work that he forgot where he was. When he stepped out, he got his bell rung at the bottom of a five-feet drop.

Coach Noble Kizer also had a winner at Purdue and kept them near the top nationally. Led by its all–Americans — Paul Moss at end, fullback Roy Horstmann, and halfback Duane Purvis — they won seven games and missed a clean sweep by moments, as a last-ditch touchdown pass by Northwestern deadlocked the game at 7–7.

An era came to an end at Chicago. After 41 years as coach of the Maroons, Amos Alonzo Stagg was asked to resign. He had reached the mandatory retirement age of 70, but he declined to accept the two advisory jobs offered him. Next year found him at the College of Pacific in Stockton, California. He showed his new boss the same letter he had written to Chicago's president four decades before: "After much thought and prayer I have decided that my life can best be used for my Master's service in the position you have offered."

At the end of the year, 13 schools left the dozen-year-old Southern Conference and formed the Southeastern Conference. The main reasons for the rupture were geographical distance, travel time and expense, a great disparity between the large and small schools in the conference, and the fact that half the teams did not play each other from one year to the next, if at all. Most of the schools in the new conference were in the Gulf states and west of the Appalachian Mountains. Those schools which stayed in the old Southern Conference were in the mid–Atlantic states and east of the Appalachians.

The cry of football brutality brought two new rule changes into effect this year. The first one tried to prevent injuries on kickoff returns by having at least five men within 15 yards of the ball when it was kicked. The second one tried to eliminate injuries from crawling after the ball carrier was downed. From now on, the ball was dead when any part of the body except hands or feet touched the ground.

1933

Michigan	(8-0-0)		Princeton	(9-0-0)	
20	Michigan State	6	40	Amherst	0
40	Cornell	0	45	Williams	0
13	Ohio State	0	20	Columbia	0
28	Chicago	0	6	Washington & Lee	0
7	Illinois	6	33	Brown	0
10	Iowa	6	7	Dartmouth	0
0	Minnesota	0	13	Navy	0
13	Northwestern	0	26	Rutgers	6
			27	Yale	2
131		18	217		8

According to Princeton line coach Tad Wieman, Jack Weller "was the best."

Beginning with his second year as head coach, Harry Kipke's defense-oriented Wolverines won 31 times, lost once, tied three, and had 17 shutouts in the last 22 games. Like athletic director Fielding H. Yost, Kipke believed in a strong defense built around a rock-hard center like all–American Chuck Bernard. On the bench was a reserve center named Jerry Ford, destined to become president of the United States.

This year captain Stan Fay replaced Newman at quarterback, Willis Ward took over for Williamson at right end, and Carl Savage was now at guard in place of Abe Marcovsky. Other than that, most of last year's championship team were back, including left end Ted Petovsky, left tackle Whitey Wistert, left guard John Kowalik, and right tackle Tom Austin. Returning backfield men were John Regeczi at fullback, left half Herman Everhardus, and John Heston, son of the great Willie, at right half.

Michigan began the defense of its national title by taking a 20-point lead over Michigan State by the end of the first quarter, and then coasting to a 20–6 win. In the next game against Cornell, three long touchdown runs gave

All-American tackle Bob Reynolds of Stanford, one of their famous "Vow Boys."

Michigan another 20-point lead. John Regeczi ran 80 yards to a score on a fake punt, Herm Everhardus raced 43 yards for a second score, and then ran back the opening kickoff of the second half 85 yards for a touchdown on the way to a 40-0 win. Behind quarterback Bill Renner, Ohio State was downed, and Chicago was beaten 28-0 as Michigan had a two-touchdown bulge before the game was ten minutes old.

The Wolverines then eased by Illinois, but not before the Illini made a few Michigan hearts skip a beat. The Wolverines stood by helplessly after a fair catch of a short Michigan punt gave Illinois a free kick, but the 30-yard field goal try just missed, and Illinois was short by a point. Everhardus provided the four winning points against Iowa on a conversion and field goal. Minnesota and Michigan sparred to a 0-0 draw, but Northwestern went under 13-0, and Michigan had its fourth Big Ten title in a row and second consecutive national championship.

After the disastrous 1931 season in which Yale overwhelmed Princeton 51-14, the Tigers hired Herbert O. "Fritz" Crisler as coach. One of the time-honored traditions at Princeton was that ex-gridiron greats worked out with the team before the Yale game, and it was said that there was one Princeton alum in uniform for each point Yale scored. Crisler handled the problem by saying he had time for advice only after practice was over. Another time-honored custom was that only alumni coached at Big Three schools, but Crisler shattered that historic legacy by speaking at every one of the 85 Princeton alumni groups around the country.

Crisler solved the alumni problem with the best medicine of all: He made Princeton a winner. The Tigers were unscored-upon until the final two games when they yielded the only touchdown of the year to Walt Winika of Rutgers and a safety to their ancient enemy, Yale. Crisler's sophomores became the best team seen at Princeton in a decade, for in their three-year sojourn within the musket-scarred walls of Old Nassau they lost only one game. They left Columbia, the East's Rose Bowl entry, behind by three touchdowns. Five members of this squad were starters for three years: guard Jack Weller, tackle Gil Lea, fullback Pepper Constable, and halfbacks Garry LeVan and Homer Spofford. Others in the lineup were centers Dan Hinman and Moose Kalbaugh, guards Charley Ceppi and John Bliss, captain Art Lane at tackle, Roy Fairman at end, halfback Chick Kaufman, and John Paul "Kats" Kadlic at quarter.

Far across the country on the opposite shore, another group of gifted sophomores appeared at Stanford, the Princeton of the West. After watching Stanford get beat by the Trojans for the fifth consecutive time the previous year, Frank Alustiza's freshman rage bubbled up as he dressed for practice the following Monday.

"They will never do that to us. We will never lose to USC."

Blocking back Bones Hamilton chimed in, "Let's make that a vow." The cheers of the locker room seconded the motion, and so the legend of the Vow Boys had its beginning.

In addition to Alustiza and Hamilton, the freshmen who made last year's oath were ends Keith Topping, Monk Moscrip, and Aly Trompas, tackles Bob Reynolds and Claude Callaway, Wes Muller at center, guard Larry Rouble, fullback Bobby Grayson, and halfback Bob Maentz. Others in the lineup were junior halfback Buck Van Dellen, senior end Lyle Smith, senior halfback Bill Sim, and back for his last year, two-time all–American guard Bill Corbus.

Southern Cal's victory string was stopped at 25 games by a scoreless encounter with Oregon State. In the next game against Cal, Cotton Warburton kept the unbeaten streak alive and well on a 59-yard scoring run in the last period to beat the Bears, 6–3. In the first half, he was dazed after making a tackle and taken to the locker room. He was still in the showers when the second half started. After being convinced the game wasn't over, he put on his uniform and returned to the game, but he never remembered his long run that day in Berkeley for the game's only touchdown.

On the following Saturday in Los Angeles, Warburton dashed 44 yards to put the Trojans in front, 7–0. Stanford came back with a 67-yard drive to even it at halftime. In the last half, Bill Corbus kicked a pair of field goals to beat USC, 13–7, and end their unbeaten streak at 27 games. The Vow Boys made good on their oath, and topped off the season with a 7–3 win over Cal in the Big Game. They accepted the Stanford ax which was given to the winner of the Big Game for the first time, and Stanford became the first team to appear in the Rose Bowl three years in a row.

A Big Three agreement kept Princeton from going to the Rose Bowl.

Army, with guard Harvey Jablonsky and halfback Jack Buckler opposite Navy tackle Slade Cutter and halfback Buzz Borries, beat the Midshipmen for win nine but Notre Dame tripped them in the tenth one, 13–12. Duke also won nine behind tackle Fred Crawford and backs Horace Hendrickson and Corky Cornelius, but lost the last one to Georgia Tech 6–0 so Columbia was invited to the Rose Bowl instead.

At Columbia, Lou Little probably did more with less material than any coach in the game. After an initial 5-4-0 year in 1930, Columbia Lou produced a pair of 7-1-1 seasons and a mark of seven wins and one loss this year. With its small enrollment and high academic standards, good backup men were a rarity at Morningside Heights. Over half the squad were enrolled in a profession such as medicine, law or engineering, and if they could play football and love the game, so much the better. The first team usually gave a good account of themselves, but the bench was often thin.

Lou Little's biggest win was in the Rose Bowl. His chief concern was over his lack of reserves, for the heat of southern California had sapped the strength of more than one team. But a storm hit the area a few days before the game and deluged the playing field with a foot of water. The fire department pumped water from the Rose Bowl around the clock, but it was uncertain until late morning whether the game would be played that day or not. On the parade route many bands played "It Ain't Gonna Rain No More." By kickoff time the Rose Bowl was half full, and the best four-dollar seats were going for fifty cents.

The rainstorm was a godsend for the underdog Columbia team. The cool weather made their slim reserves equal, and the spongy field cancelled Stanford's strong running game. Columbia scored the only points of the game on a play known as KF-79. It was a spinner play used a few times during the season and polished on the Lion stopover in Tucson. It almost worked in the first quarter, but the safety man tackled the runner on the 11-yard line.

Now it was tried again in the second period after a pass to right end Tony Matal put the ball on the Stanford 17. Columbia lined up in a single wing with an unbalanced line to the right. Halfback Cliff Montgomery took the ball from center Newt Wilder and began a complete spin. Halfway through the turn, he handed the ball to fullback Al Barabas running behind him to the left. As Barabas hid the ball on his hip, Montgomery finished his spin and faked the ball to wingback Ed Brominsky, who cut in over the left side of the line. In the Columbia huddle, short side guard Larry Pinckney switched assignments with left end Owen McDowell. Pinckney took out the right half this time while McDowell wasted the safety man, and Barabas continued his naked reverse and went into the end zone just as he had done so many times in practice.

A San Francisco sportswriter summed it up by quoting *John* 18:40: "Now Barabbas was a robber." But Stanford was robbed by more than Barabas and the clever fakes of the Lion backs. They were cheated by the wet field which caused Bob Maentz ᵗᵣ ᵍᵒ down untouched while he was running to a score. They were also done in by a remark that Columbia was only Pomona High in light blue jerseys. Stanford fumbled eight times and not just because the ball was slippery. On one fumble, Bobby Grayson got up with two broken ribs. Others in the charge of the Light Blue were Steve Dzamba at guard, and tackles Joe Richavich and Paul Jackel.

1934

Minnesota	(8-0-0)		Alabama	(10-0-0)	
56	North Dakota State	12	24	Howard	0
20	Nebraska	0	35	Sewanee	6
13	Pitt	7	41	Mississippi State	0
48	Iowa	12	13	Tennessee	6
34	Michigan	0	26	Georgia	6
30	Indiana	0	34	Kentucky	14
35	Chicago	7	40	Clemson	0
34	Wisconsin	0	40	Georgia Tech	0
			34	Vanderbilt	0
			29	Stanford (Rose Bowl)	13
270		38	316		45

A few years ago, Bernie Bierman gave Tulane its three best years in succession; at Minnesota, he created a dynasty. In his second year the Gophers were unbeaten in eight games as they won four and tied four, including a 7-3 win over Pitt which was the Panthers' only defeat of 1933. This year's team was monumental, with two squads of reserves most coaches would use as starters.

Bierman was a stern taskmaster who taught rock 'em, sock 'em football. Blocking, tackling, and execution were at the heart of his program. Practice always ended with the team lined up on the 20-yard line and Bierman standing on the far goal. Then they'd run 20 plays correctly as fast as they could before he'd let them shower. If one of the plays wasn't run to his satisfaction, he'd have them start again from square one.

Bierman was famous for his icy reserve. When he went to the hospital to visit injured Julius Alphonse, who shared right half with Art Clarkson, Alphonse had to do most of the talking. Any oratory was left to his assistants. Bierman's contribution was usually a few words which underscored what had already been said.

The game of the year was again Minnesota and Pitt. In the rematch, the Gopher strategy was to run one play, punt, and let the Panthers wear themselves down against their line patrolled by tackles Ed Widseth and Phil Bengtson, and Vern Oech and Milt Bruhn at the guards. Opposite them for Pitt were three-year men George Shotwell at center, guard Chuck Hartwig, tackle Bob Hoel, end Harvey Rooker, and quarterback Miller Munjas. In the second quarter Pitt took over on the Gopher six after a fumble, but four shots at the rhino-ribbed Minnesota line gained only four yards.

The Gophers punted away. Suddenly, Izzy Weinstock wheeled through for nine yards and lateraled to Mike Nicksick, who went 64 yards to put Pitt ahead at the half, 7–0. Bierman's dressing room speech was laconic as usual: "Two touchdowns will win it."

Both teams thrashed each other until the third period was almost over. Then Pug Lund lifted another punt to the Panthers, but the safety man, Bobby LaRue, was separated from the ball on a crushing blow by the Minnesota center, Dale Rennebohm. Right end Butch Larson corraled it for the Gophers on the Pitt 45.

Lund and Stan "the Hammer" Kostka tattooed the Panther line again and again until they were at their 22. On fourth-and-two, Alphonse took a reverse and went around right end for the score. Right guard Billy Bevan, the last Minnesota man to play without a helmet, converted to tie the game at seven apiece.

Pitt had to punt after the kickoff, and the Gophers ran it back to their 46. Again Lund and Kostka labored straight ahead until the ball rested on the Pitt 18. On last down, Minnesota finessed the Panthers again. Kostka ran into the line and gave the ball to quarterback Glenn Seidel, who pitched it back to Lund on a fake end sweep. Lund stopped and threw a pass to left end Bob Tenner on the five-yard line, who ran in for the winning score.

The 64,850 fans in Pitt Stadium were drained like the teams on the field. They alternated between admiration and swearing as Minnesota handed Pitt its only loss for the second year in a row. Two touchdowns not only won it, but the national title as well.

Stanford's Vow Boys beat the Trojans 16–0 for the second straight year, but beating Alabama in the Rose Bowl was another thing. Under coach Frank Thomas, a Rockne disciple, Alabama's fourth Rose Bowl entry in a decade was as good as any team they sent west. The Tide won all nine of its games and was national scoring champ with almost 32 points each game. They rolled up 24 points on everyone except Bob Neyland's tough Tennessee team, which held them to 13 points.

A win in the last game of the year against Vanderbilt meant a Rose Bowl invitation for Alabama. After a career that spanned three decades, it was also Dan McGugin's last game as Vanderbilt coach. The game was no contest, as the Tide won by five touchdowns and accepted the Rose Bowl offer on the following day.

The crowd of 85,000 basking in the warm California sun were treated to a demonstration of Stanford power in the first period. Alabama fumbled on its own 27, and five plays later Stanford was ahead, 7–0. The fans snapped out of their lethargy and began to shout, "We want Minnesota! We want Minnesota!"

Don Hutson and Paul Bryant, the Alabama ends, were taken out and briefed on Stanford's reverse play which had set up the easy score. No sooner was Bryant back in than he challenged his teammates, "You-all hear that? They're calling for a football team. They want to see a game and what they are getting is a footrace. No Alabama team ever heard that sort of thing before. Whatcha going to do about it?"

The Stanford line decided to play back to stop the run, so Alabama went to its passing attack. Sharpshooter Dixie Howell and Don Hutson were a passing combo as good as Dorais to Rockne and Friedman to Oosterbaan. Hutson had barn-burner speed, great hands, and more moves than a dancer in a carnival show.

Stanford had to punt after the kickoff, and Bama took over at midfield. Hutson zig-zagged until he was free, and Howell hit him for 15 yards. Then Howell completed a toss of 15 yards to Jimmy Angelich at right half. An end-around lost five yards, but a Howell to Bryant missile put the ball on the five-yard line. Stanford was now pass conscious, so Howell slipped over for the touchdown. The Tide scored in five plays just as Stanford had done, but Riley Smith's point after was blocked.

Stanford still wasn't impressed by Alabama, so they chose to kick off. The Tide rolled down the field to the six-yard line, where Riley Smith booted a field goal to put Alabama ahead, 9–7.

Reynolds again kicked off for Stanford. On the third play of the series, Howell sprinted 67 yards to a touchdown without a hand touching him. As he crossed the goal, he waved to the section whence the cry for Minnesota had come. It was now 16–7, so Joe Riley came in and promptly zipped a 30-yard pass to Hutson, who dashed the remaining 24 yards for a 22–7 halftime lead.

Alabama scored 22 points in 12 minutes against a team which had given up only two touchdowns all year. As both sides headed for the dressing room, the cheering section occupied by Alabama fans began to chant, "We want Minnesota! We want Minnesota!"

Stanford scored in the third quarter on Buck Van Dellen's 12-yard run, but eight of nine pass completions by Alabama in the first half were too much to overcome. In the final period, Howell put another one in the air from his 41, Hutson caught it on the 30 and ran in to make it 29–13. Hutson had 164 yards on passes, a Rose Bowl mark that stood for exactly 50 years.

That same day in New Orleans, the first Sugar Bowl game was played. Pop Warner's Temple Owls gave the crowd of 22,026 some double wing trickery as fullback Dave Smuckler threw to halfback Dan Testa and scored once himself. The Green Wave conjured up some fakery of their own on the kickoff. John McDaniel took the ball on the 15-yard line and ran to his right, then handed it to Claude "Little Monk" Simons, who went 85 yards down the left sideline to score. After the half, Tulane evened it on a throw from Bucky Bryan to Dick Hardy and won it in the last period as Hardy gathered in a deflected pass from Barney Mintz for a 20–14 win.

This was also the year that the Southwest Conference came into its own. The quality of football played there couldn't be ignored any longer because of two early-season wins. Both of these victories were over powerful teams, both were in Indiana, and both took place on October 6.

One game was at Lafayette between giant-striding Purdue and giant-killer Rice. The Purdue coach was Noble Kizer, one of the Seven Mules who opened holes for the Four Horsemen. Purdue had a 28-4-2 record since Kizer took over four years earlier and had not been shut out in its last 49 contests.

The game was a hard-hitting seesaw battle until the fourth quarter. With the ball on their own 43, Rice's left-handed right half, Bill Wallace, faded to his left for a pass. As he was hit by a pair of charging Purdue linemen, his pass to John McCauley fluttered only 15 yards like a wounded duck. McCauley came back to the ball, scooped it off his shoelaces, and ran 43 yards for the game's first score. Leche Sylvester added the extra point for a 7-0 lead.

Toward the end of the bitter contest, McCauley intercepted a Purdue pass on his 30 and returned it 50 yards to the Boilermaker 20-yard line. Rice tried to pull a switch by reversing the pass from McCauley to Wallace, but it was stolen by Purdue at their three. They went for a tie in the waning moments, but Red Bale at guard knocked the ball free from passer Beany Craig in the end zone. End Frank Steen fell on it for a 14-0 Rice win.

Another game bringing a Texas team national attention was played 100 miles away in South Bend. This time Notre Dame was the victim and Texas was the victor. Both squads were led by ex–Notre Dame players who brewed their own brand of Rockne's potion. In his first year as head man at Notre Dame was one of the Four Horsemen, Elmer Layden. Texas also had a first-year man as coach, Jack Chevigny, who had won one for the Gipper. Notre Dame had not lost an opening game in 38 years, and Texas was to be the sacrificial offering this year. But times had changed and so had the schedules, for Texas was not a warmup for the season ahead.

The real season began soon after the opening whistle. Notre Dame fumbled the kickoff, and in three plays Texas gobbled up the 18 yards for a score. Only two minutes had elapsed. It was not long before the situation was reversed. Texas lost a punt on its 10-yard line, and in three plays George Melinkovich had a touchdown, but Texas had a 7-6 win on a missed Irish conversion.

In the Texas-Rice quarrel, the Steers were roped and branded as Rice under Jimmy Kitts won its first conference crown. Rice scored first on a pass to Harry Witt, but Jake Verde's 90-yard interception and a Bohn Hilliard field goal made it 9-7. Three minutes remained when Rice won it, 20-9, on Ray Smith's 76-yard catch and a 35-yard theft by Harry Fouke. It was also the first year that a six-game round-robin schedule was played in the SWC.

The shape of the ball underwent its final change this year. It was first slimmed in 1912 to help the newborn passing game, and the ball was given a short circumference of 22½ inches and a measurement of 28 inches around the ends. (No reduction has ever been made in the end-to-end circumference.) In 1929 a half-inch was trimmed from the middle, and another half-inch was trimmed from the short circumference in 1934. Today's ball is about 28 inches by 21½ inches with a weight of 14 to 15 ounces.

1935

Southern Methodist	(12-1-0)		Minnesota	(8-0-0)	
39	North Texas State	0	26	North Dakota State	6
60	Austin	0	12	Nebraska	7
14	Tulsa	0	20	Tulane	0
35	Washington University	6	21	Northwestern	13
10	Rice	0	29	Purdue	7
18	Hardin-Simmons	6	13	Iowa	6
20	Texas	0	40	Michigan	0
21	UCLA	0	33	Wisconsin	7
17	Arkansas	6			
10	Baylor	0			
20	Texas Christian	14			
24	Texas A&M	0			
0	Stanford (Rose Bowl)	7			
288		39	194		46

When Ray Morrison returned to his alma mater, Vanderbilt, he left coach Matty Bell with ten seniors in SMU's starting lineup. At TCU in nearby Fort Worth, Dutch Meyer built an attack around ace passer Sammy Baugh. He used a double wing formation called the spread-and-wing, an alignment which spread the ends and put the quarterback beside a halfback in the slot inside the ends.

Both teams won their first ten games and met in the initial game from the Southwest on a national radio hookup. A Rose Bowl invitation had been offered the winner, for SMU and TCU were two of the four undefeated teams left in the country. The battle of Fort Worth on the last day in November is near the top in a long list of games which lived up to its billing and fulfillment.

The two lines eyeballing each other that day were among the best ever seen in the same game. SMU had a pair of tackles who could hold their own on any field, Maurice Orr and Truman Spain. They also had four of the best guards in the conference: Billy Stamps, Charley Baker, Paschal Scottino, and Iron Man Wetsel, with Art Johnson at center. At the ends were Maco Stewart and Bill Tipton. In the Horned Frogs' line from left to right were Will Walls, Drew Ellis, Wilbert Harrison, captain Darrell Lester, Tracy Kellow, Wilson Groseclose, and Walter Roach.

SMU came down the field in the first quarter with reverses and fake buck laterals. Bob Finley, in for ailing Harry Shuford, scored from a yard out. The Ponies repeated the process in the second quarter and drove 80 yards in five plays. Bobby Wilson burned off 21 yards around end. After two plays gained a first down, a pass from Finley to right end Maco Stewart was good for 33 yards to the nine. From there, Shelley Burt lateraled to Wilson who made a beeline for the corner and went in standing up.

SMU was out front 14–0 before Texas Christian struck back. Baugh, who could punt as well as he could pass, put one out on the SMU four-yard line.

The return punt bounced back and went out-of-bounds on the Mustang 26. With Tilly Manton and Jimmy Lawrence showing the way, TCU closed it to 14–7 at the half.

Deep in the third period, Roach intercepted a pass and ran it back to midfield. TCU battled to the Mustang 43-yard line as the quarter ended. Then Sammy Baugh connected on a pass to right half Jimmy Lawrence at the SMU 25. A pass from Baugh to Walls took it to the eight. Another Baugh toss to Lawrence in the end zone made it a brand new ball game at 14–14.

J.R. "Jack Rabbit" Smith took the kickoff and returned it to midfield. The Ponies battered their way to the Froggie 35 where the attack bogged down. On fourth-and-four, Finley faked a punt and back-pedaled to pass. He unloaded a bomb to Wilson as he was swarmed by the men in purple. Wilson leaped up at the three-yard line, jostled the ball into control as the crowd helped with body English, and tumbled into the end zone.

SMU won the game, 20–14, the conference championship, and the national title. Their win over Texas Christian put them in the Rose Bowl, the only SWC team to grace the Arroyo Seco.

Stanford's Vow Boys again overturned the Trojans 3–0, and found themselves in Pasadena for the third year in a row. Stanford drove 42 yards for a first-quarter touchdown, Bill Paulson scoring on a reverse similar to the one Columbia had used to beat them two years earlier. It was the first time Southern Methodist had been behind all year. The Vow Boys finally won a Rose Bowl game, 7–0, and Bob Reynolds became the only person to play every minute in three consecutive Rose Bowl games.

TCU went to the Sugar Bowl and beat Louisiana State in the rain. LSU scored in the second quarter when Baugh went back to pass and dropped the slick ball in the end zone. In dry weather Baugh held the ball with the laces at the heel of his thumb, and in wet weather he threw the ball with his fingers on the laces, but it didn't help him this day as he completed only three passes.

After the safety, TCU moved down the field and bare-headed Tilly Manton kicked a 26-yard field goal for a 3–2 win. Led by Gaynell Tinsley at end and Jesse Fatherree and Abe Mickal in the backfield, LSU finished fourth with nine wins and two losses.

Minnesota, with its third unbeaten season in a row and 17 straight victories, finished second. Bernie Bierman lost many of his starters from last year's national champs, but the team was so deep in talent that the difference was hardly seen. The veterans on the squad were tackle Ed Widseth, guard Vern Oech, centers Dale Rennebohm and Earl Svendson, and captain and quarterback Glenn Seidel. New starters this year were Charles "Bud" Wilkinson at guard, Dick Smith at tackle, ends Ray King, Dwight Reed, and Ray Antil, and fullback Sheldon Beise. Halfbacks were almost expendable with George Roscoe, Rudy Gmitro, Babe LeVoir, Tuffy Thompson, and Bill Matheny on the bench. Even when Julie Alphonse became ineligible at the start of the season and Glenn Seidel was lost for the year after an injury in the third game, the big Gopher machine still continued to run on all cylinders.

Another all-time thriller took place between Notre Dame and Ohio State, coached by Francis Schmidt and led by all–American guard Inwood Smith and center Gomer Jones. The Irish won their five games, and the unbeaten Bucks had four wins. Before it was over, the crowd of 81,000 was limp from the cliff-hanger finish.

Elmer Layden's Irish were all thumbs early on and trailed 13-0 at the end of three periods. Then the incredible began to unfold as Andy Pilney took an OSU punt on his own 40 and weaved his way to the Buckeye 13 before he was stopped. On third down, Pilney completed a pass to quarterback Frank Gaul on the one-yard line. Steve Miller shouldered the ball in, but the conversion caromed off the crossbar to leave it at 13-6.

After an exchange of punts, the Irish marched to the one-yard line but gave up the ball on a fumble. The Notre Dame followers groaned in disgust, for it was the sixth time that the Irish had let a scoring opportunity slip away. Only three minutes showed on the clock as Notre Dame began again from its 22.

Wally Fromhart was sent in at quarterback with instructions from the bench, and Pilney hit him on a pass good for 37 yards. Then Mike Layden, the coach's brother, completed a nine-yard toss to Pilney on the OSU 29. Another pass from Pilney to Fromhart picked up 14 yards. On the fourth play of this hurricane drive, Pilney hit Layden in the end zone for the score as the stadium erupted like a sonic boom. The roar died just as quickly as the point after touchdown squibbed low into the oncoming scarlet and gray jerseys. OSU still led, 13-12, with only two minutes left.

An onside kick by Notre Dame failed, and the Buckeyes took over at midfield. Dick Beltz went wide on an end run, but the ball was ripped loose by Larry Danbom. Hank Pojman, the Irish center, touched it last before it went out-of-bounds and Notre Dame had the ball on their own 49. The Columbus stands were in chaos as the clock showed less than 90 seconds remaining.

Pilney faded to pass. With everyone covered, he set sail for the Buckeye goal. He faked a defender on the right, side-stepped two more as he cut back over center, and gave the hip to another before he was hammered out-of-bounds on the Ohio 19.

The roar of the crowd was stilled as Pilney did not get up. He was carried off the field on a stretcher, his number 32 jersey soiled and motionless. A replacement with the unlikely name of William Shakespeare was sent in. Fifty seconds remained.

Shakespeare fired a pass which trickled through the fingers of a Buckeye defender. Forty seconds left. Everyone's heart was caught in their throat when Shakespeare retreated again and moved to his right. His blockers formed in front of him and drew the Ohio State defense with them. On the opposite side of the field, left end Wayne Millner floated through the Buckeye players to the right side. Shakespeare lofted a pass just over the hands of an Ohio halfback, and Millner had it for an 18-13 win.

A wave of Notre Dame fans overflowed the field and carried the victors to their dressing room. Others attacked one of the goal posts and uprooted it after a long siege. Then they carried the steel pipe from the stadium as a trophy. Later that evening it was found in the lobby of the Neal House, a downtown hotel.

A different spirit prevailed 300 miles northwest, for football was dying at Chicago. They didn't have a winning team, but they did have the nation's best back, Jay Berwanger, who won the first Heisman Award given by New York's Downtown Athletic Club.

The run that won the Heisman for Berwanger was made against Ohio State. Still down from their last week's loss to the Irish, Berwanger scored Chicago's second touchdown on a run which rates with the greatest. He sliced through tackle at the 20-yard line, headed for the outside, then turned back toward center. At midfield, he was sandwiched between two defensive backs. He juked each one and ran between them. Once in the clear, he outran his pursuers to put Chicago ahead, 13-0. Ohio State won it in the second half, 20-13, but Berwanger had given them a run for their money.

Along with Minnesota, Princeton was the only major unbeaten team at the end of the year and finished third. Their only loss in the past three campaigns was to Yale last year, 7-0, as the Tigers fumbled a half-dozen times in the first period, then lost on a 49-yard scoring pass from Jerry Roscoe to Larry Kelley.

Leading Princeton to its second all-winning season in three years was fiery Steve Cullinan at center, who backed up the line like a dervish. At the tackles were George Stoess, Fred Ritter, and Charley Toll, who had arms like Kong. At one guard was Tom Montgomery, with Ken Sandbach at quarter. Back for their final season for the Princeton paladins were Jack Weller at guard, Gil Lea and Hugh McMillan at the ends, halfbacks Homer Spofford and Garry LeVan, and captain Pepper Constable at fullback.

After a slow start against Penn, 7-6, and Williams, 14-7, the Tigers scored 27 last-quarter points to beat Rutgers, 29-6. Four big shutout wins followed over Cornell, Navy, Harvard, and Lehigh. Dartmouth lost, 26-6, but not before a disgruntled fan ran out of the stands and took a place in the Big Green line.

Against Yale, Princeton led 10-0 on a field goal and the coach Fritz Crisler special. Constable faked to halfback Chick Kaufman, faked an end-around to John Paul Jones, then lateraled to halfback Jack White who ran in. The Tigers added 28 fourth-period points for a 38-7 win, the last conversion being kicked at a makeshift goal post since the original had been torn down.

1936

Twenty returning lettermen and a bench full of eager sophomores again made Bernie Bierman's Minnesota mastodons three-deep at every position.

In the second game of the year with Nebraska, his veterans won it in the last minute. With 68 seconds left on the clock, Bud Wilkinson, who was moved from guard to quarterback this season, took a punt by Ron Douglas on his 28 and sidestepped charging Bob Mills. He pivoted right and then threw a lateral to Andy Uram a few yards in the rear. Uram threaded his way downfield, picking up blockers as he ran. When he crossed the goal with the only score of the game, every Nebraska player had been knocked off his feet. Bierman was almost loquacious as he said it was the best-executed spur-of-the-moment play he'd ever seen.

Minnesota (7-1-0)			Lousiana State (9-1-1)		
14	Washington	7	20	Rice	7
7	Nebraska	0	6	Texas	6
26	Michigan	0	47	Georgia	7
33	Purdue	0	13	Mississippi	0
0	Northwestern	6	19	Arkansas	7
52	Iowa	0	19	Vanderbilt	0
47	Texas	19	12	Mississippi State	0
24	Wisconsin	0	19	Auburn	6
			93	Southwest Louisiana	0
			33	Tulane	0
			14	Santa Clara (Sugar Bowl)	21
203		32	295		54

The luck of the Northmen went dry at midseason. At the end of October, Northwestern halted their four-year unbeaten span of 28 games. In Evanston's Dyche Stadium, 47,000 fans disregarded the rain to see the Gophers and Wildcats slug it out in the mud.

Minnesota's downfall began at the end of the third quarter. A short Gopher punt bounced back to their 46, and Northwestern struck quickly on a 26-yard pickup by Don Heap. Three smashes into the Minnesota line of Ed Widseth, Bob Weld, Frank Twedell, and Lou Midler, backed up by Earl Svendson and Vic Spadaccini, took the ball to the 12-yard line. On fourth-and-two Don Geyer tried a field goal, but it faded to the right of the goal post.

On the next play, Minnesota lost a lateral and the Wildcats recovered on the 13. Geyer plowed into the Gopher line but was dropped by Widseth. As they untangled themselves from the pile, Widseth drew a penalty for hitting Geyer after the whistle.

Northwestern had a first down at the one-yard stripe, and two plays into the last period Steve Toth went in for the only score of the game. The Gophers regrouped for three drives in the last quarter, but the mud and rain undid them as the Wildcat defense of halfback Ollie Adelman, center Erwin Wegner, and Hi Bender at end each recovered a fumbled lateral by the Gophers.

At the end of the season there were no major unbeaten and untied teams. In the first year of selecting the nation's top college football team, the Associated Press writers' poll chose Minnesota number one, while Northwestern was placed seventh.

Another team with three men at every position was Louisiana State.

The Tigers, paced by two-time all–American end Gaynell Tinsley, won nine out of ten games and tied Texas in the other. Their won-lost mark was almost eclipsed, however, by the arrival of the campus mascot, Mike the Tiger. Classes were dismissed as the students welcomed the big cat. Mike made trips to away games for years until too many accidents forced a halt to further travel.

LSU's high-flying Bengals returned to the Sugar Bowl where they were stomped by coach Buck Shaw's Santa Clara Broncos. The Broncos quickly took a 14–0 lead at the end of the first period on two touchdown passes, one from Nello Falaschi to Manny Gomez and the other from Bruno Pellegrini to Milt Finney. Their lead swelled to 21–7 in the third quarter when Falaschi scored on a lateral from end Frank Smith. LSU never did catch the number-six Broncos, losers only to TCU, 9–0, and fell short by 21–14.

Jimmy Crowley, one of the Four Horsemen, built Fordham into a national power. A main reason was their center, all–American Alex Wojcie-chowicz. Perennial title contender Pitt was placed on the schedule, and this year the two teams played to a second scoreless altercation. Tim Cohane, sports information director for the Rams, popularized the Fordham line as the "Seven Blocks of Granite." Other members of this famous line were guards Nat Pierce and Vince Lombardi, tackles Ed Franco and Al Babart-sky, and ends Leo Paquin and Johnny Druze. With a 5-0-1 record, the Rams entertained ideas of Rose Hill to Rose Bowl, but a 7–7 tie with Georgia and a 7–6 loss to NYU in their last two games ended the dream. Third-place Pitt went to the Rose Bowl instead and finally won at Pasadena by beating number-five Washington, 21–0.

Fourth-place Alabama had eight wins and a 0–0 struggle with Tennessee, as Joe Riley was downed a yard short of the Vol goal.

With six wins and losses to Pitt, 26–0, and Navy, 3–0, and a 13–13 tie with Southern California, Notre Dame came in eighth.

After eight years at Nebraska, D.X. Bible went back home to Texas. In those eight years, his teams won the Big Six title six times and lost only three conference games. He gave Minnesota and Pitt a good run most of the time, but the Gophers beat him four times in the last four years, and his best try against Pitt was two scoreless games. But losing to Minnesota and Pitt was no disgrace, as the Gophers lost only once in the last four years, and Pitt, with tackle Averell Daniell, often lost only to Minnesota or thumped heads with Fordham in a scoreless collision.

This year's loss to Minnesota in the final minute was hard to take, for Bible had one of his best teams. He also had some of his best players in tackle Fred Shirey, a bright spot in the line against the Gophers, sophomore center Charley Brock, underrated halfback Lloyd Cardwell, fullback Sam Francis, and a pair of spidery ends, 6'5" Elmer Dohrmann and 6'4" Les McDonald.

The loss to Minnesota hurt the Huskers, for in next week's game with Indiana, Nebraska was behind 9–0 at the intermission. Bible rallied his troops in the locker room, and showed that a team could win after playing Minnesota. He challenged their desire to win and offered starting positions

Opponents regarded Minnesota tackle Ed Widseth as a fifth man in the backfield.

to the first 11 men through the door. When he beat them to the exit, he told them they still weren't ready to play. A fight started, as friends and team-mates threw punches and knocked each other down trying to get out. The locker room was a shambles in a matter of moments, but the ninth-place Cornhuskers finished off Indiana in the second half, 13-9, and Bible used only 11 men.

In the Southwest Conference, the title chase was played in the mud. In spite of a rain-slick ball, Texas Christian's Sammy Baugh continued to throw to his favorite target, captain Walter Roach. Slingers Jackie Robbins and Dwight Sloan and receivers Jim Benton and Ray Hamilton of Arkansas were also unmindful of the rain. In the first conference game TCU out-gunned Arkansas 18-14, but was tripped up by Texas A&M, 18-7, two games later. In the last game of the conference season, TCU and SMU met in a scoreless joust, and Arkansas clinched the title with a win over Texas, 6-0, on a last-minute touchdown catch by Jim Benton.

Although Arkansas won the Southwest Conference for the first time, they did not get a bowl bid. Instead, TCU was invited next door to play in the newly-opened Cotton Bowl at Fair Park Stadium on the state fair-grounds in Dallas. The opponent for the Horned Frogs was Marquette, led by its all–American halfback, Ray "Buzz" Buivid. For the past three years Buivid was Milwaukee's finest, and was expected to help launch the Cotton Bowl along with Baugh.

Only 17,000 people braved the threatening skies to see Baugh in his last college game. In the first period, he threw 23 yards to halfback Scott

Fordham's "Seven Blocks of Granite" were, kneeling: Johnny Druze, Al Babartsky, Vince Lombardi, Alex Wojciechowicz, Nat Pierce, Ed Franco, Leo Paquin. Behind the center: Andy Palau. Backs: captain Frank Mautte, John Lock, Al Gurske.

McCall, which put the ball on the 15-yard line. Left end L.D. "Little Dutch" Meyer, the coach's nephew, kicked the Horned Frogs to a three-point lead with a 22-yard field goal.

On the first play after the kickoff, Marquette fullback Ward Cuff punted to the Froggie 15. Baugh immediately punted on first down to Art Guepe on the Marquette 40. Guepe started left, cut back, and ran 60 yards for the first TD in Cotton Bowl history.

Still in the first period, Texas Christian moved to the midfield stripe. After taking a 30-yard toss from Baugh, Meyer tip-toed down the sideline to put TCU in front again. Before the end of the half, he scored again on a pass off a fake reverse. Meyer scored all the points in the 16–6 win, but the crowd shouted for Baugh's return when he went to the bench in the closing minutes.

Baugh ended his career with 274 completions on 594 attempts for 3,437 yards. He also threw for 40 touchdowns, averaged 40.4 yards on his punts, and had a 12.7-yard average on punt returns.

Yale captain Larry Kelley won the Heisman Trophy. Against coach Harvey Harman's number-ten Penn Quakers, he was used as a decoy while Chuck Ewart caught the touchdown in the 7–0 win. In the Navy game, a punt was fumbled by the Middie safety. Kelley accidentally kicked the ball toward the Navy goal and then fell on it, after which Yale scored the winning touchdown, 12 –7.

Against Princeton, Kelley gathered in a 50-yard pass from Clint Frank and was chased by speedster Jack White. Knowing he couldn't outrun White, Kelley floored him with a stiff-arm and scored to put Yale ahead

20-16. The Tigers took a 23-20 lead in the last period on a Bill Lynch touchdown, but Frank won it for the Yalies, 26-23, with a 13-yard scoring run. In the final game with Harvard, Kelley caught another prodigious Clint Frank toss on the 10 and ran in as Yale slipped by the Crimson, 14-13.

At Mississippi a new nickname, the Rebels, was chosen for the school. Mississippi also had its first all-American, Frank "Bruiser" Kinard, who played 708 of 720 minutes this season.

1937

Pittsburgh (9-0-1)			California (10-0-1)		
59	Ohio Wesleyan	0	30	St. Mary's	7
20	West Virginia	0	24	Oregon State	6
6	Duquesne	0	27	Washington State	0
0	Fordham	0	14	California A&M	0
21	Wisconsin	0	20	Pacific	0
25	Carnegie Tech	14	20	Southern California	6
21	Notre Dame	6	27	UCLA	14
13	Nebraska	7	0	Washington	0
28	Penn State	7	26	Oregon	0
10	Duke	0	13	Stanford	0
			13	Alabama (Rose Bowl)	0
203		34	214		33

As a result of the touchdown Yale scored against Navy the previous season when Larry Kelley accidentally kicked the ball, the rule was changed. It was no longer a judgment call, for the ball was given to the opposition at the spot where it was kicked whether it was by accident or not. Numbers were also required to be put on both front and back of the jersey for the first time.

After many years of being a bridesmaid, Pitt was number one. Their only flaw was a third straight scoreless clash with third-place Fordham, whose granite line now had tackle Paul Berezney, guard Mike Kochel, and end Harry Jacunski. Pitt tried hard to lose with eight fumbles and a touchdown called back for holding.

Pitt coach Jock Sutherland, a Scotsman with a degree in dentistry, was so respected that fellow coaches called him "Doctor." Like Bierman at Minnesota, Sutherland was reserved to the point of rudeness. It was only a facade to keep shallow people at a distance, for under the cold exterior was a deeply sensitive man.

Sutherland's teams, like Bierman's, were also renowned for their Neanderthal play and quality reserves. The Panthers were so physical that Irish coach Elmer Layden, echoing Jack Wilce's sentiments about Minnesota,

Opposite: Texas Christian's Sammy Baugh, selected as quarterback on the modern all-time All-America team.

Sam Chapman went from the Cal campus to the major leagues. He played 1,368 games as an outfielder, 1,274 of them with the Philadelphia A's.

said his teams couldn't do anything for a week after playing Pitt. Layden was one-for-four against the Panthers and dropped them from the schedule.

Pitt's meat-and-potatoes entree was a hit off tackle, a play rivaled only by Gil Dobie at Cornell. From a single wing right or left, the defense was chopped down with brute power and technique of execution. Like Tennessee's Bob Neyland, Sutherland felt a play wasn't ready until it was rehearsed 500 times. The pulling linemen and backs practiced a play over and over until they achieved precision timing. The plays were designed to get four yards on first down, control the ball, and wear down the opposition. The Pitt ground game was so crushing that last year's team shut out Ohio State without throwing a single forward pass.

The only difference between the Pitt starters and reserves was the amount of playing time. Bill Daddio and Frank Souchak shared time at left end as did Fabian Hoffman and Paul Shaw on the right. The tackles were Tony Matisi, George Delich and Ted Schmidt. At the guards were Steve Petro, Dante Dalle-Tezze, and Al Lezouski, with Don Hensley backed up by Hank Adams at center. Tractor-blocker John Chickerneo divided time at quarterback with captain John Michelosen, at right half was Hal "Curly" Stebbins, and Frank Patrick and Bill Stapulis were at fullback. Left half was manned by piano-legged Marshall Goldberg and second-stringer Dick Cassiano, who saw enough time to gain 620 yards this year.

California finished second in the AP poll. Like most great teams, Cal was built around talent and conditioning. Coach Stub Allison drilled the squad in endless wind sprints, and the Bears were known as the "Thunder Team" because of their here-we-come style of play which not only wore down opponents, but manhandled them. It was a rare day when the starters played three quarters, but it happened in the second game of the double-header against the College of Pacific when Alonzo Stagg temporarily slowed down the Berkeley attack with an eight-man line.

The only game ever in doubt was the scoreless fray with the Huskies. On the opening kickoff, Cal recovered a fumble on the Washington 21 and drove to the nine-yard line but could not score. The Bears drove deep into Washington territory three more times in the first half, but still came up empty. In the last quarter Washington knocked frequently at the Cal goal, but they too were turned away. A Husky field goal by Al Cruver in the last minute just missed, and both teams had nothing to show for a day's work.

The Bears were strong at every position, especially at center where 6'4" Bob Herwig's back-up seldom got in the game. Cal had four veteran guards in Vard Stockton and Angelo Reginato on the right side and Claude Evans and Ray Hanford on the left. At the tackles were Dave de Varona, Bill Stoll, Milt Pollack, and sophomore Jack Smith. Herwig and quarterback Johnny Meek, both of whom packed better than 200 pounds, doubled as linebackers on defense and plugged up the middle. At right end, Perry Schwartz handled the defensive tackle so well that all–American wingback Sam Chapman was freed from assisting him and became an effective downfield blocker. On the opposite end of the line were Henry Sparks and Will Dolman. Dave

In 1936 and 1937, these Yale captains won the Heisman Trophy back-to-back. Clint Frank (left) was a throwback to Ted Coy in both heart and ability, while Larry Kelley is the only player in Yale-Princeton-Harvard history to score a touchdown in each of his six Big Three games.

Anderson and Ken Cotton alternated at fullback. George Cornell, Perry Thomas, and scatback Mushy Pollock saw action at halfback, but the work-horses were passing whiz and artful runner Vic Bottari at tailback and handyman Sam Chapman, who did the punting and kicked the extra points.

Cal ended its great season by beating Frank Thomas' fourth-place Alabama team in Pasadena, as they stole four Tide fumbles and four of its passes. After a typical Perry Schwartz tackle separated the safety from the ball, Schwartz recovered it on the Cal 39. The Bears went all the way, with Bottari cutting back over tackle. UC's second touchdown was a repeat of the first. They began a drive at midfield and went the distance, Bottari scoring again on a cutback over tackle. The Thunder Team met every five years thereafter at Bardelli's Restaurant on O'Farrell Street in San Francisco. Minnesota's seasoned team ran afoul of Nebraska 14–9, and Notre Dame 7–6, but six wins still brought them in fifth.

Michigan State punter John Pingel topped the nation with a 42.9-yard average, but his Spartans lost to Auburn in the Orange Bowl, 6–0. Auburn lost to Rice 13–7, and LSU 9–7, and played three scoreless affairs, one with sixth-place Villanova. The Villanova team surrendered only one touchdown and won eight of nine outings besides the tie with Auburn. Number-nine Santa Clara gave up one touchdown and safety in winning all nine of its games, including another win over eighth-place LSU in the Sugar Bowl, 6–0, and was the only major unbeaten and untied team after the bowl contests. The Broncos were first in total defense with a record which still stands, as they permitted an average of 69.9 yards each game.

A National College Football Hall of Famer in 1954, Byron "Whizzer" White of Colorado was named to the United States Supreme Court by President Kennedy.

In addition to the Sugar Bowl defeat, LSU dropped a game to Vanderbilt on a trick play. Carl Hinkle centered the ball to the quarterback, who put it on the ground behind the left guard. The quarterback then took off, pursued by the LSU team. Vandy tackle Greer Ricketson gathered up the ball and rambled 56 yards for a 7–6 victory.

Alabama won its nine games and was SEC champ, but Vanderbilt gave them a scare in the last game of the season on Thanksgiving Day. Just before the half ended, Vanderbilt trotted out the hidden ball play which had worked earlier against LSU. This time it backfired. Alabama fell on the ball and drove for its only touchdown of the day. With six minutes remaining, the Tide won 9–7 on Sandy Sanford's 23-yard field goal. But Alabama lost for the first time ever in the Rose Bowl to Cal's Thunder Team, 13–0.

Captain Clint Frank of Yale showed the same poise this year as last and won the Heisman Award. In the Dartmouth game, Yale nursed a weak two-point edge as the last stanza began. Yale was driving to put the game away when a faulty throw by Frank almost made him the goat. Halfback Bob MacLeod filched it and went 77 yards to put the Big Green's seventh-place team in front, 6–2.

A Dartmouth field goal boosted their margin to 9–2. Frank took to the air and moved the Elis to the Dartmouth 35. Only 12 ticks showed on the clock. Facing fourth-and-ten, a hush enveloped the Yale Bowl. Frank dumped off a pass to Al Hessberg, who took it on the 25. The crowd of 72,000 rose as one and cheered Hessberg all the way across the goal. The tumult stopped just long enough for Gil Humphrey to kick the tying point.

Then it erupted again to join the echoes of past games that never die.

With losses to Pitt and Carnegie Tech, 9–7, and a scoreless tussle with Illinois, Notre Dame was 6-2-1 again this year and ended in a ninth-place tie with Santa Clara.

Behind Whizzer White, Colorado led the country in scoring with 31 points per game, in rushing with 310 yards per game, and in total offense with 375.4 yards per game. White was a genuine triple-threat all–American who not only ran, passed, and punted, but he also kicked off, returned punts, kicked PATs, and called signals. White led everyone with 1,121 yards rushing, in total offense with 1,596 yards, and in scoring with 122 points. White also led the nation in all-purpose running with 246.3 yards per game, a record which has never been surpassed.

Colorado was the first team from the Rocky Mountain area to be invited to a bowl game. They took a first-quarter lead over Rice in the Cotton Bowl as White threw for one touchdown and ran back a purloined pass 47 yards for another. Then Ernie Lain hit on scoring tosses to Jake Schuehle, Ollie Cordill, and end Frank Steen and scored one himself as Rice overruled Colorado and the Whizzer, 28–14. White graduated first in his class, was elected to Phi Beta Kappa, received a Rhodes scholarship, and is today an associate justice of the United States Supreme Court.

1938

Texas Christian	(11-0-0)		Tennessee	(11-0-0)	
13	Centenary	0	26	Sewanee	3
21	Arkansas	14	20	Clemson	7
28	Temple	6	7	Auburn	0
34	Texas A&M	6	13	Alabama	0
21	Marquette	0	44	The Citadel	0
39	Baylor	7	14	Louisiana State	6
21	Tulsa	0	45	Chattanooga	0
28	Texas	6	14	Vanderbilt	0
29	Rice	7	46	Kentucky	0
20	Southern Methodist	7	47	Mississippi	0
15	Carnegie Tech (Sugar Bowl)	7	17	Oklahoma (Orange Bowl)	0
269		60	293		16

Texas Christian was the best team in the country this year. One of the main reasons was a mobile, agile, hostile line which included all–American center Ki Aldrich, a bird dog on defense who could smell out the play and then snuff it out. The line had other purple people-eaters in tackle I.B. Hale (244 pounds) and guard Forrest Kline (248 pounds). Just as hungry to eat up ball carriers were the other linemen, guard Bud Taylor, tackle Allie White, and ends Don Looney and Durward Horner.

Behind this robust line were fullback Connie Sparks, halfbacks Johnny Hall and Earl Clark, and the 1938 Heisman winner, quarterback Davey O'Brien. Ki Aldrich continued the Meyer innovation of a pulling center to lead interference on running plays. The line was just as good at dropping back to protect their passer, 5'7", 150-pound O'Brien. From this well-guarded pocket, O'Brien hurled touchdown strikes like his predecessor, Sammy Baugh.

After an early-season showdown with Arkansas, the Froggies took everyone into camp handily. One of the characteristics of this year's Purple Gang was that they answered with some points whenever the opposition scored on them. In the game with Arkansas, they not only scored immediately, but in the same way. After a 20-yard pass by the Razorbacks, a lateral picked up 48 yards to the one, from which they scored. O'Brien replied with a 31-yard run to the Porker 20, then lateraled to Sparks who took it in.

TCU met number-six Carnegie Tech in the Sugar Bowl. Carnegie had given ninth-place Holy Cross and Bill Osmanski its only loss in two years, 7-6, and had beaten Pitt and its dream backfield of Chickerneo, Cassiano, Goldberg, and Stebbins, 20-10. Carnegie's only defeat was a soul-wrencher to Notre Dame on a gross error by referee John Getchell. In the last period of a scoreless game at midfield, Tech quarterback Paul Friedlander asked the referee what down it was. "Third down," said Getchell.

Carnegie tried a run for no gain. As the team huddled for what they thought was a fourth down, Getchell came over and told them he had made a mistake. Carnegie's four downs were used up, and it was now Notre Dame's ball. The Tech team swarmed around Getchell, arguing wildly. Carnegie coach Bill Kern protested heatedly, but in vain. The Irish, who finished in fifth place, got the ball and marched to a 7-0 win.

Another hallmark of TCU was that it was never behind during the regular season. In the Sugar Bowl game with Carnegie Tech, Texas Christian drew first blood, but O'Brien missed the point after touchdown. With only seconds left until the half, George Muha scored on a long pass and kicked the Skibos ahead, 7-6.

The Horny Toads came busting out of the gate as the second half started and scored in five plays. Two long passes ate up most of the 80 yards, with the final one to Horner who caught it on the 30 and ran in. TCU was in the driver's seat again, and had answered the question about coming from behind. Carries by Muha and fullback Tony Laposki failed to crack the Froggie forwards, and ends Joe Betz and Ted Fisher chased O'Brien all day, but to no avail. O'Brien later added a 20-yard field goal in the win.

L'il Davey's number 8 jersey was retired at TCU. He led in total offense with 1,847 yards, threw 19 touchdown passes, and TCU's 164.1 passing yards per game was tops this year. In his last two seasons, he completed 187 of 401 tries for 2,426 yards, and led in passing each year with 969 yards and 1,457 yards.

Back from a tour of duty in Panama (for which he received a major's

Aerial gunner on TCU's 1938 championship team, quarterback Davey O'Brien.

cluster), Bob Neyland rebuilt the Tennessee team. He gathered a second group of flaming sophomores and led them to a second-place finish and into the glory years of Tennessee football. For the next three years his teams posted a 10-0-0 mark during the regular season, a record not often matched.

When the season began, Neyland knew his line couldn't hold up a Monday wash. His crop of sophomores were so gifted, however, that they put many of the seniors back on the bench. The ends were held by a pair of

Center Kì Aldrich of TCU.

seniors, George Hunter and captain and all–American Bowden Wyatt, who was muscled like a Greek god. At one guard was Bob Suffridge, so good he was compared to Herman Hickman. The other guard was Ed Molinski, who did his job just as efficiently but with less newsprint. At the tackles were Abe Shires and Boyd Clay, with Jim Ryke at center.

The powerplant of the Tennessee attack was George Cafego, a George Gipp type who loafed in practice but did everything right on Saturday. Cafego, called "Bad News" because he traveled so fast, was a triple-threat back who broke up more than one game with his open-field sparkle. He was also a deadly blocker who leveled many a foe when right half Bob Foxx ran the reverse or fullback Len Coffman carried the mail. The team was directed by another trip-hammer blocker, quarterback Sam Bartholomew.

Tennessee met fourth-place Oklahoma in the Orange Bowl, a game so rough that it has often been called the "Orange Brawl." On the first play of the game, Cafego flattened his man with a block so furious that it put the Sooner out of the game. Emotions began to heat up as the game progressed. Neyland sent in reserve center Joe Little to settle things down. On the first snap of the ball, Little Joe was welcomed with an uppercut to the jaw. Little chased his attacker downfield until he punched him back, and was thrown out of the game. Before it was over, Tennessee was penalized 130 yards and Oklahoma 91. The Vols pounded out a methodical 17–0 win on an eight-yard run by Bob Foxx in the first quarter, a 22-yard field goal by Wyatt in the next period, and a 19-yard reverse by Babe Wood in the final frame.

The Duke Blue Devils won the cheers in Tobaccoland. Coach Wallace Wade's team was unbeaten, untied, and unscored on in the regular season. The removal of a wart on George McAfee's foot hurt the offense so much that over half the games were won by a single touchdown. But the "Iron Dukes" dug in and held everyone scoreless – all nine teams – and finished third.

The climax game of the year was against Pitt, the nation's defending champ. The first chill of winter swept over Durham on November 26, but 52,000 forgot the freezing weather and filed into the stadium. Snow fell steadily throughout the game, but no one was disappointed. Eric "the Red" Tipton warmed their hearts with one of the greatest displays of punting seen anywhere.

After halfback Willard Eaves ran back the kickoff, a 52-yard Tipton punt was downed on Pitt's 10-yard line. Then each ran a series, and Tipton's 50-yarder went to the eight-yard line, but they returned it to their 19. The Panthers came down the field with five first downs, only to stall. Tipton rocked them back with a tremendous 65-yard haymaker which was downed on the Pitt 18.

Opposite, top: Bob Neyland's .829 winning average at Tennessee (173-31-12) is sixth best among college coaches. Bottom: Tennessee guard Bob Suffridge, a member of the modern All-America team.

In the second quarter, a short punt of 24 yards rolled out-of-bounds at the Pitt 12-yard line. Moments later, a 47-yarder was downed on Pitt's 14, and then a 48-yarder was downed on their 35. Again the Panthers' punishing ground game churned out four first downs, only to fizzle. The Iron Dukes held, and a Tipton punt of 56 yards rolled dead on the Panthers' one-foot line.

Things got worse for Pitt after the half. A 45-yard kick was downed at the Pitt 16. Another Tipton punt of 53 yards was downed on Pitt's 11. A 30-yard kick was stuck out-of-bounds on the nine-yard line. Tipton's next boot of 42 yards was downed on their 13. The Panthers got a break when a punt of 41 yards was downed at the Pitt 31. The third period ended as quarterback Bob Spangler intercepted a Panther pass on their 40-yard line.

Fullback Bob O'Mara picked up five yards to start the final quarter. On last-and-one, Tipton rolled a punt out-of-bounds on the Pitt five yard line. The Panthers attempted to punt from their end zone, but Bolo Perdue broke through to block it, caught it on the bounce, and the Blue Devils had the only score of the game.

Tipton continued to keep the pressure on as he angled one out on the Panther 11. Pitt's inability to make a first down in the second half forced them to punt again. Tipton put them back to their goal with another punt which rolled out on the Panther seven-yard line. Pitt tried to get out of the hole, but Tipton put another one out-of-bounds on their nine-yard line.

Duke made only one first down during the entire game. In the stands, Bob Neyland continually nudged Herman Hickman over Tipton's fantastic punts. In turn, Hickman nudged Neyland over Duke's boiler-plate defense of ends Bolo Perdue and Bill Bailey, tackles Frank Ribar and Bob Haas, guards Fred Yorke and Allen Johnson, and captain Dan Hill at center. The lesson in defense and punting made Jock Sutherland's last game at Pitt a very cold one, indeed, as he watched his Panthers slide to eighth place.

Duke was invited to play number-seven Southern Cal, led by guard Harry "Blackjack" Smith and captain and center Don McNeil, in the Rose Bowl. For three quarters, neither team could penetrate the other's 35-yard line. The Iron Dukes would not give, and Tipton continually backed up the Trojans with his precision punting. In the final quarter, Tipton's 25-yard pass to McAfee was good to the USC 15. But Troy held, and Tony Ruffa's 23-yard field goal looked even bigger as the seconds slowly ticked away.

A Trojan punt was recovered by Phil Gaspar on the Duke 10. The Iron Dukes still would not budge, and Tipton punted to the USC 39. Grenny Lansdell, Mickey Anderson, and Ollie Day, unable to dent the Duke defense, were replaced by Doyle Nave.

In practice, Nave and Al Krueger continually worked on play number 27, which had four variations: a long pass, short to the flat, a buttonhook, and end-around. Two minutes were left when Nave hit Krueger on a

Opposite, top: Pitt's Jock Sutherland ran his record to 144-28-14, tenth among coaches with a .812 winning average. Bottom: One of the games great punters, Eric Tipton of Duke.

27-buttonhook for a first down on the Duke 21. Then he tossed nine yards to Krueger on a 27–to the flat at the 12. On second down, an end-around to Krueger lost two yards.

With third down on the 14, Krueger ran past Tipton in the end zone on a long pass in the left corner. While the tiring Tipton was trying to keep up, Krueger took Nave's pass over his shoulder for the touchdown. It was the only score against Duke all year, but the Trojans had a 7–3 win with 41 seconds to go.

Another great front wall was the one put together by Irish line coach Joe Boland. Led by tackles Ed Beinor and Paul Kell, and Augie Bossu and captain Jim McGoldrick in the guard grooves, all head coach Elmer Layden had to do was tell his ball carriers to look good. Halfbacks Lou Zontini, Ben Sheridan, Bob Saggau, Harry Stevenson, and Mario Tonelli and Joe Thesing at full were great until they met USC's equally good line and lost their last game, 13–0. Notre Dame's eight wins and a loss put them fifth.

1939

Texas A&M	(11-0-0)		Tennessee	(10-1-0)	
32	Oklahoma A&M	0	13	North Carolina State	0
14	Centenary	0	40	Sewanee	0
7	Santa Clara	3	28	Chattanooga	0
33	Villanova	7	21	Alabama	0
20	Texas Christian	6	17	Mercer	0
20	Baylor	0	20	Louisiana State	0
27	Arkansas	0	34	The Citadel	0
6	Southern Methodist	2	13	Vanderbilt	0
19	Rice	0	19	Kentucky	0
20	Texas	0	7	Auburn	0
14	Tulane (Sugar Bowl)	13	0	USC (Rose Bowl)	14
212		31	212		14

For the second season in a row, a team from the Lone Star state wore the crown in football Valhalla. The great ones were gone — guard Joe Routt and halfback Dick Todd — but coach Homer Norton had a throne room full of replacements which took them to the top. A&M won ten games, then beat number-five Tulane in the Sugar Bowl, and paid off the bank loan on Kyle Field.

Leading the Aggie touchdown corps was 6'2", 220-pound John Kimbrough, a slashing fullback who ran like a Brahma bull coming out of the gate. Out in front of him were two whipcord guards, Marshall Robnett and Bill Audish, and two all–American tackles, Joe Boyd and Ernie Pannell. The ends were Jim Sterling and Herb Smith, who blocked Tulane's game-tying PAT in the last quarter. The halfbacks were bowl-'em-over blockers Derace Moser and Jim Thomason. Calling signals were Walemon Price and Bill Conatser.

Texas A&M's rip-roaring attack was surpassed only by its brilliant

Kenny Washington was the first UCLA player elected to the College Football Hall of Fame.

defense. They held opponents to 1.71 yards per play, lowest on record. The Aggies surrendered only 315 yards rushing and 456 yards passing all year. They led the country in rushing defense, permitting an average of 41.5 yards per game, and also in total defense, handing out a measly 76.3 yards each contest. They showed character by coming from behind to beat Santa Clara, outlasting Southern Methodist in the mud, and swamping Texas in the second half after a no-score game at intermission.

Bob Neyland's Tennessee team finished second with its second 10-0-0 season in a row. The Vol defense was so stingy that they were not just unbeaten and untied, but unscored on. It was only the eighteenth time that a major college team went through the regular season without yielding a point, and no one has done it since.

Halfway through the season, George Cafego was injured. His replacement, Johnny Butler, had already performed brilliantly. Against Alabama, he turned in an eel-hipped run without anyone touching him. He went through tackle at his 44, slanted to the outside, and flitted back and forth almost 200 yards on the way to a 56-yard scoring run. In the last game of the year against Auburn, Butler helped preserve the Vols' perfect season with a 40-yard run for the only score of the game.

With its 6-0-4 season and first unbeaten team, UCLA almost met Tennessee in the Rose Bowl. Led by its two black halfbacks, Kenny Washington and

UCLA halfback Jackie Robinson later became the first black player in major league baseball.

Jackie Robinson, UCLA drove to the Trojan goal late in the contest. The Uclans were halted six feet from the USC goal, the game ended without a score, and UCLA finished seventh. Number-three Southern Cal, 7-0-2 in the regular season, went to the Rose Bowl and ended Tennessee's perfect year.

At Cornell, Carl Snavely's Big Red won all eight games and finished number four. Snavely was the first major coach to use motion pictures of games as a coaching tool. He installed a projector in his den and scanned game films by the hour. After his wife shot the film, he used it to correct mistakes and improve the squad's performance. Another Snavely innovation was the letter each player found beside his breakfast every Monday morning. Snavely spent most of Sunday writing a fatherly letter pointing out miscues and giving praise to his boys when needed.

Snavely's boys included Kirk Hershey and Al Kelley, who had replaced Brud Holland and Carl Spang at the ends. Beside them operated two 6'3"

A&M's John Kimbrough scored the only touchdown in their game against SMU.

215-pound tackles, Nick Drahos and Fred West. At center was a mealy-mouthed agitator, Bud Finneran, sided by precision guards Howard Dunbar and Jerome Cohn. Snavely had a galaxy of triple-threat halfbacks to implement his single wing offense, Whit Baker, Hal McCullough, Jack Bohrman, and Walter Scholl. At quarterback was peerless play caller and faultless blocker Walt Matuszczak. At fullback was Mort Landsberg, who replaced captain Vince Eichler when he suffered a knee injury.

The Cayugans invaded Columbus for their biggest game of the year. In the first period, Ohio State went 86 yards to score on 19 straight running plays. The Ohio attack, which led in total offense with 309.3 yards a game, didn't show the same formation two plays in a row. At the start of the second quarter, the big Buckeye line of captain Steve Andrako at center, Charlie Maag at tackle, and their 225-pound cohorts cleared the way for another scoring drive of 72 yards. Reverses by wingback Frank Zadworney, and sweeps and slashes by tailback Jim Strausbaugh and Jim Langhurst at full made it look easy, with Don Scott at quarter finally going in.

Cornell squelched the screams in a hurry. The Ohio players were knocked off their feet by flawless blocking, and Pop Scholl went 79 yards to score. Then Scholl evaded a Buckeye tackler and threw 26 yards to Swifty Bohrman. Bohrman took it on the 37 and ran in for the score, capping it with a swan dive at the finish.

It was still two touchdowns each at the half, but the Buckeyes never recovered. Cornell did in two quick strikes what it had taken Ohio State two long marches to do. In the third quarter, Cornell took the lead on a 34-yard drive, and then stopped a Buckeye march of 53 yards on their 10. After Mort Landsberg bolted through the short side for a 41-yard gain, a Nick Drahos field goal of 27 yards gave Cornell a 23-14 win.

Led by tailback Paul Christman and two stellar tackles, Mel Wetzel and captain Ken Haas, number-six Missouri lost to Georgia Tech in the Orange Bowl, 21-7. Reverses by wingback Earl Wheby, tailback Johnny Bosch, and

George McAfee of Duke, called "the nation's most versatile back" in 1939 by the New York Sun.

quarterback Howard Ector, and a 59-yard scoring end-around by Bob Ison muzzled the Tigers' bite.

Eighth-place Duke, paced by George McAfee, won eight games. They lost only to Pitt, 14–13, but did not play in a bowl game.

After a year or two of being eclipsed by good teams around the country, two of the greatest players to put on pads brought thrills to Midwest fans. One was Heisman winner Nile Kinnick of ninth-place Iowa, and the other was Tom Harmon of Michigan.

Kinnick and his teammates made Iowa more famous for football than for its cornfields. Iowa's new coach, Dr. Eddie Anderson, fresh from a successful stint at Holy Cross, found he never had enough players. In the Purdue game there were only 14 men ready to go, and eight of them played the entire contest. Against Notre Dame, eight men again played 60 minutes, and

Last of the great drop-kickers, Nile Kinnick of Iowa.

six of them went all the way against Minnesota. In the last seven games, Kinnick missed only 18 minutes, and the team became known as the "Iron Men."

Those who served with Kinnick in the Iron Platoon were ends Dick "Whitey" Evans, Ken Pettit, who doubled as a guard, and captain Erwin Prasse. The interior line was a battle-spiced corps of tackles Jim Walker, Wally Bergstrom, who took over for Walker when he was injured, and bull-necked Mike Enich, guards Charlie Tollefson, Mike Hawkins, and Ham Snider, and centers Bill Diehl and Bruno Andruska, who replaced injured Bill Diehl. Backfield men included quarterback Al Coupee, halfback Floyd "Buzz" Dean, and sophomore fullback Bill Green, who had sprinter's speed.

After beating South Dakota in the opener, 41-0, a game in which Kinnick scored three touchdowns and drop-kicked five extra points, Iowa played Indiana. The Hawkeyes had not won a Big Ten football game at home in a half-dozen years, but they came from behind twice to down Indiana, 32-29. In the final minutes, Iowa drew a fourth-and-three in front of the goal posts. Instead of going for a tie, Kinnick threw to Prasse for the winning score.

Next week at Ann Arbor, Iowa suffered its only loss of the year. They

One of the few men with 200 coaching wins, Dr. Eddie Anderson was Coach of the Year in 1939.

took the lead on a 69-yard scoring pass from Kinnick to Buzz Dean, but Harmon tied it on a 95-yard pass interception, a Michigan record, then scored the rest of UM's points in a 27-7 win.

The next month forged the Iron Men into a legend as all four games were won by six points or less. Kinnick threw three touchdown passes to defeat Wisconsin, 19-13. In their third straight away game, Mike Enich blocked two punts which Purdue recovered in their end zone to win by the improbable score of 4-0.

Back home in Iowa City, Notre Dame shoved the Hawks around for 29 minutes but couldn't score. With less than a minute before the half, Iowa recovered a fumble on the Notre Dame four-yard line. On third down, Kinnick ran a single wing left and changed places with wingback Buzz Dean. With Kinnick still at tailback, he went in standing up and then drop-kicked Iowa to a 7–0 lead.

Notre Dame continued to march up and down the field. Two plays into the last quarter, they finally scored on a short run by fullback Milt Piepul, but the conversion faded left. Again the Irish came down the field, only to be halted on the Iowa 23. Kinnick stepped back and booted a stupendous 72-yard punt which rolled out-of-bounds on the Irish five-yard line. Notre Dame began again, but time ran out and Iowa had a one-point victory.

Minnesota came to Iowa Stadium next week, and 50,000 fans showed up to watch their Cinderella team. Minnesota held a 9–0 lead on the punting of Harold Van Every, but as the final period began Iowa scored on a drive of 80 yards to stay close at 9–7. With the dusk of evening settling over the stadium, Kinnick hit Bill Green deep in the shadows to pull it out, 13–9. Nile Kinnick's number 24 jersey disappeared among the Hawkeye fans who ran onto the field to cheer their David with the slingshot arm.

Kinnick died in World War II when his Navy plane crashed at sea. Iowa Stadium was renamed Kinnick Stadium in his honor.

At Franklin Field in Philadelphia, Tom Harmon of Michigan xeroxed Johnny Butler's great run a month before. It came just after the last-half kickoff when the crowd had hardly settled down. Harmon got the ball on his own 18 and started left. As he cut upfield, he was spun around by the Penn players. He back-pedaled to the 12, and scrambled to the far side of the field. When he reached the sideline, he turned to the goal 88 yards distant. His teammates picked off the Penn pursuers one by one, and each of them had a piece of his jersey in their hands. His bare shoulder pads bobbed up and down as he ran over, a score badly needed to tip Penn and Frank Reagan, who led 92- and 73-yard scoring drives, 19–17.

"Just as I put it on the blackboard," said coach Fritz Crisler. By the end of the year, Harmon's 102 points led the nation.

The season concluded on a sad note. The dynasty built by Stagg at Chicago ended with four lopsided losses. Chicago's president, Robert Hutchins, terminated football at the Midway and pared the Big Ten to the Big Nine, believing that football had no rightful place on a college campus. This decision, so like the decisions of others with insular intellects, shows little wisdom, and aroused a furor at the time. A school's spirit is not just in learning and theories but in the hearts of its followers. Football is a contributor to that spirit.

VI. A Second Cup of "T"

1940

Minnesota	(8-0-0)		Stanford	(10-0-0)	
19	Washington	14	27	San Francisco	0
13	Nebraska	7	13	Oregon	0
13	Ohio State	7	7	Santa Clara	6
34	Iowa	6	26	Washington State	14
13	Northwestern	12	21	USC	7
7	Michigan	6	20	UCLA	14
33	Purdue	6	20	Washington	10
22	Wisconsin	13	28	Oregon State	14
			13	California	7
			21	Nebraska (Rose Bowl)	13
154		71	196		85

Clark Shaughnessy made football history when he reinvented the T-formation. He took the game's oldest offensive alignment, redesigned it, and became the father of the modern T-formation. It was worked out with George Halas of the Chicago Bears, while Shaughnessy coached Chicago's dying program. He took a Stanford team with a 1-7-1 record and shaped them into a number-two squad which won ten games, including a Rose Bowl win over Nebraska.

The 1888 rule that made offensive linemen keep their hands at their sides eliminated the wide-open game which marked early football. The game developed into a close-knit formation which created power at the point of attack, and made the defense bunch together to stop it. This was the style of play during the mass-formation period at the turn of the century when injuries were commonplace. After the seven-man line became mandatory in 1910, the single wing was the formation used to get blockers in front of the ball carrier as at Tennessee, Minnesota, and Pitt.

Pop Warner's double wing, the Rockne shift, and the Meyer spread-and-wing all tried to split the defense and penetrate it. Shaughnessy's T-formation did not try to split the defense. Instead, he forced the defense to commit themselves by giving them fakes, brush blocks, and shifting linemen. He also added a man-in-motion, a flanker, and a quarterback under

Opposite, top: Stanford's Frank Albert, first of the modern T-formation quarterbacks. Bottom: Hall of Fame coach Clark Shaughnessy of Stanford, inventor of the modern T-formation.

Bob Westfall's 808 yards rushing almost matched Tom Harmon's 852 yards for the 1940 Wolverines.

the center. Then he kept the defense off balance with end runs, a liberal use of the forward pass, and quick openers through the line.

Shaughnessy's T-formation was the best of the old game and the new. He took football out of the power-play vogue and made it wide-open again, and his renovations caught college football completely by surprise. He also had a returning backfield which was tailor-made for his formation, for quarterback Frank Albert, fullback Norm Standlee, and halfbacks Hugh Gallarneau and Pete Kmetovic have rarely been surpassed as a unit. In addition to ends Fred Meyer, Stan Graff, and Clem Tomerlin, he upgraded the line with center Vic Lindskog, guard Dick Palmer, and sophomore tackles Bruno Banducci and Ed Stamm, and guard Chuck Taylor.

Stanford's win over seventh-place Nebraska let the rest of the country in on the new formation. The Huskers came down the field on fake reverses to wingback Butch Luther, with fullback Vike Francis keeping the ball himself and scoring the first touchdown of the game. Stanford struck back

Tom Harmon's number 98 jersey was permanently retired by the Michigan Wolverines.

quickly on an off-tackle fake to Gallarneau, who went through the hole and took out the linebacker. Left guard Taylor and Standlee also went through the hole ahead of Kmetovic, who was pulled down on the Nebraska 18 after a 29-yard gain. Another quick opener by Kmetovic put the ball on the 11-yard line. On an apparent repeat of Kmetovic's long run, Albert gave the ball to Gallarneau, faked to Kmetovic going right, and then ran back as if to pass. Gallarneau scored before anyone knew he had the ball, and it was seven apiece.

In the second quarter, Kmetovic lost a Nebraska punt in the sun. It bounced off him, and Nebraska recovered on the Stanford 35-yard line. On the first play, Allen Zikmund caught a strike from Herman Rohrig on the 10 and ran in for a 13–7 Husker lead.

Stanford scored a few plays later. Albert sent Gallarneau on a man-in-motion left as a potential blocker, and then faked to Standlee going left. Both Nebraska linebackers zeroed in on Standlee. The Stanford ends went deep and split the halfbacks. Then Gallarneau tore down the middle, and Albert hit him with a 30-yard scoring pass to put Stanford ahead at the half, 14–13.

Stanford put it away late in the third period. They drove 75 yards but were halted at the one. Harry "Hippety" Hopp punted to Kmetovic at the

39. He took a few steps left, then cut for the right corner and went all the way to make the final 21–13.

The 73–0 win by the Chicago Bears over the Washington Redskins for the pro title on December 8 convinced the football world that the T-formation was here to stay. It was Stanford's Rose Bowl win over Biff Jones' Cornhuskers, however, which sold the T-formation to college football. By the end of the decade, most teams had climbed on the T-bandwagon. In the never-ending struggle between offense and defense, Shaughnessy's brain-child fathered the split-T, wing-T, slot-T, and other brands of "T."

On the same day the T-formation was born at Kezar Stadium in San Francisco, Michigan played California across the bay in Berkeley. Tom Harmon took the opening kickoff and ran it back 94 yards to a touchdown. In the next quarter, he returned a Bob Reinhard punt 72 yards for a score. His third touchdown was an 86-yard run from scrimmage. As he neared the Cal goal, a frustrated fan named Bud Brennan made a dive for Harmon at the three-yard line, but all he got was an armful of air like everyone else that day. Harmon added an eight-yard run and a touchdown pass to Dave Nelson in the 41–0 shellacking of the Bears.

Next week, Harmon scored all 21 points in a 21–14 win over Michigan State. He ran for three more touchdowns a week later as Harvard, headed by Chub Peabody, was downed, 26–0. Against Illinois, he ran for one score, passed for another, and added a field goal as the Illini were beaten, 28–0. He ended the month of October by scoring all the points in a 14–0 win over Penn.

With 15 train cars full of fans, Michigan traveled to rain-drenched Minneapolis to play the Gophers. After a first period punting duel between Harmon and George Franck, Michigan moved 86 yards through the muck to the Minnesota one-yard line, but Harmon slipped in the mud and couldn't score. On the next exchange of punts, Minnesota fumbled the ball away at its 6. Harmon passed to Forest Evashevski for the score but missed the extra point.

Michigan again marched to the Minnesota goal, but Harmon's pass was intercepted in the end zone and brought out to the 20. Bruce Smith changed positions with Franck on the next play, and on a reverse sloshed 80 yards through the rain to score. On the verge of a two-touchdown lead, Michigan was now behind, 7–6.

Senior guards Milo Sukup and Ralph Fritz took the Wolverines inside the 10-yard line over and over, but each time their siege-gun single wing misfired to beat themselves. Minnesota won by a point and took over the top spot in the Associated Press poll.

With Red Grange in the stands, Harmon scored after Ed Frutig blocked a punt to down eighth-place Northwestern, 20–13. In his last game against Ohio State, Harmon's three scores gave him 33 career touchdowns, two more than Grange. When he left the game in the final minutes, he was a cinch for the Heisman. His 117 points headed the list, but Michigan resided in third place.

Cornell coach Carl Snavely and his 1940 captain, Walt Matuszczak.

Minnesota came from behind six times in the year to finish unbeaten, as Smith and Franck brought them home safely. Behind by one against number-ten Washington, Franck returned a kickoff 98 yards for a score. Against Nebraska, Smith tossed a 42-yard touchdown pass to defeat the Huskers, scored twice against Ohio State, and his 80-yard jaunt beat Michigan. Franck scored four times in the Iowa game, and ran 20 yards to a touchdown with an interception in the last game with Wisconsin. Smith also scored once against Wisconsin, and Minnesota ended the year number one.

On November 16, one week after Minnesota replaced Cornell as the top team in the land, Dartmouth snapped Cornell's 18-game winning streak in the famous "fifth down" game at Hanover. It was a day in which the Fates conspired to beat Cornell. In his next-to-last game at Dartmouth, coach Earl Blaik used a delayed defense which gave up the short gain and committed itself only when the ball carrier was spotted. Dartmouth played with such ferocity that by the end of the first quarter tackle Fred West, end Jim Schmuck, and both Cornell guards, Howie Dunbar and Pete Wolff, were out of the game with injuries. Cornell's other end, Kirk Hershey, was already benched with injuries from a previous game. A light snowfall during the game also hampered Cornell's passing attack, the national leader with a 186.3-yard average.

Dartmouth outplayed the Big Red for 55 minutes. Then Bob Krieger put Dartmouth ahead on a 27-yard field goal. With four minutes to go, Pop Scholl hit Bill Murphy consistently for four first downs. Mort Landsberg hurtled forward to the three. Scholl picked up two more to the one-yard line. On third down, Landsberg was stopped just short of the goal. Coach Snavely called time to stop the clock, and Cornell was penalized back to the six. On fourth down, a pass to Murphy in the end zone was batted down.

Referee Red Friesell placed the ball down on the 20-yard line, and then changed his mind when he saw it was still third down on the scoreboard. Friesell brought the ball back to the six and gave Cornell another chance. With only two seconds left, a Scholl to Murphy pass was good for a 7–3 score.

The game was hardly over when the protest began. A study of the game films revealed there was no offside and Cornell had been given a fifth down. Cornell magnanimously gave up the win, and Dartmouth accepted the 3–0 victory. It is the only time in college football history that a final score has ever been reversed.

That same day in Boston, Georgetown's unbeaten streak of 23 games ended, as Frank Leahy's Boston College Eagles handed Jack Hagerty's Georgetown squad its first loss in three years. Eagle quarterback Charley O'Rourke secured the win by dodging tacklers in the end zone before being downed. His intentional safety and free kick milked a 19–18 win and gave BC a 10-0-0 regular season and fifth-place finish. Georgetown went to the Orange Bowl where they lost 14–7 to coach Allyn McKeen's unbeaten but once-tied Mississippi State Bulldogs, the nation's number-nine team.

Tennessee again won all ten of its games for the third year in a row and finished fourth. Tennessee's star-studded team of Bob Foxx, Johnny Butler, guards Bob Suffridge and Ed Molinski, and Ed Cifers at end were pitted against Leahy's Boston College Eagles in the Sugar Bowl. Besides O'Rourke, BC's backfield had Mike Holovak and Henry "Tarzan" Toczylowski. At center was Chet Gladchuck, George Kerr and Joe Zabilski were at guard, with Gene Goodreault at end. BC stole a couple pages from Neyland's playbook by blocking a Bob Foxx punt for one score, and then getting the winning touchdown on an off-tackle play for a 19–13 win.

With eight starters returning from their national championship squad, coach Homer Norton's Texas Aggies looked forward to the coming season. Their string of victories grew to 19 as they won their first ten contests. Then they ran aground on the rock that has sunk more than one stout ship— overconfidence.

Texas A&M met Texas for its annual donneybrook on Thanksgiving

Day. The Longhorns won the toss and returned the kickoff to their 30. Fullback Pete Layden switched places with tailback Jackie Crain. Layden began a wide end run to the right and then stopped. Crain delayed two counts, then slipped unnoticed down the left sideline away from the flow of play. Layden tossed a long pass to Crain who was pulled down on the Aggie 35.

On the next play, Layden fired a pass down the middle that fell incomplete. On the third play, Layden tried the left side behind blocker Vern Martin, stopped again, and put the ball up. Wingback Noble Doss ran down the field on the right, and Layden hit him on another crossover pass to the other side. Doss took the ball over his shoulder and fell out-of-bounds on the one-yard line. On the fourth play, Layden smacked over from his fullback spot, and the Longhorns had a 7-0 lead in just 58 seconds.

The quick Texas score was all it took. John Kimbrough led the Aggie attack, but was stopped each time. The Texas line of ends Preston Flanagan and Mal Kutner, tackles Stan Mauldin, Don Williams, and Julian Garrett, guards Chal Daniel and Ted Dawson, and centers Glenn Jackson and Red Goodwin would not budge. Five Aggie bombs were intercepted, and A&M skidded to number six.

With a Rose Bowl invitation in his pocket, Norton told his boys more than once that overconfidence was killing them. After the game, he wept openly with the team in the locker room. The Aggies went to the Cotton Bowl instead and outpointed Fordham 13-12 in a hard-fought contest. After the game, Fordham center Lou DeFilippo was on crutches, and Marshall Robnett's knee was torn so badly that it ended his career. *Sic transit gloria gridiron.*

1941

Minnesota (8-0-0)			Duke (9-1-0)		
14	Washington	6	43	Wake Forest	14
34	Illinois	6	19	Tennessee	0
39	Pitt	0	50	Maryland	0
7	Michigan	0	27	Colgate	14
8	Northwestern	7	27	Pitt	7
9	Nebraska	0	14	Georgia Tech	0
34	Iowa	13	56	Davidson	0
41	Wisconsin	6	20	North Carolina	0
			55	North Carolina State	6
			16	Oregon State (Rose Bowl)	20
186		38	327		61

In a three-day meeting following the bowl games, the rules committee decided to permit unlimited substitution for the first time. This allowed players to enter and leave the game as often as needed. A second rule stated that any ball handed forward in the backfield would be considered a lateral.

A third rule said that any fourth-down incomplete pass in the end zone would not be brought out to the 20-yard line, but would be put in play at the spot where the play originated.

The Texas team that had corraled A&M last season was for real, and for six weeks UT's high-octane scoring machine was the talk of the country. Eight of the "Immortal 13," including seven starters who went all the way against the Aggies, were back, and coach Bible had one of his best teams. In the first six games, they stamped out victories with methodical similarity, beating Colorado 34-6, Louisiana State 34-0, Oklahoma 40-7, Arkansas 48-14, Rice 40-0, and Southern Methodist 34-0.

Unfortunately, the high-riding Longhorns started to believe their own press clippings, and they were halted by a Baylor team which had lost four in a row before the Texas game. The Bears' seven-man line used linemen who stunted and charged at an angle, mainly 225-pound tackle Bubo Barnett, who shadowed Jackie Crain and held him to three yards rushing. With fullback Pete Layden and end Mal Kutner on the disabled list, Texas was lucky to get a 7-0 halftime lead after a poor Baylor punt from behind their goal wobbled crazily out-of-bounds on the 10-yard line.

With only two minutes left to play, Baylor got the ball on its own 28-yard line. They connected on a series of passes for 54 yards on a drive that was just two yards short of their total yardage for the day. It was fourth-and-four with but 18 seconds left on the clock. Tailback Kit Kittrell, subbing for injured Jackie Wilson, zigged and zagged until he spotted Willie Coleman in the back corner of the end zone and hit him as time ran out. Jackie Wilson hobbled off the bench and brought the Longhorns to earth with the conversion that tied the score at 7-7.

A week later, Texas was done in completely by the Horned Frogs of Texas Christian. Again they took a 7-0 lead, but a one-touchdown edge in Texas is like trying to hold a greased pig. Behind a wall of blockers just before the half, Dean Bagley embarked on a 55-yard run to tie the score at seven. Then with two minutes to go from its 16-yard line, TCU swept to the Texas 25. Eight ticks remained when Emory Nix threw to Van Hall for the winning score, 14-7, and Texas faded to fourth. They rebounded to beat the number-nine Aggies on Turkey Day, 23-0, and scuttled Oregon 71-7 to finish as the top scorers with 33.8 points per game.

After the Texas-Baylor tie, Minnesota took over the number-one spot and was never headed. Pulling guard Helge Pukema, end Judd Ringer, and tackles Dick Wildung and 6'3", 247-pound Urban Odson, made the Gopher line like a Mack truck. Behind this punch-'em-out forward wall, halfbacks Bruce Smith and Bill Daley made the running game roll relentlessly. Bruce Smith was coach Bernie Bierman's choice as the best all-around player he'd had at Minnesota, and the Gophers finished unbeaten for the second year in a row, but it was an uphill climb most of the way.

Minnesota had sidetracked the highballing Wolverines last year, but the battle for the Little Brown Jug this season with fifth-place Michigan was a mauler. The Wolverines were paced by tackles Albert Wistert and Rube

Minnesota halfback Bruce Smith was coach Bierman's best all-around player.

Kelto, center Don Ingalls, and backfield men Tom Kuzma, George Ceithaml, and Bob Westfall. The Gophers won, but it was almost a Pyrrhic victory. Bruce Smith was carried off the field with a badly twisted right knee, and Helge Pukema was taken to a Michigan hospital. Herman Frickey, Smith's replacement, was also hurt and helped to the sideline.

The Gophers faced another rough team, Northwestern, for the second week in a row. Minnesota jumped in front on a safety in the first period, but the Wildcats came back to score and led at the half, 7-2. Because so many players were injured, especially at halfback, the Gophers were vulnerable to Otto Graham's passing, and their powerful single wing offense was held in check.

With a backfield composed of two quarterbacks and two fullbacks, Minnesota resorted to a ruse in the third period. After a punt by Bill DeCorrevont was partly blocked and rolled out-of-bounds on the Wildcat 41, quarterback Bill Garnaas informed the referee that a trick play would be coming up two plays later.

From his position at fullback, Bob Sweiger set it up with a reverse to the left. He made a point of going down in bounds so time would remain in while the referee spotted the ball on the hashmark 15 yards in from the sideline. Sweiger almost blew it with a bad case of overacting, as he said a few insulting words to a Northwestern defender and was given a polite shove for his trouble. The Minnesota center, Gene Flick, stepped between them.

All the Minnesota linemen were strung out to the right of Gene Flick. A few yards behind them, the Gopher backs spaced themselves casually. They did not huddle but stood motionless for one second. Suddenly, Flick scooped up the ball and tossed it back to Bud Higgins, a 5'7", 145-pound speedster.

Higgins took off to the right and turned the corner almost before the Wildcats reacted. The Minnesota players blocked the Northwestern man who was nearest to them. Sweiger went straight down the field and took out the last defender, and Higgins went in standing up. NU coach Lynn Waldorf called the play illegal, but the referee let it stand for an 8–7 Minnesota win.

Bruce Smith won the Heisman Award for his gutsy play. Two weeks later, he was still on the injury list against Iowa. Late in the first half, Minnesota had not made a first down and Iowa was ahead. Smith was used sparingly, but he engineered all five touchdowns and kept the Hawks at bay with his passes.

Number-two Duke was led by fullback Winston Siegfried and halfback Steve Lach, an able successor to Bill Murray, Elmore Hackney, and Ace Parker. In the line were center Bob Barnett, guards Pete Goddard and Tom Burns, tackles Bob McDonough and Mike Karmazin, and Jim Smith and Al Piasecky at the ends. The Blue Devils gained 3,350 yards in nine games, a record at the time, and were first in total offense with 372.2 yards a game.

Because of the bombing of Pearl Harbor by Japan on December 7, all large gatherings on the West Coast were cancelled. So great was the fear of further attack that all Japanese-Americans were put in detention camps. This imprisonment of loyal Americans vies with slavery as one of the darkest pages in American civil history. Instead of playing Duke in the transplanted Rose Bowl in North Carolina, end Jack Yoshihara of Oregon State, the Pacific Coast representative, was in prison on New Year's Day.

Oregon State's win over Duke was no accident. It was coach Lon Stiner's 4–3 defense, later the standard pro defense, which was the first to beat Stanford and end Shaughnessy's T-formation magic early this year. With a big, roughhewn line led by center Quentin Greenough, guards Bill Halverson, Martin Chaves, and Bob Rambo, and tackles Lloyd Wickett, Bob Saunders, and George Bain, the Beavers were long-toothed up front. The backfield had fullback Joe Day, big blocker George Peters, a left-handed wingback, Don Durdan, and a right-handed tailback, Bob Dethman, who kept opponents guessing with runs and passes to both sides. A light rain fell during the game. "Just like home," the Beavers mused.

Early in the first quarter, the Durdan-Dethman combination scored for Oregon State. They took over at midfield and moved the ball to the Duke 15. From single wing right, Dethman handed the ball to Durdan going left. Durdan stopped to put up a left-handed toss, but with no one open he ran in for a Beaver score.

The Blue Devils came right back with the Duke reverse. Tom Davis went

Albert was the second of three all–American Wistert brothers at Michigan. All played tackle, all are in the Hall of Fame, and all wore jersey number 11, which has been retired.

29 yards on one reverse, and Steve Lach ran 22 yards on another. Then Lach scored from the four-yard line on still one more reverse, and Bob Gantt's kick tied it at the half, 7–7.

After Gene Gray ran for 23 yards, Durdan retreated to toss another of his left-handed bombs. He spotted George Zellick in the end zone and hit him to put the Beavers out in front again. Duke struck back in the slam-bang third period on another Steve Lach 38-yard reverse to the Oregon State 25. A penalty put the ball on the one-yard line, where Duke scored to tie it at 14–14.

In just two minutes, Oregon State scored again and went in front for good. This time it was a right-handed toss from Bob Dethman to Gene Gray, who gave the hip to a would-be tackler on the 28 and went in to score. The play covered 70 yards for the longest pass play in Rose Bowl history.

Oregon State led 20–14 as the last quarter started. Duke marched down to the State nine-yard line, where it was second-and-one for a first down.

Bill Dudley of Virginia is the only player to win an MVP award in college, military, and pro ranks.

Mississippi coach Harry Mehre flanked by Merle Hapes (41) and Junie Hovious.

With the linebackers close and the backs deep, Duke's play-caller, Tommy Prothro, decided it was a good spot to throw a pass between them. The ball was tipped by the receiver and fell into the hands of an orange-jerseyed defender.

Duke was turned away by the interception, the fourth one of the day for Oregon State. Along with three fumbles recovered by the Beavers, it was the seventh turnover lost by the Blue Devils.

A safety was added to make it 20–16 when Durdan was tackled in the end zone by Mike Karmazin. It was another of those last-quarter safeties which kept defeat from the door. Instead of a kick from the end zone and a possible blocked punt for a touchdown, Oregon State got a free kick from their 20. Durdan booted one far downfield into Duke territory, and the Beavers were out of danger. The mighty Dukes were toppled, and Wallace Wade lost another Rose Bowl game, this time near the Atlantic shore.

Notre Dame, under new coach Frank Leahy, was third. They won eight, tied Army 0–0, and handed tenth-place Navy and Bill Busik their only loss, 20–13. Leahy was a line coach who helped build the Seven Blocks of Granite under Jim Crowley at Fordham, and he had with him as his line coach, Johnny Druze, one of the Seven Granite Blocks who brought savvy to the Notre Dame line. Standouts for the Irish were center Wally Ziemba, guard Bernie Crimmins, captain Paul Lillis at tackle, end Bob Dove, halfbacks Steve Juzwik and Bill Earley, and fullback Fred "Dippy" Evans.

Number-six Fordham beat number-seven Missouri, which led in rushing with 307.7 yards each game, in the Sugar Bowl on tackle Alex Santilli's blocked punt, 2–0. A muddy field hurt the great backs, Fordham's Jim Blumenstock and low-slung passing fullback, Steve Filipowicz, and Mizzou's Harry Ice and Bob Steuber.

Coach Aldo "Buff" Donelli's Duquesne team finished the year undefeated, including a 16–0 win over Mississippi State and its great running back, Blondy Black. In his three years as coach, his teams won 23 contests, were tied once by Detroit, 10–10, in the first year, and were beaten once the previous year, a 14–6 loss to Harry Mehre's Mississippi team and its two backfield aces, Junie Hovious and Merle Hapes. This season eighth-place Duquesne was first in total defense with 110.6 yards, in rushing defense with 56 yards, and scoring defense with 2.9 points per game. Led by halfback Phil Ahwesh and Al Demao, a replica of Duquesne's 1936 all–American center, Mike Basrak, it was the last round for many squad members who had been together for three years, often competing against each other on the two first teams Donelli used.

Georgia, under third-year coach Wally Butts, won national recognition. Leading the Bulldogs was halfback Frank Sinkwich, the "Jaw-Jaw" boy, whose lower mandible was broken in the second game of the year. In spite of the brace attached to his helmet and drinking his meals through a straw until November, his 1,103 yards rushing was the best. He also set an Orange Bowl mark of 382 yards total offense in a 40–26 win over Texas Christian.

Captain Bill Dudley of Virginia was the country's scoring leader with 134 points. After his touchdown runs of 67 and 79 yards beat North Carolina, 28–7, for the first time in a decade, he was carried off the field by his teammates. The only defeat for coach Frank Murray's eleven was a 21–19 loss to Yale on two missed conversions by Dudley, who took no steps when he kicked, but swung his leg like the pendulum on a clock.

1942

This season saw the transition from peacetime to an all-out war program. Many colleges figured to field strong teams, only to find their rosters depleted by players who had joined Uncle Sam's military. Lineups changed from one week to the next, and many great players, and scores of lesser ones, never came back. In many cases the coach himself was now in the military, and any hope for a winning season was based on young coaches up from the ranks, untried sophomores, military rejects, and fuzzy-cheeked freshmen who were eligible to play this year.

The two decades of growth which resulted in the T-formation and unlimited substitution also brought a year of innovation and experiment. New coaches tried new systems, and many teams used an offense which was part

T-formation and part single wing. New personnel were shuttled in and out
and from position to position in order to find a winning combination. The
game itself was in transition as fertile brains brought further implementation and germination, slowed down only by World War II.

Ohio State	(9-1-0)		Georgia	(11-1-0)	
59	Fort Knox	0	7	Kentucky	6
32	Indiana	21	14	Jacksonville Air Base	0
28	Southern California	12	40	Furman	7
26	Purdue	0	48	Mississippi	13
20	Northwestern	6	40	Tulane	0
7	Wisconsin	17	35	Cincinnati	13
59	Pitt	19	21	Alabama	10
44	Illinois	20	75	Florida	0
21	Michigan	7	40	Chattanooga	0
41	Iowa Pre-Flight	12	13	Auburn	27
			34	Georgia Tech	0
			9	UCLA (Rose Bowl)	0
337		114	376		76

In his second year as coach, Paul Brown made Ohio State the top team.
Gone was the elephantine line, and in its place were lean performers like
tackles Chuck Csuri and Bill Willis, guards Hal Dean and all–American Lin
Houston, center Bill Vickroy, and end Bob Shaw. During the summer,
Brown told his men to be ready to scrimmage on the first day of practice,
which they did. This regimen gained the Bucks more points in the last period
than any other quarter. Behind in the Indiana game, they shifted to the T-
formation and scored three times in the second half to win it. Against
number-nine Michigan and all–American guard Julie Franks, Ohio's
receivers scored twice after outrunning the Wolverine secondary. They lost
to Wisconsin, but 21 Ohio State players became sick on the way to Madison.

In practice sessions, a water bucket was not allowed on the field, and
no one was on the grass unless injured. Brown's team was well-drilled in
blocking and tackling, and as tough mentally and physically as a commando
unit. His single-wing men were captain George Lynn at quarter, wingback
Les Horvath, tailback Paul Sarringhaus, and fullback Gene Fekete. He ran
the T-formation about 25 percent of the time, the first Big Ten coach to
employ it.

Frank Sinkwich of Georgia was the country's flashiest back. His 2,187
yards total offense was first to pass 2,000 yards in a year. The Bulldogs'
diamond-hard line of tackle Gene Ellenson, guard Walter Ruark, and center
Leo Costa made them a contender for national honors. Sophomore tailback
Charley Trippi was so highly rated that "Fireball Frankie" was moved to fullback where his quick getaway and strong leg drive could be used best. With
wingback Lamar Davis, this power-primed trio made Georgia second in the
nation and their 429.5 yards per game total offense best in the land.

Sinkwich helped Georgia to its first SEC title and won the Heisman for

Georgia's first Heisman Trophy winner (1942), tailback Frank Sinkwich.

himself. The Bulldogs showed the stuff of champions, as they overcame a 10–0 third-quarter deficit against Alabama and exploded for three last-period touchdowns, two to end George Poschner and a midair fumble returned by Andy Dudish for a 21–10 win. They also gave number-five Georgia Tech, with guard Harvey Hardy, and Clint Castleberry and Eddie Prokop in the backfield, its first loss, 34–0. Then they beat UCLA, led by guard Jack Lescoulie, ends Milt Smith and Herb Wiener, and Bob Waterfield at quarter, 9–0, in the Rose Bowl. They lost to an Auburn squad hot at season's end, the only T-formation team Georgia faced all year.

Harry Stuhldreher, quarterback of the Four Horsemen, coached Wisconsin to a winning season. The Badgers had that endangered species, a veteran at every position, and were the only team to beat Ohio State. With center Fred Negus, quarterback Jack Wink (whose 101-yard interception wrecked Great Lakes 13–7), end Dave Schreiner, halfback Elroy "Crazy Legs" Hirsch, and Pat Harder at full, the Badgers won with the pass or run. Wisconsin men in the Atlantic and Pacific fighting wrote home to cheer the best Badger team in three decades. They almost won it all except for a 7–7 tie with number-six Notre Dame, and a 6–0 letdown loss to Iowa a week after their win over Ohio State, to earn a third-place showing.

Number-four Tulsa led in scoring offense with 42.7 points and in scoring defense with 3.2 points per game. Cal Purdin's running and the tosses of Glenn Dobbs to Saxon Judd made Tulsa first in passing with 233.9 yards per game. Henry Frnka's team finally lost to number-seven Tennessee in the Sugar Bowl, 14–7.

Boston College led in rushing defense with 48.9 yards per game, and had two men on the All-America team, end Don Currivan and fullback Mike Holovak. Behind the pass blocking of weight lifter Gil Bouley at tackle, quarterback Mickey Connelly soon made Eagle partisans forget "Chucking Charley" O'Rourke. After three early-season wins, the BC juggernaut downed Wake Forest 27–0, Georgetown 47–0, Temple 28–0, Fordham 56–0, and Boston University 37–0. Only traditional rival Holy Cross remained.

On the Saturday after Thanksgiving, the Eagles played Holy Cross at Boston's Fenway Park. Unlike most coaches, Denny Myers boasted big about his club, and didn't worry too much about the defense. Even when Holy Cross ran up a 20–0 lead, people still thought BC would win. Sophomore George Connor out-muscled Gil Bouley throughout the 55–12 defeat, Holy Cross had the upset of the year, and the proud Eagles roosted in the number-eight spot.

The loss was a blessing in disguise for the Boston College team. A victory party was scheduled later that evening at the Cocoanut Grove in Boston. That night, it burned to the ground, and 400 people died, including cowboy movie star Buck Jones.

Glad to be alive, BC met tenth-place Alabama in the Orange Bowl and led 14–0 at the end of the first period. Like their counterpart in the Rose Bowl eight years before, Alabama scored 22 points in the second quarter and went on to win, 37–21.

1943

Notre Dame	(9-1-0)		Iowa Pre-Flight	(9-1-0)	
41	Pitt	0	32	Illinois	18
55	Georgia Tech	13	28	Ohio State	13
35	Michigan	12	33	Iowa State	13
50	Wisconsin	0	25	Iowa	0
47	Illinois	0	21	Missouri	6
33	Navy	6	19	Fort Riley	2
26	Army	0	46	Marquette	19
25	Northwestern	6	28	Camp Grant	13
14	Iowa Pre-Flight	13	13	Notre Dame	14
14	Great Lakes	19	32	Minnesota	0
340		69	277		98

With the bloody legions of Mars encircling the globe, almost 200 colleges discontinued football this year. Many of them gave up the sport when

Tom Hamilton, a Navy player and coach, and later admiral, instituted a training program that helped keep college football alive during the war.

the Army said its trainees on college campuses would not have time for football. Those colleges that did play fielded a team full of men who could not pass the Army physical, and 17-year-olds not yet eligible for the draft. Gas rationing and transportation restrictions curtailed travel, and many teams played a home-and-home series with nearby schools.

The fortunate teams were the ones with a Navy program which allowed trainees to participate in varsity sports. New recruits who had played for one team the year before now were at another school, often a traditional rival. Wisconsin's Elroy Hirsch and Minnesota's Bill Daley now wore a Michigan uniform, and Illinois guard Alex Agase played for Purdue, and became the only Big Ten player to make all–American at two different schools.

Commander Tom Hamilton was the man behind the physical fitness program for naval aviation cadets. Navy pre-flight schools were set up at Iowa, Georgia, North Carolina, and St. Mary's in California. With seasoned personnel, many of them ex-pros, and ex-college coaches to train them, these pre-flight schools were among the best teams in the country. Of the top ten teams this year, four were service teams, and two of them were pre-flight schools. Football at these Navy schools was curbed because the training program lasted only 12 weeks, with a new class coming and going every two weeks. If one of these classes finished in midseason, the coach had to find good replacements in a hurry.

When Frank Leahy changed to the T-formation at Notre Dame, the rush to the new system began in earnest. Leahy was forced to do so because he had a great passer, Angelo Bertelli, who could fake handoffs but could not run. He also had two good halfbacks — Creighton Miller, who led the nation in rushing with 911 yards, and a Navy transfer from Illinois, Julie Rykovich. This talented trio took Notre Dame to the rushing and total offense titles with 313.7 and 418 yards per game, respectively.

In addition to all–Americans Miller and Bertelli (who won the Heisman), the Irish had two all–Americans in the line, guard Pat Filley and tackle Jim White. When Bertelli was called into the service, he was replaced by another potential all–American, Johnny Lujack. It was Notre Dame's greatest team to date.

The Irish won the national title by beating the three best teams in the nation. Their season was 30 seconds too long, as they lost to number-six Great Lakes in the last moments of the last game. Steve Lach dropped a depth charge on Notre Dame with a 46-yard scoring pass to Paul Anderson to sink the Irish.

With a roster full of ex-pro players, including Dick Todd of Texas A&M and the Washington Redskins, Iowa Pre-Flight finished second. Coached by Lieutenant Don Faurot, the Seahawks used the split-T formation which he had invented two years before at Missouri.

The split-T differed from a straight-T in that the quarterback did not spin and fake but moved along the line of scrimmage and kept the ball or tossed it back according to the reaction of the defensive end. The line was also spaced wider to eliminate the need for power blocking in order to open a hole. The hole was already created by the greater spacing, and a lineman's main task was to hold the hole open briefly until the runner went by. Offensive philosophy was quickly changing from a short-yardage game of two-on-one blocking to brush blocks and quick openers which capitalized on defensive errors to go for the long gain.

The split-T did not need a three-way back or pulling linemen to make a play work as in the single wing. Neither did it need a quarterback who could pass or fake as in the regular-T. Its success depended on deception like the straight-T, and as a quarterback could run with the ball or throw it, so many yards were gained by a halfback run which turned into a pass. It was developed for linemen who were good blockers but not great ones, and for average backs who were not triple-threat players.

Benefiting from their Navy training programs, Michigan and Purdue shared the Big Ten title. Led by backfield men Tony Butkovich and Babe Dimancheff, unbeaten Purdue was fifth. With ten ex–Badgers on its team,

Michigan beat Wisconsin easily. Aided by all–American tackle Merv Pregul-
man, and Bob Wiese and captain Paul White in the backfield, they beat Minnesota for the first time in a decade, lost only to Notre Dame, and finished
third.

Navy ended up fourth in the Associated Press poll. Led by all–
American tackle Don Whitmire of Alabama, now matriculating at Annapolis, Navy won eight games and was beaten only by Notre Dame. The Middies
took everyone in tow on the Atlantic coast, including Army and its all–
American center, Casimir Myslinski.

Behind ex–Vol guard Jim Myers, now playing in Durham, Duke led in
scoring defense with 3.8 points, in rushing defense with 39.4 yards and in
total defense with 121.7 yards per game. Tom Davis' passes to ends Bob
Gantt and Benny Cittadino took Eddie Cameron's squad to the scoring title
with a 37.2-point average. The number-seven Blue Devils were defeated only
by Navy, 14–13.

The oddest game of the year was between Illinois and Ohio State. The
game supposedly ended in a 26–26 tie with the ball on the Illini 35-yard line.
Both teams were undressing in the locker room when the referee told them
there was an offside on the last play. "The game cannot end on a penalty,"
he intoned.

Both teams trotted back to the field, some of the players without any
shoes on. John Stungis, an 18-year old freshman, split the uprights with a
field goal and Ohio won, 29–26.

At the College of Pacific, 81 years young A.A. Stagg was in his fifty-
fourth straight year as head football coach. Led by all–American tackle Art
McCaffrey, his COP Tigers had a won seven, lost two record, and Stagg was
chosen coach of the year.

1944

Army (9-0-0)			Ohio State (9-0-0)		
46	North Carolina	0	54	Missouri	0
59	Brown	7	34	Iowa	0
69	Pitt	7	20	Wisconsin	7
76	Coast Guard Academy	0	26	Great Lakes	6
27	Duke	7	34	Minnesota	14
83	Villanova	0	21	Indiana	7
59	Notre Dame	0	54	Pitt	19
62	Penn	7	26	Illinois	12
23	Navy	7	18	Michigan	14
504		35	287		79

Army football was at the summit again. The Black Knights of the Hudson gunned down everyone on their way to the title. They averaged 56 points
each contest, fifth best for a major college, and the modern record. They
were also first in scoring defense with 3.9 points, and in rushing with 298.6
yards per game.

Coach Earl Blaik had so many men on his squad that he used two separate teams. It was not a two-platoon system with separate offensive and defensive units, but a team with two complete two-way squads. One team was called the Veterans, and had Dick Pitzer and Ed Rafalko as ends, tackles Al Nemetz and Bill Webb, guards Johnny Green and Joe Stanowicz, and center Bob St. Onge. The backs were Doug Kenna, Max Minor, Dale Hall, and Bobby Dobbs. The other team, called Plebes, had end Barney Poole, tackle DeWitt Coulter from Texas A&M, guard Art Gerometta, and Herschel Fuson at center. In the backfield were quarterback Tom Lombardo, halfback Glenn Davis, and fullback Felix "Doc" Blanchard.

Blaik said the best game he ever saw was when his two teams went at it in scrimmage. Even the PAT kicker, Dick Walterhouse, was tops, for he had a record-setting 47 conversions during the year. The team also tied the mark of 36 pass interceptions, and set a record of 8.2 touchdowns each contest (74 in nine games).

Davis and Blanchard — Mr. Outside and Mr. Inside, as George Trevor first called them — were undoubtedly the best one-two punch ever to grace a gridiron. At 5'9" and 170 pounds, Davis could run the 100-yard dash in 9.7 seconds. Blanchard, at a little over six feet and 205 pounds, was just a shade behind in the 100 at ten seconds flat. These twin tornadoes complemented each other perfectly, for Davis was a good passer and Doc a fine receiver. A favorite play was a direct pass to Davis at tailback, who then tossed a quick pass out to the flat, where Blanchard took off like a bee-stung buffalo. Davis was also one of the best blockers on the squad, while Blanchard did the punting and kicked off.

Army's trouncing of Notre Dame was the worst defeat in Irish history. The Cadets hadn't beaten Notre Dame in 13 years or even scored on them in the last five games, and the revenge was sweet. Eight interceptions aided the Cadets. Army was so high they had 20 points in ten minutes, Blanchard ran into head linesman Dave Reese and put him out of the game, and by halftime it was 33–0. Their last score was on an interception by tackle Harold Tavzel, who cavorted in the end zone like a cat in a catnip store.

The Navy game was played in Baltimore's Municipal Stadium. Navy had its own share of stars with end Leon Bramlett, top punt returner Hal Hamberg, and Arkansas transfer Clyde "Smackover" Scott from Smackover, Arkansas, two all–Americans from Alabama (halfback Bob Jenkins and tackle Don Whitmire), and all–American guard Ben Chase. At the end of three periods Army was in front 9–7, when Davis intercepted a pass and ran it back to midfield.

Army struck quickly as Blanchard clipped off 25 yards from right end. On the last 25 yards to the goal, Blanchard got the call on almost every play. The Cadet answer to the Sherman tank battered the Navy line for three yards, then for four, and again for another three yards. With first down on the ten, it was Doc once more, as he whammed into the end zone standing up.

"This is the only man," said Army line coach Herman Hickman, "who can run his own interference."

Earl "Red" Blaik had a 166-48-14 record (a .759 average) at Dartmouth and Army.

The next time Army got the ball, Davis took a shovel pass from Lombardo on a run to the short side called "The California Special." He veered inside the end and headed for the sideline. Then he turned the corner and sped to the goal like quicksilver. Navy, in the number-two spot before the game, dropped to fourth, but their per-game rushing defense of 53.8 yards was still tops.

Although Davis and Blanchard usually played only a quarter and seldom more than a half, Davis ran for three touchdowns in each of the games with Brown, Penn, North Carolina, Notre Dame, and Villanova. His total of 120 points was high for the year. He scored 20 touchdowns and passed for two more, yet he handled the ball on only 68 plays. He had an incredible 12.4 yards each time he got his hands on the ball. Blanchard scored nine touchdowns during the year and had a 7.1-average per carry. Both of them were chosen on almost every All-America team.

At Ohio State, Paul Brown's replacement, Carroll Widdoes, had a successful season. Behind its veteran line, the Buckeyes won all nine games.

Army's touchdown twins: Glenn Davis (left) and Doc Blanchard.

A mainstay in the Ohio line was Bill Willis at tackle, a three-year letterman who failed his Army physical. Others deferred from military duty were a pair of all–Americans, end Jack Dugger and guard Bill Hackett. Another all–American, Les Horvath, a dental student, won the Heisman Trophy. He

Dental student Les Horvath was the first Buckeye to win the Heisman (1944). As a dentist, he helped fit high school players with mouth guards.

was a tailback in the single wing, but was at quarterback when Ohio State went to the T-formation. With him in the backfield were freshmen Bob Brugge, Dick Flanagan, and Ollie Cline. Against Michigan, both teams went back and forth until the Bucks had the last seesaw, and Widdoes was coach of the year. Along with the Heisman, it was the first time both awards went to the same school.

Another team which had a winning season without military personnel was Oklahoma A&M, now Oklahoma State. Coach Jim Lookabaugh's Cowboys beat everyone except the Norman Naval Air Station squad. In the backfield was an 18-year old sophomore, Bob Fenimore, whose 1,758 yards total offense was the best in the nation. Fenimore, a single wing tailback who could run and pass, ran for 902 yards and threw for 856. In the Cotton Bowl, Jim Spivatal's 52-yard scoring run helped A&M down TCU, 34–0.

Military teams again flourished. Besides Army and Navy, four service teams were in the top ten. Randolph Field placed third and Bainbridge Naval Station finished fifth. Iowa Pre-Flight came in sixth and Fourth Air

Force was tenth. Southern Cal, Michigan, and Notre Dame were seventh, eighth, and ninth.

1945

Army	(9-0-0)		Navy	(7-1-1)	
32	Louisville Air Base	0	49	Villanova	0
54	Wake Forest	0	21	Duke	0
28	Michigan	7	28	Penn State	0
55	Melville Navy Base	13	20	Georgia Tech	6
48	Duke	13	14	Penn	7
54	Villanova	0	6	Notre Dame	6
48	Notre Dame	0	33	Michigan	7
61	Penn	0	36	Wisconsin	7
32	Navy	13	13	Army	32
412		46	220		65

Army was undefeated for the second year in a row, and again was national champion. They were victorious in all nine starts, and lengthened their win streak to 18 games. Graduation trimmed Blaik's two indomitable units from last season, but this year's team was just as good, and maybe a bit better. The Texas Aggies gave another transfer, right end Hank Foldberg, and Mississippi State sent Tom McWilliams to join Blanchard and Davis as running mates. Arnold Tucker took over at quarterback to complete one of the best backfields to step on any gridiron at any time.

The third game with number-six Michigan was before a sellout crowd of 70,000 at Yankee Stadium. During the game, Fritz Crisler, the Michigan coach, took advantage of the rule which permitted unlimited substitution. He repeatedly sent in fresh troops to slow the Army legions, but the irresistible force of Army's blistering attack gradually wore down the Wolverines.

Crisler's deployment of new men sent in as a unit helped popularize the two-platoon system, for coaches everywhere saw that rested players could play a better game. They realized, too, that separate squads with specialized personnel would also improve the game, for most players are better at either offense or defense than they are at both.

Army met Notre Dame one month later at Yankee Stadium. The Irish had Frank Dancewicz at quarter, halfbacks Phil Colella and Elmer Angsman, and fullback Frank Ruggerio. At center was Bill Walsh, and making the first of his four appearances was lineman Bill Fischer. Before they left in the first half, Davis scored three times and Blanchard twice. In a repeat performance, Army ripped number-nine Notre Dame for the second straight year.

Army wasted no time with Navy, the number-two team, coached by submarine commander Oscar Hagberg. The Touchdown Twins never let Navy close enough to shake hands. By the end of the first quarter, Blanchard

Alabama coach Frank Thomas had a 141-33-9 record, winning almost 80 percent of his games.

scored twice and Davis added a touchdown run on a sizzling scamper of 49 yards to send Navy down to defeat.

The Black Knights were in a class by themselves and one of the greatest teams of all time. They led the nation in rushing offense with 359.8 yards each game, in total offense with 462.7 yards per game, and in scoring with a 45.8-point average. Their rushing average of 7.64 yards per play (3238 yards on 424 plays) and 7.92 yards gained each play (4164 yards on 526 plays) still are records. Davis, the California Comet, scored 18 touchdowns this year, but he was upstaged by Blanchard, who scored 19 times. Blanchard was the nation's scoring leader with 115 points, while Davis had a whopping 11.74-yard average each time he touched the ball (1197 yards on 102 plays). Army's one-two punch was also one-two in the voting for the Heisman Award, for Blanchard came in first with Davis second for the second year in a row.

Navy had a good season until they met Army. Led by center Dick Scott and captain Dick Duden and Leon Bramlett on the ends, it wasn't until the sixth game with Notre Dame that a touchdown was made through the Navy line. The 6–0 Irish lead was good until the last period when Clyde "Smackover" Scott intercepted a pass and returned it 60 yards to knot the score. At the end of the game, Notre Dame passed to the Navy one-yard stripe, but Skip Minisi's tackle prevented a touchdown. The game ended after two cracks at the stubborn Navy line. A week before, Minisi caught the pass from Bob Hoernschemeyer that beat eighth-place Penn.

Alabama did not field a team during 1943, but in just two short years they were back near the top. Frank Thomas started to rebuild with his 1944 war babies, and his success this year was due to a pair of all–Americans, Vaughn Mancha at center and tailback Harry Gilmer. This season's squad was first in total defense, allowing only 109.9 yards per game. The Tide was also first against the run, holding opponents to 33.9 yards per game.

Alabama was second only to Army in total offense, most of it gained on the passing of Harry Gilmer, a 158-pound, six-footer with a rubber-like arm. Gilmer had peripheral vision which let him spot receivers from the corner of his eye, and he had long, slender fingers which helped him grip the ball. He also had the amazing ability to pass while leaping in the air, and his strong arm permitted him to flick it short or release it long. He was cool under pressure and seldom intercepted. His average of 64.8 percent on pass completions was a record at the time.

Number-three Alabama spoiled Southern Cal's perfect record of eight wins in eight Rose Bowl appearances. The Tide scored once in the first quarter, and added two more touchdowns in the second period for a 20-0 halftime lead. They scored again after the half to make it 27-0 before the Trojans finally made a first down. Alabama let everyone know why they were first in defense by holding USC to six yards rushing and 41 yards total offense.

A step behind Alabama in defense was Indiana, a team which gave up only one touchdown in its last five games. Coached by Bo McMillan, the Praying Colonel from Centre College, Indiana had its first undefeated season and won the Big Ten title for the first time. Sprinkled throughout the team were top-drawer personnel, including all–American end Pete Pihos, who finished the season at fullback when the starter was injured. Michigan coach Fritz Crisler said Ted Kluszewski and all–American end Bob Ravensberg were the best pair of ends he'd seen all season. In spite of Bo's concern over his 200-pound "pore l'il boys" in the line, the Hoosiers gave everyone their comeuppance all year.

In the annual battle with Purdue for the Old Oaken Bucket, the Boilermakers couldn't dent the Indiana line. McMillan used a four-man line and four linebackers which never let Purdue get closer than the Hoosier 35-yard stripe. Purdue had one scoring chance just before halftime when Indiana fumbled on its 20-yard line. Three plays went nowhere and the fourth was intercepted.

After being held to no score at halftime, Indiana went to work. They mounted a touchdown drive of 77 yards on king-sized bites of yardage, as Pihos went in from the one-yard line on the seventh play. The Hoosiers scored again before the quarter was over when Kluszewski stole an airborne fumble from Ed Cody deep in Purdue territory, Pihos later scoring again from a yard out.

In the fourth quarter, the Hoosiers scored two more touchdowns. They drove 65 yards, with quarterback Ben Raimondi tossing a seven-yard touchdown to Kluszewski, later a baseball star for the Cincinnati Reds. On the next Indiana march, Raimondi threw another short scoring pass to end Louis Mihajkovich for a 26-0 win. For taking the Hoosiers to a number-four finish with nine victories and a tie, McMillan was voted coach of the year.

Oklahoma A&M had an unbeaten season for the first time. They won all eight games, gave Oklahoma its worst defeat, 47-0, and finished fifth. Bob Fenimore's 1,641 yards total offense led the nation. He had 1,048 yards running and 593 on passes, and was the first player to lead in total offense two years in a row. His 5,099 yards total offense is still a school mark.

Under Jim Phelan, St. Mary's won seven games, lost only to UCLA by six points, and finished seventh. Among their wins was a 26-0 whitewashing of Rose Bowl-bound Southern Cal. The team was led by "Squirmin' Herman" Wedemeyer, a unanimous choice for all–American halfback, and later a television star as "Duke" on *Hawaii Five-O*.

Most of the team was seventeen years old, with two sophomores and eight freshmen on the starting squad. The Galloping Gaels were the most exciting team of the year, as Phelan's boys played a wide-open game full of tricks and razzle-dazzle. One of their plays, a hook-and-lateral with a second lateral, was a pass from a halfback to an end, who in turn tossed a lateral to one back, who then lateraled to another back. Against Nevada, the play was good for 74 yards and a touchdown. It began with a short pass from Wedemeyer to end Ed Ryan, who tossed it back to quarterback Denis O'Connor, who threw it to Spike Cordeiro, who took it the rest of the way. In the Sugar Bowl, St. Mary's lost to the hard-riding Cowboys of Oklahoma A&M, 33-13.

Military men came back from the service in ever-increasing numbers, and rosters changed from week to week as these veterans returned to school. In Texas, Bobby Layne and Doak Walker, his high school teammate, were discharged from the Merchant Marine the last week of October. Layne returned to Texas, where he had already raised eyebrows with his freshman tosses to end Hub Bechtol, while Walker enrolled at Southern Methodist, where his high school coach, Rusty Russell, was on the staff.

On the very day that Layne and Walker were separated from the Merchant Marine, the Longhorns lost their only game of the year, a 7-6 squeaker to Rice. One week later, Layne and Walker faced each other as opponents when Texas met the SMU Mustangs.

Early in the game, Walker scored on a 32-yard dash to give SMU a 7-0 lead at halftime. In the final period, Layne got the Steers going with a touchdown pass to Dale Schwartzkopf to draw close at 7-6. Late in the game, the Longhorns got a break when Layne intercepted a Walker pass. A few plays later, Layne threw to Peppy Blount in the end zone for a 12-7 Texas win.

Tenth-place Texas met Missouri, the Big Six champ, on New Year's Day in the Cotton Bowl. Texas scored first on a 48-yard touchdown pass from Layne to halfback Joe Baumgardner. Missouri came back in four plays on a 65-yard scoring pass from quarterback Bill Dellastatious to end Roland Oakes. Jim Kekeris added the point after to tie the game. Layne then scored two times to Missouri's once to give Texas a 21-14 halftime lead. The crowd didn't think it could get better, but it did.

On the third play of the second half, Missouri fumbled on its own

20-yard line and Texas recovered. The Longhorns scored in two plays on two completed passes by Layne, and it was 27–14.

The Tigers narrowed it to 27–21 on Howard Bonnett's 21-yard touchdown run as the final quarter started. Texas charged back with Layne flipping a lateral to halfback Ralph Ellsworth and then breaking downfield. Ellsworth faded back and uncorked a beauty to Layne, who caught it on the 25 and ran over. Missouri kept pace on a 42-yard run by Lennie Brown, Bob Hopkins finally scoring to make it 33–27. The Longhorns scored as Layne took a lateral from Ellsworth to end the festivities at 40–27.

It was the greatest offensive display the Cotton Bowl had seen, and a near-perfect day for Bobby Layne. He had a hand in each of his team's 40 points, scoring four touchdowns himself, passing for two more, and kicking four extra points. He hit on 11 of 12 passes, nine of them to end Hub Bechtol.

1946

Notre Dame	(8-0-1)		Army	(9-0-1)	
26	Illinois	6	35	Villanova	0
33	Pitt	0	21	Oklahoma	7
49	Purdue	6	46	Cornell	21
41	Iowa	6	20	Michigan	13
28	Navy	0	48	Columbia	14
0	Army	0	19	Duke	0
27	Northwestern	0	19	West Virginia	0
41	Tulane	0	0	Notre Dame	0
26	Southern Cal	6	34	Penn	7
			21	Navy	18
271		24	263		80

With World War II over and blue-bearded Mars no longer in command, players and coaches returned to college to finish their education and play a little football. Back from two years with the Navy in the Pacific theater, Frank Leahy took up where he left off at Notre Dame. His Fighting Irish of 1943 were national champs, and so was this year's team.

At Notre Dame, Leahy carved out a career rivaling that of Knute Rockne. Although not as animated as Rockne, Leahy was just as successful as his old coach and often compared with him. Leahy did not enjoy the popularity Rockne did as an after-dinner speaker, but in front of a blackboard before his fellow coaches and players, Leahy had no equal. His desire for perfection was matched only by Dobie at Cornell, and only Neyland at Tennessee equaled his attention to detail. He had the intensity of Howard Jones, and ate and drank football like Yost and Shaughnessy. In practice, he constantly exhorted his players to "pay the price."

Leahy could not miss with the veterans who returned to the Golden Dome after the war. The line bulged with all–Americans, including three

Many rate Johnny Lujack as Notre Dame's greatest quarterback.

all-time Notre Dame greats: guard Bill Fischer, end Leon Hart, and Holy
Cross transfer George Connor at tackle. Linemen from the 1943 champs
were end Jack Zilly, tackle George Sullivan, guard Joe Signaigo, and backs
Fred Earley and all-time Irish great, quarterback Johnny Lujack. Returning
from the 1942 team were end Paul Limont, tackle Ziggy Czarobski, guards
Bob McBride and Bud Meter, and backfield men Gerry Cowhig, Jim Mello,
Corwin Clatt, Bob Livingstone, and Russell Ashbaugh.

Two-time all–American Leon Hart is a member of the all-time Notre Dame team.

Also greeting Leahy were these players from wartime squads: backs George Ratterman, Frank Tripucka, Terry Brennan, Bill Gompers, John Panelli, and linemen Bob Skoglund, John Mastrangelo, Jack Fallon, Marty Wendell, Fred Rovai, and Bill Walsh. New linemen were Jim Martin, George Strohmeyer, Ralph McGehee, and backs Emil Sitko, Mike Swistowicz, Coy McGee, Ernie Zalejski, and Floyd Simmons.

Two-time defending national champion Army again made a run for the crown. The ends were still Barney Poole and Hank Foldberg. Tackles Nemetz and Coulter had been replaced by Shelton Biles and Goble Bryant, another transfer from the Texas Aggies. Joe Steffy joined Art Gerometta at guard, and at center was Jim Enos backed up by Bill Yeoman. The backfield of Tucker, Davis, and Blanchard now had Rip Rowan at right half. Army was still a great team, but diplomas had thinned the ranks considerably.

The Big Rabble ran into trouble right away. In the first game a tackler hit Blanchard's knee, it bent the wrong way, and he sat out two games. He didn't scrimmage or do any more kicking, but he was in the lineup against Michigan.

Number-six Michigan met the Cadets at Yankee Stadium, and Army ran into more trouble on the fourth play. Tucker hurt the wrist and shoulder

Frank Leahy's record is unequalled among modern-day coaches.

of his throwing arm, but he remained in the game. With Blanchard and Tucker both injured, Davis took over.

Michigan was ahead by a touchdown when Davis went through right guard on the Wolverine 41 and cut to the outside. At the 15-yard line, he faked inside and the safety man bought it. In one fluid move, he leaned outside and ran in for the touchdown.

Just before the half, Army took the lead on another Davis score. On fourth-and-18 from the Michigan 23, Tucker gave the ball to Davis on a handoff. The left side of the Michigan line poured through and knocked Davis loose from the ball as he took it. Two Wolverines dived for the ball and missed. Running to his right, Davis fielded it on the hop, jumped in the air and threw a scoring strike to Bobby Folsom for a 13–7 halftime lead.

Michigan tied the score after the second-half kickoff. In the last period, Army drove to Michigan's seven. Blanchard turned left end and legged it for the goal. He was hit at the three, but carried two tacklers into the end zone for the winning points.

No game excited more people than Army–Notre Dame at Yankee Stadium. It was a showdown between the two top elevens to see who was number one. It was also a grudge match, for Notre Dame wanted to avenge the humiliating defeats of the last two years, and Army wanted to prove that it could beat the big boys and not just weak wartime teams. Among the 74,000 were 100 men who wore the Purple Heart and watched as guests of the Military Academy.

After both teams made a pair of first downs in the opening stanza, the action picked up in the next quarter. Davis tossed a lateral to Blanchard, who dashed around left end for 23 yards to the Notre Dame 23. The Cadets chanted for a touchdown, but the Irish started to push the Black Knights back. Davis tried left end but was tackled for a five-yard loss. A pass from Davis fell incomplete, and another Davis-to-Blanchard lateral failed as Davis lost nine yards. With fourth-and-14 on the Irish 37, a Davis punt was returned to the Notre Dame 12.

The Irish now put on their best drive of the day. Lujack threw to Skoglund for 25 yards, and Cowhig swept through tackle for 20. Harvey Livesay was sent in as another linebacker, but Notre Dame kept coming. Lujack passed to Cowhig for two yards. Gompers got five. Lujack got one on a quarterback sneak. Yankee Stadium was pandemonium as the Irish reached Army's four-yard line. On fourth-and-two, Notre Dame faked into the middle and gave the ball to Gompers around right end. Gompers strung it out but was overtaken on the three, a yard short of a first down.

The Irish had driven 85 yards only to come up snake eyes. Army punted out of danger, but Tucker intercepted a pass on his own 40 and returned it 30 yards on the last play of the half.

In the third period, Tucker stole another pass and ran it back 32 yards to the Army 42. On the next play, Blanchard tore around left end. He was in the open when Lujack hit him at the ankles like a sickle cutting wheat. He dropped after a 21-yard gain at the Irish 37, but Lujack had saved a certain touchdown.

Then Blanchard made four yards, and Tucker passed to Foldberg for 13. The din was deafening as the ball was spotted on the Irish 20. Terry Brennan intercepted a pass on his seven-yard line, and the uproar subsided as if turned off by a switch.

In the last frame, it was Army which kept coming. A last-down play was short by inches at the Irish 33. Not long after, Sitko intercepted a Tucker pass on his 10-yard line. Seconds later, Tucker had his third interception. Blanchard caught a Tucker pass out-of-bounds on the Notre Dame 20 with 48 seconds left, but it was brought back and the game ended zip to zip.

The game proved nothing, although Army retained its number-one spot in the ranking as it had since the middle of October. The Black Knights from Storm King Mountain were still unbeaten, but their victory string had ended at 25 games.

The Army-Navy game was another classic. It was also the last college game for B&D, whose great careers had led Army to three unbeaten years on the gridiron. Navy, on the other hand, was rebuilding under its new coach, Captain Tom Hamilton. Without their wartime transfers, Navy lost its opener to Columbia, beat Villanova for its only win, and lost its last six games.

Navy could not get going at the start. After an exchange of fumbles, Army got the ball on its 37-yard line. Then Tucker threw to Davis, who sped 46 yards down the sideline until he was pushed out-of-bounds. After Blanchard picked up a yard, Davis took an overhand pitch from Tucker and ran in standing up from 14 yards out. Jack Ray's point after was good.

Army had scored in four plays and made it look easy. Early in the second quarter, Navy drove 81 yards to a score. "Pistol Pete" Williams and Myron Gerber made half of it on the ground, and sophomore quarterback Reaves Baysinger did the rest with an 11-yard toss to Art Markel and a 32-yarder to end Leon Bramlett. Baysinger took it in on a quarterback sneak from two yards out. Navy was making a game of it, but Bob Van Summern's point after was tipped by an Army lineman, and the Cadets still led, 7–6.

Army came right back with an 81-yard touchdown march. All of it was overland with Blanchard and Davis carrying the mail. On a trap play at midfield, Blanchard angled for the sideline and went all the way. Jack Ray's conversion made it 14–6.

After Bill Yeoman intercepted a pass on the Navy 38, Army scored again in three plays. Davis tossed to Poole for eight and ran for four. As Blanchard went on a man-in-motion left, Davis took a direct pass from center and threw a 26-yard pass to Blanchard for the touchdown. Jack Ray's third point after was good, and Army was riding high with a 21–6 halftime lead.

Army drove to the Navy 32 after the second-half kickoff. It looked like the Cadets were going to put the game away with another score, but on fourth-and-two they chose to kick. The punt went only ten yards, and Navy had the ball on its 22.

Navy came to life and went 78 yards to score. Williams, Gerber, and Pete Hawkins hacked away at the Army defense. An 18-yard pass to Markel took the ball near the goal. Hawkins ran in from the two but missed the PAT, and Army led, 21–12.

After the kickoff, Army went for the first down on fourth-and-one on its 34. Navy put in an extra guard, Ken Schiweck. Army faced an eight-man line, and Blanchard was stacked up for no gain. Schiweck lined up as a flanker, and Baysinger hit him on a forward pass. Hawkins gained 16 yards to the five-yard line. Then Baysinger tossed a lateral to Billy Earl as the last quarter started. With a flick of his wrist, Earl threw to captain Bramlett in the end zone for a touchdown. The crowd was a near riot as the conversion failed again, and Army still led, 21–18.

On the first play after the kickoff, Davis dashed 29 yards around end to the Navy 39. It looked as if Army was moving, but a pass by Davis was intercepted far downfield by Pete Williams.

In the waning moments, a Williams pass to Phil Ryan for 17 yards helped take Navy to the Army 23. Two minutes remained.

UNC's Charlie "Choo-Choo" Justice was one of the last great triple-threat backs.

Three times Navy was stopped for no gain. On fourth down, Lynn Chewning broke through for 20 yards. 90 seconds to go.

It was first down and three yards to the score that would topple Army. Chewning hit the line but was stopped for no gain. The crowd ran on the field, but the guards could push them back only inches. Another Chewning whack at the line gained nothing.

Navy tried to stop the clock and drew a penalty. On third down at the eight-yard line, Hawkins faked at the line and threw the ball back to

Williams, who ran for the goal. The Army line drove him into the crowd at the five-yard stripe with nine seconds left. The official ruled that Williams was still in-bounds, and in the wild melee the gun sounded before Navy could run another play.

Army's undefeated streak of 28 games was still intact, but the narrow win cost Army its third straight title. Notre Dame, which was second all year, swapped places with the Cadets in the last AP poll. Army's Earl Blaik was voted coach of the year.

Notre Dame was first in total offense with 441.3 yards and in rushing with 340.1 yards each game. Their 141.7 yards total defense and scoring defense of 2.7 points per game was also the best. Tackle George Connor of the Irish won the first Outland Trophy as the best interior lineman of the year.

Glenn Davis won the Heisman. His 354 points and 59 touchdowns were marks which stood 30 years. His career rushing average of 8.26 yards per try (2,957 on 358 plays) is still a record.

Number-three Georgia led in scoring with 37.2 points, and was the only unbeaten and untied team at year's end. Headed by Charley Trippi, they won 11 games, including a 20–10 Sugar Bowl win over ninth-place North Carolina and Charlie Justice.

Number-ten Rice beat seventh-place Tennessee in the Orange Bowl on eight first-period points. With Y.A. Tittle at quarter, number-eight LSU played Arkansas to no score in the Cotton Bowl.

A Rose Bowl pact between the Big Ten and Pacific Coast Conferences was started this year, an agreement that has lasted to this day. Behind linemen Max Wenskunas, Lou and Alex Agase, and Sam Zatkoff, backs Perry Moss, Julie Rykovich, and Buddy Young of fifth-place Illinois helped down the number-four Uclans, 45–14. Russ Steger's 68-yard interception scored for the Illini, and UCLA's Al Hoisch had a 103-yard kickoff return, still a Rose Bowl mark.

1947

Notre Dame	(9-0-0)		Michigan	(10-0-0)	
40	Pitt	6	55	Michigan State	0
22	Purdue	7	49	Stanford	13
31	Nebraska	0	69	Pitt	0
21	Iowa	0	49	Northwestern	21
27	Navy	0	13	Minnesota	6
27	Army	7	14	Illinois	7
26	Northwestern	19	35	Indiana	0
59	Tulane	6	40	Wisconsin	6
38	Southern Cal	7	21	Ohio State	0
			49	Southern Cal (Rose Bowl)	0
291		52	394		53

Notre Dame was unbeaten for the second year in a row and repeated as national champion. The Irish were again deep at every position, and sometimes the reserves were as good as the starters. In the backfield with Heisman-winning quarterback Johnny Lujack were halfbacks Terry Brennan and Emil "Six-Yard" Sitko, and fullbacks Jim Mello and Cornie Clatt. Lujack hit on 61 of 109 of his passes for 791 yards. Frank Tripucka had enough game time to connect on 25 of 44 passes. From left to right the linemen were Jim Martin, George Connor, Bill Fischer, George Strohmeyer, John Mastrangelo, Ziggy Czarobski, and Jack Zilly. Last season, when sophomore end Leon Hart came to look at the Notre Dame campus, line coach Ed "Moose" Krause went out into a rainstorm to meet Hart at the train station and get him bedded down for the night.

"No football player is worth pneumonia," Krause's wife insisted.

"You only say that because you've never seen Hart," said Ed.

During the season only Northwestern was able to score more than once against the Irish. Terry Brennan returned the opening kickoff 97 yards to a touchdown against Army, a series which was subsequently suspended because of heavy betting on the game. Outside the stadium, Brennan's dad was still talking with friends and never saw his son's great run. Southern Cal held the Irish to a slim 10–7 halftime lead, but the floodgates opened after a 76-yard touchdown run by Emil Sitko on the first play of the second half.

The other top team of 1947 was Michigan. It was Crisler's last team and his masterwork. He had been building it for two years with his war veterans, and most of them were now seniors. Many sports writers, including Grantland Rice, thought Michigan was equal to, if not better than Notre Dame.

Crisler's two-platoon system featured almost two complete teams for offense and defense. His previous teams had separate offensive and defensive linemen, but this season's squad used different backfields as well. The offensive linemen were light but quick, and able to hold their own against heavier opponents. At the ends were Dick Rifenburg and Bob Mann, the lean and mean tackles were Bill Pritula and captain Bruce Hilkene, and Dominic Tomasi and Stu Wilkins were the guards. Center John White passed the ball in Crisler's tricky spin system with the mechanical efficiency of a vacuum tube. The defensive line included Ed McNeill, Ralph Kohl, Quent Sickles, Joe Soboleski, Alvin Wistert, and Len Ford, linebackers Dick Kempthorn and Dan Dworsky, and defensive backs Bump Elliott, Jack Weisenburger, Wally Teninga, and Gene Derricotte. Place-kicker Jim Brieske hit 52 of 57 conversions.

The offensive backfield was one of the best, for a quartet of better ball handlers has seldom lined up together. At quarterback was Howard Yerges, clever as a treeful of owls at calling plays, on the wing was Bump Elliott, Jack Weisenburger was at full, and at tailback was Bob Chappius (pronounced happy us), an Air Corps vet who was shot down in World War II.

Crisler's backs were also light and fast, and his version of the single wing

Above: SMU's Doak Walker had a "knack for pulling off great deeds," said head coach Matty Bell. Opposite: Texas quarterback Bobby Layne.

even surpassed the trickery of Pop Warner's. The ball was usually centered to Weisenburger at fullback, who then began the numberless spins and fakes. Like a spinning bombshell, Weisenburger whirled, handed the ball to the tailback beside him, slipped it to the wingback or end coming across in front of him, or kept it himself and tore into the line, sometimes giving it to the quarterback on a buck lateral. A Houdini with the pigskin, Weisenburger often fooled the coaches with his legerdemain.

All this sleight-of-hand was turned loose from half a dozen different formations. The Wolverines bewildered their opponents with an endless

display of half spinners and full spinners, end-arounds, reverses, buck laterals, and quick openers in which the ball changed hands three or four times. Crisler also had a few T-formation plays called the alumni-T, just to let the old grads know that Michigan was keeping up with the times.

Crisler's passing game was equally potent. Chappius hit on 49 of 86 passes for 976 yards to lead the Big Ten for the second year in a row. Michigan's 173.9 yards passing, total offense of 412.7 yards, and 38.3 points per game led the nation.

The struggle for number one between Notre Dame and Michigan reversed itself four times during the year. After Michigan gave Pitt its worst beating ever, they were voted the top spot. The Irish supplanted them when Minnesota and Illinois each held the Wolverines to two touchdowns. Michigan regained first place as they started to run up big scores again, and the Fighting Irish squeaked by Northwestern. In November, Notre Dame won big, and on the final ballot they were voted number one.

On New Year's Day, Michigan equaled the score of its point-a-minute team in the first Rose Bowl game by inundating eighth-place Southern Cal, 49–0. A clamor arose for the Wolverines as the best team in the country. The AP took a special poll, and this time Michigan won by 226 to 119 votes. The December vote, however, remained final and Notre Dame kept its number-one spot.

In the second and last meeting between Bobby Layne and Doak Walker, Southern Methodist bested Texas by a single point. The Mustang coach, Matty Bell, gave the Dallas fans something to yell about right from the start. The kickoff was taken by Frank Payne who started to his right, then gave the ball to Paul Page running left. Page was convoyed 80 yards downfield by a picket line of blockers before he was pulled down on the Texas 19.

After three tries at the Longhorn line proved futile, Dick McKissack caught a Walker pass for a first down on the Texas four. On the following play Page scored on another reverse around the left side, and the Ponies were out in front with a 7–0 lead.

Texas came back in the second period after Byron Gillory's punt return of 40 yards. From the Mustang 30-yard line, Layne picked up 19 yards on a pair of passes to Dale Schwartzkopf and Max Bumgardner. Fullback Tom Landry went through tackle for the last 11 yards, and it was a spanking new game at seven each.

Just before the half, SMU went ahead for keeps. Walker and wingback Gil Johnson switched positions and lined up in a single wing left. From the Mustang 45, Johnson hit Walker on a curl-in pass over the line. Walker cut for the outside and sped down the sideline until he was knocked out-of-bounds at the one-yard stripe. On the next play, McKissack took it in for a 14–7 lead.

In the final frame, Texas gobbled up 72 yards on three quick strikes by Bobby Layne. He hit Schwartzkopf, Peppy Blount, and Gillory, who then scored. The point after was no good, and Texas lost its only game, 14–13, to wind up in fifth place.

Southern Methodist won all its games until it played Texas Christian in the finale. The Purple Gang had 12 points before the Mustangs got out of the gate. With the half ending, Walker faded back to pass, found no one open, and galloped 65 yards to score. After the half, Walker directed another touchdown drive of 50 yards to put the Ponies ahead by a point, 13–12.

There were 90 seconds left when TCU's Lindy Berry retreated to his 20-yard line and unleashed a long one to Morris Bailey at midfield. Bailey took it in full stride and kept on to the SMU goal. He was trapped on the Mustang 15 and lateraled to Charlie Jackson, who was downed at the eight-yard line by Bobby Folsom. On the first play, Berry pitched back to Pete Stout, who dropped the ball at the 10. After two Mustangs had their hands on it, Stout found the handle and ran over for the go-ahead score of 19–13.

It wasn't over yet. Walker fielded the kickoff and picked a path behind his blockers to the Froggie 30. The clock showed under a minute as Walker and Johnson again changed places. On third down, Johnson threw to Walker at the nine-yard line. There were 15 seconds left when Walker ran to the right and drew the Purple and White defenders with him. Johnson drifted left and connected with captain Sid Halliday for the tying touchdown.

Walker's leg-weary conversion hooked left to end the game, 19–19. SMU was conference champ, and Walker was hoisted to the shoulders of the crowd in a cheer. He gained 119 yards rushing, 136 passing, and 216 on six kick returns for a 471-yard total.

With only a tie to mar a perfect year, SMU played unbeaten Penn State in the Cotton Bowl. The 13–13 final revealed SMU's third-place rank and the number-four finish of the Lions. Led by guard Steve Suhey, PSU was the defensive champion, giving up 76.8 yards and three points each game. They also led in rushing defense, yielding 17 yards per game, the lowest ever recorded.

Army's 32-game unbeaten streak was broken early in the year by Columbia. Lou Little had one of his better backfields with quarterback Gene Rossides, halfback Lou Kusserow, and fullback Ventan Yablonski, but the player who ran the Cadets ragged was end Bill Swiacki. Swiacki's diving finger-tip catch in the end zone made it 20–14. Another sliding Swiacki catch on the three-yard line set up the 21–20 victory. His catches were voted the most decisive and spectacular of the season. Army guard Joe Steffy won the Outland Trophy as the year's best lineman.

After they played their last game as seniors a year later, Rossides and Kusserow approached coach Little.

"Thank you," they said, "for everything you've done for us."

"I never did anything for you boys," Lou replied in return. "You did everything for me."

Coach George Munger's Penn Quakers were another team giving Army trouble this year, as they played to a 7–7 tie. With all–American center Chuck Bednarik, tackle George Savitsky, and Skip Minisi in the backfield,

Penn had its first unbeaten season in 40 years and finished seventh with seven wins. Most of them were battle-steeled veterans, but they trained like sophomores. "They still had enthusiasm, that old college try," said Munger.

Under a new head coach, Johnny Vaught, Mississippi won the SEC title for the first time. On the way to a 9-2-0 year, they downed Kentucky and George Blanda, 14-7, and beat Tennessee for the first time, 43-14. Charlie Conerly was the passing leader with 1,367 yards on 133 of 233 attempts for a .571 average. His prime target, Barney Poole, was the year's leading receiver.

Back for their last year were Alabama's war babies, now all seasoned players. In the senior line were center Vaughn Mancha, guard Johnny Wozniak, and tackle Tom Whitley, all four-year men. The backfield also had four-year veterans in slick passer Harry Gilmer and in running backs Lowell Tew and Norwood Hodges. Two consecutive losses to Tulane, 21-20, and Vanderbilt, 14-7, made them dig in, but they won the rest of their games to end sixth. A 27-7 loss to Texas in the Sugar Bowl gave them an 8-3-0 mark.

1948

Michigan	(9-0-0)		Notre Dame	(9-0-1)	
13	Michigan State	7	28	Purdue	27
14	Oregon	0	40	Pitt	0
40	Purdue	0	26	Michigan State	7
28	Northwestern	0	44	Nebraska	13
27	Minnesota	14	27	Iowa	12
28	Illinois	20	41	Navy	7
35	Navy	0	42	Indiana	6
54	Indiana	0	12	Northwestern	7
13	Ohio State	3	46	Washington	0
			14	Southern Cal	14
252		44	320		93

Michigan and Notre Dame were again the two best teams in the land. A narrow win over Purdue early in the year hurt the Irish vote, and a come-from-behind tie in the last game put them in the runner-up spot. Michigan, on the other hand, registered a second unbeaten season in a row and extended its win streak to 23 games.

Having accomplished what he set out to do — a national champion team and a Rose Bowl win — Crisler retired as Michigan coach and became athletic director for the Wolverines. Bennie Oosterbaan, Michigan's all–American end, became coach. He inherited a squad whose defense returned virtually intact, and the names of Rifenburg, Derricotte, and captain Tomasi became the new heroes in maize and blue. Oosterbaan called Dworsky and Kempthorn "the greatest pair of linebackers Michigan has ever had," a pair who led Michigan to a 4.9-point scoring defense, the nation's best.

To replace Michigan's 1947 dream backfield, who had gone the diploma route, Oosterbaan installed Pete Elliott at quarterback and Tom Peterson as the spinning fullback. Two sophomores were at halfback, Chuck Ortmann at tailback and Leo Koceski on the wing. Ortmann was an able passer and runner, while Koceski was a good receiver and ran the reverse as well as anyone. Bob Erben was now offensive center, while sophomore Al Wahl, later an all–American tackle, worked at both offense and defense.

Oosterbaan was voted coach of the year, making it the first time this award went to two different coaches at the same school two years in a row. Oosterbaan represented the change that was taking place in coaching. He wore a sweatshirt and baseball cap in practice, often mixing it up with his squad when a demonstration was needed. His style was controlled fun, a departure from previous coaches, who were more like military drill instructors. The changing times dictated a change, for players were no longer fearful of authority. They now responded to coaching authority earned by respect, and an appreciation for players who were expected to sacrifice their skins for the good of the team.

Notre Dame had not lost in three years, and their unbeaten string was at 28 games. Only two ties smudged their three-year record: the dead-even heat with Army in 1946, and the tie with Southern Cal this year. Their 21 consecutive wins surpassed by one the total amassed by Rockne's first teams and his last.

Although Notre Dame lost Lujack, Connor, and Czarobsky, the Irish were still a powerful unit. Frank Tripucka at quarterback was joined by Brennan, Sitko, and Panelli in the backfield. Up front were center Bill Walsh, guards Marty Wendell and captain Bill Fischer (this year's Outland Trophy winner), tackles Ralph McGehee and Jack Fallon, and ends Jim Martin and Leon Hart.

Hart was first among Notre Dame receivers with 16 catches. He also averaged 9.8 yards on the end-around, good enough to be their top ball carrier. Leahy always beamed over Hart's 25-yard run with a pass against USC and then shaking off eight tacklers. "It was the most destructive run I've ever seen." he enthused.

Hart's catch of Tripucka's pass put the Irish ahead in the second quarter. On the last play before halftime, Tripucka was injured, and sophomore Bob Williams came in at quarterback.

After intercepting a pass in the third quarter, the Trojan attack came to life. Mixing up their runs and passes, Dean Dill and Jack Kirby moved toward the Notre Dame goal. Five minutes into the final period, Bill Martin scored to tie it at seven.

With the momentum on their side, USC made a carbon copy of its first touchdown. Dill and Kirby teamed for another 42-yard drive, and Martin went in for a second time to put Troy ahead.

There was 2:35 left when Bill Gay took the kickoff and ran to his left. A wall formed in front of him and shook him loose at the 20. He cut back

SMU's Kyle Rote drives through the line.

toward midfield and outran the Southern Cal defenders until he was pulled down on the 12-yard line.

The Irish had a reprieve. Williams faded to pass and threw to Gay in the flat. The pass was incomplete, but SC drew a flag for pass interference, and Notre Dame had a first down on the one. From there, Sitko took it in for the score. Steve Oracko calmly kicked the game into a 14–14 tie with 35 seconds to go.

On the train ride back home the Irish were still chanting, "God bless you, Steve Oracko. God bless you, Bill Gay."

Behind Charlie "Choo-Choo" Justice, North Carolina came in third. They had nine wins, tied William and Mary 7–7, and gave number-eight Georgia its only regular-season loss, 21–14. Like Crisler and Neyland, Tarheel coach Carl Snavely used the single wing. From his tailback spot, the triple-threat choo-choo ran, passed, bottled up the enemy with his quick kicks, and led the nation with a 44-yard punting average. UNC's only loss was to number-five Oklahoma in the Sugar Bowl, 14–6, as Bud Wilkinson, in his second year at OU, was about to rewrite football history.

SMU's Doak Walker won the Heisman Award. The SMU backfield of

Walker, Page, McKissack, and Johnson was strengthened by the addition of sophomore Kyle Rote. Walker boosted his chance for the Heisman by faking a pass late in the Texas A&M game, then sweeping around left end for the winning touchdown, 20–14.

With Bobby Layne gone, it was Walker against Clyde Scott of Arkansas. A Porker drive stalled after Scott returned the kickoff 61 yards, but Scott ran the next punt to the SMU 42. Three carries by Scott put it on the three, and from there Leon Campbell ran over.

A few plays later Scott was knocked unconscious, never to play for Arkansas again. Never impartial with the cards, Fate also dealt SMU a cruel hand, for Walker was knocked out on the same play. Both of them had to be assisted from the field.

Campbell took up where he left off before Scott was downed. Not long after, he got the ball on his 32 and went through left tackle. He cut back and was escorted down the sideline 68 yards for his second touchdown to put the Razorbacks in front, 12–0.

With Walker on the bench, the Mustangs limped along like a pony without a shoe. With less than four minutes to play, Gil Johnson connected on four straight passes to move the ball past midfield. From his wingback position, Rote took a reverse and rambled 35 yards to the Arkansas eight-yard line. From there, Rote lugged it over for the first SMU score. Walker trotted out and kicked the point after to make it 12–7.

SMU continued its derring-do. There were 50 seconds to go when Johnson threw to Wayne Burnett on the Porker 21. With 16 seconds left, Walker came in to give the game his magic touch.

A Johnson-to-Walker pass was intercepted, and the miracle was denied momentarily. The frantic Fayetteville fans received a rude jolt when Arkansas was penalized for offside. SMU still had the ball, and the Porkers lined up on their 16-yard line.

The clock had 12 ticks left. Johnson dropped back again, sidestepped the Arkansas rush, and completed one to Zohn Milam. Milam came down out of bounds, and the crowd relaxed once more.

There was time for one more play. Johnson faded to pass as the last five seconds slipped away. The gun went off, but Johnson threw to Page, who stepped over for the winning touchdown, 14–12, and the Ponies had earned a tenth-place finish.

The angry crowd ran on the field to see about the penalty which had wrenched victory from their grasp. Arkansas tailback Gordon Long became a hero in defeat as he led the officials to safety. He received a commendation from President Harry Truman and was awarded the Swede Nelson Sportsmanship Trophy for 1948.

Led by Norm Van Brocklin's tight spiral passes, Oregon had its best season in years. They won nine games, lost to national champ Michigan, tied Cal for the Pacific Coast Conference title, and ended ninth. Oregon lost to SMU in the Cotton Bowl, 21–13, and was the first PCC team to play in a bowl game other than the Rose Bowl. The Cotton Bowl was enlarged from 47,000 to 67,000 seats for the game, and was called "the house that Doak built."

Coach Lynn "Pappy" Waldorf put fourth-place Cal on the football map with an unbeaten season. Tackle Jim Turner and Jackie Jensen at full were the big guns for the Bears, but Bob Voigt's number-seven Northwestern team beat them in the Rose Bowl, 20–14.

In the first period, NU's Frank Aschenbrenner ran 73 yards for a score, and Jensen almost equaled it with a 67-yard touchdown dash. The game kept the crowd on the edge of their seats, as Cal held on to a 14–13 lead until late in the contest. With three minutes to go, Ed Tunnicliffe sewed it up for the Wildcats with another long run of 43 yards for the winning touchdown.

Red Blaik's two-platoon system helped rebuild Army into a sixth-place finisher. The Cadets won their first eight games and tied Navy in the closing minutes, 21–21. Counting the last two outings of 1947, Blaik ended the year with another unbeaten string of 11 games. The Cadets showed a solid front with guard Joe Henry and captain Bill Yeoman at center. The Penn game was also won in the final moments, as Army marched from its 26-yard line to the Penn 15. With 15 seconds left, Johnny Trent caught an Arnie Galiffa pass in the end zone for a 26–20 Army win.

1949

Notre Dame (10-0-0)			Oklahoma (11-0-0)	
49 Indiana	6		46 Boston College	0
27 Washington	7		33 Texas A&M	13
35 Purdue	12		20 Texas	14
46 Tulane	7		48 Kansas	26
40 Navy	0		48 Nebraska	0
34 Michigan State	21		34 Iowa State	7
42 North Carolina	6		39 Kansas State	0
28 Iowa	7		27 Missouri	7
32 Southern Cal	0		28 Santa Clara	21
27 Southern Methodist	20		41 Oklahoma A&M	0
			35 LSU (Sugar Bowl)	0
360	86		399	88

Notre Dame lost 13 men by graduation, but coach Frank Leahy had little trouble molding his returning lettermen into national champions again. Co-captains Hart and Martin were back at end and tackle, respectively, with Ralph McGehee at tackle and Bill Wightkin the other end. The guards were now Bob Lally and Frank Johnson, with Walt Grothaus at center and Bob Toneff at defensive tackle. The backfield still had Bob Williams at quarterback and fullback Emil Sitko. The halfbacks were Frank Spaniel and Larry Coutre.

The Notre Dame attack ground out 434.8 yards total offense each game

In 17 seasons at Oklahoma, Bud Wilkinson fashioned a 145-29-4 record for a winning .826 average, eighth among coaches.

to lead the nation. Emil Sitko gained 712 yards rushing and closed out his four-year career with 2,226 yards on 362 carries for a 6.1 average and 25 touchdowns. Bob Williams threw for 16 touchdowns and completed 83 of 147 passes for 1,347 yards. Hart caught 19 passes for 257 yards and five touchdowns, and won the Heisman Award and Maxwell Award as the player of the year.

This year it was Southern Methodist which gave the Irish a scare in the last game. With Doak Walker on the sideline nursing an injured leg, Kyle Rote became a one-man gang as he took the fight to the Irish. Notre Dame led at the half 13-0, but Rote scored in the third quarter to cut it to 13-7. The Irish came back to take a two-touchdown lead, but early in the final period Johnny Champion ran 64 yards to the Notre Dame one. Rote took it in to make it 20-14. Moments later, the Dallas stands went wild with joy as Rote scored again, but Irish linebacker Jerry Groom got a hand on the point after to keep it at 20-20.

Notre Dame showed its championship caliber by coming right back with a 57-yard touchdown march. They went overland in ten straight-ahead plays, with halfback Billy Barrett going over at the corner from six yards out. Not a single pass was thrown.

SMU came back on a drive from its 20, but at the Irish 28 Rote was stunned momentarily. A Fred Benners pass put them on the five-yard line, but on fourth down Rote's pass was intercepted by Groom, and the game ended a few minutes later at 27–20.

Notre Dame had completed another undefeated season for the fourth year in a row, and their unbeaten string was at 38 games. They were at the top of the football world.

At Oklahoma, Bud Wilkinson was commencing a success story second to none in college football. His team won 11 games this year, including a Sugar Bowl win over LSU. After losing their first game the previous year, Oklahoma was now riding a 21-game winning streak. OU also won the Big Seven crown for the second year in a row, a feat they continued with monotonous regularity through 1959. Gone from last year's squad were guard Buddy Burris and quarterback Jack Mitchell, whose 23.6-yard punt return average (922 yards on 39 returns) is an all-time record. Mitchell was helped by his wife, Jeanne, who drilled him on the plays which OU ran in its games.

Wilkinson's football education had come a long way since he played for Bernie Bierman at Minnesota. During the war, he was assistant coach at Iowa Pre-Flight, where Don Faurot had used the split-T formation. Wilkinson installed the split-T at Oklahoma because modern defensive play gave different assignments to the defense on each play. A defensive end could charge, drift out, or drop back. In the split-T the quarterback ran, lateraled, or passed according to what the defensive end did. Wilkinson felt his success was due to the way the Sooners took advantage of the reaction by the defense. Wilkinson also acknowledged his debt to the defensive ideas of Bob Neyland at Tennessee, who was a disciple of Pot Graves, line coach for Percy Haughton at Harvard.

Wilkinson's real contribution was his personal touch which sparked the Sooners, for he had a deep integrity and moral fiber that everyone respected. Like Lon Stagg, Wilkinson was a disciplined individual who could hardly say a bad word about anyone.

Wilkinson thought this year's team was the equal of any he had at Oklahoma. The Sooner line included ends Bobby Goad and Jim Owens, tackles Wade Walker and Leon Manley, guards Stan West and Dee Andros, and center Charley Dowell. At quarterback was Darrell Royal, Lindell Pearson and George Thomas (who was first in scoring with 117 points), were the halfbacks, and at fullback was Leon Heath. The excellent quality of this team is revealed by the fact that five of them later became head coaches.

Oklahoma had two teams of almost equal ability. They were not separate offensive and defensive units, but each team played both ways and was alternated about every seven minutes. OU was the country's best in rushing defense with 55.6 yards per game, and Wilkinson was selected as the coach of the year.

Led by all–American guard Rod Franz, third-place Cal won all ten games, but was shaded by sixth-place Ohio State in the Rose Bowl, 17–14. They lost in the last few minutes just like the year before. Bob Celeri went back to punt near his goal, but the center snap bounced at his feet. He tried to punt on the run, but the ball dribbled out on the Cal 13. Jim Hague kicked the winning points, the first Rose Bowl win by a field goal.

Army won nine contests, inflated its unbeaten string to 20 games, and snapped Michigan's win streak at 25 with a 21–7 win. A tenacious defense nabbed four passes and held the Wolverines to three completions. The two-platoon system started last year by Blaik kept the Army players fresh. The running of Jim Cain and Gil Stephenson, and Arnie Galiffa's passes to Dan Foldberg gave number-four Army a balanced attack. In the 38–0 win over Navy, the Middies never crossed the midfield stripe once.

Jess Neely's Rice Owls won all their Southwest Conference games, and then beat North Carolina in the Cotton Bowl, 27–13. The team had a lot of war vets who were now in their last year, and they blocked and tackled with the cool efficiency of pros. They lost only to number-nine LSU in the second game, 14–7, but their ten wins earned them a fifth-place finish.

The only close shave on the way to the conference crown was with Texas, which was always pushing someone to the throne room. The Steers moved in front early on a blocked punt by Ray Stone that rolled out of the end zone for two points. Texas pushed over a pair of touchdowns to lead 15–0 late in the third frame.

The Owl veterans then buckled down. Their stubborn-jawed line-backers, 232-pound Joe Watson and 212-pound Gerald "Bones" Weatherly, shut down the Texas attack. On offense, the hammer-and-anvil blocking of the Rice forwards opened holes for Billy Burkhalter and Gordon Wyatt and gave protection for the passing of Vernon Glass. In a matter of moments, Texas led only by one. With eight ticks left, Jim "Froggie" Williams kicked an 18-yard field goal for a 17–15 win, and the Owls flew high from then on.

Michigan lost to Army and Northwestern, 21–20, played Ohio State to a 7–7 tie, and was seventh. Led by Clayton Tonnemaker at center, tackle Leo Nomellini, and ends Gordy Soltau and Bud Grant, Minnesota handed Ohio State its only loss, 27–0, but defeats by Michigan, 14–7, and Purdue, 13–7, put them eighth.

College of the Pacific ended in the top ten for the only time in its history. After a 7–6 win over San Francisco, COP had a 56.8 average in its next ten games, with the 34–7 win over Cincinnati the lowest score. Quarterback Eddie LeBaron's tosses to end John Rohde, and scoring by halfbacks Eddie Macon, Don Brown, and Bruce Orvis helped Bill McFarland set a new mark of 54 conversions.

VII. Football in Transition

1950

Oklahoma (10-1-0)			Army (8-1-0)		
28	Boston College	0	28	Colgate	0
34	Texas A&M	28	41	Penn State	7
14	Texas	13	27	Michigan	6
58	Kansas State	0	49	Harvard	0
20	Iowa State	7	34	Columbia	0
27	Colorado	18	28	Penn	13
33	Kansas	13	51	New Mexico	0
41	Missouri	7	7	Stanford	0
49	Nebraska	35	2	Navy	14
41	Oklahoma A&M	14			
7	Kentucky (Sugar Bowl)	13			
352		148	267		40

The big news early in the season was that Notre Dame's four-year un-beaten streak expired at 39 games. It was stopped by Stu Holcomb's Purdue team which built a 21–0 halftime lead. Notre Dame closed to seven on scores by Jim Mutscheller and John Petitbon, but a Dale Samuels pass to Mike Maccioli widened Purdue's winning margin to 28–14. Gone from the Irish attack were the precision passing and endless backs which made Notre Dame unbeatable during the past four years. It was bound to happen sooner or later, but the pressure was off and Frank Leahy could sleep nights again.

The flowering of Oklahoma football came into full bloom this year as the Sooners went all the way to the top. Wilkinson lost 18 of his first 25 men and all of his starters except Leon Heath, but he rebuilt the Sooners into na-tional champs. One of the main reasons for OU's success was all–American tackle Jim Weatherall. Other good reasons were Frank Anderson at end, co-captains Harry Moore at center and Norm McNabb at guard, and safety Buddy Jones.

OU won all ten of its games and went to the Sugar Bowl for the third year in a row. After derailing North Carolina and the great choo-choo, Charlie Justice, two years ago, and destroying Louisiana State last year, the Sooners quickly became America's favorite team. Except for an opening-season loss to Santa Clara in 1948, 20–17, Oklahoma had not lost in three years. It would be 1959 before OU under Wilkinson was to lose a conference game.

Oklahoma's opponent on New Year's Day was Kentucky, winner of the Southeastern Conference for the first and only time. The man behind Kentucky's success was Paul "Bear" Bryant. The Wildcats also won ten games and were number three nationally. Then they dropped their last game to Tennessee, 7–0, on a snow-covered field and skidded to seventh place.

Bryant was ready for Oklahoma. He planned to put the ball in the air, use his ace punter, Dom Fucci, to keep OU in its own territory, and pressure the Sooner quarterback with his defense, whose 4.8 points and 153.8 yard total defense per game led the nation that year. He defensed the split-T by having his pair of all–American tackles, Walt Yowarsky and Outland winner Bob Gain, float wide from time to time. This gave Bryant four ends, which took away the quarterback option to keep the ball or lateral it.

Kentucky had to punt after the kickoff. On the second play by Oklahoma, Yowarsky and Gain broke through and shook the quarterback loose from the ball, then recovered it on the Sooner 26. On the next play, Babe Parilli passed to Shorty Jamerson in the end zone, and it was 7–0 with less than three minutes gone.

Just before the half, UK scored again. They went 81 yards in seven plays, most of it on a 51-yard pass from Parilli, "Sweet Kentucky Babe," to right end Al Bruno. Bruno was brought down short of the goal, but Jamerson bucked over for his second touchdown, and Kentucky was ahead by 13 points.

During the season, the Sooners came from behind to win in the Texas A&M, Texas, and Nebraska games, and it looked like their second-half pizazz would carry them to victory again. In the third quarter, Oklahoma marched 68 yards deep into "Youkay" territory, only to be thrown back at the two-yard line.

Not long after, Kentucky covered another Oklahoma fumble. They pushed to the Sooner nine-yard line where their attack short-circuited. After a field goal try by Bob Gain went astray, the Sooners got going for their only score, a drive kept alive by a pair of fourth-down plunges by Leon Heath. Quarterback Claude Arnold pitched out to halfback Billy Vessels, who then lofted a 17-yard pass to Merrill Green in the end zone to make it 13–7.

Oklahoma lost its last chance on another fumble with seven minutes left at their 32. Kentucky moved to the Sooner 13-yard line before they had to surrender the ball. The gun sounded as a last-ditch pass by Vessels was intercepted at midfield.

Oklahoma's winning streak was terminated at 31 consecutive victories. The UK defense, led by their pair of eat-'em-alive tackles, Gain and Yowarsky, recovered five of Oklahoma's seven fumbles. In the first half, Yowarsky had caused or been in on three of them and was voted the game's most valuable player.

Earl Blaik had Army rolling for the third consecutive year. Their unbeaten streak of 28 games went back to 1947, only to be ended in the game with Navy. They were first in scoring defense with 4.4 points allowed per game, and Jim Cain and Gil Stephenson led a group of lean-limbed backs on the attack. The quarterback and punter for the team was Bob Blaik, the coach's son.

The free-wheeling Army team scored 258 points in its first seven games, but it was deluged by a Bay Area rainstorm and only beat Stanford 7-0 on a pass from Blaik to Dan Foldberg. Still weary from their West Coast trip, coach Eddie Erdelatz's Middies outmuscled the Cadets and pinned them to a second-place finish.

Both Navy touchdowns came in the second period. After Navy intercepted a Blaik pass, the first of five pilfered by the Midshipmen, Navy sailed to its first tally, quarterback Bob Zastrow scoring from the seven-yard line. With 20 seconds left in the half, Zastrow threw 30 yards to end Jim Baldinger for the touchdown.

The Cadets made it 14-2 after the half when Bill Rowekamp and Bob Volonnino tackled Zastrow behind his goal for a safety.

The last quarter was wild. Both teams lost the ball twice on fumbles, three Army passes were intercepted, and a Navy punt was blocked. Army knocked at Navy's goal three times, but came up empty on each try. They lost the ball on an interception at the 21. Then they gave it up on downs at the 22. They got the ball back again and went to the six, only to lose it on a fumble. After a punt was blocked on the nine they moved to the three, but lost it again on John Gurski's second interception of the period.

After chasing others to the title for the past few seasons, Texas finally was SWC champion. They were unbeaten except for a one-point loss to Oklahoma in the final moments. Their veteran line with guard Bud McFadin, tackle Ken Jackson, and Don Menasco at linebacker kept the number-three Steers in every game.

When Texas met unbeaten Southern Methodist, the Ponies were number one and riding the crest of five victories. Both squads raced neck and neck like two horses in the home stretch. Texas moved in front on fullback Byron Townsend's dive over the line, and SMU tied it on a Kyle Rote touchdown. Texas countered with another blast by Townsend, and SMU matched it with Rote's second score. Texas went ahead on a pass from quarterback Ben Tompkins to end Ben Proctor. SMU quarterback Fred Benners passed to end Ben White for a touchdown, but the missed conversion left it 21-20. A safety made it 23-20, and Texas was home by a nose.

Fresh from two years at Kansas and two at Navy, coach George Sauer, Nebraska's 1933 all-American fullback, took over at Baylor and gave Texas another close game with his new T-formation. The score was knotted at 20-20 late in the contest when Texas safety Bobby Dillon gathered in a punt and parked it in the Bears' end zone 84 yards away for the winning points, 27-20.

Texas lost its second game in the Cotton Bowl to Tennessee in the last three minutes, 20-14. Coach Blair Cherry, who was Bible's successor, Wes Fesler at Ohio State and Harry Stuhldreher at Wisconsin, resigned at the end of the season because of the pressures of big-time football.

At Tennessee, General Neyland, who won his star in World War II, still disdained the T-formation. The Vols won ten games with their single-wing offense, losing only to Mississippi State, 7–0, early in the year. At tailback was Hank Lauricella, who threw 27 yards to Bert Rechichar for the winning score against Kentucky.

In the Cotton Bowl, Texas led at the half, 14–7. The Vols' superb defensive line of Ted Daffer, Pug Pearman, Bill Jasper, Bud Sherrod, and Doug Atkins shut out Texas in the second half. After fullback Andy Kozar scored Tennessee's second touchdown, Pat Shires missed the conversion which would have tied the game and was fighting back the tears when he returned to the bench.

"Don't worry about it, Pat," Neyland said to his dejected place-kicker. "We didn't come out here to tie them."

It was not long before Tennessee drove 43 yards to a score to turn back the Steers. Inasmuch as Oklahoma and Texas lost in bowl games and Tennessee won, Vol fans thought they were number one. But in those days the vote was taken before the bowl contests, and Tennessee had to be content with fourth place.

Number-five California was unbeaten for the third straight year except for a 7–7 tie with Stanford. Fullback Johnny Olzewski and all–American guard Les Richter led Cal to the Rose Bowl for the third year in a row. Again UC lost in the last period, as ninth-place Michigan came from behind to win, 14–6. Two Don Dufek scores and a stubborn defense won it for the Wolverines.

Coach Charlie Caldwell's Princeton team was another single-wing squad which caused a few ripples. Like Bierman and Neyland, Caldwell's single wing was based on two-on-one blocking to insure short but sure gains. When the end and wingback took out the defensive tackle, Caldwell's power sweep was similar to Jock Sutherland's great teams at Pitt. When the Tigers were rolling, the spins and laterals looked more like Fritz Crisler's Wolverines.

The Princeton line, led by center Redmond Finney, gave the Tiger backs plenty of running room. Triple-threat tailback Dick Kazmaier was the big weapon in the Princeton attack, especially on the run or pass option play, but on the wingback reverse Bill Kleinsasser and Bob Unger were a joy to watch. No less a magician on the pivots and fakes was Jack Davison at fullback. All got superior blocking from quarterback George Chandler.

Counting the last four games of 1949, Princeton now owned a winning streak of 13 after going through the season unbeaten. They won the Big Three title handily by beating Harvard 63–26, and Yale 47–12, in successive wins. Their 38.8-point average was the best in the country and gave them a sixth-place finish. Charlie Caldwell was chosen coach of the year.

The last game was against Dartmouth on the "day of the big wind." Hurricane Flora broke plate glass windows and uprooted trees along the eastern seaboard. The referee handed the ball to the center on every play to keep it from being blown away. A punt into the open end of Palmer Stadium

Princeton great Dick Kazmaier later became president of the National Football Foundation and Hall of Fame.

was useless, while a punt with the wind zoomed downfield like a rocket. Kazmaier scored one touchdown in the 13–7 win, a 37-yard scurry with the wind which whisked him along like a bionic man in football pads.

Caldwell was amazed at the scramble to the T-formation. He didn't like the way the quarterback had his back to the play as he faded to pass. He also thought his single wing had as much deception as the T, and that its clever maneuvers were just as crowd-pleasing. Caldwell gave three reasons for the switch to the T: alumni displeasure at not keeping up with new ideas, players who mistakenly thought the single wing was outdated, and coaches who had to fill stadiums with interesting football.

With halfback Sonny Grandelius and two-way Dorne Dibble at end, Biggie Munn's Michigan State squad beat Michigan 14–7 for the first time since 1937, lost only once and finished eighth.

Led by fullback Fred Cone, Frank Howard's Clemson team beat Miami in the Orange Bowl 15–14, as guard Sterling Smith nailed Frank Smith for a last-period safety to come in tenth at 9-0-1.

Ohio State's Vic Janowicz won the Heisman as a junior. He beat out other deserving juniors such as Johnny Bright of Drake, who had 2,400 yards total offense. He also outvoted sophomore Bobby Reynolds of Nebraska whose 157 points led in scoring, and senior worthies Reds Bagnell of Penn and Kyle Rote of SMU.

Don Heinrich and Hugh McIlhenny gave Washington a one-two combo which made UW the coast's most exciting team. Heinrich's 134 completions on 221 attempts for 1,846 yards and a .606 average was the nation's best. "Hurryin' Hugh" had 1,107 yards rushing and a 6.8-average per carry. McIlhenny was one of the few ball carriers who didn't have to be told to cut in the open field in order to escape a pursuer from behind.

1951

Tennessee (10-1-0)		Michigan State (9-0-0)	
14 Mississippi State	0	6 Oregon State	0
26 Duke	0	25 Michigan	0
42 Chattanooga	13	24 Ohio State	20
27 Alabama	13	20 Marquette	14
68 Tennessee Tech	0	32 Penn State	21
27 North Carolina	0	53 Pitt	26
60 Washington & Lee	14	35 Notre Dame	0
46 Mississippi	21	30 Indiana	26
28 Kentucky	0	45 Colorado	7
35 Vanderbilt	27		
13 Maryland (Sugar Bowl)	28		
386	16	270	114

Disaster struck Earl Blaik of Army a month before the season began. Ninety cadets were caught possessing or distributing exam information, and they were dismissed from the Military Academy for violations of the honor code. Most of last season's strong squad were missing when practice started. With a team made up of plebes and yearlings (freshmen and sophomores), the brave old Army team carried on through a year of two wins and seven losses.

In his next-to-last season as coach, General Neyland turned out another national champion at Tennessee. Operating from Neyland's bone-jarring single wing attack, all–American tailback Hank Lauricella again was the Vols' gazelle-gaited ground gainer. His stylish triple-threat talents included

Michigan State tackle Don Coleman was named on Notre Dame's all-opponent team for three consecutive years: 1949, 1950, and 1951.

the quick kick, a big part of the Tennessee offense. Lauricella specialized in the coffin-corner punt, rated the best since Harry Kipke rolled them out in the corner for Michigan three decades earlier.

General Neyland's last great team dispelled any doubts that the single wing formation was through. A stickler for meticulous play execution, Neyland's Big Orange team ran plays with blackboard perfection. The Vols also felled opponents downfield with precision blocking that would have made Rockne himself drool. A main cog in the Tennessee attack was Jim Hahn. From his wingback position, he cut down would-be tacklers and helped the Volunteers roll up big scores in almost every game. Noticeably absent, however, was the General's perennial parsimonious defense, for this year's champs were touched for 116 points, anathema to any Neyland follower. But offense was now the name of the game, and it was no longer a rout when Tennessee scored two touchdowns.

Last year's Tennessee fans thought their team was number one after surviving the bowl games best. Because the polls had closed in December, the Vols finished fourth in 1950. The situation was reversed this year, as Tennessee was voted national champion and then lost to Maryland in the Sugar Bowl. Even the Fates did not lean on Neyland too hard, for it took them only a year to make it right for the General and his followers.

In preparation for its entrance into the Western Conference, Biggie Munn had Michigan State moving in championship form. This season's squad won all its games, was in and out of the top spot throughout the year, and placed second to Tennessee in the final AP and UPI votes (United Press International coaches' poll), which began in 1950. After their only loss last year, the Spartans won the last six games and now had a winning streak of 15.

Although Michigan State football was well on the way to its best years, the Spartans did not look like champions much of the time. In six of their nine games, they came from behind or broke a tie to win. Typical was the Ohio State game in which the Green and White gladiators were behind ten points with ten minutes to play. After getting close at 20–17, they pulled it out with two minutes left. Left half Tom Yewcic took a pitch from quarterback Al Dorow and faked a run right. Then he fired a long cross field pass to Dorow, who caught it on the OSU 11 and ran in for the win.

In the Spartan line were center Jim Creamer, guards Frank Kapral and Deane Garner, tackles Marv McFadden and Don Coleman, and ends Bill Carey and Bob Carey. Defensively, they had guard Dick Kuh, tackle Bill Horrell, and ends Joe Klein and Ed Luke. At linebacker were Ed Timmerman and Bill Hughes, the halfbacks were Rex Corless and John Wilson, with Jim Ellis at safety.

Tackle Don Coleman was on everyone's All-America team. In a day of two-platoon specialists on either offense or defense, Coleman played both ways and on special teams for three years. Against Penn State, he made every Spartan tackle on kickoffs and punts. After fullback Dick Panin scored on the first offensive play and Michigan State beat Notre Dame for the second year in a row, Frank Leahy said Coleman "was the best lineman we've faced all year," repeating what he had said last season. Coleman's number 78 was retired, the first jersey so honored at Michigan State.

Jim Tatum's Maryland squad rolled through nine wins with a 39.2-point average to lead the nation, and then beat number-one Tennessee in the Sugar Bowl. It was the first time a team from College Park was unbeaten and untied, and it ranked them third.

Maryland play-caller Jack Scarbath, one of the best split-T quarterbacks in the country, kept the defense guessing with his pitch-or-keep deception on the option play. With halfbacks Chet Hanulak, Ralph Felton, and Bob Shemonski to take the option pitch when fullback Ed "Mighty Mo" Modzelewski didn't, the Terps' backfield was the equal of any in the land. In their line were ends Paul Lindsay and Lou Weidensaul, tackles Joe Moss and Stan Jones, guards Pete Ladygo and Bob Ward (Maryland's first all-American), and center Tom Cosgrove. On defense were guards Ed Kensler and Bill Maletzky, tackles Dick "Little Mo" Modzelewski and Bob Morgan,

Wisconsin's Alan Ameche was the first freshman to lead the Big Ten in rushing, and he finished his career with 3,212 yards.

and Paul Nestor and John Alderton at the ends. Roy Martine and Dave Cianelli were linebackers, Bernie Faloney and Ed Fullerton were at half-back, with Joe Petruzzo at safety. In the Sugar Bowl, the Terps' separate offensive and defensive units dominated the General's Tennessee Volunteers, and the Maryland fans chanted "We're number one" all the way back to College Park.

For the second time in five years, Ray Eliot had Illinois in the Rose Bowl

Bobby Dodd had a winning .713 game average at Georgia Tech (165-64-8).

on New Year's Day. Stellar players for the fourth-place Illini were guard Chuck Studley, center Chuck Boerio, quarterback Tommy O'Connell, half-back John Karras, fullback Bill Tate, and safety Al Brosky, the all-time career interception leader with 29.

Illinois was unbeaten in ten games, including a 40-7 win at Pasadena over number-seven Stanford. The only blot was a 0-0 tie with Ohio State, now coached by Woody Hayes. One week later, Sam Rebecca clinched the Big Ten title for the Illini with a 26-yard field goal against Northwestern for the only points of the game.

Eighth-place Wisconsin's total defense of 154.8 yards per game and 5.9 points scoring defense led the nation, but in the second game the Illini gave

Coach Johnny Vaught built Mississippi into a football power with a 190-61-12 record (a .745 average).

Wisconsin some of its own medicine. The Badgers had a first down three feet from the goal, but linebacker Chuck Boyle taunted the Badger quarterback: "Send Ameche at me!" Ameche thundered at Boyle like a wild horse, but Boyle lassoed him for a three-yard loss. After four plays, the ball rested on the six-yard line, and Illinois went on to win, 14–10.

Coach Eliot liked to call it the proper state of mind. A locker room orator cut from the same cloth as Knute Rockne and Bill Roper, his glowing speeches appealed to his young charges. During World War II, he held hands with his 17-year-old players, and even now his genuine emotion touched the hearts of hardened veterans who knew the meaning of honesty, courage, and honor.

Ray Eliot called it heart. "You must have heart," he told his team. "You who lack the heart, you who have lost the spirit and hope, you who have lost self-confidence—you are *dead,* sir. You are done. You must have heart."

Frank Gifford would have liked to play for Eliot. Gifford was a great believer in heart, or as he called it, desire. The ABCD's of football—and life—have always been ability, brains, courage, but the greatest of these is desire. "Desire," Gifford said, "is the key. Physically, there isn't much difference in players; mentally, there's a tremendous difference. You have to *want* to make the sacrifices to keep going."

Many writers have said that Gifford was the most ill-used back in modern college football. Strong enough to hit the line and shifty around the ends, he was skilled in throwing from the halfback option or catching a pass himself. He could punt and was called the "Trojan Toe" for his place kicking accuracy. He was Southern California's best offensive player, yet he toiled on defense for coach Jeff Cravath. Here, his sure tackling and pass defense talents also stood out.

In his senior year, Gifford was the starting tailback under SC's new coach, Jess Hill. He led the Trojans to a 7-3-0 record and helped end California's three-year unbeaten string in Pacific Coast Conference play. Behind 14-0 at the half, Gifford rallied the Trojans for a 21-14 win, including a 70-yard touchdown run for Southern Cal's first score.

Gifford, master of the big play, saved the best for last. As the game neared its end, another dazzling run by Gifford put the ball deep in Cal territory. USC tried the option play with Gifford ready for a pass or run. Cal's all-American guard, Les Richter, had the angle on Gifford and was set to throw him out-of-bounds. Gifford whipped the ball underhanded, like a softball pitcher, beneath Richter's upraised arms. The ball zinged straight to Dean Schneider, who caught it for the tying score.

There was more. With time running out on fourth down, yet another Gifford run of 48 yards put the ball on the Cal two-yard line. On the last play of the game, Gifford went over for the winning touchdown. His jubilant teammates carried Gifford off the field on their shoulders.

Mississippi's Arnold "Showboat" Boykin also ended his career in a blaze of glory. In his last game he scored all seven touchdowns, still a record, as the Rebs beat Mississippi State, 49-7.

Another southern team which made history this year was coach Bobby Dodd's fifth-place Georgia Tech team. They didn't lose in 12 outings, and only a 14-14 tie with Duke tainted their perfect season. Dodd gave full credit to his coaching staff for putting together a team which did not beat itself with mistakes. Led by guard Ray Beck, tackle Lum Snyder, and quarterback Darrell Crawford on offense, and defensive tackle Lamar Wheat, the White and Gold were hard to beat. In the waning moments of the Orange Bowl game, they intercepted a pass, and then Pepper Rodgers kicked a field goal to down Baylor 17-14 and give them their eleventh win.

Princeton again finished in sixth place. They won another nine games and ran their winning streak to 22 straight. Cornell was beaten 53-15, Harvard 54-13, and Yale 27-0, and the Tigers were awarded the Lambert Trophy for the second year in a row as the best team in the East. The orange-striped knights also won the Big Three crown for the fifth consecutive time, surpassing Percy Haughton's four straight titles from 1912 to 1915.

Dick Kazmaier was the back of the year and outdistanced all others in the Heisman voting. He led the nation in total offense with 1,827 yards on 861 rushing and 966 passing. He scored nine touchdowns, passed for another 13, and completed 62.6 percent of his passes. In three seasons he gained 4,357 yards and threw 35 touchdown passes, not bad for an outdated single wing tailback.

George Sauer had Baylor in the running again with a ninth-place finish. Larry Isbell and Stan Williams succeeded Adrian Burk and end John Ison as the Bears' passing threat, and guided them to an 8-2-1 mark, one of their best. They placed second in the conference for the third year in a row, but Isbell and battery mate Williams at end had the Green and Gold in every game.

Under coach Joe Kuharich, the San Francisco Dons had their first perfect season and their first all–American, Ollie Matson. They won all nine games, and then abandoned football. "All-the-way Ollie" was the leading rusher in the nation with 1,566 yards, just four short of Fred Wendt's 1948 record. Matson also scored 21 touchdowns, one short of the 22 scored by Bobby Reynolds last year. His 226.3-yard average this season in all-purpose running made him second to the 1937 record of Whizzer White.

The Dons also had a good passing game with quarterback Ed Brown throwing to ends Merrill Peacock, Ralph Thomas, and 6'7" Bob St. Clair. Brown was backed up by Bill Henneberry who took over when Brown was injured in the second game. In the last game of the year Loyola went up and down the field but couldn't score a touchdown, although their quarterback, Don Klosterman, led the country in passing with 1,843 yards. The Dons finished the year with the best rushing defense in the land, holding opponents to 51.6 yards each game. Members of this rib-popping defense were guards Vince Tringali and Greg Hillig, 6'5", 243-pound Mike Mergen and 6'3", 225-pound Gino Marchetti at the tackles, ends Bob Weibel and Bob St. Clair, and linebackers Burl Toler and Roy Giorgi.

1952

Michigan State (9-0-0)			Georgia Tech (12-0-0)		
27	Michigan	13	54	The Citadel	6
17	Oregon State	14	17	Florida	14
48	Texas A&M	6	20	Southern Methodist	7
48	Syracuse	7	14	Tulane	0
34	Penn State	7	33	Auburn	0
14	Purdue	7	30	Vanderbilt	0
41	Indiana	14	28	Duke	7
21	Notre Dame	3	45	Army	6
62	Marquette	13	7	Alabama	3
			30	Florida State	0
			23	Georgia	9
			24	Mississippi (Sugar Bowl)	7
312		84	325		59

Biggie Munn's Spartans were unbeaten for the second year in a row and were national champs. They had another nine wins and enlarged their win streak to 24 games. Coach Munn took full use of the two-platoon system.

He put three offensive and defensive teams on the field and simply ran opponents into the ground.

The Spartans were loaded not only with ability but brains. They ran offensive patterns from the single wing, double wing, straight-T, split-T, wing-T, and short punt formations. It took speed and intelligence to master these multiple assignments, and slow thinkers and slow movers found themselves on the bench most of the time. Fresh players were shuttled in and out constantly, and Munn's troops had to be sharp mentally and physically. Munn called it "a game of chess at high speed."

Only Oregon State and Purdue put a damper on Biggie Munn's manifold legions. In the second game of the year, Oregon State, which finished 2-7-0, took MSU down to the wire. The Spartans missed a field goal try with seven seconds to go, but a Beaver penalty gave Gene Lekenta another attempt, which was good. Purdue also held MSU to only two touchdowns, but Michigan State waylaid a Boilermaker pass late in the game to save the seven-point win.

Biggie Munn was voted coach of the year. One of his chief tasks had been to rebuild the Spartan offensive line which was decimated by diplomas. The defensive platoon finished the year as the country's best against the rush, limiting opponents to 83.9 yards each game. Standout linemen were center Dick Tamburo and guard Frank Kush. The light but fast backfield was paced by halfback Don McAuliffe and Tom Yewcic, now at quarterback.

At Georgia Tech, Bobby Dodd also got maximum use out of the two-platoon system. Each man on the squad played either offense or defense, and not one regular or sub was used both ways in the same game. The team had so much depth that injuries to key men hardly slowed the Tech attack. They won all 12 games, including a Sugar Bowl win over seventh-place Mississippi, and were second.

Dodd called this year's Rambling Wreck the best team he had seen at Tech since he joined the staff in 1931. The defense was a shade behind number-eight Tennessee, whose 166.7 yards per game total defense was first. Center Pete Brown, co-captains George Morris at linebacker and offensive tackle Hal Miller, end Buck Martin on offense, and halfbacks Leon Hardeman and Bobby Moorehead were rated all–American. Other top men were guard Orville Vereen and end Cecil Turner on defense, and offensive guard Ed Gossage.

The second game of the year with Florida was one of the two close games they had. It was won in the last seconds on a field goal by Pepper Rodgers, who duplicated his game-winning performance of last New Year's Day. The other close game was with number-nine Alabama, led by halfbacks Bobby Marlow and Corky Tharp. The Tide took a first-period lead on a field goal by Bobby Luna. Georgia Tech crashed back with a touchdown, and then turned away three scoring drives by Alabama in the second half for the win.

Notre Dame's 7-2-1 mark put them third. They tied Penn 7–7 in the opener, then beat tenth-place Texas 14–3. The Longhorns had ends Tom

Don McAuliffe (left), Spartan captain, with coach Biggie Munn.

Stolhandske and Carlton Massey, guards Harley Sewell and Phil Branch, and a top backfield of T. Jones at quarter, and Gib Dawson, Billy Quinn, and Dick Ochoa. A week later the Irish lost to Pitt, 22–19, but came back to win six of their last seven games.

In one of the big games of the year, two-way player Johnny Lattner of Notre Dame helped upset Oklahoma 27–21. He set up the second Irish score by intercepting a pass and returning it to the Sooner seven-yard line. In the next Irish drive, he caught a pass and took it to the OU 27. On the winning march, he banged 17 yards to the Oklahoma seven on a key play. All-purpose Lattner was also credited with two game-saving tackles on Billy Vessels and Buddy Leake.

In the last game of the year, Southern California came to South Bend unbeaten in nine games, but was upended by Notre Dame 9–0. The Trojans lost the ball five times on interceptions and fumbled three times in the frigid weather. One of the fumbles on the USC 19 led to the only touchdown of the game. The Irish drove inside the 10-yard line, and then picked up a first down on the four with their sucker shift, which pulled the Trojans offside. Another Southern Cal fumble on the Notre Dame goal turned the ball over to the Irish on their one-yard line.

Oklahoma, beaten only by Notre Dame and tied by Colorado in its opener, 21–21, finished in fourth place. In the Sooner line were all–American center Tom Catlin and tackles Ed Rowland and Jim Davis. Eddie Crowder at quarter, halfbacks Buddy Leake and Billy Vessels, and Buck McPhail at fullback gave OU a versatile attack which was first in scoring with a 40.7-point average.

On the way to the Heisman Trophy, Vessels rushed for 1,072 yards and passed for another 209. He scored 15 times as a sophomore, missed most of the previous year due to an injury, and had 18 this season for a total of 35 career touchdowns. Like many skillful runners, Vessels was neither big nor fast, but quick. He ran at top speed in a step or two, and often hit the hole as the block was being made. He also had great balance, and when he was hit he stayed upright while the tacklers seemed to slide off. Then his quick acceleration put him in high gear almost immediately.

Southern Cal lost only to Notre Dame. When the Trojans met UCLA for the right to play in the Rose Bowl, both teams were unbeaten. Number-five USC was led by tailback Jim Sears, end Don Stillwell, center Lou Welsh, guard Bob Cox, and tackles Charley Ane and Bob Van Doren. Number-six UCLA had an ace tailback in Paul Cameron, a triple-threater whose faking on the option play set up many scoring passes to ends Ernie Stockert and Ike Jones. The Uclan defense was led by guard Jim Salsbury, tackle Charley Doud, and linebackers Terry Debay and all–American Donn Moomaw.

UCLA held a 12–7 halftime lead on Pete Dailey's field goal, a safety, and a Bill Stits score when guard Elmer Willhoite ran back a stolen pass 72 yards to the Bruin eight. Sears, who scored on a 70-yard play after getting a lateral from Al Carmichael on the UCLA 36, now threw to Carmichael in the flat for a 14–12 win.

Led by linebackers George Timberlake and Marvin Goux, the Trojans, who were first in scoring defense with 4.7 points each game, finally gave Pacific Coast fans something to cheer about. After six humiliating losses to Big Ten teams, USC beat Wisconsin in the Rose Bowl, 7–0. Tackle Dave Suminski, end Don Voss, Jim Haluska at quarter, and fullback Alan Ameche kept the Badgers in it, but they lost on a last-half Rudy Bukich pass to Carmichael.

Although coaches at major schools objected, the NCAA Rules Committee changed the substitution rule and abolished two-platoon football at the end of the year. The change was made in behalf of over 50 small colleges who had abandoned big-time football because they could no longer compete financially. They were not able to afford the large coaching staff with its offensive and defensive specialists, and the cost of larger squads with more scholarships which did not fill their empty stadiums.

The Football Rules Committee acted in behalf of all schools, whether big or small. The new rules stated that any player who was removed from the first and third periods could not return to action in those two quarters. Players removed before the final four minutes of the second and fourth quarters could return in the last four minutes before the half and at the end of the game.

1953

Maryland (10-1-0)			Notre Dame (9-0-1)		
20	Missouri	6	28	Oklahoma	21
52	Washington & Lee	0	37	Purdue	7
20	Clemson	0	23	Pitt	14
40	Georgia	13	27	Georgia Tech	14
26	North Carolina	0	38	Navy	7
30	Miami (Florida)	0	28	Penn	20
24	South Carolina	6	34	North Carolina	14
27	George Washington	6	14	Iowa	14
38	Mississippi	0	48	Southern Cal	14
21	Alabama	0	40	Southern Methodist	14
0	Oklahoma (Orange Bowl)	7			
298		38	317		139

Number-one Maryland was unbeaten in the regular season and champs of the new Atlantic Coast Conference, as the Southern Conference divided again. It was the culmination of a dream for ex–Terp football coach Curley Byrd, now Maryland's president. Unhappily, the Sooners ended their perfect year in the Orange Bowl.

Maryland led in scoring defense with a 3.1 points per game average. Jim Tatum's Terps were also first in rushing defense, holding opponents to 83.9 yards per game. One reason for Maryland's defensive strength was that they made the switch to one-platoon football better than most squads. Quarterback Bernie Faloney had played in the defensive backfield the year before, and Maryland tackles Stan Jones and Bob Morgan were the backbone in last season's one-way lines. Center John Irvine, guard Jack Bowersox, and end Marty Crytzer were the blockers in front of halfbacks Ron Waller and Chet Hanulak, and fullback Ralph Felton. In the defensive backfield were Joe Horning and Dick Nolan, whose 90-yard punt return for a touchdown against Clemson was a new Maryland mark.

Notre Dame was number one for the first eight weeks of the season. After the tie with Iowa, they slipped to second place. During the game, they faked injuries twice in order to gain more time. With Iowa leading in the first half, the Irish faked an injury to stop the clock, then pushed over a touchdown to knot the score. Near the end of the game, the ninth-place Hawkeyes led again, but Notre Dame again faked another injury. The clock was stopped, and with two seconds to go left end Jim Shannon caught a touchdown pass to tie the score. It was a ploy as old as the game, but Leahy's critics never let him hear the end of it.

Leahy called this year's team his best ever. The line was first rate with tackles Frank Varrichione and Art Hunter, guards Ray Lemek and Minnie Mavraides, and center Jim Schrader. Quarterback Ralph Guglielmi and captain Don Penza at right end aided the Irish passing attack. Fullback Neil Worden and halfbacks Johnny Lattner and Joe Heap gave Notre Dame a husky ground game.

Lattner won the Heisman Trophy with his 60-minute performance in game after game. He was tireless on defense and seemed to get stronger as the game wore on. He intercepted four passes during the season, caught 13 on offense, and was the team's punter. It was none other than Lattner who passed Gipp's 3,064 yards in all-purpose running with a new Notre Dame mark of 3,116 yards.

Leahy collapsed at halftime against Georgia Tech and retired at the end of the season. His 107-13-9 record for a .864 average is second to Rockne's and ahead of George Woodruff's 142-25-2 record (a .846 average) and Percy Haughton's 96-17-6 (a .832 average).

Another team which successfully made the transition to one-platoon play was Michigan State, which finished in third place. Many Spartan players were established stars in either offense or defense, but now they had to learn new aspects of the game as if it was their first day of practice. Defensive end Don Dohoney mastered the techniques of offensive play so well that he became an all–American. Other MSU players who stood out both ways were center Jim Neal, tackle Larry Fowler, and end Ellis Duckett.

The Spartans won their first four outings and padded their win streak to 28 games, the longest in Michigan State history. Purdue stuck them with their only loss, 6-0, but they ended the regular season with eight wins. The Purdue contest was the only time they did not come from behind to win, a feat they performed often. Michigan State and seventh-place Illinois both had five wins and a loss in Big Ten play, but the Spartans went to Pasadena. The Illini's J.C. Caroline was the country's top rusher with 1,256 yards, but MSU's pony express backfield of Tom Yewcic, LeRoy Bolden, Billy Wells, and Evan Slonac was no less exciting.

In the Rose Bowl, desire ignited the ability, brains, and courage of the Spartans. Down 14–0 against UCLA, MSU blocked a punt to slice the lead to 14–7 just before the half. Then they took the second-half kickoff and marched to the tying touchdown. Quick openers with Yewcic handing off to a halfback or fullback built a 21–14 lead by the end of the third quarter. The Bruins narrowed it to 21–20 before Billy Wells returned a Paul Cameron punt 62 yards to a touchdown and a 28–20 win.

Oklahoma finished the season with an 8-1-1 record and was ranked number four, just as in 1952. They lost their opening game to Notre Dame by almost the same score as the previous year, and then tied Pitt, 7–7. OU won its last nine games and began a string which was to become the longest winning streak in college football history.

After the first two games Wilkinson switched his personnel, trying to find his best two-way men. Max Boydston went from end to fullback and back to end, and halfback Buddy Leake shared the quarterback job with Gene Calame. The strength of the OU squad was its intrepid line, where guard J.D. Roberts won all–American recognition. By the end of the year, Oklahoma led the nation in rushing with an average of 306.9 yards each game.

The Sooners crowned their season by beating Maryland in the Orange Bowl. The high-flying Terrapins were held in check by the OU line that stopped Maryland twice in the first half, once on the four-yard line and again on the six. Oklahoma then drove 80 yards in the second quarter for the game's only points, with halfback Larry Grigg scoring on a 25-yard dash. Injured Maryland quarterback Bernie Faloney came off the bench and took the Terps to the OU 30, but the Sooner defense again stiffened and held on to win.

Other than the Rose Bowl loss to Michigan State, fifth-place UCLA lost to Stanford by a single point. They blew a 20–7 halftime lead, as Stanford quarterback Bob Garrett, the country's top passer with 118 of 205 for a .576 average and 1,637 yards, completed 18 of 27 passes and kicked three conversions to down the Uclans, 21–20.

UCLA coach Henry "Red" Sanders called his team a one-platoon version of his 1952 squad, and he praised their team spirit, that of practicing and playing hard. Sanders said he learned how to handle players from his coach at Vanderbilt, Dan McGugin, the fundamentals of blocking and tackling while an assistant to Josh Cody at Clemson, and the single wing from his friend, Bob Neyland.

The Cotton Bowl provided the biggest New Year's Day excitement. Sixth-place Rice with its twin terrors, Dick Maegle and Dave "Kosse" Johnson, hosted Alabama in the annual affair. The Tide went in front on a touchdown by Tommy Lewis, but Maegle put Rice ahead 7–6 with a dashing 79-yard scamper. Then quarterback Bart Starr directed Alabama to the five-yard line but fumbled. Maegle was off on a 95-yard gallop for another score when Lewis leaped off the Alabama bench and brought Maegle down on the Tide 38-yard line. Maegle was promptly awarded a touchdown as 75,504 fans stared in disbelief. Maegle added another scoring caper of 34 yards and was the game's MVP as Rice won it readily, 28–6.

Georgia Tech had its 31-game unbeaten string of 29 wins and two ties halted by Notre Dame. The number-eight Engineers were 8-2-1 after a 13-6 loss to Alabama and a 0-0 split with Florida. Led by center Larry Morris and tackle Bob Sherman, they stopped tenth-place West Virginia in the Sugar Bowl and became the first team to win three successive bowl games. Hard running by Glenn Turner, Leon Hardeman, and Bill Teas enabled Pepper Rodgers, who shared the quarterback post with Bill Brigman, to toss scoring passes to ends Sam Hensley, Jim Durham, and Henry Hair to give the Yellow Jackets an early lead and a 42-19 win.

1954

Ohio State	(10-0-0)		UCLA	(9-0-0)	
28	Indiana	0	67	San Diego Navy	0
21	California	13	32	Kansas	7
40	Illinois	7	12	Maryland	7
20	Iowa	14	21	Washington	20
31	Wisconsin	14	72	Stanford	0
14	Northwestern	7	61	Oregon State	0
26	Pitt	0	27	California	6
28	Purdue	6	41	Oregon	0
21	Michigan	7	34	Southern Cal	0
20	Southern Cal (Rose Bowl)	7			
249		75	367		40

It took Woody Hayes just four years to produce an undefeated season at Ohio State. They won seven conference games, the first team to do so since Stagg's 1913 champions. The Buckeyes were unbeaten in ten games and voted national champs in the AP poll. UCLA, however, was voted number one by the UPI coaches' poll.

A main reason for Ohio State's success was the bulldozer blocking of its personnel. End Dean Dugger and fullback Hubert Bobo (who also did the punting) paved the way for Buckeye halfbacks Howard "Hopalong" Cassady and Bob Watkins. Above all, 6'2", 250-pound guard Jim Parker cleared out the enemy whenever the yardage was critical. His straight-ahead blocking gave birth to the Bucks' "three yards and a cloud of dust" offense. On end runs, Parker pulled out like a runaway rhino to smooth the path for Cassady and running quarterback Dave Leggett.

Other members of Woody's platoon who performed notably were center Ken Vargo, guard Dave Williams, tackles Dick Hilsinki and Frank Machinski, and end Dick Brubaker. Equally important were the reserves, many of whom were 60-minute performers. They were halfbacks Jerry Harkrader and Jim Roseboro, center Bob Thornton, guard Jim Reichenbach, tackle Don Swartz, and end Bill Michael.

Hopalong Cassady was a local boy like Chic Harley who could crush opponents with a single play. In the Wisconsin game, the Badgers were driving to increase their 7-3 lead. Cassady stole a pass and returned it 88 yards for a touchdown to turn the game around. In the last game of the year, Michigan was knocking at the Buckeye goal to take the lead. After a goal-line stand late in the game, Cassady's 60-yard sprint set up the touchdown which broke the deadlock and let Ohio finish the season unbeaten.

It didn't take long for Woody Hayes to make his personality known nationwide. At student of military history like "Hurry Up" Yost, Hayes looked at a football field and a battlefield in the same way. The Rose Bowl had been deluged by a rainstorm before the game, and the field was a soggy mess. When the Buckeye and Trojan marching bands chewed it up even more at halftime, Woody was irate. "Let's keep them off the grass," he growled.

The Rose Bowl officials were speechless. The bands had rehearsed a month, and Woody was asked to clarify his remark.

"Listen," he began, "millions of people saw them on television this morning during your Rose Bowl parade, so who cares if they don't strut their stuff on the football field at halftime? The field is already ankle-deep in mud. Let's save what's left for the football players."

Woody was overruled. A Buckeye win didn't mellow him, for he allowed no one to talk to his players after the game.

"Nobody talks to my kids," Woody said resolutely. Then at the traditional postgame interview, he kept the sportswriters waiting 20 minutes before he let them in.

While Woody Hayes was auditioning for the year's Mr. Grouch award, Red Sanders of UCLA was voted coach of the year. Sanders was one of the new breed of coaches who mixed discipline with fun. His style was to give a personal demonstration on proper technique, often punctuating his performance with a pun or caustic comment. A dedicated disciple of Neyland's single wing offense, his teams embodied hard-charging linemen, backs who could block as well as run, and a triple-threat tailback who could run, pass, and punt.

UCLA led the nation in rushing and scoring defense, holding opponents to 73.2 yards and 4.4 points per game. Their 28 pass interceptions were also tops. Besides the deep men, UCLA's success was due to its 4–4 defense of four linemen and four linebackers that choked off the quick openers of the T-formation.

The Uclans were also first in the country in scoring with 367 points for an average of 40.8 points per game. In the line were captain John Peterson at center, guards Sam Bogoshian, Jim Salsbury, and Hardiman Cureton, tackles Joe Ray and all–American Jack Ellena, and ends Bob Long and Bob Heydenfeldt. At quarterback was Terry Debay, the wingback was Jim Decker, in the tailback slot was Primo Villanueva, with Bob Davenport at fullback.

Oklahoma won all ten games and increased its winning streak to 19 straight. This year's OU team won because of outstanding personnel instead of squad depth as before. In Max Boydston and Carl Allison, the Sooners had two quality ends. The line was above average with guard Bo Bolinger, tackle Don Brown, and all–American center Kurt Burris. Left half Buddy Leake and quarterback Gene Calame also helped keep the OU victory string alive.

The Sooners mowed down opponents like grain at harvest time. The team may have lacked explosive power, for all of their touchdowns were

Ohio State's Jim Parker, a guard on the modern all-time All-America team.

scored on sustained drives. The third-place Sooners won the Big Seven title for the seventh straight time, but conference rules did not permit a repeat visit to the Orange Bowl.

Frank Leahy's successor at Notre Dame was 25-year old Terry Brennan. He led the Irish to a number-four finish with nine wins and a loss to Purdue, 27-14. Purdue quarterback Len Dawson was responsible for all 27 points, as he threw four scoring passes and kicked three extra points. Dawson said that Purdue usually gave Notre Dame a good go because many squad members hadn't made the team there, so they enrolled at Purdue and loved nothing better than to beat the Irish. Ralph Guglielmi's 3,117 yards passing made him the first Irish signal-caller to exceed 3,000 yards.

Coach Eddie Erdelatz took Navy to seven victories, won the Lambert Trophy as the East's top team, and came in fifth. They lost to Pitt, 21-19, and Notre Dame, 6-0, after fumbling the tying touchdown at the goal. It was the best Navy team since 1945.

Leading the Middies was quarterback George Welsh, a split-T operator who ran the option play like a master. An able runner and passer, his main target was all-American Ron Beagle at end, who also made the option play work with his bull-like blocking.

The Army-Navy game showcased the two top offensive teams of the year. The seventh-place Cadets also won seven and lost two, and finished as the rushing leader with 322 yards each contest. They were also first in total offense with 448.7 yards per game, but they were outdueled by the Middies in a wild 27-20 thriller which kept the 100,000 fans in Philadelphia's Municipal Stadium roaring from start to finish. The win over Army was the fourth in five tries for Eddie Erdelatz, a record which was matched by Welsh himself when he took over as Navy coach two decades later.

Navy's appearance in the Sugar Bowl was the first time they had been in a bowl game since they tied Washington 14-14 in the 1924 Rose Bowl. Injuries and sickness hurt them before the game, but the Sailors still dominated Mississippi in a 21-0 win.

Led by all-American tackle Rex Reed Boggan, Johnny Vaught's sixth-place Mississippi Rebels finished the year as the nation's defensive leader, holding opponents to 172.3 yards total offense each game. Halfbacks Allen Muirhead and Jim Patton and fullback Paige Cothren took them to nine wins and a 6-0 loss to Arkansas. But it was their uninspired play against the Middies that riddled their number-one defense with first downs (20-5) and total yards (450-121). Navy fullback Joe Gattuso picked up 111 yards rushing and scored twice, with halfback John Weaver getting the other points.

Maryland won seven but lost to Miami and UCLA, tied Wake Forest 13-13, and came in eighth. Center John Irvine, guards Jack Bowersox and Tom McLuckie, end Bill Walker, halfback Ron Waller, fullback Dick Bielski, and defensive back Joe Horning starred.

Wisconsin fullback Alan "the Horse" Ameche won the Heisman. He earned his nickname because his running style was more like a gallop than a sprint. He averaged 4.7 yards per carry, and hometown friends later gave him 3,212 dollar bills, one for each yard he gained. He was the meat of coach Ivy Williamson's attack and kept the number-nine Badgers in contention when he was suited up.

Coach Bowden Wyatt brought Arkansas in tenth. In the lineup were fullback Hank Moore, halfbacks George Walker and Preston Carpenter, and all-American guard Bud Brooks. They won eight but lost 21-14 to SMU on Frank Eidom's scoring catch, the only touchdown pass against them all year. They also lost to LSU 7-6, and Georgia Tech in the Cotton Bowl, 14-6. SMU end Ray Berry later caught passes from John Unitas for the Baltimore Colts and coached New England to the Super Bowl.

At the end of the year, Michigan State athletic director and former Spartan coach, Biggie Munn, spoke out against one-platoon football. He said it brought back the 220-pound player who could withstand the rigors of 60-minute football, and forced the "good little man" from the game. He thought football had stepped backward to the early days when mass was more important than finesse.

Football equipment also took a verbal beating. Researchers said the face guard did not protect the wearer, and that it was "legalized murder." They also claimed knee pads did not protect the knee. The biggest criticism was leveled at shoe cleats, which dug into the turf and prevented a player from pivoting. Jammed into the ground while running, the ankle and knee joint suffered injury, especially when hit by another player from the side.

1955

Oklahoma (11-0-0)			Michigan State (9-1-0)		
13	North Carolina	6	20	Indiana	13
26	Pitt	14	7	Michigan	14
20	Texas	0	38	Stanford	14
44	Kansas	6	21	Notre Dame	7
56	Colorado	21	21	Illinois	7
40	Kansas State	7	27	Wisconsin	0
20	Missouri	0	27	Purdue	0
52	Iowa State	0	42	Minnesota	14
41	Nebraska	0	33	Marquette	0
53	Oklahoma A&M	0	17	UCLA (Rose Bowl)	14
20	Maryland (Orange Bowl)	6			
385		60	253		83

Oklahoma won all 11 games and expanded its winning streak to 30 victories. They were voted number one in both the AP and UPI polls. The Sooners were not a brawny outfit like the 1949 champions and did not handle the ball as well as the 1952 squad, but their lightning-limbed offense had the highest marks in rushing with 328.9 yards per contest, in total offense with 410.7 yards, and in scoring with an average of 36.5 points.

The Sooners capped their season with an impressive win over Maryland in the Orange Bowl. Their team speed was so fast that they ran off plays before Maryland could set its defense. After stopping a Maryland drive on the OU five-yard line and giving up a touchdown in the second quarter, Oklahoma zipped past the Terps in the last half. Tommy McDonald lit the fire on a 33-yard punt return in the third period. Then he caught the Terrapin defense napping with his specialty, the halfback option pass, which was good for 19 yards. Two plays later he ran around end four yards for the tying touchdown, and the real estate rush was on.

Wilkinson called McDonald the best halfback he ever coached. He could not only carry the mail, but he could deliver it through the air with his running pass, a play in which he completed 70.8 percent of his tosses. During the season, McDonald had a rushing average of 6.8 yards each carry and scored 16 touchdowns.

Oklahoma's first-team line from left to right included Joe Mobra, Cal Woodworth, Bo Bolinger, Jerry Tubbs, Cecil Morris, Ed Gray, and John Bell. Backfield men were quarterback Jim Harris, halfbacks McDonald and Bob Burris, and fullback Billy Pricer.

In its second season under coach Duffy Daugherty, Michigan State finished in the number-two spot. Daugherty was voted coach of the year, but gave credit for his success to the Spartan team. He called captain Carl "Buck" Nystrom "the best guard I've seen in my nine years at Michigan State." He also praised quarterback Earl Morrall, who passed for 941 yards, completed 42 of 68 passes for a .617 mark, and averaged 42.9 yards on his punts.

Morrall had a stand-up passing style which was beautiful to see. He held the ball high over his helmet and released it with a flip of his wrist. It more than compensated for his scrambling, which gave the crowd a fit as he looked for a receiver. Morrall said his success was due to his peripheral vision, a talent which allowed him to spot secondary receivers when the primary one was covered. Just as fascinating was his slick ball handling, which made fans feel they were watching a master craftsman at work.

Maryland was unbeaten until they met Oklahoma in the Orange Bowl and finished in third place. Led by its all–American center and linebacker Bob Pellegrini, guard Jack Davis, tackles Ed Heuring and Mike Sandusky, and end Russ Dennis, the Terps were first in rushing defense with 75.9 yards per game. Early in the year, they stopped number-four UCLA with minus 26 yards total offense. Maryland signal-caller Frank Tamburello, with quick pops to halfback Ed Vereb, was one of the best split-T workmen around. But injuries to fullback Tom Selep and tackle Joe Lazzarino disabled the Terrapin entry in Jim Tatum's last season at College Park.

Big Ten champ Ohio State could not return to the Rose Bowl, so Michigan State took their place. Clarence Peaks scored once and tossed to John Lewis for the other, but after Sam Brown was hurt Ronnie Knox brought UCLA down the field on passes to Rommie Loudd and Jim Decker, with Doug Peters diving over to tie it at 14 a piece.

In the final minutes, MSU's Gerry Planutis missed a field goal try, but UCLA was penalized to the five-yard line for unsportsmanlike conduct. On the next play, Knox was rushed and threw to an ineligible man, and the ball was spotted at the one-yard line. Knox punted to his 34, but the Uclans interfered with the catch and were penalized another 15 yards to the 19-yard stripe.

The comedy of errors continued. Michigan State fumbled the ball but recovered. Then the Spartans were penalized 15 yards for holding, but Earl Morrall got ten back on a completed pass. Michigan State fumbled once more and again recovered. MSU threw a kicking tee on the field and drew a five-yard penalty for delay of game. With seven seconds left, Dave Kaiser kicked the Spartans to victory with a field goal from the 31-yard line.

With guard Jim Parker still out front, Hopalong Cassady won the Heisman Award. He was also aided by a sure-handed backfield that fumbled less than once a game. In his four years at Ohio State, Cassady scored 222 points, surpassing the school record of 201 points scored by Chic Harley during World War I, and played 55 minutes of every game for the fifth-place Buckeyes.

Texas Christian, under coach Abe Martin, won the SWC title and finished sixth. Shifty Jim Swink, a tricky runner from the Lone Star state where halfbacks grow like prairie grass, was the nation's top scorer with 125 points. TCU won nine games and lost only to Bear Bryant's Texas Aggies, 19–16. Against tenth-place Mississippi in the Cotton Bowl, TCU had a 13–0 lead but the Rebs cut it to 13–7 by halftime. Late in the game, Mississippi faced a fourth-and-three at the Froggie 45. Quarterback Eagle Day hit Paige Cothren on a first down, and Ole Miss soon had a 14–13 win.

Led by guard Franklin Brooks, number-seven Georgia Tech was first in scoring defense with 4.6 points allowed a game. They had eight wins, tied Tennessee 7–7, and lost to Auburn on two missed conversions, 14–12. The 7–0 win over Pitt came after Bobby Grier, the first black man to play in the Sugar Bowl, interfered with end Don Ellis on a pass, and Tech had a first down at the goal, where quarterback Wade Mitchell went over behind Jimmy Morris at center. Two Pitt drives were halted, once at the one-yard stripe before the half, and at the five-yard line in the closing minutes.

Terry Brennan's veteran team at Notre Dame won eight games, lost to Michigan State and USC, 42–20, and came in ninth.

1956

Oklahoma (10-0-0)			Tennessee (10-1-0)		
36	North Carolina	0	35	Auburn	7
66	Kansas State	0	33	Duke	20
45	Texas	0	42	Chattanooga	20
34	Kansas	12	24	Alabama	0
40	Notre Dame	0	34	Maryland	7
27	Colorado	19	20	North Carolina	0
44	Iowa State	0	6	Georgia Tech	0
67	Missouri	14	27	Mississippi	7
54	Nebraska	6	20	Kentucky	7
53	Oklahoma A&M	0	27	Vanderbilt	7
			7	Baylor (Sugar Bowl)	13
466		51	275		88

Oklahoma won all its games again and swept to the national title for the second year in a row. The murderous Sooner attack was first in the land with 391 yards rushing, 481.7 yards total offense, and 46.6 points per game. They were also second in total defense with 193.8 yards per game, and topped the AP poll all year except for one week in October and another in November.

In their second game, the Sooners used five teams in burying K-State, and set a modern mark of 32 straight wins. After branding the Texas Longhorns with their worst loss in half a century, Oklahoma was called "the greatest football team of all time."

After giving Notre Dame its worst-ever defeat at home, OU was flat. Colorado blocked a punt for one touchdown, switched from the single wing to a T-formation and scored on a pitchout, then added a third on a double reverse for a 19–6 halftime lead.

Wilkinson was mad at intermission. He told his squad that they didn't deserve to wear the red jerseys they had on. He was concerned about the game, the team, the tradition, the streak.

The second half was an entirely different game. Oklahoma, with workman-like precision, took the kickoff and drove 80 yards to a touchdown. In the third quarter, the Sooners scored again for a 20–19 lead. When Colorado plugged the middle to stop the handoffs of Jim Harris to Billy Pricer, Harris went wide with a delayed pitchout to Tommy McDonald or Clendon Thomas. Colorado was turned back, and OU had its thirty-sixth consecutive victory.

The Sooners closed the season with four more runaway wins. They moved across the Plains like a June tornado, engulfing Iowa State, Missouri, Nebraska, and Oklahoma A&M. In the Nebraska game, Oklahoma ran and passed for 656 total yards. OU now had 40 unbroken wins, surpassing the 39 set by the University of Washington.

The Sooner line operated with mechanical efficiency. They rose up as one and bucked ahead three or four yards at a crack, a sight as inspiring as a punt turning over or the end-over-end wobble of a field goal. The men in this unit who moved as one man were all–American center Jerry Tubbs, guards Bill Krisher and Joe Oujesky (who replaced injured Ken Northcutt), tackles Ed Gray and Tom Emerson, and ends John Bell and Don Stiller.

The mainspring of Oklahoma's success was Bud Wilkinson. He organized the football program at every level from recruiting to readiness to public relations. A man of high moral principles, he had no trouble getting athletes from the Bible Belt who were his kind of people. His players were from church-going families all over the state, and the OU campus made them feel the warmth of the small-town atmosphere they grew up in. They did not feel like a tiny cog in a large football factory, and they were given as much adulation as any Saturday hero ever received.

Wilkinson's preparation for a game began as early as Sunday morning when scouting reports were discussed. On Sunday evening the finished report was given to the squad. Monday was devoted to offensive plans and Tuesday to defensive plans. By Wednesday lunch, these reports were in the hands of the players, who were told to digest them by afternoon practice. Habit patterns of OU opponents were detailed, and by game time the Oklahoma players knew as much about the other team as they did about themselves.

Wilkinson's success bred alumni fever throughout the state. OU grads quietly informed talented players that the Norman campus still provided a quality education in an unsophisticated setting reminiscent of a former time. With the zeal of a religious crusade, many Oklahoma boys felt it their duty to play for the Big Red team. With the possible exception of Notre Dame and a few state schools, this evangelical spirit was felt nowhere else.

In playing for coach Neyland at Tennessee, Bowden Wyatt had fulfilled the first of his life's ambitions. After a successful program at Wyoming and Arkansas, Wyatt was back coaching at his alma mater to complete his second ambition. In his second year as coach of the number-two Vols, Wyatt compiled a perfect 10-0-0 season and was voted coach of the year.

Tennessee played Bobby Dodd's Georgia Tech team in Atlanta for the SEC crown early in November. Both men had learned under Bob Neyland at Tennessee, and both teams reflected the emphasis on defense and kicking which Neyland taught. The game became a classic Neyland struggle of hammer-hard defense, giving the ball to the other team on a punt, and playing for the breaks.

In the first quarter, Johnny Majors quick-kicked 68 yards on first down to the Tech 17-yard line. Kenny Owen and Johnny Menger each rolled a Georgia Tech punt dead inside the Tennessee five-yard line. Just before the half, another Majors punt died on Tech's two-inch line. At halftime, the score was still 0-0.

The third quarter produced the only touchdown of the game. The Vols sent one man deep and one short on a weak-side run-or-pass option play. Buddy Cruze, the short receiver, caught the ball on the Tech 35 and turned upfield. As he cut sharply, two defensive backs plowed into each other on the tackle, and Cruze raced to the one-yard line. On the next play, Tommy Bronson took it in and that was the ball game, 6-0. Before it was over, four Tennessee punts were blown dead inside the five-yard line and five more inside the 10, mainly off the toe of tailback Bobby Gordon.

Back in Knoxville 200 miles to the north, the downtown section celebrated the victory with blaring horns and parading cars far into the night. On the Tennessee campus, the slogans on the locker room wall silently saluted the General's philosophy: "the team that makes fewer mistakes WINS."

In the Sugar Bowl, these words undid the Vols as Baylor intercepted four passes for a victory, after UT had lost only six interceptions during the regular year. While guards Bill Glass of Baylor and John Gordy of Tennessee banged heads, Del Shofner set up the first Baylor score with a 54-yard run to lead at halftime, 6-0. Sammy Burklow's conversion put Tennessee ahead 7-6, but they gave it back in the last period on a fumble at their 15-yard line, which led to the winning touchdown by Buddy Humphrey.

After an apprenticeship in the Palouse country of Washington state, Forest Evashevski took over at Iowa. The Hawks won their first Big Ten title since 1921, and were ranked number-three nationally. Iowa boasted an aggressive defense led by tackle Alex Karras and an attack which kept opponents guessing. Quarterback Ken Ploen could throw long or short, and the running game used a wing-T, or flanker-T formation, with single wing blocking power.

Iowa's only loss was to seventh-place Michigan in November. The Wolverines went out in front on a 25-yard field goal by all–American end Ron Kramer, but Iowa took advantage of two Michigan miscues to lead at the half, 14-3. Michigan took the last half kickoff and marched 69 yards to a touchdown, and then put on an 80-yard drive for a 17–14 victory with six minutes remaining.

On the next weekend, Iowa scored in the first five minutes against Minnesota, and then stopped the Gophers six times inside their territory for a 7–0 win. One week later, end Jim Gibbons caught a 17-yard scoring pass to defeat Ohio State 6–0, and tie them for the Big Ten lead. Next week Michigan dumped the Bucks, 19–0, and the Hawkeyes went to Pasadena where they downed tenth-place Oregon State, 35–19. Beaver coach Tommy Prothro quarterbacked Duke in the 1942 Rose Bowl, but this was his first trip to Pasadena since the wartime game was played in North Carolina.

Fourth-place Georgia Tech's sinewy single wing offense led them to victory in every game except the loss to Tennessee. The interior line of tackles Carl Vereen and Ormand Anderson, guards Don Miller and Allen Ecker, and Don Stephenson at center cleared out the opposition like a rush-hour policeman. When both guards pulled and joined all three backs on their power sweeps, it was like a cattle drive in front of the ball carrier. Bobby Dodd's gifted backfield of Wade Mitchell, Toppy Vann, Paul Rotenberry, George Volkert, and Kenny Owen had smooth sailing all year.

The Engineers played only as hard as they needed to against Kentucky, but Southern Methodist was a bit tougher. Don Miller's blocked punt brought a safety, but it took a third-quarter drive to catch the Ponies, 9–7. It also took a fourth-period score to beat Duke 7–0. Then came the rematch with Pitt and all–American end Joe Walton in the Gator Bowl. Quarterback Corny Salvaterra starred for Pitt, but Jerry Nabors at end caught the go-in-front pass to lead at the half, and Tech never lagged in a 21–14 win.

Bear Bryant's fifth-place Texas Aggies breezed through their season with a 9-0-1 record, and were slowed down only by Houston in a 14–14 tie. On a hurricane-swept afternoon at Kyle Field in College Station, they gave TCU its only conference setback, 7–6, as Loyd Taylor's conversion was good. An even greater cause for rejoicing was the 34–21 victory over Texas, A&M's fourth win at Austin in 32 tries. Halfback John David Crow and Jack Pardee at fullback put zest in the Aggie attack. Out in front of them were center Lloyd Hale, guards Dennis Goehring and Dee Powell, tackles Charley Krueger and Jim Stanley, and ends Gene Stallings and Bobby Keith. Although A&M won the SWC title, they did not go to the Cotton Bowl due to recruiting violations by overzealous alumni.

Miami won the state title with 20–7 wins over both Florida and Florida State. Miami coach Andy Gustafson (Army backfield coach during the Blanchard-Davis era) had another strong backfield in quarterback Sam Scarnecchia, halfback John Varone, and Don Bosseler at fullback, their leading rusher. Miami also led in total defense and rushing defense with 189.4 yards and 106.9 yards each game. When the final AP poll was taken in December, Miami had an 8-0-1 mark and finished sixth. Their season was blunted only by a 7–7 tie with Georgia until they lost their last game to Pitt, 14–7.

With injuries crippling not only sophomore tackles and ends, but also junior guards and center, Notre Dame was 2-8-0, including a 47–14 defeat by ninth-place Michigan State. Paul Hornung took up the slack and carried home the Heisman. He hit on 59 of 111 passes, and had 420 yards on 94 tries for a 4.5-yard average.

Guard Jim Parker of Ohio State won the Outland Trophy as the year's best lineman. Stanford's John Brodie was the nation's top passer as he connected on 139 of 240 for 1,633 yards and a .579 average. The Ivy League officially came into being with a de-emphasis in football and a round-robin schedule. Jim Brown of eighth-place Syracuse set an all-time record by scoring 43 points in a single game. In the Cotton Bowl he scored three touchdowns and made good on three extra points, but the last one in the final quarter was blocked by Chico Mendoza to preserve a 28–27 Texas Christian win.

1957

Auburn	(10-0-0)		Ohio State	(9-1-0)	
7	Tennessee	0	14	Texas Christian	18
40	Chattanooga	7	35	Washington	7
6	Kentucky	0	21	Illinois	7
3	Georgia Tech	0	56	Indiana	0
48	Houston	7	16	Wisconsin	13
13	Florida	0	47	Northwestern	6
15	Mississippi State	7	20	Purdue	7
6	Georgia	0	17	Iowa	13
29	Florida State	7	31	Michigan	14
40	Alabama	0	10	Oregon (Rose Bowl)	7
207		28	267		92

Coach Ralph "Shug" Jordan brought Auburn its first national title as they won all ten of their games. The Tigers won with a defense which shut out six teams and allowed only four touchdowns in four different games. They led the nation in scoring defense as they surrendered an average of 2.8 points per game. They were also first in rushing defense, yielding 67.4 yards per game, and in total defense with a 133-yard average. Members of this junkyard dog defense were center Jackie Burkett, guards Tim Baker and Zeke Smith, tackles Ben Preston and Cleve Wester, and ends Jerry Wilson and Jim Phillips, who won all–American honors.

Just before the season began, Jordan banished his starting quarterback for disciplinary reasons. Lloyd Nix, a third string, left-handed halfback, took over the signal-calling job and moved the team with flawless instinct. Nix didn't need to throw much as the slaughterhouse line and running backs Tommy Lorino and Billy Atkins gave Auburn a take-it-to-'em ground game. The War Eagles operated from a full house, regular T-formation using a give to the backs on a straight-ahead belly series.

The season opener set the style of future games. The huge Auburn line, which outweighed Tennessee 23 pounds per man, immobilized the Vols in a

7–0 win. In the Kentucky game, a recovered fumble on the Wildcat 30 and a roughing penalty on UK tackle Lou Michaels put the ball on the six-yard line, where Auburn scored for a 6–0 victory. Georgia Tech was held off twice inside the Tiger 10-yard line, and all the scoring came on a 21-yard Billy Atkins field goal. Atkins scored all of Auburn's points in their first three SEC games and finished the year with a total of 82, second in the conference to LSU's Jim Taylor with 86.

By now, the Tiger defense was the best in the land. Florida had two first downs in the third quarter when the Auburn reserves came in. Mississippi State was able to score first, the one time the Tigers were behind all year, but that's all the Maroons could get. Georgia was stopped inside the War Eagle four-yard line eight straight times before they had to give it up. In a series interrupted 41 years over the issue of expense money for players, Auburn gave Alabama its fourth beating in a row. Violations of NCAA rules kept Auburn from participating in post-season play.

After a first-game loss to Texas Christian, Woody Hayes had Ohio State back on target. They finished second in the AP vote, but the UPI coaches' poll tabbed them in the top spot. Scorning the pass, the Buckeyes ran the ball 85 percent of the time. Of their 3,126 total yards, 2,681 were gained on the ground.

Ohio's running attack was most evident in the showdown with Iowa for the Big Ten title and Rose Bowl bid. Late in the game, the Hawkeyes led Ohio State, 13–10. Starting from their own 32, quarterback Frank Kremblas fed the ball to fullback Bob White on almost every play. Five straight smashes into the Iowa defense took it to the Hawkeye 10-yard line. Halfback Dick LeBeau went straight ahead for two, then back to White again for five yards and into the end zone on the next play for the win.

Oregon hadn't been to the Rose Bowl for 38 years, but this year they were back as Pacific Coast champs. Oregon coach Len Casanova was not too concerned about Ohio State's great running game, for he knew his 5'6", 198-pound left guard, Harry Mondale, would make his presence felt with his submarine charge into the Buckeye backs. Oregon also had a good running attack, for halfback Jim Shanley and fullback Jack Morris were the best one-two riveters seen on the western slope in years. With quarterback Jack Crabtree tossing to ends Ron Stover and J.C. Wheeler, the Ducks would be in the ball game.

Ohio State was favored by 19 points. The big spread seemed justified when they marched 79 yards to a touchdown in the first quarter. The Bucks surprised everyone with a 37-yard pass from Kremblas to end Jim Houston, Kremblas then going in from the two. Oregon came back in the second period on an 80-yard drive using pitchouts, keepers, and short passes. Shanley scored on a pitch from the five-yard line, and it was a level seven at the half.

Oregon offense was so effective that they didn't have to punt once, and their defense played Ohio State to a standstill. In the final frame, Don Sutherin's 34-yard field goal gave Ohio a 10–7 lead. Again the Ducks came back and moved to the Buckeye 24, only to fumble. Oregon outgained and outdowned Ohio State, but coach of the year Woody Hayes had a three-point win.

Led by center Dan Currie, Michigan State opened with a 54–0 win over Indiana, a game which saw seven different men score. In the Cal game, MSU's ground attack took a back seat as they won on three touchdown passes, 19–0. Against the Wolverines, halfback Walt Kowalczyk ran amuck as the Spartans beat up Michigan 35–6, for their worst loss in 22 years. Purdue handed Michigan State its only defeat, 20–13, as the Boilermaker line caused ten Spartan fumbles, captured five, turned two into scores, and held MSU quarterback Jim Ninowski to minus 36 yards trying to pass. The Spartans finished with an 8-1-0 year and came in third.

Oklahoma looked like they would never lose as they added to their victory mark every week. Texas scored first on a 10-yard toss from Walt Fondren to Monte Lee. The Longhorns finally bit the dust in the third period when Jakie Sandefer scored to give OU the lead, and Texas was soon the forty-fourth victim.

Dallas Ward's Colorado team gave the Sooners their biggest scare. After Bill Krisher blocked Colorado's second conversion, Clendon Thomas scored the tying touchdown in the last frame, and quarterback Carl Dodd kicked the winning PAT to make it 14–13.

The Oklahoma consecutive win streak ended three weeks later at 47 games, the longest on record. They were shut out by Notre Dame, 7–0, and their national record of scoring in 123 straight games also came to an end. The vaunted Oklahoma attack gained only 98 yards rushing and 47 through the air. The last quarter shazam which had carried OU to victory so often was stillborn. Instead, the Irish drove 80 yards in eight minutes on 19 plays to the three-yard line, largely on carries by Nick Pietrosante and Pat Doyle. On the final one, Bob Williams faked a handoff and then pitched out to Dick Lynch, who streaked around right end to score. The Oklahoma fans gave the Irish a standing ovation at game's end. The fourth-place Sooners completed the year with a 10-1-0 record, as they beat Duke in the Orange Bowl 48–21.

Eddie Erdelatz brought Navy in fifth. With the band playing the Belgian national anthem for ex-king Leopold, who was in the stands, the Middies helped Boston College dedicate its new stadium. Erdelatz used all 33 players, as his split-T offense with roll-out quarterback Tom Forrestal proved too much for the Eagles. Navy dropped out of the top ten after losing to North Carolina 13–7, but climbed back in after a convincing win over number-ten Notre Dame, with Ray Wellborn going over all three times. In the following game, Navy failed to capitalize on five chances inside the Duke 30-yard line, and had to settle for a 6–6 tie.

With its jitterbug defense of stunts and blitzes, the Navy line, anchored by 6'2", 235-pound tackle Bob Reifsnyder and 5'11", 204-pound guard Tony Stremick set itself for the Army-Navy game. Army, which lost only to Notre Dame, 23–21, on a fourth quarter field goal by Monty Stickels, had sever wins. But Army halfback Bob Anderson was held to 18 yards rushing and halfback Pete Dawkins had only 63 yards. Referee Albie Booth tossed Army tackle Bill Melnik out of the game for punching out one of Reifsnyder's teeth. Captain Ned Oldham scored once on a six-yard sprint around end and again on a 44-yard punt return in a 14–0 win. Navy beat Rice in the Cotton Bowl, 20–7, to conclude a 9-1-1 season.

Alex Karras of sixth-place Iowa won the Outland Trophy as the year's best lineman. Karras liked to call himself a Greek kid just trying to get an education, but he was really a tough hombre who did not accept shabby treatment on or off the field. He reminded people of Wilbur Henry, another great lineman whose quickness and intelligence made him a shade better than the man opposite him. Karras had four or five different moves, but he used a little hop to the outside most of the time. Any lineman who tried to anticipate these moves found Alex making a surprise lunge to the other side. Karras beat those he faced with brains as well as brawn, and opponents who mean-mouthed him soon found themselves on their butt with a pleasant rejoinder from Alex.

The Heisman Trophy went to John David Crow of Texas A&M. After winning their first eight games A&M was in first place, but they lost to Rice 7–6, and Texas 9–7, and came in ninth. Texas tied Baylor 7–7, and lost 19–12 to Southern Methodist, quarterbacked by Don Meredith. Led by King Hill and Frank Ryan at quarter, end Buddy Dial, and fullback Howard Hoelscher, Rice lost to Texas 19–14, Duke 7–6, Clemson 20–7, and Navy for an eighth-place rank. Behind guard Jackie Simpson and tackle Gene Hickerson, quarterback Ray Brown took number-seven Mississippi to a 39–7 win over Texas in the Sugar Bowl and a 9-1-1 record.

1958

Louisiana State (11-0-0)			Iowa (8-1-1)		
26	Rice	6	17	Texas Christian	0
13	Alabama	3	13	Air Force	13
20	Hardin-Simmons	6	34	Indiana	13
41	Miami (Florida)	0	20	Wisconsin	9
32	Kentucky	7	26	Northwestern	20
10	Florida	7	37	Michigan	14
14	Mississippi	0	28	Minnesota	6
50	Duke	18	28	Ohio State	38
7	Mississippi State	6	31	Notre Dame	21
62	Tulane	0	38	California (Rose Bowl)	12
7	Clemson (Sugar Bowl)	0			
282		53	272		146

For the first time since 1912, there was a scoring change in the rules. The conversion following a touchdown was now worth two points upon crossing the goal by a run or pass. Kicking the ball through the goal post was still valued at one point, but the ball was centered from the three-yard line instead of the two. The rule on substitutes was liberalized so that any player could return to the game once each quarter. Previously, only the 11 men who started the quarter could re-enter.

Louisiana State had not had a perfect season in exactly half a century. Coach Paul Dietzel not only gave them a perfect year, but a bowl game victory, the national title, and coach of the year honors for himself. A big reason for LSU's success was Dietzel's use of the new substitution rules.

Dietzel's LSU squad was really three teams in one. The first squad was called the "Go Team" and was made up of the best men. They were a double-duty crew who played both offense and defense. The second squad, called the "White Team," was made up of 11 men who played only on offense. The third squad was called the "Chinese Bandits," and got more space on the sports pages than third-team players usually get. They played only on defense.

The Tigers had a first-class backfield in quarterback Warren Rabb, halfbacks Billy Cannon and Johnny Robinson, and Red Brodnax at fullback. Dietzel used a wing-T formation with one halfback out as a flanker. With his blocking ability, Brodnax gave Rabb protection on passes and cleared the way when Cannon or Robinson carried the ball. Center Max Fugler, guard Larry Kahlden, tackle Charles Strange, and end Billy Hendrix gave the line stability.

The Chinese Bandits showed their stuff in the second game of the year against Alabama, coached for the first time by Bear Bryant. Like third-stringers everywhere, the Bandits tried a little harder. They throttled an Alabama drive and made them settle for a field goal. In the second half, Rabb tossed to Robinson for a touchdown, and Cannon scored the other for the victory.

After six wins in six starts, LSU moved into the top spot in the AP poll. In the seventh game, unbeaten Mississippi came to town looking for Tiger meat. Ole Miss also boasted a 6-0-0 mark, and 67,720 showed up for the showdown.

It was the first time Tiger Stadium was a sellout, and the first of many great games LSU and Ole Miss played over the next few years. The Tigers turned back the Rebels early in the first quarter with a goal-line stand, and then went in front, 7-0, on Rabb's keeper just before the half. The Bayou Bengals scored again in the last period to preserve their number-one rating.

Being number one has often been a curse more than a blessing, and Mississippi State, winner of three games, almost caged the LSU tiger. A Billy Stacy touchdown put State ahead at the half, but the Bengals caught them in the third period to take a 7-6 win. A Maroon field goal just missed in the final seconds and LSU dodged the bullet.

Louisiana State closed its perfect year with a victory over Clemson, 7-0. It was LSU's first Sugar Bowl win, as Cannon threw a nine-yard scoring pass to Mickey Mangham in the third stanza. In the last quarter, the Bandits were sent in to halt a last-minute Clemson threat and maintain LSU's one-touchdown margin.

The Chinese Bandits gained such a following that their fans started coming to the games in coolie hats. Whenever the Bandits came into a game with their backs to the wall, the rousing chant of "Defense, Defense!" rocked Tiger Stadium. They did not cheer in vain, as the Banditos surrendered no touchdowns all year.

Iowa finished second in both the AP and UPI polls. They led the country in total offense with an average of 405.9 yards each game. At quarterback for the Hawkeyes was Randy Duncan. He had three good ends in Don Norton, Curt Merz, and Bob Prescott. The Hawks were also deep in halfbacks with Bob Jeter, Willie Fleming, Bob Jauch, and Kevin Furlong. Captain John Nocera and Don Horn provided plenty of power at fullback. The line was a barbed-wire outfit with Don Suchy at center, guards Gary Grouwinkel and Don Shipanik, and tackles John Burroughs and Mac Lewis.

Except for a vexing 13–13 tie with Air Force and a loss to Ohio State, the Hawks picked everyone clean. The game with the Buckeyes was 7–7 at the end of a quarter, 21–21 at the half, and 28–28 at the end of three periods before number-eight Ohio State put ten fourth-quarter points on the scoreboard for the win.

Iowa's Rose Bowl victory over Cal was a sad epitaph on the breakup of the Pacific Coast Conference. The Hawks set a record of 516 yards total offense, 429 yards rushing, and a 7.5-average gain on their 69 plays. Bob Jeter rushed for 194 yards on nine carries for a 21.6-yard average, all Rose Bowl marks.

Earl Blaik of Army had everyone talking about his lonely end formation. In order to combat his opponents' defensive strength, his squad lined up in a wing-T and unbalanced line, with the end 15 yards out from the strong-side tackle. The team ran right or left depending on which side of the field the ball was spotted at the end of the previous play. With lonesome end Bill Carpenter already in position while his teammates were in the huddle, Army could strike quicker than if they had to wait for him to get set.

Blaik's formation was intriguing because everyone wanted to know how the lonesome end knew what the next play would be. Was it done by hand signals from the bench? Was it done by touching another part of the body (skin on skin), or was it done by touching the jersey (skin on cloth)? "Very simple," Blaik explained after the season was over. "The position of the quarterback's feet told Carpenter what the play would be."

The lonesome end was not simple to Army's foes. It spread the defense and allowed bigger holes for the Army backs to run through. It opened up the passing game so much that by the end of the year Army led in passing with a 172.2-yard average. It also helped halfback Pete Dawkins win the Heisman Trophy. Army was third with eight wins and a 14–14 tie with Pitt, led by Mike Ditka in the first of his three years as Pitt's top receiver.

Most of Auburn's good-field, no-hit team were back as they were again unbeaten in ten games but were tied by Georgia Tech, 7–7. Led by Outland Award winner Zeke Smith at guard, the Tigers shut out Tennessee in the opener, 13–0. Kentucky gave them a handful again until the last period when Jimmy Laster took a pitchout and dashed 43 yards to a touchdown and an 8–0 win.

In the next game, Georgia Tech quick-kicked the ball away all day waiting for Auburn to make an error. They finally gave the ball to the Engineers on an interception which led to the tying touchdown, and Auburn's win streak ended at 17 in a row.

Florida was just as gristly. The Gators led by three on a 23-yard field goal, but Auburn passed their way to a 6–3 lead. Florida came back with a march to the one-yard stripe, where they fumbled, and Auburn gave up a safety for a 6–5 win. The Tigers again were first in total defense with 157.5 yards and in rushing defense with 79.6 yards each game, and came in fourth.

Fifth-place Oklahoma finished the year with ten wins and a loss. They were hard pressed to beat Oregon 6–0 in the second game as the Ducks sent their linebackers through the gaps in the wide-spaced Sooner line, while the ends shut off the sweeps.

A week later Oklahoma played Texas, and both teams knocked each other down for 60 minutes. Texas held an 8–0 halftime lead on a pass from Rene Ramirez to George Blanch. Oklahoma replied with a third-period score but failed to make the conversion on a pass, and it stayed 8–6. Early in the last period, guard Jim Davis fought through the Texas line, captured a handoff and went 24 yards for a Sooner touchdown. This time the conversion pass was good to make it 14–8. Vince Matthews came in at quarterback for Texas and completed six passes in a 74-yard drive to the OU seven-yard line. From there, Bobby Lackey hit Bob Bryant on a jump pass to tie it, kicked the extra point for a 15–14 win, and was mobbed by his teammates. Oklahoma closed the year with its eleventh straight Big Eight title, their 4.9 average scoring defense was first, and beat number-nine Syracuse in the Orange Bowl, 21–6.

After a 37–6 warmup against Detroit, coach Ben Martin's Air Force team tied Iowa and showed they were ready for the heavyweights. After five wins, the Falcons crashed the top ten and ended sixth with a 9-0-2 mark. Their other tie was a scoreless dogfight with tenth-place Texas Christian in the Cotton Bowl. In between they beat Stanford 16–0, Colorado State 36–6, Utah 16–14, Oklahoma State 33–29, and Colorado 20–14. In the Utah game, both teams scored twice in the final period, but Utah was penalized on the conversion and failed its second two-point try.

Led by tackle Dan Lanphear, Milt Bruhn's Wisconsin Badgers tied Ohio State 7–7, lost only to Iowa 20–9, and were seventh.

College of the Pacific led the nation in rushing with an average of 259.6 yards each game. COP's Dick Bass was the leading runner with 1,361 yards and top scorer with 116 points.

1959

Syracuse (11-0-0)			Mississippi (10-1-0)	
35	Kansas	21	16 Houston	0
29	Maryland	0	16 Kentucky	0
32	Navy	6	43 Memphis State	0
42	Holy Cross	6	33 Vanderbilt	0
44	West Virginia	0	53 Tulane	7
35	Pitt	0	28 Arkansas	0
20	Penn State	18	3 Louisiana State	7
71	Colgate	0	58 Chattanooga	0
46	Boston University	0	37 Tennessee	7
36	UCLA	8	42 Mississippi State	0
23	Texas (Cotton Bowl)	14	21 LSU (Sugar Bowl)	0
413		73	350	21

The NCAA Rules Committee widened the goal posts this year from 18 feet six inches to 23 feet four inches. Major-college field goal kickers responded by making good on 192 of 380 attempted, including a 52-yarder by Randy Sims of Texas A&M. The rule on substitution was changed to permit one player to enter the game any time the clock was stopped. This allowed specialists such as field goal kickers to get into the game and made it possible to send instructions to the players without fear of penalty.

Coach Ben Schwartzwalder's Orangemen from Syracuse won the national title, and were the country's best in five major categories. They were first in total offense with 451.5 yards, in rushing with 313.6 yards, and in scoring with 39 points each game. They also topped the nation in total defense, allowing 96.2 yards per game, and in rushing defense, yielding an average of 19.3 yards, second lowest on record. At the end of the season, Syracuse was the only major unbeaten and untied team in the land, and Ben Schwartzwalder was coach of the year.

Syracuse crowned its season by beating Texas in the Cotton Bowl. On their first series, Syracuse quarterback Dave Sarette called a pass to Ernie Davis. He took the halfback-to-halfback toss from Ger Schwedes, which covered 85 yards for a Cotton Bowl record, and scored as the Syracuse cannon boomed its applause.

In the next period, the Orangemen marched 80 yards to the Texas two, where the Longhorns held. It took four cracks to cross the goal again, but on the last one Davis scored and the cannon gave him another ovation. Just before the half, four Syracuse holding penalties and the Texas goose egg brought a few punches. Ben Schwartzwalder and Darrell Royal rushed onto the field, but since everyone kept their helmets on, no damage was done.

Texas came out smoking after the half and went 69 yards to score on a pass from Bobby Lackey to Jack Collins. Then Davis intercepted a pass and returned it to the Longhorns' 24. After fullback Art Baker tried the line and Schwedes tried the end for no gain, Davis popped through to the Texas three-yard stripe. From there, Schwedes went in. A Texas touchdown in the final period was not enough, and Syracuse had its first perfect season.

Linemen on this championship Syracuse squad were left end Gerry Skonieczki, left guard Roger Davis, Al Bemiller at center, right guard Bruce Tarbox, inside tackle Bob Yates, Maury Youmans at outside tackle, and right end Fred Mautino.

Johnny Vaught brought Mississippi in number two. Football fever gripped the state as the Rebs won their first six games. The fever became epidemic as the gusto in the mint juleps kept pace with the consecutive victories. Then came the epic contest with LSU. After six games, Louisiana State was in first place and Mississippi was third. Ole Miss had given up one touchdown in six games, while LSU yielded only a pair of field goals.

The game was advertised as the greatest ever played in the South. Tickets were harder to come by than a jug of good white lightning, and scalpers did a land-office business. Scores of people dressed as band members and cheerleaders marched in with the real units, and then looked for a seat once they were inside. The 68,000 who bought a ticket were joined by hundreds more who stood shoulder-to-shoulder in Tiger Stadium.

The crowd was not disappointed. The two teams probed each other trying to find a weakness. After Billy Cannon fumbled on his own 21, Ole Miss drove toward the LSU goal. With the fans on their feet screaming wildly, Mickey Mangham nailed Jake Gibbs on the three-yard line to end the threat. Tackle Bob Khayat pumped through a 22-yard field goal to give Mississippi a 3–0 lead.

In the last half, coach Vaught kept the Tigers off balance with first-down punts on three successive possessions. With Ole Miss nursing its slim lead, tackle Lynn LeBlanc halted Gibbs for a 10-yard loss near midfield. The Rebels punted on third down hoping for a Tiger miscue, but Ole Miss made one instead. Billy Cannon fielded the punt on the 11-yard line and began his run to immortality. All 11 Ole Miss players had a shot at Cannon, but he zigzagged past them all. When he pulled up 89 yards later, he not only won the game but the Heisman Trophy for himself.

Tiger Stadium was bedlam for several minutes. When play was resumed, Mississippi drove down to the LSU two-yard line. With the stadium rocking and only 18 seconds left, Doug Elmore was stopped inches short of the goal on fourth down to give Louisiana State a 7–3 victory. Those who survived the cardiac climax joined in the wild celebration which went on in the stands for hours.

The LSU-Mississippi Sugar Bowl rematch was a poor imitation of their first encounter. Bobby Franklin at quarter and fullback Charley Flowers kept the steam up, while Cowboy Woodruff, Larry Grantham, and George Blair scored in a 21–0 Rebel win. Ole Miss was the national leader in scoring defense, giving up just 21 points in ten games. LSU also lost a 14–13 decision to Tennessee during the regular season for a nine-and-two record to finish number three.

There was a three-way lockup in the Southwest Conference for the first time in 45 years. Texas, Texas Christian, and Arkansas all had five wins and a loss in conference play. Arkansas halted TCU on an 18-yard field goal by

Fred Akers, 3–0. TCU beat Texas on Harry Moreland's 56-yard scoring run in the last period, 14–9. A Kleo Halm catch led to a late Texas win over Arkansas, 13–12.

Number-four Texas went to the Cotton Bowl where they lost to Syracuse for a 9-2-0 mark. Seventh-place Texas Christian lost to LSU 10-0, and to Clemson 23-7 in the first Bluebonnet Bowl in Houston and ended 8-3-0. Arkansas, which was ninth at nine and two, lost to Mississippi earlier in the year, but stopped Georgia Tech, led by its all–American center, Maxie Baughan, in the Gator Bowl, 14–7, to end Bobby Dodd's chain of bowl-game wins at eight.

Georgia won the SEC title and came in fifth. After a 30–14 loss to South Carolina, the Dawgs were unbeaten. Included was a 21–10 win over Florida on Charley Britt's 100-yard scoring return with an intercepted pass, but they were pushed to the limit in a 14–13 win over Auburn. The clock showed five minutes to go when Bulldog guard Pat Dye recovered a fumble on the Tiger 45, and quarterback Fran Tarkenton began the long march goalward. On last down from the 13 with 25 seconds left, Tarkenton moved right and threw left to end Bill Herron for the score. Georgia's tenth win was over Missouri in the Orange Bowl, 14–0, on two Tarkenton six-pointers to Bill McKenny and Aaron Box, and Durward Pennington's two PATs.

It was a poor year in the Big Ten as Wisconsin won the title despite two defeats in the conference. Their ranking was sixth, but they finished with a 7-3-0 mark after losing to Washington in the Rose Bowl, 44–8. This was the first year of the AAWU (Athletic Association of Western Universities), made up of Cal, UCLA, USC, Stanford, and Washington). It was also the year which ended the Big Ten dominance in the Rose Bowl over Pacific Coast teams.

Washington's only loss was to USC, 21–15. Their coach was Jim Owens, an ex–Oklahoma end who put backbone into the UW teams. Scrimmages were often a fight between one squad and another, and no Husky player entered a game with tape on. This regimen paid off, for it took them to ten wins and a number-eight rating.

Number-ten Alabama's 45.7 yards per game pass defense led the nation. They lost to Georgia, 17–3, and to Penn State, 7–0, in the first Liberty Bowl, and tied both Tennessee and Vanderbilt by scores of 7–7.

VIII. The College Football Explosion

1960

Minnesota (8-2-0)			Mississippi (10-0-1)		
26	Nebraska	14	42	Houston	0
42	Indiana	0	21	Kentucky	6
7	Northwestern	0	31	Memphis State	20
21	Illinois	10	26	Vanderbilt	0
10	Michigan	0	26	Tulane	13
48	Kansas State	7	10	Arkansas	7
27	Iowa	10	6	Louisiana State	6
14	Purdue	23	45	Chattanooga	0
26	Wisconsin	7	24	Tennessee	3
7	Washington (Rose Bowl)	17	35	Mississippi State	9
			14	Rice (Sugar Bowl)	6
228		88	280		70

The substitution rule was loosened this year to allow each team to send in one substitute between successive downs without penalty. Last year it had to be done when the clock stopped, but this year it was permitted while the clock was still running. It allowed the coach to consult with the quarterback more often, and permitted the use of specific plays in certain situations.

Since the widening of the goal posts last year, the number of field goals increased to a high of 224. Field goal scoring had doubled with wider goal posts, and they decided 38 games.

Minnesota was national champ. Under coach Murray Warmath, the Gophers climbed from the cellar in 1959 to a first-place tie with Iowa in the Big Ten. Warmath was chosen Coach of the Year, and Minnesota guard Tom Brown won the Outland Trophy.

When Iowa and Minnesota met in Minneapolis, both teams had six wins in six games. Iowa was ranked number one and Minnesota was number three. Both squads were so high that fumbles dotted the early going. The Gophers got a break on an Iowa punt when the ball was centered over the kicker's head. Minnesota scored three plays later on a pitchout from quarterback Sandy Stephens to halfback Bill Munsey. Iowa scored in the second period on a Tom Moore field goal, and Minnesota led at the half, 7–3.

After the intermission, Iowa capped a 55-yard drive with a 20-yard touchdown run on a trap play by halfback Wilburn Hollis. On the next

Minnesota guard Tom Brown won the Outland Award, and the Chicago Tribune Trophy *as MVP of the Big Ten in 1960.*

series, the Gophers marched 81 yards in 11 plays to regain the lead. The two squads had swapped touchdowns, but at the end of three quarters it was still Minnesota, 13–10.

Minnesota broke the game open in the last period when fullback Roger Hagberg shook loose on a 42-yard scoring burst. Not long after, Gopher tackle Bobby Bell recovered a Hawkeye fumble on the Iowa 19, and four plays later Jim Rogers scored again for Minnesota to give them a 27–10 victory. With eight wins and a loss, Iowa ended the year at number-three.

On the following Saturday, Purdue gave Minnesota its only regular season loss. Warmath's juggernaut used the same bruising line play he had learned as a guard under Robert Neyland at Tennessee, but the Gophers were no match for the speedy Boilermaker backs. Minnesota slid to fourth place, but regained the top spot after beating Wisconsin in the last game. They moved on to Pasadena where they lost to Washington's headhunters.

While Minnesota and Iowa were locking horns for the number-one spot, Mississippi was improving on the previous year's 10-1-0 mark. They suffered a midseason letdown against Arkansas and LSU, but survived on the toe of Allen Green. In the Arkansas game, Green kicked a 39-yard field goal with only three seconds to go for a win. One week later, he kicked two field goals to tie LSU. In the win over Tennessee, the Rebs scored after the opening kickoff and never gave up the lead. In the final regular-season contest, Jake Gibbs hit 13 of 15 passes, mostly to Art Doty and Bobby Crespino but also to John Brewer and Ralph Smith, to rout Mississippi State. James Anderson was fullback, Richard Price was at guard, and Bob Benton at tackle. After the Sugar Bowl victory, second-place Ole Miss was the only major unbeaten team, but the Football Writers Association of America voted them the top spot.

The glory of the Naval Academy was Joe Bellino, this year's Heisman winner. Bellino continued his heroics where he left off in last year's Army-Navy classic. Instead of getting a record-setting fourth touchdown in the 43–12 victory over Army, Bellino insisted that senior Rollie Brandquist make Navy's final score.

Bellino had 18 touchdowns this year, including both scores in a 14–7 win over Notre Dame, and four more against Virginia, one on a 90-yard run from scrimmage. On the very first play of the Army-Navy game Bellino raced 58 yards to the Army 41-yard line, then scored moments later to give Navy a lead they never surrendered. When the Cadets closed it to 17–12 and threatened to overtake the Middies, Bellino intercepted a goal-line pass on the last play of the game. Navy was dumped by tenth-place Duke during the year, 19–10, and lost to Missouri in the Orange Bowl, 21–14. They finished fourth with nine wins and two defeats.

Bellino's records as the Navy bombardier include a 21.9-yard career average on all kick returns, still the Academy mark. His retired number 27 jersey hangs in the Naval Academy field house.

On the same Saturday that Purdue downed Minnesota, Missouri beat Oklahoma 41-19 for the first time in 15 years, and took over first place. On the next weekend, Missouri's brief reign was over as a 23–7 Kansas win knocked them from the top rung. Their perfect season was gone, but Kansas had to forfeit the game because of an ineligible player. Missouri ended in fifth place, defeated Navy in the Orange Bowl, and had a record of ten wins and a loss.

The 72,212 Orange Bowl fans, including President-elect John F. Kennedy, were treated to two long runs in a matter of minutes. The first occurred when Greg Mather picked up a Missouri lateral and dashed 98 yards for a score to put Navy ahead, 6–0. Moments later, Norm Beal stole a Navy pass and ran 90 yards down the left sideline to tie it. Bill Tobin kicked the first of his three extra points, and Dan Devine's Tigers were never behind after that.

With all 11 starters back, including one-eyed quarterback Bob Schloredt, halfback George Fleming, center George Pitt, and a junior college transfer at tackle, Ben Davidson, Washington's brawling bunch finished sixth. They lost only to Navy, 15–14, on a field goal in the last 14 seconds. Schloredt's collarbone was broken in the UCLA game, but Bob Hivner directed the team to narrow victories over the Uclans, 10–8, Oregon State, 30–29, Oregon, 7–6, and Washington State, 8–7. In the last game, fullback Don McKeta had a deep gash closed with ten stitches, then caught the winning two-point conversion. With Schloredt at the helm in the Rose Bowl, the play-with-pain Huskies led Minnesota, 17–0, then coasted to an easy win and also had a 10-1-0 season.

Seventh-place Arkansas won the SWC title outright this year. They started with a bang, but defeats by Baylor, 28–14, and Mississippi dropped them from the top ten. They won their last four games to finish the regular season with eight wins.

Arkansas had two tinglers along the way. In the Texas game, Porker coach Frank Broyles evened the score for last year's one-digit defeat by Darrell Royal. A furious battle brought the game down to the last minute with Texas on top by two. Mickey Cissell came off the bench, placed the kicking tee on the Texas 20, and booted Arkansas to a 24–23 win with 16 ticks to go. Cissell duplicated his coronary against Rice. For over 59 minutes the Owls and the Hogs rubbed the ground bare in the middle of the field. Again Cissell left the bench, put the tee on the 16-yard line, and kicked the only points of the game with 25 seconds left.

In the Cotton Bowl, Lance Alworth provided the Hogs with the thrills. A high pass from center forced him to punt on the run, but he rolled it out on the one-yard line. Later on in the third period he returned a punt 49 yards to put Arkansas in front, but Duke scored in the last three minutes to skin the Porkers, 7–6.

Ohio State won seven, had a 35–12 loss to Iowa and 24–21 defeat to Purdue, and was eighth. Alabama was ninth with eight wins. They lost to Tennessee 20–7, tied Tulane 6–6, and Texas 6–6 in the Bluebonnet Bowl on field goals by Tommy Brooker and the Steers' Dan Petty.

1961

Alabama (11-0-0)			Ohio State (8-0-1)		
32	Georgia	6	7	Texas Christian	7
9	Tulane	0	13	UCLA	3
35	Vanderbilt	6	44	Illinois	0
26	North Carolina State	7	10	Northwestern	0
34	Tennessee	3	30	Wisconsin	21
17	Houston	0	29	Iowa	13
24	Mississippi State	0	16	Indiana	7
66	Richmond	0	22	Oregon	12
10	Georgia Tech	0	50	Michigan	20
34	Auburn	0			
10	Arkansas (Sugar Bowl)	3			
297		25	221		83

By now, college football gripped the national awareness as no other sport had done, and in some parts of the country it was followed with religious zeal. Attendance at college football games passed 20 million for the first time in 1960. It was a bad year for Babe Ruth as Roger Maris poked 61 home runs and Whitey Ford hurled 29 consecutive scoreless innings in the World Series to erase the Babe's marks, but not even these could compete with talk about Oklahoma's downfall or the mediocrity of Notre Dame.

College football had turned to a wide-open attack like the pro ranks. As the offense opened up the game, the popularity of the split-T began to wane. Its place was taken by the wing-T or slot-T, in which the end was spaced wide and a halfback put in the slot between the tackle and end. This point-getting machine was run by well-trained quarterbacks who had learned their lessons in high school and now showed up at college in record numbers. They not only could throw the ball, but they knew how to move it with the right play and could take charge of a team.

Hamilton Fish, Harvard's all–American tackle in 1908 and 1909, was once asked to comment on the modern college game. "The main difference," he observed, "is the shape of the ball." Then he added, "It's opened up the game." He was right, as the ball was in the air more often because of its slimmer shape. In the last year before the rebirth of the T-formation (1939), college teams threw the ball 37.4 percent of the time for 132.8 yards per game. This year they tossed it 44.8 percent for 189.4 yards per game. It would be the last year passing yards averaged less than 200.

In order to keep pace with the never-ending battle between offense and defense, coaches began using a countermeasure known as the three-deep defense. Three men were placed deep to pick up any receivers who went down for long passes thrown from the wing-T formation. In this three-deep defense, at least three linebackers were close to the line of scrimmage to stop the running attack through the line or around the flanks.

In just four years Bear Bryant had turned Alabama football around and brought them a national championship. He ended the four humiliating defeats by Auburn, and made the winless season a thing of the past. Five wins, four losses, and a tie in his first year was the closest he came to a losing season as coach of the Tide. In that first year, 42 reported for practice, but by the opening game only 25 remained. The reputation he built at Texas A&M, when he took his first Aggie squad to the hills of central Texas, had preceded him. Bryant was known as a tough teamster whose teams were hitters, but he also built champions.

In its first five games, the Tide gave up 22 points and won on defense as much as offense. After quarterback Roman Gabriel put North Carolina State up by seven, Alabama held them to minus five yards rushing. They shut out their last five opponents and finished first in scoring defense with 2.2 points per game. In the Tide defense were linebackers Lee Roy Jordan, John O'Linger, and Darwin Holt, ends Dick Williamson and Tommy Brooker, tackles Billy Neighbors and Charlie Pell, guards Jimmy Wilson and Jimmy Sharpe, and backs Mike Fracchia, Cotton Clark, and Butch Wilson.

By the first week in November, Alabama climbed into second place behind Texas. When Texas Christian knocked over Texas in their annual slugfest, the Tide was the only major unbeaten and untied team remaining, and they topped everyone in total defense with 132.6 yards per game. They ended the year with a 10–3 win over Arkansas in the Sugar Bowl, as quarterback Pat Trammell ran 12 yards to a score and Tim Davis added a 23-yard field goal to give Alabama a 10–0 halftime lead. Arkansas made it 10–3 on a third-period Mickey Cissell field goal, and then had Alabama on the ropes in the last minute as a scoring pass from quarterback George McKinney grazed the fingertips of halfback Lance Alworth.

Bear Bryant got his nickname when he wrestled a bear at a county fair as a teenager. He was a man of deep character who built his teams with boys whose parents said grace at meals and had given their sons the deeper values of Bible and home. Bryant knew that character was the spark which turned talent into winners, and he put into his players the desire to be the best.

No less important was his emphasis on work and sweat. Up at three in the morning, he was making plans with his staff when the sun came up at six. He drove his players until they could play with pain and pride as if they were already men. Every once in a while he lost a player for driving him too hard, but usually he got more out of his players than they knew they had.

From his place on the coaching tower in practice, his voice came down through a bullhorn like thunder. With a grin which was the closest he could get to a smile, he dominated the team like a father-confessor. "God doesn't see more than Coach did," said Joe Namath, "and Coach probably sees more people." At Kentucky, George Blanda had echoed the same sentiment years before, "Seeing that face for the first time — granite, grim, gritty, I thought, 'This must be what God looks like.'" Namath summed it up best, "It's simple to understand why Bryant was a great leader. People follow an honest man who earns their respect."

After an opening-game tie with Texas Christian, Ohio State won its last eight games and finished second. Like Alabama, the Buckeyes were halfway down the top ten, climbing from seventh to sixth to fifth by the end of October. When Texas was bumped out of first place, Ohio State moved up behind Alabama in the final three polls, and was also unbeaten but tied once.

With his offensive and defensive platoons, Woody Hayes put a wild caveman crew on the field. Center Bill Armstrong, guards Rod Foster and Tom Jenkins, tackles Daryl Sanders and Bob Vogel, and ends Tom Perdue and Chuck Bryant gave the Bucks a line which could hold its own with anyone. The backfield of John Mummey at quarter, halfbacks Paul Warfield and Matt Snell, and all–American fullback Bob Ferguson was one of the Buckeyes' best. Six smooth wins in conference put Ohio on the road to Pasadena.

Trouble developed because the Rose Bowl pact between the Big Ten and the Pac-8 had terminated, and as yet there was no formal agreement. The Buckeyes were eventually chosen by the Rose Bowl selection committee, but the Ohio State faculty council rejected the offer by a 28–25 vote, stating overemphasis as the reason.

"I don't agree with those 28 no votes," Woody told an alumni group at a dinner in Cleveland, "but I respect the integrity of the men who cast them, if not their intelligence."

Back in Columbus, the faculty veto stirred up the students. They marched on the governor's house, but he was out. They came back to the campus in an ugly mood. Then co-captain Mike Ingram spoke up. "Listen," he said, "no one is more disappointed in the faculty vote than the players — and they're all back in their dorms learning to live with that decision. If they can, then you can."

The crowd slowly melted away. It pleased Woody that one of his boys had pointed them in the right direction.

Number-six Minnesota met UCLA in the Rose Bowl. The Bruins led on Bobby Smith's field goal, but Gopher linemen Robin Tellor and Julian Hook at guard, tackles Bobby Bell and Carl Eller, and ends Bob Deegan and Tom Hall shut off the Uclans. Sandy Stephens scored twice, Bill Munsey once, Tom Loechler added three PATs for a 21-3 Minnesota win, and UCLA made it five for five in Pasadena.

Darrell Royal had Texas on a rampage with his new formation, the single wing-T. It was a wing-T alignment with the tailback deep as in the single wing, and the fullback one step ahead and one step out. It let quarterback Mike Cotten mix in the options of the T-formation, and it gave single wing power right or left, depending on which side the wingback and fullback lined up. With this well-honed offense, the Steers gained 545 yards in an early-season game with Washington State. Later on, halfbacks Jim Saxton, Jack Collins, and Jerry Cook ran wild for 354 yards against ninth-place Arkansas. Texas held the top spot for the first two weeks in November, but giant-killer Texas Christian knocked them from their lofty perch with a 6-0 win. Texas ended up in third place, stole five passes to turn back Mississippi,

12-7, in the Cotton Bowl, and finished the year with ten wins and a loss.

When Mississippi and LSU met on the first week in November, Mississippi was unbeaten for the fourth straight year. The Rebs had six wins and were ranked number two behind Michigan State. Louisiana State lost its opener, but won five games in a row and was ranked sixth. In the Ole Miss line were tackle Jim Dunaway and guard Billy Ray Jones. LSU had guards Roy Winston and Monk Guillot, and tackle Billy Booth. At quarterback for Mississippi was Doug Elmore, with Billy Ray Adams at fullback. LSU halfbacks were Wendell Harris and Jerry Stovall, and fullback Earl Gros.

The Rebels had a 7-3 lead when Jerry Stovall got LSU going late in the third period with a 57-yard run to the Ole Miss 23. After a successful fourth-and-five play, Stovall scored to put LSU ahead for good in a 10-7 victory. LSU had spoiled the Rebels' perfect season for the fourth consecutive year, this time ending a 21-game unbeaten streak. Louisiana State finished number four, beat seventh-place Colorado (coached by Sonny Grandelius) in the Orange Bowl 25-7, and ended the year with ten wins and one loss. After five straight bowl wins, Mississippi lost to Texas in the Cotton Bowl, finished fifth with nine wins and two defeats, and topped the country in total offense with 418.7 yards each game.

With five wins, including a win over Notre Dame for the sixth straight time, Michigan State was number one midway through the season. But on the same day that LSU beat Mississippi, Minnesota gave Michigan State its first defeat, 13-0, and they fell to sixth place. One week later they lost to Purdue, 7-6, and skidded to ninth place. The Spartans won their final two games to finish number eight with seven wins and two losses. When Duffy Daugherty was hanged in effigy, he rebuked his detractors by asking them what was wrong with a 7-2-0 record.

In tenth place was Utah State, the nation's scoring leader with an average of 38.7 points each game. Led by tackle Merlin Olsen, this year's Outland Award winner, Utah State also led the nation in rushing defense, allowing 50.8 yards per game. Their only loss was to Baylor, 24-9, in the short-lived Gotham Bowl in New York, and they finished with nine wins, one loss, and a tie.

Ernie Davis won the Heisman Trophy, the first black man to be chosen. He averaged 5.5 yards per carry this year, and set career records at Syracuse with 35 touchdowns and 220 points, in rushing with 2,386 yards, and in all-purpose running with 3,414 yards.

1962

Two rule changes occurred this year. The first was the result of a roughing-the-kicker penalty on the final play of last season's Notre Dame-Syracuse game. Under the old rule, there was no second try on a missed field goal if time had expired, but the rule also said a game could not end on a penalty, so no one left the stadium waiting for the replay. The Irish made good on a second attempt and won, 17–15. The new rule resolved the conflict and was made retroactive to include Notre Dame's win over Syracuse.

Southern California (11-0-0)			Wisconsin (8-2-0)		
14	Duke	7	69	New Mexico State	13
33	Southern Methodist	3	30	Indiana	6
7	Iowa	0	17	Notre Dame	8
32	California	6	42	Iowa	14
28	Illinois	16	7	Ohio State	14
14	Washington	0	34	Michigan	12
39	Stanford	14	37	Northwestern	6
13	Navy	6	35	Illinois	6
14	UCLA	3	14	Minnesota	9
25	Notre Dame	0	37	USC (Rose Bowl)	42
42	Wisconsin (Rose Bowl)	37			
261		92	322		30

The second change concerned touching down a punt inside an opponent's 10-yard line. The old rule considered this a touchback, and the ball was brought out to the 20. Now the punt was dead where it was grounded. This added to the crowd excitement as they watched the ball to see how close it came to the goal.

In his third year as head man, John McKay brought Southern Cal a national title and was voted coach of the year. He built the Trojan offense around his three B's, Beathard, Bedsole, and Brown. Quarterback Pete Beathard's passes usually ended up in the hands of all–American end Hal Bedsole, and Willie Brown, the team's rushing leader, was the first of many high-stepping halfbacks McKay brought to USC. Fullback Ben Wilson put muscle into the Troy attack. He lined up deep behind the quarterback, who was under center Larry Sagouspe, with Brown one step behind him in an I-formation, and Ken Del Conte as flanker. The rest of the line included end Ernie Pye, tackles Marv Marinovich and Gar Kirner, and guards Pete Lubisich and all–American Damon Bame.

The unsung heroes of the Trojan camp were the defense. They forced Iowa to make mistakes and then shut them out. When they handed the Huskies their only defeat of the year, they put themselves on the inside track to the Rose Bowl. The defense also kept the Trojans in the game with UCLA. With five minutes left, the Uclans led 3–0, but Brown's great reception set up a score, and the defense forced another turnover for the win. Southern Cal moved into first place in mid–November and held it for the last three weeks, ending the schedule by blanking Notre Dame.

Wisconsin finished second and topped the nation in scoring with 31.7 points per game. They were coached by Milt Bruhn and led by quarterback Ron VanderKelen, the Big Ten's MVP and total offense champion with 1,237 yards. His main target was 6'5" end Pat Richter, but he dumped off to halfbacks Lou Holland and Gary Kroner coming out on pass patterns, something most teams weren't doing at the time. At the other end was Ron Carlson with Ralph Kurek at fullback. The interior line had tackles Roger Pillath and Roger Jacobazzi, guards Steve Underwood and Steve Schenck, and center Ken Bowman. The only defeat for the Badgers was to Ohio State, but they won the Big Ten title with an 80-yard drive in the final four minutes to down the tenth-place Gophers.

For sustained thrills, the Rose Bowl game was hard to beat. USC marched to the Wisconsin 13 and lined up for a field goal. With Beathard holding, he stood up and tossed to Ron Butcher on a tackle-eligible pass for a score. VanderKelen ran and passed Wisconsin to the USC one, where Kurek went in to even the count.

Damon Bame's interception set up a second-period score by Wilson. After quarterback Bill Nelsen threw 45 yards to Brown, halfback Ron Heller ran 25 yards for a 21-7 USC halftime lead.

On the first series after the half, Bedsole took a short Beathard pass and went 57 yards down the sideline for a score. Wisconsin charged back on VanderKelen's passes to the Troy 17, and then ran in to make it 28-14. Beathard made good on three third-down passes, the last a 23-yarder to Bedsole which ran it to 35-14. After Tom Lupo's interception, Beathard hit end Fred Hill for 31 yards and a 42-14 lead as the last quarter started.

Then the fireworks began. VanderKelen threw to Richter at midfield. After he hit Carl Silvestri for 15, Holland scored from the USC 13, and it was 42-21 with 11:40 to go. A Trojan fumble led to another score to make it 42-28 with 8:32 left.

After USC went to the Badger 33 and lost the ball on downs, Wisconsin drove to the Trojan 4 and lost it on an interception. The ball was centered over the head of Trojan punter Ernie Jones, but he fell on it for a safety. It was 42-30 with 2:40 remaining.

Bill Smith returned the free kick to USC's 43. VanderKelen threw to Holland for six and Richter for 18. From the Troy 19, he hit Richter to make it 42-37 with one minute to go, but time ran out on the frenzied fans before Wisconsin could run a play.

VanderKelen completed 33 of 48 attempts for 401 yards, all Rose Bowl marks. Richter's 11 receptions are also a record, and his 163 yards gained were one short of Don Hutson's mark. Four scoring passes by Pete Beathard were also a new record.

After coming close the last three seasons, Mississippi had its first perfect year and finished third. Paced by tackle Jim Dunaway and guard Don Dickson, the Rebels had the nation's best total defense, permitting 142.2 yards per game. In the season opener, a fumble and bad center snap by Memphis State led to a 21-7 Mississippi victory. Ole Miss finally broke the LSU jinx by holding them to 70 yards rushing in a 15-7 win, the first in five years. Leading Tennessee 7-0 in the third period, halfback Louie Guy raced the length of the field with an interception to open the gate on a 19-6 win. Against Mississippi State, sophomore quarterback Jim Weatherly turned a busted

John McKay's 16-year mark at USC was 127-40-8 (a .749 average).

play into a 13–6 Rebel win. In the Sugar Bowl, quarterback Glynn Griffing took Ole Miss to a 17–13 win over Arkansas, their tenth of the year.

After Texas beat the Sooners for its fourth win in October, the Steers climbed to the top rung. Ernie Koy's punts held off OU all day, and barefoot Tony Crosby's 16-yard field goal early on became the winning margin, 9–6. The game almost ended in a riot as both squads swarmed angrily on the field at the finish.

On the following Saturday against Arkansas, the Razorbacks threatened to add to their 3–0 lead with a march to the Longhorn goal. As fullback Danny Brabham stabbed for the touchdown, he was met by linebackers Johnny Treadwell and Pat Culpepper. The ball squirted loose like oil from a gusher, and Joe Dixon fell on it for a Texas touchback. The Longhorns won it 7–3 on a 90-yard drive, tailback Tommy Ford scoring with 16 seconds left.

A week later Rice tied the Steers 14–14 and pushed them out of the top spot. On Thanksgiving Day against ancient rival Texas A&M, the Longhorns overcame a 3–0 third-period deficit with two touchdowns in the final 15 minutes to down the Aggies 13–3 and finish number four. In the Cotton Bowl, Texas lost to LSU, 13–0, and ended this year with nine wins, a loss, and a tie.

With sophomore Joe Namath at quarterback, Alabama won eight games and took over first place in November. But no sooner were they number one when Georgia Tech turned them out, 7–6. Alabama gambled on a two-point conversion late in the game, but missed. They recovered the onside kick, but missed again when they lost the ball on an interception. Behind linebacker Lee Roy Jordan's 33 solo tackles in the Orange Bowl, the Tide halted number-eight Oklahoma 17–0, and finished fifth with ten wins and a loss.

After winning big over Oklahoma State, 34–7, and Tulsa and TCU by identical scores, 42–14, Arkansas left Baylor behind with a 28–0 lead. Then cool Don Trull, the nation's top passer with 1,627 yards on 125 of 229 for 54.6 percent, blitzed the Porkers with three scoring passes and Arkansas was lucky to win, 28–21.

On the next weekend, the title-bound Steers gave the Razorbacks their only regular-season loss. Southern Methodist then kept Arkansas hearts in a dither with a 78-yard drive for a 7–0 lead which held up into the last period. Late in the game, the Porkers scored on an 11-yard run by Jesse Branch. Quarterback Billy Moore's two-point conversion attempt was dropped, and SMU still led, 7–6. Then Tommy McKnelly kicked Arkansas into a 9–7 lead with a 27-yard field goal. The Mustangs tried a field goal from the Porker 17 in the last minute, but Mike Hales blocked it for an Arkansas win. The sixth-place Hogs lost to Mississippi in the Sugar Bowl, and finished with nine wins and two losses.

In his first year as head coach, Charles McClendon took LSU to a seventh-place finish. His Tigers lost only to Mississippi, were tied by Rice 6–6, and led the country in scoring defense, allowing 3.4 points per game.

In the Cotton Bowl, LSU won its ninth game as the defense shut out Texas, while Lynn Amedee was good on two field goals and Jimmy Field ran 22 yards to score.

Coach Rip Engle had ninth-place Penn State in a bowl game for the fourth straight year. Led by end Dave Robinson, tackle Chuck Sieminski, and fullback Roger Kochman, they had nine wins, lost only to Army, 9-6, and to Florida in the Gator Bowl, 17-7.

Oregon State quarterback Terry Baker was the Heisman winner and total offense leader with 2,276 yards. He had career marks of 4,979 yards on 1,503 running and 3,476 passing. His 99-yard scoring run, a Liberty Bowl record, beat Villanova, 6-0. Beaver end Vern Burke led receivers with 1,007 yards on 69 catches.

1963

Texas (11-0-0)		Navy (9-2-0)	
21 Tulane	0	51 West Virginia	7
49 Texas Tech	7	28 William & Mary	0
34 Oklahoma State	7	26 Michigan	13
28 Oklahoma	7	28 Southern Methodist	32
17 Arkansas	13	21 VMI	12
10 Rice	6	24 Pitt	12
17 Southern Methodist	12	35 Notre Dame	14
7 Baylor	0	42 Maryland	7
17 Texas Christian	0	38 Duke	25
15 Texas A&M	13	21 Army	15
28 Navy (Cotton Bowl)	6	6 Texas (Cotton Bowl)	28
243	71	320	65

Led by Outland winner Scott Appleton at tackle, Texas had its first perfect season in 43 years and was national champion. Darrell Royal was coach of the year, and the team reflected his conservative football philosophy of ball control, tight defense, and infrequent use of forward passes. "When the ball is put in the air, more things bad can happen than good," said Royal.

Texas was in second place when they met number-one Oklahoma in their annual showdown. A 17-12 win over defending champ USC put Oklahoma at the top, but this game was a romp as the Steers showed OU how to run the split-T option. Duke Carlisle gained 66 yards on keeper plays, and ran for one score and passed for another. Texas took over number one and held it for the rest of the year.

Barefoot kicker Tony Crosby was the hero for the next three weeks. Arkansas was dispatched with two conversions and a field goal. The Rice Owl was held to 39 yards rushing as Tony clipped its wings with an extra point and a 22-yard three pointer. For his third encore, Crosby unsheathed his shoeless extremity and downed SMU with two extra points and another field goal.

In its eighth win of the year, Texas outlasted the Baylor Bears. For almost three quarters it was a scoreless standoff. Then the Longhorns put together a drive, fullback Tommy Stockton scoring from the one-yard line. Texas fumbled away a last-period insurance touchdown chance on the Baylor 13 with 1:53 to go. Aided by a 15-yard penalty, quarterback Don Trull moved the ball to the Texas 19 with a half-minute left. Trull aimed for the end zone again, but Carlisle speared it to end the Baylor threat. Trull was the country's top passer for the second straight year with 2,157 yards on 174 of 308 attempts for 56.5 percent.

TCU went down next, and Texas took on the Aggies. After a Crosby field goal of 17 yards, A&M scored on two long passes from Jim Keller to Travis Reagan and George Hargett for a 13-3 last-quarter lead. Texas pushed over a score, but it was still 13-9 as the two-point conversion failed. With 1:19 remaining, Carlisle ran in for a 15-13 victory, and the Horns had hooked everyone on the trail.

With Carlisle in the backfield were tailback Tommy Ford, fullback Harold Philipp, and wingback Joe Dixon. The line from left to right included Ben House, Appleton, George Brucks, Dave McWilliams, Tommy Nobis, Staley Faulkner, and Charles Talbert.

Led by Roger Staubach at quarterback, Wayne Hardin's Navy crew was the number-two team. With Staubach completing 17 of 22 passes, Navy left West Virginia in dry dock. A week later against William and Mary, he threw for 206 yards and gained 91 running for a new Academy total offense record of 297 yards.

Against Michigan, Staubach bettered his week-old record with 307 yards total offense. He hit 14 of 16 passes, one a 54-yarder to John Sai for a 20-0 halftime lead. "The greatest quarterback I've ever seen," said Michigan coach Bump Elliott.

Navy had its hands full with Southern Methodist on the night before Texas defeated the Sooners in Dallas. Guard Fred Marlin put Navy ahead with his second field goal, 28-26, but the Ponies came back to take the lead, 32-26, on a one-yard plunge with 2:05 to go. Navy steamed backfield to the Mustang seven-yard line. With only seconds left, a Staubach pass was tipped, juggled a moment, then dropped as 38,000 in the Cotton Bowl watched breathlessly.

The VMI game contributed the year's most unusual touchdown. A long field goal try by Navy's Fred Marlin fell short in the end zone, and a VMI player cornered it and spiked it to the turf. Marlin, seeing the ball was still in play, fell on it for a much-needed touchdown, as the Keydets went down to defeat stubbornly.

Navy gave Pitt its only loss. The Middies intercepted four passes, recovered a fumble, and held the Panthers to 76 yards on the ground. Notre Dame and Maryland were both defeated by big scores. Navy continued to roll against Duke, including Sai's 93-yard scoring run from scrimmage, the longest by a Navy man.

Along with 33 other games around the nation, the Army-Navy game was postponed a week because of President Kennedy's death. Army went down for the fifth year in a row, but they were at the Navy goal as quarterback Rollie Stichweh tried to call time out when the gun sounded, a reversal of the historic 1946 encounter.

Number-two Navy returned to Dallas to meet number-one Texas in the Cotton Bowl. With Navy in a nine-man line, the Longhorns went airborne. Duke Carlisle unloaded a 58-yard touchdown bomb to wingback Phil Harris, and then hit him with a 63-yard scoring strike. Carlisle added a touchdown himself, Harold Philipp got the other, and it was 28-zip. Staubach scored in the last quarter, but it was not enough to catch the stampeding Longhorns.

Led by 6'3", 237-pound Dick Butkus, Illinois won the Big Ten title in the final game by stopping ninth-place Michigan State, 13-0. They were third, beat Washington in the Rose Bowl, 17-7, and ended with an 8-1-1 mark. Butkus called defensive signals, then prowled up and down ready to pounce on anyone in his way.

Butkus made people forget that Ray Nitschke had been a linebacker at Illinois. With two tackles like 234-pound Bill Minor and 262-pound Archie Sutton to hold the middle, he often blitzed on his own. In the Minnesota game, he was in on 17 tackles and caused two fumbles. Against Ohio State, he was in on 23 tackles. By the end of the regular year, Butkus had 144 tackles and caused seven fumbles. Contact was his meat, and when practice was cancelled because of rain, he often became angry and even morose.

Number-four Pitt had four wins in four games for the first time in a quarter-century. Their coach was John Michelosen, a quarterback on Pitt's 1937 national champs. Michelosen kept the two deep men in Jock Sutherland's single wing formation, but he added a quarterback under center and an end spaced 15 yards from the tackle with a wingback in the slot between them. The result was a wide-open attack combining power, passing, and deception. In its opener, Pitt rolled up 27 first downs to six as UCLA was beaten 20-0. Against Washington, quarterback Fred Mazurek hit on 11 of 16 passes, then snared a fourth-period pass on the Pitt 13 to halt the Huskies, 13-6. After giving Cal a touchdown on an 85-yard kickoff return, Pitt beat its third West Coast team in a row, 35-15. In the next game with West Virginia, Mazurek, called "Mr. Moto" by his teammates, caught an 11-yard pass from tailback Paul Martha to keep Pitt in the game. Then in the final quarter, Martha scored on a 46-yard run to down the Mountaineers, 13-10.

Pitt's only loss was to Navy. Their red-dog defense, led by tackles Ernie Borghetti and John Maczuzak, dumped Staubach for 93 yards, but he still hit on 14 of 19 to cage the Panthers. Navy stole four passes, two by Mazurek and two by backup Ken Lucas, and all four led to scores. Pitt rebounded to win its last five games and finished with nine wins, including a 31-20 win over

Miami (Fla.) and quarterback George Mira, whose 2,318 yards total offense was the country's best. Only in the 28-0 defeat of Army did Michelosen revert to the power game he knew so well. In the stands keeping a scorecard on the performance of his players was Pittsburgh chancellor Edward H. Litchfield, the man many people felt was the power behind the Panthers' crowd-pleasing game. But Michelosen needed no outside help, even though the students had a great time at the games with their own version of the situation:

> Michelosen, Michelosen, he's our man,
> If he can't do it, Litchfield can.

Auburn's terrific tandem of tailback Tucker Frederickson and T-formation quarterback Jimmy Sidle helped take them to a fifth-place finish. Frederickson was the SEC's best blocker, and Sidle ran for 1,006 yards, just ten shy of this year's rushing leader, Memphis State's Dave Casinelli. End Howard Simpson, guard Bill Van Dyke, and linebacker Bill Cody cemented the defensive unit. Down 12-0 against Tennessee, Sidle hit on two touchdown passes and scored one himself for a 23-19 win. Florida was held to 52 yards rushing and one first down, as the Gators were shut out, 19-0. Mississippi State handed Auburn its only regular-season loss, 13-10, on Justin Canale's 36-yard field goal in the final seconds. The Tigers won three more games, including the first win over Alabama in five seasons on a Woody Woodall field goal, but their Orange Bowl loss to Nebraska put them at nine and two.

After a successful tenure at Wyoming, where he brought the Cowboys four Skyline Conference titles in his first five years, Bob Devaney had Nebraska in gear again. In his second year, the Cornhuskers won nine of ten games, lost to Air Force, 17-13, and finished number six. The only close games were a 14-7 win over Minnesota on a 65-yard pass from quarterback Dennis Claridge to end Tony Jeter, a 13-12 defeat of Missouri as the Tigers missed a two-point conversion, and a 20-16 triumph over Oklahoma State.

In the first of many games over the next two decades, the Big Eight title was settled by the Oklahoma-Nebraska game at the end of November. Devaney went with what got him there, his big, husky line led by 269-pound guard Bob Brown and 245-pound tackle Lloyd Voss. While helping Nebraska build a 29-7 lead, they shook five fumbles out of number-ten OU and held them to 98 yards rushing. Behind this forward wall, Husker backs Rudy Johnson, Kent McCloughan, and Fred Duda ran for an average of 262.6 yards each game, the best in the land. Nebraska went on to the Orange Bowl where they defeated Auburn, 13-7. They scored on the second play of the game on a 68-yard run by Dennis Claridge, added two field goals by Dave Theisen, and finished with ten wins and a loss.

Mississippi opened the season by playing Memphis State in a scoreless tilt and ended it with another tie against Mississippi State, as the Rebels' Billy Carl Irwin knotted it 10-10 on a last-period field goal. In between, they won seven games and finished in seventh place. The Rebel line of center Kenny Dill, guard Stan Hindman, tackle Whaley Hall, and end Allen Brown was the nation's best in rushing defense and scoring defense, allowing an average of 77.3 yards and 3.7 points per game, respectively. Against Alabama in the Sugar Bowl, the quarterback fireworks between Joe Namath and Perry Lee Dunn did not take place, as Namath was benched in favor of Steve Sloan, and the Rebs lost six of 11 fumbles. Tim Davis was the hero as he kicked four field goals in a 12–7 Tide win.

After its Sugar Bowl win, number-eight Alabama had a 9-2-0 record. In each defeat, they could not overcome a 10–0 deficit. With seven minutes left against Florida, the Tide drove 77 yards to score but lost 10–6, as Bear Bryant suffered his first loss at home. In the Auburn game, Benny Nelson scored on an 80-yard run, but once again the Tide came in short, 10–8.

1964

Alabama (10-1-0)			Arkansas (11-0-0)		
31	Georgia	3	14	Oklahoma State	10
36	Tulane	6	31	Tulsa	22
24	Vanderbilt	0	29	Texas Christian	6
21	North Carolina State	0	17	Baylor	6
19	Tennessee	8	14	Texas	13
17	Florida	14	17	Wichita State	0
23	Mississippi State	6	17	Texas A&M	0
17	Louisiana State	9	21	Rice	0
24	Georgia Tech	7	44	Southern Methodist	0
21	Auburn	14	17	Texas Tech	0
17	Texas (Orange Bowl)	21	10	Nebraska (Cotton Bowl)	7
250		88	231		64

With the NCAA rules permitting almost unlimited substitution this year, two-platoon football was back for the first time since 1952. The new rule allowed the coach to send in as many players as he wanted when the clock was stopped. Only two players could be sent in while the clock was running.

The day of the two-way player had gone the way of the knee-length bathing suit and five-and-dime store. With so many quality players throughout the country, there was room for specialists who could block or tackle or kick. They excelled in one phase of the game, they were often fresh and rested, and they gave the game greater technical skill and stepped-up action. The result was more crowd appeal, as football became the all–American game.

With Joe Namath out of the Bear's doghouse, Alabama won all its regular-season games and was the champ. Behind center Gaylon McCollough and guard Wayne Freeman, Namath ran Georgia's ends for three touchdowns. He ran for two more against Tulane and scored one against Vanderbilt, but the win over North Carolina State was costly. After a toss to end Tommy Tolleson, Namath left with a knee injury which hobbled him the rest of his career.

Florida had hopes of repeating last year's upset, but after fullback Steve Bowman tied the score, a David Ray field goal put the Tide ahead with 3:30 remaining. Jim Hall tried a field goal for the Gators on the last play, but it veered right and Alabama had its closest call. LSU was turned back with three interceptions, one for 33 yards and a touchdown by Hudson Harris.

Georgia Tech put up a struggle before Namath broke the game open just before the half. With the ball at midfield and 1:47 to go, Namath went into the game and in 29 seconds the Tide had a touchdown. Alabama recovered the onside kickoff, and in a few more seconds they had a 14–0 halftime lead. Auburn went down as Ray Ogden returned a kickoff all the way from the end zone, and Alabama finished unbeaten. Their perfect season collapsed in the Orange Bowl, as Texas gave Alabama its only loss of the year.

At Arkansas, their perfect season did not end on New Year's Day, as Frank Broyles brought them home in second place with an all-winning season for the first time in 55 years. Ken Hatfield got things under way in the opener with a 28-yard punt return in the second quarter. A 55-yard drive was helped by a 23-yard Bill Gray to Jerry Lamb pass, with Jim Lindsey going around end 18 yards to score. Oklahoma State tied it in the third period, but the Hogs pounded back 64 yards for the winning touchdown. The Cowboys had another shot after an Arkansas fumble, but the Razorback defense made State settle for a 37-yard field goal by Charles Durkee.

In the next game, Tulsa stunned Arkansas with a 14–0 lead, their second touchdown coming on a five-yard pass from Jerry Rhome to Howard Twilley. Late in the second period, Razorback linebacker Ronnie Caveness stole a halfback pass on the Tulsa 12 for a quick score. Moments later, Caveness recovered a fumble, and a field goal made it 14–10 at the half. It was all Arkansas in the third quarter, as the Porkers piled up 21 unanswered points. Rhome finished the year as the country's best passer, as he connected on 224 of 326 attempts for 68.7 percent, 2,870 yards, and 32 touchdowns.

Arkansas continued with impressive wins over TCU and Baylor. Then came the shoot-out with defending champion Texas. Again Ken Hatfield ignited them by returning a punt 81 yards for a score and a 7–0 halftime lead. The lone touchdown stood up until Texas tied it early in the final stanza. Then quarterback Fred Marshall hit Bobby Crockett on a 34-yard pass to put Arkansas in front, and Tom McKnelly added the extra point. Texas came back and scored with a minute and a half to go. They gambled on a two-point conversion, but the Porker defense smothered it for the close win.

Arkansas shut out their last five regular-season opponents, and ended up as the nation's defensive scoring leader, permitting 5.7 points per game. Hatfield was the top punt returner for the second straight time, averaging 16.7 yards both years. After a come-from-behind win over Nebraska in the

Cotton Bowl, Arkansas was the only major unbeaten and untied team in the country, and national champion in the eyes of many. "I certainly consider us number one," said Broyles, this year's coach of the year winner.

For reversing Notre Dame's football fortunes, Ara Parseghian shared the coach of the year award with Frank Broyles, the first time there was a dual winner. Parseghian moved Jim Carroll from offensive guard to linebacker, Dick Arrington went from tackle to guard, and Jack Snow was shifted from halfback to split end. He was also lucky to have newcomers Nick Eddy at halfback, defensive end Alan Page, linebacker Jim Lynch, and 6'5", 260-pound defensive tackle Kevin Hardy. After six wins in six starts, Notre Dame was in first place, and quarterback John Huarte, who didn't win a letter last year, was on his way to winning the Heisman Trophy.

Only Southern Cal stood between Notre Dame and the national championship. With Huarte connecting on 11 or 15 passes for 176 yards and a touchdown to Jack Snow, the Irish took a 17-0 halftime lead. USC coach John McKay's hope for a quick second-half score came true as the Trojans took the kickoff and drove to a touchdown. Then Notre Dame fumbled the ball away on SC's nine-yard line, and a touchdown was brought back on a holding call.

Southern Cal promptly uncoiled 82 yards for a score. Mike Garrett and Ron Heller moved it on the ground, and quarterback Craig Fertig completed five passes, the final one to Fred Hill, and it was 17-14 with four-and-a-half minutes remaining.

"We've got 'em now," shouted McKay from the sideline.

The Irish had to punt after the kickoff, and Garrett ran it back 18 yards to the Notre Dame 35. A Fertig to Hill connection gave them a first down on the 17. Two plays later, Hill caught a Fertig toss for a touchdown, but he was ruled out-of-bounds.

With the cheers of the crowd choked off in their throats, USC ran 84-Z on fourth-and-eight. Rod Sherman split wide left, ran downfield five steps, zigged out and in, and Fertig hit him to give the Trojans a 20-17 win with 1:33 to go. The Coliseum crowd erupted again, as Notre Dame slumped to third place with nine wins while Southern Cal checked in at the number-ten spot.

Michigan missed an unbeaten year by one point and finished number four. They had hard-hitting linebackers in Frank Nunley and Tom Cecchini, and defensive tackle Bill Yearby and offensive tackle Tom Mack were highly rated. The ends were well-manned by captain Jim Conley, John Henderson, Bill Laskey, and Ben Farabee.

Air Force was grounded 24-7 as quarterback Bob Timberlake and fullback Mel Anthony ran for 250 yards. Using wing-T option plays, pitchouts, and power sweeps, sophomore halfbacks Carl Ward and Jim Detwiler helped send Navy down, 21-0. Two touchdowns in the final quarter beat Michigan State 17-10, but three Michigan fumbles aided Purdue's 21-20 win. The Wolverines let a 19-0 lead over Minnesota slip away, but ended on top, 19-12. Northwestern was stopped 35-0, Illinois 21-6, and Iowa 34-20. In the

Rose Bowl playoff with ninth-place Ohio State, Rick Volk intercepted two passes to help turn back the Bucks, 10–0. Michigan ended its season in Pasadena by beating number-eight Oregon State 34–7, as Mel Anthony put an 84-yard run from scrimmage in the record book.

Another team which missed a perfect season by one point was fifth-place Texas. On their first series they drove 72 yards for a score in a 31–0 win over Tulane, but were in arrears to Army at halftime, 6–3, before winning, 17–6. Texas Tech was beaten 23–0, and Oklahoma lost for the third time in the last four years by the same score, 28–7. The Longhorns' 15-game winning streak ended in the one-point loss to Arkansas. Rice was stopped 6–3 on field goals by Dave Conway of 27 and 37 yards and 25 unassisted tackles by Tommy Nobis. The 7–0 win over SMU was also a toughie, and so was the 20–14 win over Baylor on a 25-yard pass from quarterback Marv Kristynik to end George Sauer, Jr., with 1:51 to go. Texas finished with big wins over TCU, 28–13, and Texas A&M, 26–7.

In the first Orange Bowl played under the lights, Texas led Alabama at the half, 21–7, on a 79-yard scoring run by Ernie Koy, a 69-yard pass play from Jim Judson to Sauer, and a Bama fumble which was converted into a touchdown. The Tide came back on two scoring passes from Joe Namath to Wayne Trimble and Ray Perkins, added a David Ray field goal, but fell short as Namath was downed inches away from the goal line in the final quarter.

Bob Devaney's Nebraska team finished sixth again this year. Devaney continued his mastery of Minnesota with a second straight win over the Gophers, 26–21. The defensive line of tackles John Strohmeyer and Dick Czap and middle guard Walt Barnes held South Carolina to three yards rushing in a 28–6 win. A scoreless game with Missouri ended in the last quarter when end Langston Coleman dropped the Mizzou quarterback in the end zone for a safety. The final score mounted to 9–0 on a 37-yard pass from quarterback Bob Churchich to Kent McCloughan. Kansas, paced by Gayle Sayers, was the eighth victim, 14–7, as end Freeman White scored on a 92-yard pass, and Kansas was later stopped on the one-yard line. Oklahoma State became win number nine, 27–14. Nebraska dropped its last two games, as a 7–3 fourth-quarter lead slipped away twice, once to Oklahoma, 17–7, and to Arkansas in the Cotton Bowl.

Louisiana State, with its pro-style flanker-T installed by coach Charles McClendon, finished number seven. In the opener, tackle Mickey Cox blocked a Texas A&M punt in the end zone and flanker Doug Moreau left-footed a 34-yard field goal for a 9–6 win. In the next game Rice was beaten 3–0 on a 28-yard field goal by Moreau in the last three minutes. Starting quarterback Pat Screen was injured in the 20–3 win over North Carolina, but Billy Ezell came on to lead LSU to a 27–7 victory over Kentucky. Safety man White Graves intercepted a Youkay pass and returned it 99 yards for a score, and Moreau added two more field goals.

Against Tennessee, Moreau's 21-yard field goal matched Fred Martin's 28-yarder in a 3–3 tie. In the Ole Miss game, the Rebs led 10–3 with six minutes left when LSU covered a fumbled punt on the 47. Three plays later, Billy Masters had Ezell's 19-yard pass to draw near, 10-9. On the conversion, Ezell rolled right behind center Rich Granier and guard Remi Prudhomme and threw to Moreau. The ball was tipped, then hugged by Moreau for the win.

LSU lost to Alabama and to Florida, 20-6, on a make-up game postponed by Hurricane Hilda, but met Syracuse in the Sugar Bowl. Syracuse runners Floyd Little and Jim Nance were contained until Moreau tied it, 10-10, on a 57-yard pass and then got an eighth win on a 28-yard field goal with four minutes remaining, 13-10.

1965

Alabama	(9-1-1)		Michigan State	(10-1-0)	
17	Georgia	18	13	UCLA	3
27	Tulane	0	23	Penn State	0
17	Mississippi	16	22	Illinois	12
22	Vanderbilt	7	24	Michigan	7
7	Tennessee	7	32	Ohio State	7
21	Florida State	0	14	Purdue	10
10	Mississippi State	7	49	Northwestern	7
31	Louisiana State	7	35	Iowa	0
35	South Carolina	14	27	Indiana	13
30	Auburn	3	12	Notre Dame	3
39	Nebraska (Orange Bowl)	28	12	UCLA (Rose Bowl)	14
256		107	263		76

The NCAA rules committee relaxed the rules on free substitution even more this year. Each team was permitted to send in as many players as they wanted after each score, between periods, or after each change of possession. Two substitutes could be sent in at any time before the ball was snapped.

By the end of October, the three top teams in the country were Michigan State, Arkansas, and Nebraska. They remained in that order until the final regular season poll when Alabama and UCLA were added to the first five in both the AP and UPI polls. UPI did not take another poll, but AP did because of the previous year's unrest after Texas beat Alabama in the Orange Bowl and Arkansas beat Nebraska in the Cotton Bowl. For the first time, therefore, AP cast its final vote after the bowl games in January.

All five top teams played in a bowl game on New Year's Day. The Orange Bowl was now a night game, the last of NBC's bowl game tripleheader. Arkansas' second straight perfect season ended in the Cotton Bowl, and UCLA outpointed Michigan State in the Rose Bowl. By kickoff time in the Orange Bowl, it was winner take all between Alabama and Nebraska.

Alabama's race to the national title was done the hard way. In their opener, they struggled to overcome a 10–0 Georgia lead, but pushed ahead by the fourth quarter, 17–10. With Georgia in possession on their own 20 and time running out, Kirby Moore hit Pat Hodgson with a short pass. Hodgson lateraled to Bob Taylor who took it all the way for a score. A Moore to Hodgson repeat was good on the two-point try, and Georgia had done it by one.

From then on, Alabama began its long climb to the top. Ole Miss had the Tide on the canvas in the last period, 16–7, but an Alabama field goal cut it to 16–10 with five minutes left. Then Steve Sloan led an 89-yard touchdown drive in a come-from-behind win. Alabama won the rest of its games except for the tie with Tennessee, as time ran out for the Tide on the Vols' four-yard line.

In four years Bob Devaney had taken Nebraska to four straight bowl games, and made the Cornhuskers the boss of the Big Eight in the mid-1960s. Ends Freeman White and Tony Jeter, tackle Dennis Carlson, and guard LaVerne Allers made Nebraska's offensive line the best in the midlands. Running backs Harry Wilson, Fred Duda, and 5'7", 153-pound Frank Solich gave Nebraska the top ground game in the nation with 290 yards per game. The Huskers beat everyone by ten points except Missouri, which was downed on a last-quarter field goal by Larry Wachholtz, 16–14, and Oklahoma State, 21–17. Their 28 points in the Orange Bowl was enough for victory, but it was the Huskers' misfortune to run into a fired-up Alabama team.

Although they were outweighed in the line, the Tide took it to the Huskers and won in the trenches. They stunted on defense and closed down the Nebraska running attack for a 24–7 halftime lead. Nebraska was forced to go to the air, and quarterback Bob Churchich hit on three scoring tosses, two to Tony Jeter and one to Ben Gregory. But Alabama also won it upstairs, as Steve Sloan threw for 296 yards. Wide receiver Ray Perkins had 159 yards and ten catches, two for scores. When the smoke had cleared, Alabama had 39 points and was number one, while Nebraska faded to fifth.

At Michigan State, Duffy Daugherty finally gave the Spartans a championship. At the end of the regular season, they were the second team with a perfect record of ten wins in ten games. The Spartans had the best scoring defense, giving up 6.2 points per game, and they had the best defense against the rush, permitting 45.6 yards each game. On two successive weekends, Michigan was held to minus 51 yards and Ohio State was 22 yards in the red. A month later, Notre Dame had 12 yards in the negative column.

The Spartans dripped with talent. At defensive end was 6'8", 280-pound Bubba Smith. "You don't feed him, you oil him," wrote a sportswriter. At middle guard was Harold Lucas. Behind them were linebacker Ron Goovert and cornerbacks George Webster and Don Japinga. On offense were center Boris Dimitroff, guards John Karpinsky and Dave Techlin, tackles Jerry West, Buddy Owens, Don Bierowicz, and ends Gene Washington and Bob Viney. Quarterback Steve Juday often threw to Clint Jones and Dwight Lee coming out from halfback.

The Rose Bowl game was a rematch between Michigan State and UCLA. The Spartans had defeated UCLA in their season opener, but the Uclans had disposed of USC and its Heisman Award winner, Mike Garrett, the country's leading rusher with 1,440 yards, and both teams met in Pasadena again. UCLA surprised everyone by leading at halftime, 14–0. The momentum continued to be with UCLA in the second half, as they held the Spartans three times on fourth-and-one. In the last period, fullback Bob Apisa took a pitchout and went 32 yards down the sideline for a Michigan State score. On the conversion, the holder stood up and tried to complete a two-point pass, but Jerry Klein nicked it and UCLA still led, 14–6.

The Spartans now began to dominate the Bruin team. After a punt was partially blocked, they came down the field and scored with 31 seconds to play. Again Michigan State tried for a two-point conversion. Bob Apisa caught the pitch and headed for the flag. Dallas Grider and Bob Stiles met Apisa and took him down short of the goal to save the victory. Stiles was kayoed on the hit and had to be brought around to accept the MVP Award. Tommy Prothro and the Uclans finally had a Rose Bowl win, for neither had won it before, and Prothro was coach of the year.

In addition to Nebraska and the Spartans, Arkansas was the third team with a perfect record of ten wins which went down to defeat on New Year's Day. A national championship also eluded the Razorbacks, but not before they laced together two unbeaten seasons and 22 consecutive wins, the longest in Porker history.

In their opener, the Hogs got off to a great start with a 21–0 halftime lead over Oklahoma State. When the Cowboys tried to make a comeback, Larry Elliott's 69-yard punt return set up a score to put it out of reach, 28–14. Tulsa had a 12–10 halftime lead in the next game, but was blanked after that in a 20–12 win.

Tulsa again led the nation in total offense with 427.8 yards and in passing with 346.4 yards per game. Tulsa quarterback Bill Anderson tossed a record 509 passes, connecting on 296 for 3,464 yards, 30 touchdowns, and 58.2 percent to head the list. Howard Twilley was first in scoring with 127 points, and his 134 catches for 1,779 yards are both all-time season records. Twilley's 261 receptions and 32 touchdowns are also career marks for receivers.

After TCU and Baylor were put away, Arkansas met Texas, led by Outland winner Tommy Nobis, in another showdown. Motels hung out "no vacancy" signs for 150 miles around, and at the game it was standing room only. No one was disappointed. "I never saw a better college football game," said television announcer Lindsey Nelson.

The Arkansas defense scored two early touchdowns. After a Bobby Nix punt was fumbled on a hit by Jim Williams at the Texas five-yard line, it was recovered in the end zone by Martine Bercher. The Longhorns drove to the Arkansas 20, where Tom Trantham stole a bobbled handoff in midair and went 77 yards to make it 13–0.

The second period was just as hectic. A Porker drive with Jon

Brittenum throwing and Bobby Burnett crashing inside pushed the Arkansas lead to 20–0. Stung by the Razorback barrage, the Steers sprang to life. They passed their way downfield and got on the boards with a 35-yard field goal by Dave Conway. Another Texas drive netted a touchdown to slim it to 20–10 at halftime.

Texas still had the edge after the half. Their first march ended in a 34-yard field goal, but the next drive hit paydirt as Marv Kristynik skirted end on a 14-yard touchdown run, and a two-point conversion made it 21–20. Conway added a third field goal, another 34-yarder, and the Steers' lead went to 24–20.

Arkansas responded to the 24 unanswered Texas points with an 80-yard drive. Brittenum to Crockett was on everyone's lips as they connected on five passes for 68 yards, the last one a diving catch near the sideline. Brittenum wedged in for the score, and 42,000 Fayetteville fans slapped each other crazily in the 27–24 win. The Razorbacks had bulldogged the number-one Longhorns and were a shoo-in for the top spot in the next weekly poll.

Arkansas won its last five games as the offense scored big, and was the top scorer in the country with 32.4 points per game. In the Cotton Bowl, their two-year win streak that had uprooted everything in its path could only score one touchdown. Arkansas took the lead on a Brittenum to Bobby Crockett pass, but halfback Joe Labruzzo's touchdowns gave LSU a 14–7 halftime lead. Both teams punched each other out in the last half but neither could score.

The scintillating Cinderella team from the Southwest would not wear the golden slipper this year, either. After the bowl games, the AP voted Alabama national champ, with Michigan State, Arkansas, UCLA, and Nebraska ending in that order. Number-six Missouri stopped Florida in the Sugar Bowl, 20–18, and number-seven Tennessee turned back Tulsa in the Bluebonnet Bowl, 27–6. Louisiana State, Notre Dame, and USC rounded out the top ten.

1966

Notre Dame (9-0-1)			Michigan State (9-0-1)		
26	Purdue	14	28	North Carolina State	10
35	Northwestern	7	42	Penn State	8
35	Army	0	26	Illinois	10
32	North Carolina	0	20	Michigan	7
38	Oklahoma	0	11	Ohio State	8
31	Navy	7	41	Purdue	20
40	Pitt	0	22	Northwestern	0
64	Duke	0	56	Iowa	7
10	Michigan State	10	37	Indiana	19
51	Southern Cal	0	10	Notre Dame	10
362		38	293		99

Ara Parseghian had a powerhouse at Notre Dame. The Irish won by four touchdowns over everyone except Purdue and Michigan State, and their offense of 36.2 points each game topped all comers. Led by linebacker John Pergine and safety Tom Schoen, their 3.8 points in scoring defense was second to Alabama's 3.7 points per game.

Many of the sophomores who missed a national championship by a minute-and-a-half were now seniors. Back on defense were linebacker-captain Jim Lynch, Alan Page at end, tackles Kevin Hardy and Pete Duranko, and on offense, guard Tom Regner and halfback Nick Eddy. In the backfield were two-year starters Larry Conjar at fullback and halfback Rocky Bleier. Sophomore standouts were offensive tackle Bob Kuechenberg, Terry Hanratty at quarterback, and end Jim Seymour, whose 13 catches for 276 yards against Purdue are both Notre Dame single-game records.

Nick Eddy never got in the Michigan State game because of a bad shoulder, and Hanratty and center George Goeddeke left with injuries. MSU took a 10-0 lead on Regis Cavender's short spurt and a 47-yard field goal by barefoot Dick Kenney. Coley O'Brien came in at quarterback and hit halfback Bob Gladieux on a 34-yard pass to make it 10-7 at intermission. Joe Azzaro's 28-yard field goal on the first play of the final quarter knotted it at 10-10.

With the ball on their own 30 in the last minute-and-a-half, Parseghian sent in orders not to risk an interception. As Notre Dame rushed impotently into the line on four straight plays, the Spartan players on the sideline taunted them, "Get off the field if you've given up." Parseghian said afterward, "I didn't want to risk giving it to them cheap," but in *Sports Illustrated* Dan Jenkins wrote, "They TIED one for the Gipper."

Parseghian had played the percentages and won. As he said with some truth, "When you're number one and you only get tied, you can't lose." On the far side of the field Duffy Daugherty had a different opinion, "We ought to be number one and Notre Dame ought to be number one-A." In the middle were 80,000 people in East Lansing and millions of fans who continue to debate the issue.

On the following week, Notre Dame was still in first place by three votes. The Irish were number one while Michigan State was number two as they had been from the second week in October, and they stayed in that position until the final ballot.

Michigan State was also bulging with talent. In the backfield with black quarterback Jimmy Raye were fullback Bob Apisa and halfbacks Clint Jones and Dwight Lee. Up front were tackle Jerry West, guard Tony Conti, and end Gene Washington. The defense had tackles Pat Gallinagh and Nick Jordan, Bubba Smith at end, halfback Jess Phillips, and linebackers Charley Thornhill and George Webster (voted by MSU fans as their "all-time greatest player"), his number 90 jersey being retired at season's end.

Michigan State won all its games easily except for the Notre Dame tie and the Ohio State game. Illinois was held to 17 yards on the ground and

Bob Griese's stats at Purdue included 308 of 609 pass completions for 3,402 yards, and 28 touchdowns.

Northwestern got only six, and it was 28–0 over Purdue when the reserves came in. Ohio State held an 8–3 margin in the rain until late in the third period. Jimmy Raye's passes began to find their mark, and Bob Apisa scored to cap an 82-yard drive. Dick Kenney faked a kick on the conversion, then tossed a two-point pass to holder Charley Wedemeyer for the win.

Alabama was one of the few teams which had a good claim on the national title three straight years. They won all 11 games and were the only major unbeaten and untied team at the end of the year. Six teams were shut out, the last four in a row, and they finished as the country's best team in scoring defense.

Bear Bryant also came up with another top quarterback, Ken "Snake" Stabler. With ends Ray Perkins and Wayne Cook to throw to and good pass protection from tackles Jerry Duncan and Cecil Dowdy, Stabler hit 16 of 19 passes to down Ole Miss 17–7, nine of them to Perkins for a school mark. The Tide was tested only once more by Tennessee, as the Vols had a 10–0 halftime lead and Stabler hadn't completed a pass. Then Stabler connected on seven of nine tosses, and scored himself early in the last period. A two-point pass made it 10–8. A Steve Davis field goal won it 11–10 with three minutes left, but they almost lost it as a field goal attempt by Gary Wright from the Tide 20 went wide with 16 seconds to go.

Alabama played sixth-ranked Nebraska in the Sugar Bowl, and their 34–7 win was even more impressive than last year. By the end of the first period it was 17–0, and the once-beaten Huskers never got on the scoreboard until the final quarter. Stabler's rapier arm cut the heavier Nebraska team to ribbons, as he completed 12 of 17 passes for 218 yards. Since the wire services did not vote after the bowl games this year, Alabama's lopsided win changed nothing, and they remained the number-three team.

Georgia's fourth-place Dawgs did not play Alabama, so they shared the SEC title. Georgia downed Ole Miss 9–3 as fullback Ronnie Jenkins zoomed 46 yards through the center for the game's only touchdown. Ninth-ranked Miami stopped the Bulldogs in the next game, 7–6, for their only loss. Behind this year's Heisman winner, Steve Spurrier, Florida took a 10–0 lead, but the Dawgs won it in the second half, 27–10, as tackle Bill Stanfill began to spend time in the Florida backfield, and safety Lynn Hughes ran back a hurried pass 50 yards for a score. Georgia was also down by ten against Auburn but came on to win, 21–13. The Bulldogs gave eighth-place Georgia Tech their first loss, 23–14, and met Southern Methodist in the Cotton Bowl. On the first play of the game halfback Kent Lawrence ran 74 yards to a touchdown, and the number-ten Mustangs became Georgia's tenth victim, 24–9.

UCLA had nine wins and a loss and finished in fifth place. With Gary Beban throwing the ball and Mel Farr running it, the Uclans beat Pitt 57–14, Syracuse 31–12, and Missouri 24–15. In the next game, Rice held a 24–16 lead but fumbled twice with four minutes to go. One fumble was turned into the tying touchdown on a 33-yard Beban to Hal Busby pass, and the other was the winning margin, 27–24, as Kurt Zimmerman kicked a 17-yard field goal with seven seconds showing on the clock. On the following weekend, Penn State was buried, 49–11, under an avalanche of 533 yards total offense and 31 first downs. UCLA's only loss was to Washington, 16–3, but they rebounded to beat Southern Cal 14–7, as Norm Dow took over for Beban who was out with a broken ankle.

Neither Michigan State nor the Uclans made a repeat trip to the Rose Bowl. Instead, Purdue made its first trek to Pasadena and met Southern Cal, in spite of USC's worst-ever defeat at the hands of Notre Dame. Number-seven Purdue, losers only to Notre Dame and Michigan State, was coached by Jack Mollenkopf and led by quarterback Bob Griese, tight end Jim Beirne, and safety John Charles. Griese was the team's punter and place-kicker, and set a Big Ten record in total offense with 4,829 career yards.

Purdue ran off nine first downs and took a 7–0 lead, but USC came back with nine first downs for a 7–7 tie two minutes before intermission, halfback Don McCall going in from a yard out. Late in the third period, Perry Williams scored his second touchdown and Griese added another extra point to make it 14–7. USC drove down the field for a score as the Trojan fans went into a furor, with Troy Winslow passing to Rod Sherman, who cut behind George Catavolos. On the two-point attempt Troy tested Catavolos again, but he intercepted the toss to save the win, and the Boilermaker fans broke into a cheer heard all the way back to West Lafayette.

1967

Southern California	(10-1-0)		Tennessee	(9-2-0)	
49	Washington State	0	16	UCLA	20
17	Texas	13	27	Auburn	13
21	Michigan State	17	24	Georgia Tech	13
30	Stanford	0	24	Alabama	13
24	Notre Dame	7	17	Louisiana State	14
23	Washington	6	38	Tampa	0
28	Oregon	6	35	Tulane	14
31	California	12	20	Mississippi	7
0	Oregon State	3	17	Kentucky	7
21	UCLA	20	41	Vanderbilt	14
14	Indiana (Rose Bowl)	3	24	Oklahoma (Orange Bowl)	26
258		87	283		141

After five years, John McKay and USC were back with another national title. The main reason was tailback, O.J. Simpson. At 6'2" and 210 pounds, O.J. had 9.4 speed. He could squirt through a hole or turn the flank in a moment. Once in the open, he kept tacklers off balance with his quick moves and flashing speed. A workhorse in the Trojan backfield, he carried the ball 30 or 40 times a game. Even with the defense stacked against him, he led the country with 1,415 yards on 266 carries for a 5.3 average.

The Trojans looked like world-beaters right from the start. Washington State was outmanned, and 164 yards gained by O.J. on 30 carries helped defeat Texas. Michigan State was in front at halftime, 17–14, but O.J. and quarterback Steve Sogge overtook them in the second half. Sogge completed 14 of 16 attempts for the day, O.J. had 190 yards on 36 carries and tossed a seven-yard pass to flanker Jim Lawrence for the winning touchdown.

USC's next three opponents went down like dominoes. O.J. had 163 yards against Stanford and 169 against number-five Notre Dame. Down 7–0 at the half, the Trojan comeback was led by linebacker Adrian Young, who snagged four interceptions in the game. In the next game with Washington, O.J. bolted 86 yards for one touchdown, and tossed a 17-yard pass to split end Earl McCullouch for another. O.J. rushed for 235 yards on 30 carries, and was only three yards short of the 1,000-yard mark in six contests.

Wins over Oregon and Cal followed before USC lost to Oregon State, which finished seventh. The Beavers bumped Purdue from second place with a 22–14 win, beat Washington State 35–7, tied UCLA 16–16, and overcame USC in successive games. With seven wins, including a 17–15 win over Penn State (which came in tenth), top-rung UCLA met USC to decide the trip across town to Pasadena.

UCLA was led by its Heisman winner, quarterback Gary Beban. They took the lead on a 12-yard run by Greg Jones. Southern Cal tied it at the end of the first quarter as Pat Cashman stole a Beban pass in the flat and returned it 55 yards for a touchdown.

The Trojans revived after UCLA's Zenon Andrusyshyn missed a field goal. McCullouch went 52 yards on a reverse and caught a pass to put the ball on the Bruin 13. From there, O.J. slashed into the end zone for a 14–7 halftime lead. After a second UCLA field goal try was blocked by 6'8" Bill Hayhoe, Beban's 53-yard scoring pass to George Farmer evened it in the third quarter.

In the last period, Andy Herrera swiped a Trojan pass. Beban directed a 65-yard drive to put the Uclans ahead, tossing to Rich Spindler and then to Dave Nuttall for the score. Hayhoe's big paw deflected the point after to keep the count at 20–14.

Toby Page replaced Sogge at quarterback. With third down on the Trojan 36 he called a 23-Blast, Simpson's favorite play. O.J. darted between guard Steve Lehmer and tackle Mike Taylor. Downfield, end Ron Drake blocked the safety as O.J. cut back to the middle and went all the way. Rikki Aldridge kicked USC to the Rose Bowl with a 21–20 win, and the roar in the Coliseum was like Times Square at midnight on New Year's Eve.

After the game in the Trojan locker room, Beban shook Simpson's hand, "O.J., you're the best." Simpson replied, "Gary, you're the greatest. It's too bad one of us had to lose."

In the Rose Bowl USC beat Big Ten champ, Indiana. Led by Adrian Young, Tim Rossovich, and Gary Magner, the Trojans held the Hoosiers to 189 yards total offense, as O.J. scored on two short bursts to win the MVP Award. USC tackle Ron Yary won the Outland Trophy, and Mike Battle was

USC's O.J. Simpson lighting the afterburner.

the top punt returner in the country with 570 yards on 47 returns for a 12.1-yard average.

Coach Doug Dickey's Tennessee team finished in the number-two spot. After an opening game loss to UCLA, sophomores Steve Kiner and Jack Reynolds took over as linebackers. No one scored 20 points on the Vols again, and they won their last nine games.

Tennessee handed eighth-place Alabama its only loss during regular-season play. UT defensive backs Al Dorsey and Charlie Fulton stole three passes to end Bama's 25-game unbeaten streak and avenge last year's one-point defeat. A week later, LSU was beaten on a field goal with only a minute left. A win over Ole Miss avenged eight straight wins by the Rebs, as half-backs Walt Chadwick and Richmond Flowers ran behind the blocking of center Bob Johnson, guard Charley Rosenfelder, and tackle John Boynton.

Second-place Tennessee lost to third-place Oklahoma in the Orange Bowl. OU piled up a 19-0 halftime lead, but Jimmy Glover got the Vols going with a score to cut it to 19–17 in the second half. Oklahoma defensive back Bob Stephenson stole a pass from quarterback Dewey Warren and ran it back to stretch it to 26–17. Tennessee scored with 4:05 left to make it 26–24. With the ball on the 26-yard line and 14 seconds showing, a Karl Kremser field goal went wide, and 77,993 fans took a few minutes to unwind.

Under its new coach, Chuck Fairbanks, Oklahoma finished the year with ten wins and a 9–7 loss to Texas on Rob Layne's field goal and a score by quarterback Bill Bradley. Two missed field goals and two end-zone steals by Texas undid the Sooners. Four teams were blanked, as all–American nose guard Granville Liggins and linebacker Don Pfrimmer made the OU center tough going, and Oklahoma's 6.8 points per game scoring defense headed the list. Missouri never crossed midfield in the first half, and tailback Ron Shotts scored the lone touchdown which stopped Mizzou, 7–0. Kansas was overcome 14–10 on a touchdown pass from quarterback Bob Warmack to tight end Steve Zabel with 62 seconds to go. One week later, wingback Eddie Hinton raced 23 yards with a fourth-quarter touchdown to turn back Nebraska, 21–14.

"It's fun while it lasts," said Fairbanks afterward. "Two of these in a row is tough on you." He didn't know the Orange Bowl had number three waiting for him just around the corner.

Fourth-place Indiana had its own Aladdin's Lamp this year. After five wins in five contests, the Hoosiers made it into the top ten. All over the state the greeting was, "Keep the big red ball rolling," as people gave each other a little red ball. For turning them around from 1-8-1 to 9-2-0, Johnny Pont was chosen coach of the year, and Indiana's best season since 1945 earned them a first-ever appearance in the Rose Bowl.

The Hoosiers won game after game, as they came up with just enough points to win. Kentucky was done in 12–10 as a fourth-down pass was tipped into Al Gage's hands for a touchdown. Kansas was beaten 18–15 as Dave Kornowa won the kicking job with a field goal. A score in the last 53 seconds sunk Iowa, 21–17. Michigan gave way to a touchdown drive in the final two minutes, 27–20. Wisconsin lost 14–9 as their last-down pass sailed over the end zone. Michigan State was halted 14–13 before Minnesota ended the fun and games, 33–7, but the cardiac kids came back to outpoint number-nine Purdue for the Old Oaken Bucket, 19–14.

Most final-minute action was provided by quarterback Harry Gonso, halfback John Isenbarger, and flanker Jade Butcher. It was tackle Doug Crusan, guard Gary Cassells, and linebackers Ken Kaczmarek and Jim Sniadecki, however, who kept the Hoosiers in each game. Dame Fortune put them on their own in Pasadena, but they gave a good account of themselves against the USC champions.

Wyoming had successive 10-1-0 seasons under Lloyd Eaton and was sixth. They led in rushing defense with 42.3 yards per game, but blew a 13–0 halftime Sugar Bowl lead and lost to LSU, 20–13.

1968

Ohio State (10-0-0)			Penn State (11-0-0)	
35	Southern Methodist	14	31 Navy	6
21	Oregon	6	25 Kansas State	9
13	Purdue	0	31 West Virginia	20
45	Northwestern	21	21 UCLA	6
31	Illinois	24	29 Boston College	0
25	Michigan State	20	28 Army	24
43	Wisconsin	8	22 Miami (Fla.)	7
33	Iowa	27	57 Maryland	13
50	Michigan	14	65 Pitt	9
27	USC (Rose Bowl)	16	30 Syracuse	12
			15 Kansas (Orange Bowl)	14
323		150	354	120

The game that had been slowly maturing for decades finally came of age this year. A main factor was the offensive explosion which produced more points, more total yardage, and more passes attempted and completed than ever before. For the first time, total offense for both teams went over 600 yards with 657 yards per game, and the combined points exceeded 40, as a new high of 42.4 was reached. This modern dilemma was verbalized by Frank Broyles of Arkansas, whose Porkers led SMU 35-0 at the start of the last period, but barely escaped with a 35-29 win. "A 35-point lead just isn't safe anymore," said Broyles afterward.

One reason for the high scores was a new rule which stopped the clock after a first down. A team which was behind no longer had to toss an incomplete pass on purpose to save time, but could run the ball for a first down to stop the clock. A record high of 150.1 plays per game added to the excitement. Finally, player numbers became standardized: backs wore 1-49, interior linemen were 50-79, and ends had 80-99.

Ohio State's sophomore-studded team got everyone's attention in a hurry. SMU and Jerry LeVias were beaten and so was Oregon. Then came Purdue, led by nose guard Chuck Kyle, quarterback Mike Phipps, and Leroy Keyes, last year's top scorer with 114 points.

At the half, the game still had no score. Then Ted Provost intercepted a Phipps pass and returned it 34 yards for the first score of the game. Moments later, a State drive took them to the Purdue 14. Right end Jan White wasn't open, so quarterback Bill Long ran in for the second score. Purdue went down as Keyes got 19 yards rushing and Phipps was held to minus four yards passing.

After knocking Purdue out of the top spot, the Buckeyes were number two behind front-runner USC. In November, the Bucks and Trojans switched spots after Ohio State's smashing win over Michigan. One week later, Notre Dame held O.J. to 55 yards on the ground and tied USC 21-21. The Irish lost only to tenth-place Purdue, 37-22, Michigan State, 21-17, and came in fifth at 7-2-1.

For the second year in a row, Heisman winner O.J. Simpson led in rushing with 1,709 yards. The match between the number-one Buckeyes and number-two Southern Cal led to numerous luncheons and dinners graced by celebrities like Bob Hope and Governor Ronald Reagan, but on New Year's Day it was winner take all.

After a scoreless first period, Ron Ayala kicked a 21-yard field goal and O.J. scored on an 80-yard touchdown run to give USC a 10-0 lead. Ohio State tackles Dave Foley and Rufus Mayes knew they had to tighten their belts. After a pep talk by quarterback Rex Kern, the Bucks drove to a touchdown, fullback Jim Otis going over for the score. With three seconds to go in the half, Jim Roman added a field goal to level it at 10-10.

Another field goal by Roman in the third quarter gave Ohio State a 13-10 lead. The two teams slugged it out until the last period, when the Buckeyes recovered a fumble on the Trojan 21. On the second play, Kern lofted a pass to Leo Hayden in the end zone to give Ohio a 20-10 lead. Moments later O.J. fumbled the ball away on his 16, and Kern quickly threw to Ray Gillian to make it 27-10. A last-minute USC score closed it a bit, but Ohio State was number one, and the 9-1-1 Trojans tailspinned to fourth.

After a long apprenticeship to Rip Engle, Joe Paterno gave Penn State an unbeaten season in his third campaign as head man. The first half of the year saw come-from-behind wins over West Virginia and Army. Against Army, a wild second half was settled when the Cadets tried an onside kick. Tight end Ted Kwalik scooped up the crazily bounding ball and dashed 53 yards for the touchdown that clinched the bitterly contested victory.

One week later, Penn State met Miami and its star defensive end, Ted "Mad Stork" Hendricks. Using his long, flapping arms like levers, Hendricks pried apart the blockers and forced the quarterback into a pitchout, then tackled the runner. The Lions wisely avoided his end, as halfback Charlie Pittman scored three second-half touchdowns to keep the Staters unbeaten.

Penn State finished with wins over Maryland, Pitt, and Syracuse. Up front in the 4-4-3 defense were ends Gary Hull and John Ebersole, and tackles Mike Reid and Steve Smear. The linebackers were Denny Onkotz, Jim Kates, Jack Ham, and Mike Smith. Deep men were Pete and Paul Johnson and safety Neal Smith, a ball-hawking unit who stole 25 passes and recovered 17 fumbles this season. In the offensive line were tackles Steve Bradley and John Kulka, guards Tom Jackson and Charlie Zapiec, and center Warren Koegel.

In the Orange Bowl, the Staters met Pepper Rodgers' Kansas team, led by quarterback Bobby Douglass. Kansas had a 14-7 lead in the last quarter after a 47-yard punt return by Don Shanklin led to the second score by fullback John Riggins. With 76 seconds to go, a 47-yard pass put the ball on the three-yard line, and quarterback Charlie Burkhart bootlegged it in as time ran out.

Penn State was still entitled to a conversion. A pass was knocked down, but Kansas drew a penalty for having 12 men on the field. On the second try,

Bob Campbell ran in to give the Lions a one-point win, and Paterno was coach of the year. Penn State was second, while Kansas ended seventh with a 9-2-0 mark.

Texas gained a 20-20 tie with Houston in its opener, but lost the next one to Texas Tech, 31-22. James Street took over at quarterback, and Darrell Royal's wishbone offense started to rev up. In the wishbone-T, the backs line up in a Y-formation with the fullback where the fork begins and the quarterback at the base of the Y. Designed by assistant coach Emory Bellard, it was run oriented, an outgrowth of Royal's dislike of passing.

Oklahoma State became the first victim, 31-3, and Texas was on the long climb up again. Oklahoma was defeated 26-20 as the Longhorns marched 85 yards with 2:37 to go, Happy Feller kicking three field goals, the last one a 54-yarder which hit the crossbar and bounced over. A ding-dong battle with Arkansas followed, but the Texans wrapped it up in the second half, 39-29.

After big wins over Rice, 38-14, and SMU, 38-7, Baylor lost 47-26 as the Longhorns gained 557 yards, 212 of them by Chris Gilbert, the first player to rush for 1,000 yards three seasons in a row. On the following weekend TCU was beaten 47-21 with another jet-fueled Longhorn performance of 490 yards, Steve Worster gaining 183 yards this time. Texas A&M was downed in the season-ender 35-14, and the Steers closed out the year with a win over Tennessee in the Cotton Bowl, 36-13. With the tie and defeat, their nine straight wins brought them a third-place finish.

At Arkansas, Frank Broyles had quarterback Bill Montgomery go to the air lanes in his offense of "two split people and two runners." In the Texas game, Arkansas threw 35 passes while the Longhorns threw only eight, a tactic which brought coach Royal much criticism even though he won. Against Texas A&M, Edd Hargett, who led the Aggies to the SWC title last year and rewrote most of the A&M passing records, hit on 28 of 55 passes, but Montgomery completed 20 of 28 for a 25-22 Arkansas win. In the Sugar Bowl, Arkansas handed number-eight Georgia its first loss, 16-2. They scored on a 27-yard Montgomery to Chuck Dicus pass and three Bob White field goals to finish number six with a 10-1-0 record.

Led by all-American defensive back Roger Wehrli, Missouri was ninth at 8-3-0. Quarterback Terry McMillan's three touchdowns took Mizzou to a 35-10 win over Alabama in the Gator Bowl.

One of the best games of the year was played between Harvard and Yale in the de-emphasized Ivy League. For the first time in 50 years, both teams faced each other with perfect records.

Yale's offense got in gear early as quarterback Brian Dowling scored once himself and passed for two more to Calvin Hill and Del Marting. The 22-0 lead looked like a runaway. Harvard coach John Yovicsin sent Frank Chiampi in at quarterback, and he trimmed it to 22-6 with a 15-yard scoring pass to Bruce Freeman.

Early in the second half Yale fumbled a punt on its 25, and the Crimson recovered. In three plays Gus Crim scored to slice it to 22-13. Yale struck back as the last quarter started and went 45 yards in seven plays. Dowling went around right end to put Yale safely in front again at 29–13.

Ten more minutes ticked away. Stung by the white hankies the Yale partisans waved and their chant, "You're number two," Harvard renewed the attack. They went 69 yards to the Yale 15, where Chiampi tossed another touchdown pass to Freeman with 42 seconds left. While the fans screamed at a penalty on the conversion, Harvard made good on its second try and it was 29–21.

Harvard's Bill Kelly covered the onside kick just past the midfield stripe as the crowd went goofy. Chiampi picked up 14 yards on an end run and 15 more when his face mask was grabbed. In five plays, Harvard drove to Yale's eight-yard line. With three seconds to go, Chiampi hit Vic Gatto on a touchdown pass and it was 29–27. Then his two-point toss to Pete Varney knotted it 29–29, and Yale coach Carmen Cozza was fit to be tied himself.

·1969

Texas	(11-0-0)		Penn State	(11-0-0)	
17	California	0	45	Navy	22
49	Texas Tech	7	27	Colorado	3
56	Navy	17	17	Kansas State	14
27	Oklahoma	17	20	West Virginia	0
31	Rice	0	15	Syracuse	14
45	Southern Methodist	14	42	Ohio University	3
56	Baylor	14	38	Boston College	16
69	Texas Christian	7	48	Maryland	0
49	Texas A&M	12	27	Pitt	7
15	Arkansas	14	33	North Carolina State	8
21	Notre Dame (Cotton Bowl)	17	10	Missouri (Orange Bowl)	3
435		119	322		90

The Longhorns' nine-game win streak continued through 1969 as they made it 20 in a row and took over first place at the end of November. Their wishbone-T led the nation in rushing with 363 yards per game, and was the best scoring machine ever in the SWC.

The Steers started their season with a low-scoring win over Cal, but then the deluge began with impressive defeats of Texas Tech and Navy. The Texans overcame a 14-0 Oklahoma lead to beat OU for the eleventh time in 13 years. Huge scores over Rice and SMU followed. Against the Mustangs, all four starting backs — James Street, Steve Worster, Ted Koy, and Jim Bertelsen — each had more than 100 yards rushing. Astronomical point totals continued, as the Steers stampeded hapless Baylor, TCU, and Texas A&M.

At the end of November, the number-one Longhorns met number-two Arkansas for the Cotton Bowl bid and the national title. The crowd was still

Steve Owens set seven NCAA records, five Big Eight marks and three other school marks to earn the Heisman Trophy in 1969.

buzzing over President Nixon's arrival by helicopter when Arkansas fell on a Texas fumble on the first play of the game. In less than two minutes Bill Burnett scored and the Razorbacks led, 7–0. Another Texas fumble in the third quarter gave Arkansas a 14–0 lead, as they scored five plays later on a 29-yard pass from Bill Montgomery to Chuck Dicus.

Texas scored on the first play of the final period. Street faded to pass, then sped 42 yards to a touchdown. On the conversion, Street slid along the line, then went in to make it 14–8.

Texas scored again with 3:58 left. On fourth-and-three at their own 43, Darrell Royal gambled to win. After a fake handoff, Street connected with tight end Randy Peschel on a 44-yard pass down the sideline to the Arkansas 13. Ted Koy punched out 11 yards through the middle, and on the next play Jim Bertelsen banged over for the tying touchdown. Happy Feller booted home the winning point, and President Nixon presented the Longhorns with a plaque proclaiming them number one.

Notre Dame made its first appearance in a bowl game since 1925 and met Texas in the Cotton Bowl. The Irish took the lead on a 26-yard field goal by Scott Hempel, and made it 10-0 on a 54-yard pass from quarterback Joe Theismann to end Tom Gatewood. A 74-yard drive by the Longhorns cut it to 10-7 by the half.

Texas took a 14-10 lead on a last-quarter 77-yard march in which they threw no passes, wisely evading defensive tackle Mike McCoy. Notre Dame went 80 yards on its next possession, Theismann passing 26 yards to half-back Jim Yoder to make it 17-14.

Texas fought back with a drive from its own 24 to the Notre Dame 28. Three running plays gained eight yards. With 4:26 to go on fourth-and-two, a pitch to Koy was good for a first down. Three more plays picked up eight yards, and it was fourth-and-two on the 10-yard line. Street tossed to split end Cotton Speyrer, who caught the ball on his knees at the Notre Dame two. Billy Dale scored three plays later to give Texas a victory with 68 seconds left. The Irish lost only to Texas and Purdue, 28-14, tied USC 14-14, and finished in fifth place with an 8-2-1 record.

Penn State had another 11-0-0 year, but again Joe Paterno's team placed second. Most of their blue-collar defense was back, including Outland winner Mike Reid, as they blocked three punts, recovered nine fumbles, and stole 24 passes. Against Colorado, they intercepted three passes by quarterback Bob Anderson, while holding him to four yards rushing and 8 of 26 passes.

Kansas State proved a tough foe in the early going, but an interception of a Lynn Dickey pass on fourth-and-two turned them back in the final period. Syracuse was just as thorny, as they held a 14-0 lead. With ten minutes left, a Lydell Mitchell score and a two-point play made it 14-8. Three minutes later, Franco Harris tied the score, and Mike Reitz kicked the winning point.

With only a 31-24 loss to Colorado, Missouri met Penn State in the Orange Bowl. Ten first-quarter points beat the Tigers, as Mike Reitz kicked a 29-yard field goal, and Charlie Burkhart hit Mitchell on a 28-yard touchdown toss. Seven Missouri passes were intercepted, prompting Tiger coach Dan Devine to say, "That's the best defensive unit I've seen in 20 years of football coaching." Missouri finished number six with a 9-2-0 record, and Joe Paterno politely told President Nixon what he could do with his plaque.

After New Year's Day, Southern Cal was one of three unbeaten teams left. Only the Notre Dame tie hurt them, and they finished third. Among their three last-minute wins was a 26-24 shading of Stanford on Ron Ayala's 34-yard field goal with no time left.

When the Trojans met UCLA both had 8-0-1 records, with the Bruin tie coming at the hands of Stanford, 20-20. USC's defensive line was called "The Wild Bunch," and had ends Charlie Weaver and Jim Gunn, tackles Al Cowlings and Tody Smith, and middle guard Bubba Scott. They sacked

Bruin quarterback Dennis Dummit ten times and stole five passes, but he hung in to direct two scoring drives, tossing to Gwen Cooper for a 12-7 UCLA lead with 3:07 remaining.

In the final seconds, three passes by USC quarterback Jimmy Jones took it to the UCLA 43, but after four straight misses time ran out. The joy of the Bruin fans ended in a groan, for a flag was down for pass interference. Jones loaded up again and threw to the corner of the end zone where Sam Dickerson made a diving catch for a 14-12 win, and the Trojan fans who came through the cliffhanger had their fourth straight ticket to Pasadena.

Coach of the year Bo Schembechler survived a heart attack just before the Rose Bowl game, and was not on the bench to watch USC beat his Wolverines, 10-3. Ron Ayala and Tim Killian traded field goals to tie it at the half. In the third period, flanker Bob Chandler scored on a short pass to give the Trojans ten wins and a tie, while Michigan finished ninth with 8-3-0.

Ohio State was in first place throughout the season until Michigan beat them in their traditional mid-November fray. For two months they had one of the best records ever in college football as they beat TCU 62-0, Washington 41-14, Michigan State 54-21, Minnesota 34-7, Illinois 41-0, Northwestern 35-6, Wisconsin 62-7, and Purdue 42-14. But the loss to Michigan nosedived them to fourth. A Columbus carpetmaker sent Woody Hayes a rug to remind him how the season ended, for into it was woven:

1969: Michigan 24, Ohio State 12
1970 . . . ?

The Sugar Bowl matched Bill Montgomery of Arkansas against quarterback Archie Manning of Ole Miss. The Rebs scored first on Bo Brown's 69-yard run and Cloyce Hinton's 52-yard field goal to take Ole Miss to a 24-12 halftime lead. In the last period, Glenn Cannon of Mississippi intercepted a pass in his end zone and later recovered a fumble on his 28 to preserve a 27-22 Rebel win. Arkansas, which led in scoring defense with 7.6 points per game, fell to seventh place with nine wins and two defeats, while Mississippi was eighth with an 8-3-0 record.

Linebackers Mike Anderson and George Bevan made LSU's defensive rush tops with 38.9 yards per game. The tenth-place Tigers lost only to Ole Miss 26-23, but their nine wins never brought a bowl bid, for they paled beside the glamor of Notre Dame, Archie Manning, and top passer John Reaves of Florida with 2,896 yards, whose team stopped SEC champ Tennessee in the Gator Bowl, 14-13.

Oklahoma fullback Steve Owens was the Heisman winner. His 138 points and 1,523 yards rushing topped the country, and his 56 career touchdowns are still a three-year mark.

IX. The National Pastime

1970

Nebraska (11-0-1)			Notre Dame (10-1-0)	
36 Wake Forest	12		35 Northwestern	14
21 Southern Cal	21		48 Purdue	0
28 Army	0		29 Michigan State	0
35 Minnesota	10		51 Army	10
21 Missouri	7		24 Missouri	7
41 Kansas	20		56 Navy	7
65 Oklahoma State	31		46 Pitt	14
29 Colorado	13		10 Georgia Tech	7
54 Iowa State	29		3 Louisiana State	0
51 Kansas State	13		28 Southern Cal	38
28 Oklahoma	21		24 Texas (Cotton Bowl)	11
17 LSU (Orange Bowl)	12			
426	189		354	108

In the 60s, the ideas of equal opportunity and everyone is equal became confused. Coaches became concerned about the mood of college life and how it would affect football. In the spring of 1970, 3,500 Nebraska students demonstrated against the Vietnam War, but 14,000 students at the intra-squad game that same afternoon helped remind people that not everyone had lost their way.

Bob Devaney could easily have been elected governor, for he put Nebraska on the map more than the corn or beef had ever done. He recruited heavily within the state, for he believed an athlete played better where he grew up. With a roster full of hometown boys, Nebraska fever became evident across the state. "Nebraska Number One" buttons were as common as the pure beef burgers, and bumper stickers proclaimed "Go Big Red." Many homes had a lampshade shaped like a Nebraska football helmet, and pets wore red sweaters when the weather was cold. On away games, planes full of Husker fans showed up in red jackets and huge cowboy hats.

The USC tie put Nebraska third behind Texas and Ohio State, but on New Year's Day both front-runners were upended. "It's all yours," Devaney told his squad before they met Louisiana State in the Orange Bowl. "All you have to do now is go out and win it."

Nebraska did just that, but not without a struggle. LSU was the defensive rushing leader again with 52.2 yards per game, and was led by tackles Ronnie Estay and John Sage, safety Tommy Casanova, and linebacker Mike Anderson. Coach of the Year Charles McClendon had Art Cantrelle at tailback. Nebraska's defense was led by middle guard Ed Periard, linebacker Jerry Murtaugh, tackle Dave Walline, and halfback Bill Kosch. On offense was tackle Bob Newton.

The Cornhuskers took a 10–0 first period lead on a touchdown by Joe Orduna and a Bob Rogers three-pointer. Two field goals by Mark Lumpkin in the next two quarters trimmed it to 10–6. Then the Tigers scored on a Buddy Lee to Al Coffee pass of 31 yards to make it 12–10 at the end of three. A last-quarter drive won the title for Nebraska, as quarterback Jerry Tagge nosed in from one yard out. Louisiana State settled in seventh place with a 9-3-0.

After three wins in three games, Notre Dame was third behind Texas and Ohio State. After seven wins, they held the top spot for one brief week. When the Irish lost to Southern California, they dropped to sixth and remained there until New Year's Day.

Notre Dame took over second place when they beat Texas in a return match in the Cotton Bowl. The Texas wishbone formation was stopped by the Irish defense which put their linebackers in a wishbone alignment opposite the Texas backfield. Notre Dame's wishbone defense caused nine fumbles and closed the gate on the Longhorn attack, limiting them to 216 yards rushing.

After Eddie Phillips ran 63 yards on the first play, Texas scored on a 23-yard field goal by Happy Feller. The Irish came back with a 26-yard Joe Theismann scoring pass to Tom Gatewood, Notre Dame's all-time receiver. Safety Tom Eaton nailed a Texas fumble on the kickoff, and the Irish went in soon after. Notre Dame scored again early in the second period, but Texas hammered away for 86 yards to shave it to 21–11. Scott Hempel's 36-yard field goal made it 24–11 at the half to end the day's scoring.

Quarterback Joe Theismann rewrote the record book at Notre Dame. His 526 yards on 33 completions against USC this year is a single-game record. He set season records this year with 155 completions on 268 tries, in passing with 2,429 yards for 242.9 per contest, and in total offense with 2,813 yards. His three-year career marks include 290 of 509 attempts for 57 percent, 31 touchdown passes, and 4,411 yards passing, all Irish firsts. He also broke Gipp's total offense record with 5,551 yards.

After their loss to Notre Dame, Texas fell to number three in the AP poll, but UPI still voted them number one. The Cotton Bowl loss ended their winning streak at 30 games, the Longhorn mark. Texas was the country's leading ground gainer with 374.5 yards and first in scoring with 41.2 points per game.

Darrell Royal's wishbone-T became the most-copied formation of the seventies. It is sometimes called the triple option since the quarterback has three choices once he gets the ball. He can give it to the fullback, pitch it to a halfback, or keep it himself, depending on the reaction of the defensive

Heisman winner Jim Plunkett of Stanford led the Pac 8 in passing and total offense for three straight years (1968–1970).

end. If he keeps it, the quarterback becomes a fourth ball carrier in this rush-inclined offense. On the flanks are a split end and a tight end who can be used as blockers, decoys, or pass receivers.

First-year coach Bill Battle guided Tennessee to a fourth-place finish with 11 wins and a loss. Fullback Curt Watson gave the Vols offensive might. Jackie Walker was at linebacker, and in the backfield were Bobby Majors and Tim Priest, leaders of a defensive secondary which nabbed 35 passes this season, an SEC record. UT lost only to number-ten Auburn, 36–23, in a contest plagued by 14 turnovers, but they recovered to shut out Alabama, 24–0. After piling up a 24–0 first-quarter lead over Air Force in the Sugar Bowl on a pair of scores by halfback Don McLeary, a field goal by George Hunt, and a touchdown pass from quarterback Bobby Scott to Gary Theiler, the Big Orange eased to a 34–13 win and its best won-lost record in two decades.

Ohio State's sensational sophomores were now seniors, and they led the Buckeyes to a 9-1-0 record, a Rose Bowl trip, and a number-five rank. Back was nose guard Jim Stillwagon, the Outland winner, and behind him were the secondary of Tim Anderson, Jack Tatum, Harry Howard, and Mike Sensibaugh, who led in interceptions with eight. Except for a 10–7 win over Purdue and a 20–9 victory over Michigan in their last two outings, the Bucks beat everyone by at least two touchdowns. In the doorway to the practice field was the rug with last year's Ohio-Michigan score emblazoned on it, and after stomping on it all season, Ohio put the Wolverines away in the last period and found itself facing Stanford and Heisman winner Jim Plunkett. Michigan, with linebackers Marty Huff and Mike Taylor, tackle Dan Dierdorf, and guard Henry Hill, was ninth.

Plunkett's statistics were impressive. His career records were 52 scoring passes, 7,544 yards passing, and 254.4 yards per game total offense, all new records. Even more impressive was Plunkett's humanity. His parents were blind and he helped care for his mother after his dad died.

Ralston (a workaholic whose enthusiasm was infectious) had a few tricks for Ohio State. Eric Cross ran 41 yards on a flanker reverse, and Plunkett went 13 yards on a quarterback draw. Jackie Brown ran in from the four, but John Brockington scored twice from a yard out and Ohio State led 14–10 at the half.

The teams swapped field goals in the third period. On the first play of the final quarter, the Buckeyes had fourth-and-one at the Stanford 19. Linebacker Ron Kadziel stopped Brockington short of the first down, and Ralston's ardor became epidemic.

Five straight passes by Plunkett took it to the two-yard line, where Brown scored to put Stanford ahead 20–17. Another touchdown pass to Randy Vataha made the final score 27–17. Up in the stands, Plunkett's blind mother heard the cheers that said her son's team had won and earned an eighth-place finish.

Arizona State led the nation with 514.5 yards total offense per game. They beat North Carolina in the Peach Bowl, 48–26, to cap their perfect season of 11 wins and come in sixth.

1971

This was the year of the Big Eight, as Nebraska, Oklahoma, and Colorado finished one-two-three. Nebraska held the top spot in every weekly poll, and became the first team since the turn of the century to win 13 games. After beating a good Alabama team in the Orange Bowl, Nebraska received all 55 first-place votes.

The Huskers' slot-I or spread-I formation had Jeff Kinney at tailback, and Jerry Tagge again was the nation's top passer with 143 of 239 for 59.8 percent. The offense also had tackle Carl Johnson, guard Dick Rupert, and slotback Johnny Rodgers, a 5'9", 173-pounder who could beat you whenever he caught a pass, ran a reverse, or fielded a kick. His 15-yard average (1,983 yards on 132 plays) each time he touched the ball is an all-time record. Defensive standouts in the line were Outland winner Larry Jacobson at tackle, guard Rich Glover, and end Willie Harper. Safety Bill Kosch and cornerbacks Jim Anderson and Joe Blahak gave the Cornhuskers one of the best defensive backfields in the country.

Nebraska (13-0-0)			Oklahoma (11-1-0)		
34	Oregon	7	30	Southern Methodist	0
35	Minnesota	7	55	Pitt	29
34	Texas A&M	7	33	Southern Cal	20
42	Utah State	6	48	Texas	27
36	Missouri	0	45	Colorado	17
55	Kansas	0	75	Kansas State	28
41	Oklahoma State	13	43	Iowa State	12
31	Colorado	7	20	Missouri	3
37	Iowa State	0	56	Kansas	10
44	Kansas State	17	31	Nebraska	35
35	Oklahoma	31	58	Oklahoma State	14
45	Hawaii	3	40	Auburn (Sugar Bowl)	22
38	Alabama (Orange Bowl)	6			
507		104	534		217

A step behind Nebraska was Oklahoma. The Sooners operated from the wishbone-T installed last year by Chuck Fairbanks. The explosive OU attack was first in the nation in scoring with 44.9 points, in total offense with 566.5 yards, and rushed for 472.4 yards each game, an all-time high. In the lightning-swift backfield were quarterback Jack Mildren, fullback Leon Crosswhite, and halfbacks Greg Pruitt and Joe Wylie. The offense included ends Jon Harrison and Al Chandler, guard Ken Jones, and center Tom Brahaney. On defense were end Ray Hamilton, tackle Derland Moore, linebacker Steve Aycock, and safety John Shelly.

When both teams met on Thanksgiving Day, they had been one-two most of October and November. Anyone who had seconds on the turkey and trimmings missed the first score of the game, a darting 72-yard punt return by Rodgers after OU's first series. The Sooners countered with a field goal, but Kinney went over at the end of a 54-yard march to make it 14–3. Oklahoma came back with two long drives, Mildren dashing in from the 3, and then took a 17–14 halftime lead on a 24-yard pass from Mildren to Harrison.

In the third period, Nebraska went 53 yards and 61 yards to regain the lead at 28–17, with Kinney going over on short yardage both times. Behind 11 points for the second time in the game, Oklahoma drove 73 yards to make it 28–24, Mildren again scoring from the three. With 7:05 left in the game, the Sooners forged ahead as Mildren tossed 16 yards to Harrison to cap a 69-yard effort.

Down 31–28, Nebraska muscled up for one final push to the Sooner goal 74 yards away. On third-and-one from their own 35, Kinney swept end for

17 yards. Moments later, it was third-and-eight from the OU 46, but Tagge tossed 11 yards to Rodgers, who caught the ball lying down. In the next few minutes, Nebraska moved to the Oklahoma 15. From there, Kinney got the ball four straight times. With his jersey in shreds he scored the winning points, and the Cornhuskers were on the way to the Orange Bowl.

Oklahoma finished the year in the Sugar Bowl against Auburn. Led by Terry Beasley and Heisman winner Pat Sullivan, Auburn had a good season until the final two games, when they were deflated by Alabama and Oklahoma. In some ways, Oklahoma's win over the Tigers was more decisive than Nebraska's dismantling of Alabama, for the score was 19-0 after one quarter and 31-0 at the half.

Colorado, which lost only to Nebraska and Oklahoma, ended third. Coach Eddie Crowder had top players in guard Bud Magrum, tackles Jake Zumbach and Herb Orvis, and halfback Charlie Davis. Against Oklahoma State, Davis rushed for 342 yards, a record for sophomores. Winners over Louisiana State, 31-21, and Ohio State, 20-14, the Buffaloes got their tenth win in the Bluebonnet Bowl, 29-17, after Robert Newhouse put Houston on top with two scores.

Before losing to Nebraska and diving to fourth, Alabama won 11 straight. Behind guard John Hannah and Jim Krapf at center, halfback Johnny Musso spearheaded the wishbone-T. Against both Tennessee and Houston, tight end Dave Bailey caught two scoring passes from quarterback Terry Davis. Alabama ended the regular season with a win over previously unbeaten Auburn, 31-7, as the Tide's swarming defense, which looked like a jailbreak on every series, was never better. Led by defensive end Robin Parkhouse and linebackers Jeff Rouzie and Tom Surlas, the Tigers were held to 27 yards rushing, seven first downs, and never went past midfield after the half. When Oklahoma and Auburn lost on Thanksgiving weekend, everything was ready in the Orange Bowl for the title game between number-one Nebraska and number-two Alabama, but it was a blowout as three Tide fumbles led to quick scores, and the Huskers' longest unbeaten streak stood at 32 games.

Tackle Dave Joiner and backs Lydell Mitchell and Franco Harris took Penn State to a fifth-place finish. Mitchell led the nation in scoring with 29 touchdowns and 174 points, both modern records. Except for a narrow 16-14 win over Air Force, the Lions from Mt. Nittany won their first ten games easily. Their only loss was to Tennessee, 31-11, but they rebounded to beat Texas in the Cotton Bowl. Trailing 6-3 at halftime, quarterback John Hufnagel began the second-half scoring display with a 65-yard touchdown pass to Scott Skarzynski, and it was Katy-bar-the-door for a 30-6 win.

The Wolverines checked in sixth. They won 11 games, including a much-publicized win over Ohio State, but it was Wocdy Hayes who got the headlines. As deeply allergic to Ann Arbor as Pasadena, this year's game at Michigan made Woody break out again.

With a minute to go, Tom Darden intercepted a Buckeye pass on the Michigan 32. "Interference," bellowed Woody, but no flag was thrown. His

Alabama's all–American guard John Hannah became a mainstay in the line for the New England Patriots.

rage took him onto the playing area, where he got a flag for being on the field. While his assistants tried to restrain him, he tore a cloth down-marker on the sideline to pieces and drew another 15-yard penalty. Michigan ran out the clock to safeguard a 10-7 win and its best season in years.

Michigan's 6.4 points and 63.3 yards rushing defense each game led the nation, but it couldn't stop Stanford in Pasadena. The Wolverines led at the half on Dana Coin's 30-yard field goal, but Stanford pulled even in the third frame on a 42-yarder by Rod Garcia. Michigan had a 10-3 lead in the final period when Stanford's Reggie Sanderson took the center snap on a fake punt and gave it to Jackie Brown who ran 31 yards to a first down. Quarterback Don Bunce completed one to Bill Scott at the Michigan 24. Brown turned the corner from there, and it was ten apiece.

Not long after, Stanford's Jim Ferguson gave up a safety in the end zone. Michigan punted after the free kick, and Stanford had the ball on its 22 with 1:48 to go. Bunce hit on five passes in a row to tight end Scott, flanker John Winesberry, and split end Miles Moore. Garcia's 31-yard three-pointer with 16 seconds left gave Stanford a 13-12 win and a tenth-place finish.

Georgia and Arizona State, both 11-1-0, came in seventh and eighth. Vince Dooley downed brother Bill in the Gator Bowl 7-3, as a Jimmy Poulos score spiked Ken Craven's North Carolina field goal, and ASU aced Florida State in the first Fiesta Bowl, 45-38. Ten-and-two Tennessee was ninth after a Liberty Bowl win, as two Arkansas field goals by Bill McClard fell short by one, 14-13.

For the second straight year, Cornell's Ed Marinaro was the country's leading rusher. His average of 174.6 yards each game (4,715 yards in 27 games) is still an all-time career record.

1972

Southern California	(12-0-0)		Oklahoma	(11-1-0)	
31	Arkansas	10	49	Utah State	0
51	Oregon State	6	68	Oregon	3
55	Illinois	20	52	Clemson	3
51	Michigan State	6	27	Texas	0
30	Stanford	21	14	Colorado	20
42	California	14	52	Kansas State	0
34	Washington	7	20	Iowa State	6
18	Oregon	0	17	Missouri	6
44	Washington State	3	31	Kansas	7
24	UCLA	7	17	Nebraska	14
45	Notre Dame	23	38	Oklahoma State	15
42	Ohio State (Rose Bowl)	17	14	Penn State (Sugar Bowl)	0
467		134	399		74

Coach of the Year McKay's Trojans were loaded. All but one starter returned to the offensive line, including Booker Brown, Dave Brown, Pete Adams, and Steve Riley. In the defensive line were John Grant, Jim Sims, Jeff Winans, and Dale Mitchell, and linebackers Charles Anthony and Rich Wood. Defensive backs were Charles Phillips, Artimus Parker, Marv Cobb, and Charles Hinton.

At quarterback was senior Mike Rae, who shared the job with sophomore Pat Haden. The wide receivers were Lynn Swann, Edesel Garrison, and the coach's son, J.K. McKay. At tight end were Charlie Young and Jim Obradovich. Rounding out this team swimming in depth and talent were fullbacks Sam "Bam" Cunningham and Manfred Moore, and tailbacks Rod McNeill and Anthony Davis.

USC struck quickly and scored often. No one came close to beating them. Several teams picked up points late in the game when the reserves came in, and they held the top spot all year.

Anthony Davis quickly became the Trojan's latest tailback sensation.

He broke a scoreless combat in the Oregon game with two long second-half scoring runs, and led the charge which beat UCLA. The Bruins failed to tie it early on after tight end Jack Lassner came up with a fumble. Behind quarterback Mark Harmon, tailback Kermit Johnson and fullback James McAlister took it to the Troy 17, but Efren Herrera's field goal was no good. It was in the UCLA game that Davis added glitter to his performance, as he slid in the end zone and did a shimmy while on his knees.

Against Notre Dame, Davis gave a performance which spoke for itself. He returned the opening kickoff 97 yards for a touchdown and scored twice on short runs to give USC a 19-10 halftime lead. His next touchdown was on another short burst, but the Irish kept pace at 25-23. Davis took the following kickoff and ran it back 96 yards to quiet Notre Dame, and later scored on an eight-yard run.

Once-beaten Ohio State got to Pasadena by topping number-six Michigan, 14-11. Michigan had the best scoring defense for the second year in a row with 5.2 points allowed each game, but against the Bucks they beat themselves. With ten wins in ten starts, a tie would have put the Wolverines in the Rose Bowl. Twice they had fourth-and-short yardage inside the Ohio 10-yard line, but both times they tried for a first down and failed on each occasion.

The Columbus crowd did its best to help Michigan's decision against a field goal. With 13 seconds left and Michigan on the Buckeye 41, they poured onto the field and leveled the goal post at the Ohio end. Armed with a scorecard, Woody Hayes chased them back into the seats and bade the game go on. The security guards moved in, and the game was finished without a field goal or post.

In the Rose Bowl, the brutish Buckeyes had a 7-7 tie when USC scored the first five times it had the ball after the half. Sam Bam dived over the goal four times, and Davis ran 20 yards for the other. Ninth-place Ohio State coach Hayes praised USC, "They are the best college football team I've ever seen," he said.

Behind center Tom Brahaney, tackle Dean Unruh, and quarterback Dave Robertson, Oklahoma ran in overdrive with Greg Pruitt, Joe Wylie, and Leon Crosswhite. Backed by sophomores Rod Shoate at linebacker and safety Randy Hughes, tackles Derland Moore and Ray Hamilton, and nose guard Lucious Selmon made the middle of the OU line a fortress. Oklahoma gave up only two field goals in its first four games, while on their way to the rushing title of 368.8 yards each game. Then Colorado stopped the Sooner land rush, and OU fell to eighth-place and began the long climb up.

In a "rematch of the game of the century," Oklahoma fumbled the ball away four times. Nebraska lost the ball three times on fumbles, and three on interceptions. It was not a "Battle of the Heisman," either, as Pruitt went out with an injury, and Johnny Rodgers gained five yards in four carries, returned one punt for seven yards, and caught three passes for 41 yards. Oklahoma won it in the last quarter on a 41-yard field goal by Rick Fulcher.

Oklahoma was second after a Sugar Bowl win over tenth-place Penn

Nebraska coach Bob Devaney won 80.6 percent of his games (136-30-7).

State, led by defensive end Bruce Bannon and linebacker John Skorupan. But when it was found that OU had used an ineligible player, the Big Eight zinged them with a probation which forbade any bowl games for two years and no national TV for 1974 and 1975.

Texas finished in third place. After their early-season loss to Oklahoma, the Longhorns also began the long climb back. In the battle of the wishbone attacks, Texas met Alabama on New Year's Day in the Cotton Bowl. The Tide took a 10–0 lead on a 50-yard field goal by Greg Gantt and a 31-yard touchdown run by Wilbur Jackson. Texas won it in the second half, as quarterback Alan Lowry scored on a three-yard run in the third period, and then bootlegged it 34 yards to the winning touchdown with 3:20 left. The 17–13 win was their tenth of the season against one defeat.

Number-four Nebraska finished with a 9-2-1 record. Many of the great ones were back, and hope for a third straight national title ran high. But their 23-game winning streak came to an end in the LA Coliseum as UCLA beat them in their first game, 20–17. Later in the year, a 23–23 tie with Johnny Majors' upstart Iowa State team did them in. Another field goal in the Oklahoma game completed their downfall. Johnny Rodgers won the Heisman

Award and Rich Glover was the Outland winner, making it the first time these trophies were won by two players from the same team. In his last game as Cornhusker coach, Bob Devaney switched Rodgers to tailback. He scored four touchdowns and passed for a fifth to give Nebraska a 40-0 third quarter lead and a third straight win in the Orange Bowl, as Notre Dame was outclassed, 40-6.

At Auburn, coach Shug Jordan's quarterback had never taken a snap from center, and most of his starters were walk-ons. Yet by the end of the year they lost only one game to Bert Jones and LSU, 35-7, beat eighth-place Tennessee, 10-6, and ended fifth.

One of the most incredible moments in southern football took place in the Auburn-Alabama game. The Tide was victorious in all ten of its starts, and had been number two throughout November. Alabama scored in the second quarter, but the PAT was blocked by Roger Mitchell. The Tide added a field goal for a 9-0 halftime lead, and it ballooned to 16-0 by the end of three quarters.

Auburn was awakened in the last period by a 42-yard Gardner Jett field goal with 9:50 to go. The Tide took the kickoff, but was stopped at midfield. On fourth down, linebacker Bill Newton came through untouched to block the Bama punt. Dave Langner took the ball on the hop and dashed into the end zone with 5:30 left.

Then the instant replay began. Alabama got the kickoff and made three first downs again. On fourth down at midfield, Bill Newton came through untouched once more to block the kick. Dave Langner fielded the ball on the bounce and raced to the end zone with the tying points. Gardner Jett's conversion was good for a 17-16 win, and the best-selling bumper sticker in the South was born: "Punt Bama Punt." The Tigers moved on to the Gator Bowl where they beat Colorado, 24-3, for their tenth win.

Alabama's tenth win was over Virginia Tech, 52-13, as they held Don Strock, the top passer and total offense leader in the land, to 98 yards passing and intercepted him four times. After their loss to Auburn, Bama fell to fourth place, and then faded to number seven when Texas beat them in the Cotton Bowl.

Howard Stevens ended his career at Louisville with 193.7 yards per game in all-purpose running, the all-time mark.

1973

Notre Dame had been badly beaten at the end of last season, but new men in the defensive line made the difference this year. Freshman Ross Browner joined sophomore Jim Stock on the flanks, and a pair of 270-pound tackles, sophomore Steve Niehaus and junior Mike Fanning, gave the Irish a formidable front four.

Ross Browner let everyone know early that he came to play. He scored the first two points against Northwestern by blocking a punt which rolled out of the end zone, and had five tackles on the afternoon. On Notre Dame's first series, quarterback Tom Clements hit tight end Dave Casper for 15 yards, and halfback Eric Penick scored on a 16-yard run to begin the rout of the Wildcats.

Notre Dame (11-0-0)		Ohio State (10-0-1)	
44 Northwestern	0	56 Minnesota	7
20 Purdue	7	37 Texas Christian	3
14 Michigan State	10	27 Washington State	3
28 Rice	0	24 Wisconsin	0
62 Army	3	37 Indiana	7
23 Southern Cal	14	60 Northwestern	0
44 Navy	7	30 Illinois	0
31 Pitt	10	35 Michigan State	0
48 Air Force	15	55 Iowa	13
44 Miami (Florida)	0	10 Michigan	10
24 Alabama (Sugar Bowl)	23	42 USC (Rose Bowl)	21
382	89	413	64

Defense helped win the next four games. Safety Luther Bradley broke up two passes and intercepted a third against Purdue, and Denny Stolz's Michigan State offense didn't cross the Irish goal for the fourth straight year. MSU's points came on a field goal by Dirk Kryt and Ray Nester's interception. Rice was held to 63 yards rushing and Army got only ten yards on the ground.

A 7-7 tie with Oklahoma had knocked USC out of the top spot, but they were the best team the Irish faced so far. After taking a 13-7 halftime lead, Penick's 85-yard touchdown run touched off the cheers which lasted until the final gun. Troy made it 20-14 on a 27-yard Pat Haden to Lynn Swann scoring throw, but a third Bob Thomas field goal closed the scoring. USC had only 66 yards on the ground, and their unbeaten streak ended at 23 games.

Notre Dame took over the number-five spot and then stopped Navy with 77 yards rushing. Pitt was tougher, as freshman Tony Dorsett gained 209 yards running. After swamping Air Force and Miami, the Irish had their first perfect season since 1949.

Number-one Alabama met number-three Notre Dame in the Sugar Bowl for the national title. The Irish finished second in total defense with 201.3 yards allowed per game, and held the Alabama wishbone to no yards in the first period. Three passes from Tom Clements to split end Pete Demmerle were good for 59 yards, and fullback Wayne Bullock's score made it 6-0 Notre Dame at the end of one.

Quarterback Gary Rutledge put Alabama up by one on a Randy Billingsley run, but Al Hunter ran back the kickoff 93 yards for a Sugar Bowl record. A two-point play and a 39-yard field goal by the Tide's Bill Davis gave Notre Dame a 14-10 halftime lead.

A touchdown by each team ended the third period at 21-17. In the fourth quarter, Richard Todd came in at quarterback for Alabama. Todd handed off to Mike Stock and faded left. Stock ran right and tossed to Todd, who raced 25 yards to put the Tide ahead at 23–21. A 19-yard Bob Thomas field goal with 4:26 left gave the Irish a one-point lead. A daring 35-yard pass from the end zone to Robin Weber in the final minutes preserved the thin margin and won the title, while 11-1-0 Alabama fell to fourth.

Ohio State had been number one since the first of October, and for the sixth straight year the Ohio-Michigan contest determined the Big Ten champ and Rose Bowl representative. Veterans manned each team. Michigan had Dennis Franklin at quarterback, halfbacks Clint Haslerig and Chuck Heater, and Ed Shuttlesworth at fullback. Tackle Dave Gallagher and halfback Dave Brown were noteworthy on defense. On the Buckeye side were offensive tackles Kurt Schumacher and Outland winner John Hicks. Cornerback Neal Colzie and linebackers Randy Gradishar, Rick Middleton, and Vic Koegle gave Ohio State a 4.3-point scoring defense, the nation's best.

Both teams were high-scoring vehicles, but defense is what the crowd saw that day. Ohio led 10-0 at the half on Blair Conway's field goal and a Pete Johnson run. Michigan's Mike Lantry left-footed a 30-yard field goal in the final frame, and Franklin's rollout tied it soon after to give the Wolverines a 10-0-1 record. Moments later Franklin left with a shoulder injury, and he and the sixth-place Wolverines saw the Rose Bowl game on TV.

In Pasadena, the revenge was a joy for Woody Hayes and the Buckeyes. USC played them tough with a 14-14 halftime tie and a 21-14 third-quarter lead, but three touchdown smashes by fullback Pete Johnson told who was winning in the pits. Ohio scored four times in the second half for a convincing win and a number-two finish, while the 9-2-1 Trojans skidded to eighth place.

New coach Barry Switzer's Oklahoma wishbone rolled on with receiver Tinker Owens, tackle Eddie Foster, guard John Roush, and new men in quarterback Steve Davis and halfback Joe Washington. On defense were linebacker Rod Shoate, end Gary Baccus, and nose guard Lucious Selmon, sided by his brothers, Lee Roy and Dewey.

After tying USC and overtaking Miami 24–20, the Sooners won ten games, including a 27-0 win over Nebraska, the pass defense leader with 39.9 yards allowed per game. New coach Tom Osborne's Huskers lost to Missouri 13-12 and tied Oklahoma State 17-17, but got a ninth win over Texas in the Cotton Bowl, 19-3, to finish number seven, while 10-0-1 Oklahoma, barred from bowl play, was third.

Penn State was victorious in a dozen games, but a 16–9 win over Louisiana State in the Orange Bowl only ranked them fifth. Steve Rogers scored first, but a 44-yarder by PSU's Chris Bahr made it 7–3 after a period. A Tom Shuman to Chuck Herd 72-yard pass and Heisman winner John Cappelletti's lunge gave the Lions a 16-7 halftime lead. A third-quarter safety ended the scoring.

Arizona State's 28-7 win over Pitt in the Fiesta Bowl dealt them an 11-1-0 year and a ninth-place finish. Coached by Frank Kush, ASU led in total offense and scoring for the second year in a row. Quarterback Danny White's 17.2 yards on every completion is the career high, while the other half of the ASU attack, halfback Woody Green, had a career mark of 125.1 yards each game.

Minus the last of the four Brezina boys, Mark, Bill Yeoman's Houston team, led by D.C. Nobles at quarter and linebacker Deryl McGallion, also won 11, lost to Auburn, 7–0, and tied for ninth.

1974

Oklahoma (11-0-0)			Southern California (10-1-1)		
28	Baylor	11	7	Arkansas	22
72	Utah State	3	16	Pitt	7
63	Wake Forest	0	41	Iowa	3
16	Texas	13	54	Washington State	7
49	Colorado	14	16	Oregon	7
63	Kansas State	0	31	Oregon State	10
28	Iowa State	10	15	California	15
37	Missouri	0	34	Stanford	10
45	Kansas	14	42	Washington	11
28	Nebraska	14	34	UCLA	9
44	Oklahoma State	13	55	Notre Dame	24
			18	Ohio State (Rose Bowl)	17
473		92	363		142

OU swept along averaging 507.7 yards total offense, 438.8 yards rushing, and 43 points per game, all top figures. Leading the attack were Steve Davis at quarter, halfback Joe Washington, fullback Jim Littrell, and ends Tinker Owens and Wayne Hoffman. The line had center Kyle Davis, guards John Roush and Terry Webb, and tackles Mike Vaughan and Jerry Arnold. On defense were nose guard Dewey Selmon, tackle Lee Roy Selmon, end Jimbo Elrod, linebacker Rod Shoate, and safeties Randy Hughes and Zac Henderson.

In the opener, the Sooners scored 21 last-quarter points to subdue Grant Teaff's tough Baylor Bears. Another nine points in the final period turned back Texas: split end Billy Brooks tied it on a 40-yard run and Tony DiRienzo won it with a 37-yard field goal. By the end of the year, OU's unbeaten streak was at 29 games, the longest in the nation. "Oklahoma is the best team I've ever seen — ever," said Kansas State head coach Vince Gibson.

The UPI coaches' poll did not rank Oklahoma since they still were on probation. After the bowl games, AP's writers and broadcasters gave the Sooners 51 of 60 first-place votes. "We're not in the business of policing college football," said AP. "As long as Oklahoma continues to field a deserving team, we'll rank it."

USC came in second in the AP poll, but was voted number one by UPI.

It was not an easy climb for the Trojans, as they lost their opener and tied the seventh game. Quarterback Steve Bartkowski led Cal to the USC 17 in the last minute, but a wide field goal brought a tie. "Cal deserved to win," growled coach McKay.

The Trojans played well enough to win five games in between the loss and the tie. Graduation had taken some of the squad's best blockers, but tight end Jim Obradovich, tackle Marv Powell, and guard Bill Bain helped take up the slack. On defense, the team was held together by linebackers Rich Wood and Ed Powell, end Gary Jeter, tackle Art Riley, nose guard Otha Bradley, and Charles Phillips, Marv Cobb, and Danny Reece in the backfield.

The Trojans jelled as a team against Stanford. They scored on their first offensive series and never looked back. "SC put together one of the finest combinations of defense and offense I've ever seen," said Stanford coach Jack Christiansen. A week later against Washington, Anthony Davis became the first player in conference history to gain 1,000 yards three straight years.

In the last game, Notre Dame took a 24-0 lead when USC made one of the greatest comebacks ever seen anywhere. It began with a Pat Haden swing pass to Davis for a score as the half ended.

Davis caught the second-half kickoff, cut behind a block by Ricky Bell, and sped 102 yards down the left sideline to score. Three mminutes later Davis scored again, and three minutes after that he had another touchdown and a two-point conversion to make it 27-24. Then Haden threw to J.K. McKay for a score, and USC was in front by ten with only 9:23 gone. Another Haden to McKay scoring pass made it 41-24 as the third quarter ended.

Kevin Bruce recovered his second Irish fumble as the final period started. Haden passed to Shelton Diggs for a touchdown, and USC had doubled the score. Then Charles Phillips ran back his third interception 58 yards for another touchdown to end the scoring at 55-24. Only 1:44 of the last period had elapsed.

USC had scored 55 points in 17 minutes. Haden hit on eight of eight, Davis scored 26 points, and McKay had four catches, two for touchdowns. As the trio came off the field, coach McKay put his arms around them. "Never have there been three smaller kids who have done so much so often," he said proudly.

For the third year in a row, it was USC and Ohio State in the Rose Bowl. The Buckeyes had ten wins, but were elbowed from the top spot by Michigan State, 16-13, a game in which the Bucks scored on the last play, but it was ruled that the gun had fired before the ball was snapped. At quarterback for Ohio State was Bible-reading Cornelius Greene, Pete Johnson at fullback, Brian Baschnagel at wingback, and Heisman winner Archie Griffin. Up front were center Steve Myers, tackle Kurt Schumacher, and Van DeCree at end. For the defense were tackle Pete Cusick, cornerback Neal Colzie, and linebackers Bruce Elia, Arnie Jones, and Ken Kuhn.

Archie Griffin of Ohio State won the Heisman Trophy his junior and senior years.

Chris Limahelu put Troy in front with a 30-yard first period field goal. Ohio State took a 7–3 halftime lead on a two-yard plunge by Champ Henson, but not before a punt by USC's Jim Lucas grazed his foot. Lucas shorthopped it and ran 16 yards for a first down.

After a scoreless third quarter, a USC touchdown put them in front by three. Ohio seesawed back into the lead with a scoring drive, and Tom Klaban's 32-yard field goal made it 17–10. With two minutes left, Haden completed a 38-yard pass to McKay in the end zone to draw within one. A diving catch by Shelton Diggs on the two-point pass gave Southern Cal a last-minute win.

Ohio State and Michigan switched places after the Rose Bowl game. The Buckeyes ended fourth and the 10-1-0 Wolverines were third. For the past three years Michigan's record was a glowing 30-2-1, but no Pasadena trips. They had won all their games except for two losses and a tie with Ohio State. With wingback Gil Chapman, fullback Chuck Heater, tailback Gordon Bell, and a healthy Dennis Franklin at quarter, their backfield had speed to burn. Linebacker Steve Strinko and safety Dave Brown took Michigan to a 6.8-point scoring defense, best in the land for the third time in four years. But Tom Klaban's four field goals, the last one a 45-yarder, gave Ohio a 12–10 win and another Rose Bowl trip.

Alabama's record for the past few years was even more gaudy than Michigan's. For the second year in a row and third time in four years, they were unbeaten in regular-season play, including this year's 21–16 opening day win over Maryland and its Outland winner, defensive end Randy White. Their closest game was with Florida State, as quarterback Richard Todd was out with injuries and running backs Willie Shelby and Calvin Culliver couldn't get a score. But two Bucky Berrey field goals, the last a 36-yarder in the final minute, gave Alabama an 8–7 win. The Bear's defense, however, was solid as usual, as ends Mike Dubose and Leroy Cook, linebacker Woody Lowe, and deep men Ricky Davis and Mike Washington held together a scoring defense not far behind Michigan's.

Alabama met Notre Dame in a rematch on New Year's Day in the Orange Bowl. Wayne Bullock and Mark McLane scored on short runs before Danny Ridgeway's 20-yard field goal made it 13–3 at halftime. Alabama scored with 3:13 to go on Todd's 48-yard pass to Russ Schamun. Tight end George Pugh's catch closed it to 13–11. Then Todd passed to mid-field, but Reggie Barnett's interception ended Ara Parseghian's career on a winning note. The number-two Tide sank to fifth place, while the 10-2-0 Irish, which lost to USC and Purdue, 31–20, and was first in total defense with 195.2 yards and rushing defense with 102.8 yards each game, was sixth.

Penn State and Auburn, both 10-2-0, were seventh and eighth, respectively. State chilled Baylor's first showing in the Cotton Bowl, 41–20, while Auburn trampled Texas in the Gator Bowl, 27–3.

Nebraska beat Florida in the Sugar Bowl, 13–10, to end ninth at 9-3-0. Led by running back Rob Carpenter, Miami of Ohio tied Purdue, 7–7, and was tenth after their tenth win over Georgia in the Tangerine Bowl, 21–10, to give coach Dick Crum an unbeaten year.

Freddie Solomon, Tampa's running quarterback, ran for 1,300 yards for a 118.2-yards per game average, a record. His 3,299 yards on 557 carries is also a career record for quarterbacks.

1975

Oklahoma	(11-1-0)		Arizona State	(12-0-0)	
62	Oregon	7	35	Washington	12
46	Pitt	10	33	Texas Christian	10
20	Miami (Florida)	17	20	Brigham Young	0
21	Colorado	20	29	Idaho	3
24	Texas	17	16	New Mexico	10
25	Kansas State	3	33	Colorado State	3
39	Iowa State	7	24	Texas El Paso	6
27	Oklahoma State	7	40	Utah	14
3	Kansas	23	21	Wyoming	20
28	Missouri	27	55	Pacific	14
35	Nebraska	10	24	Arizona	21
14	Michigan (Orange Bowl)	6	17	Nebraska (Fiesta Bowl)	14
344		154	347		127

Oklahoma's veteran team repeated as national champions. The offensive team had tackle Mike Vaughan, guard Terry Webb, a pair of good split ends in Tinker Owens and Billy Brooks, quarterback Steve Davis, halfback Joe Washington, and fullback Jim Littrell. On the defense were Jimbo Elrod at end, nose guard Dewey Selmon, tackles Anthony Bryant and Outland winner Lee Roy Selmon, safety Scott Hill, and cornerbacks Zac Henderson and Sidney Brown.

Oklahoma and Ohio State again dominated the race to number one. The Sooners survived early-season scares when a 20–7 lead over Miami and first-period leads of 14–0 over Colorado and 10–0 over Texas evaporated. Miami came up short, but not before they scored ten last-quarter points. Then a Dave Williams touchdown throw to Billy Waddy came close, but a Colorado conversion went wide with 1:19 remaining. Texas came closer with a 17–17 tie on a 43-yard Russell Erxleben field goal before OU put it away.

The Sooners' 28-game winning streak came to an end against Kansas. Oklahoma scored on a 52-yard Tony DiRienzo first-period field goal. Early in the year, Kansas coach Bud Moore had moved Nolan Cromwell from defensive back to quarterback. In his first game against Oregon State, Cromwell ran for 294 yards, a rushing record for quarterbacks. The loss was Barry Switzer's first at Oklahoma, and forced the Sooners from second place.

OU bounced back with a 20–0 halftime lead over Missouri, but the Tigers forged ahead with 27 second-half points to lead late in the last period. On fourth-and-one, Washington raced 71 yards for a touchdown, then took the two-point toss to win it with 4:20 to go. Nebraska moved into second place for two weeks until the Sooners gave them their first loss, and OU finished the regular season number three behind unbeaten Ohio State and Texas A&M.

Coach Emory Bellard's Texas Aggies had a great year until December, including a 20–10 win over Texas. With Pat Thomas and Lester Hayes in the defensive secondary, and a linebacking corps of Ed Simonini, Garth Ten-Napel, and Bob Jackson, A&M was first against the run with 80.3 yards and in total defense with 183.8 yards per game. On offense were halfbacks Skip Walker and Bubba Bean, wishbone fullback George Woodard, split end Carl Roaches, guard Bruce Welch, and field goal kicker Tony Franklin's buggy-whip leg. But after ten wins, the Aggies dropped out of the top ten with losses to Arkansas, 31–6, and USC, 20–0, in the Liberty Bowl, John McKay's last game as coach of the Trojans.

Returning for their last year at Ohio State was the senior backfield of Corny Greene, Brian Baschnagel, Pete Johnson, and Archie Griffin. In the defensive backfield were Craig Cassady (Hopalong the Great's son), Ray Griffin (Archie's younger brother), and Tim Fox, with stellar guard Ted Smith in the offensive line.

Other than Michigan, the Buckeyes were tested only by Penn State. Chris Bahr kept the Lions close with three field goals, but Ohio held a one-point lead late in the game. On third down and 11 to go, Griffin pulled in a

23-yard Green pass at the Penn State 45. Johnson carried the ball seven times in the next nine plays, driving in from the 11-yard line for a 17–9 Buckeye win.

The Big Ten title again came down to the Ohio-Michigan game. The bone-bruising contest brought eight turnovers, as Michigan's defense ended Griffin's 31 regular season 100-yard games and his 33 career games of 100 yards, both all-time marks. His 46 yards gave him 5,177 yards on 845 tries for a 6.13 average, the first man at a major school to gain over 5,000 yards. Ohio State won the game, 21–14, and a trip to Pasadena for the fourth time in a row, while Griffin again won the Heisman Award, the only player to win it twice. Ohio's crunching attack led in scoring with 34 points per game, Johnson getting 25 touchdowns the hard way, and Tom Skladany's 46.7-yard punting average was the nation's best.

Ohio State met PAC-8 champ UCLA in the Rose Bowl. Although the Buckeyes had beaten UCLA early in the year, 41–20, and were unbeatable for two periods, the score was still 3–0 at the half. The Bruin's tied it on Brett White's field goal, and then took a 16–3 third-quarter lead on two touchdown passes from quarterback John Sciarra to flanker Wally Henry. Ohio cut it to 16–10, but Wendell Tyler's 54-yard touchdown dash made it 23–10 at the gun.

"We're a better team now," said UCLA's coach, Dick Vermeil. Four good reasons were up front, where nose guard Cliff Frazier and linebacker Dale Curry steadied the defense, and guards Phil McKinnely and Randy Cross helped knit the offensive line.

The Buckeye's Rose Bowl loss dropped them to fourth place, and the 9-2-1 Bruins, with a loss to Washington, 17–13, and a 20–20 tie with Air Force, finished number five. With new rules permitting number two teams to play in a bowl game, Oklahoma beat Michigan 14–6 in the Orange Bowl, and was voted national champion. The eight victories, two losses, and a pair of ties against Stanford, 19–19, and Baylor, 14–14, settled Michigan in eighth place.

Arizona State ended the year with a perfect record, the only unbeaten and untied team left. Their last win was over Nebraska in the Fiesta Bowl. ASU scored on a 27-yard field goal by Dan Kush, the coach's son. ASU blitzes put quarterback Vince Ferragamo on the bench, but Terry Luck came on to give the Huskers a 7–3 lead. A 33-yard Kush field goal made it 7–6 at the half.

Monte Anthony's second touchdown for the Cornhuskers in the third quarter lifted it to 14–6. Fred Mortenson replaced Dennis Sproule at quarterback, and on fourth-and-one he tossed a 10-yard scoring pass to John Jefferson, then tied it 14–14 on a two-point pass to wide receiver Larry Mucker. Nebraska center Rik Bonness and ASU linebacker Larry Gordon were ejected for fighting, and a 29-yard field goal by Kush won it with 4:29 left. ASU finished number two and Frank Kush was voted coach of the year, while the 10-2-0 Cornhuskers ended up in ninth place.

Texas lost to Oklahoma and Texas A&M, got a tenth win over Colorado in the Bluebonnet Bowl, 38–21, and was sixth. Arkansas, which lost to

Texas, 24–18, and Oklahoma State, 20–13, won number ten in the Cotton Bowl against Georgia, 31–10, and ended seventh.

For the third year in a row, Alabama won 11 of 12 games and was third. This year, however, it wasn't a bowl game that Alabama lost, but its opener to Missouri, 20–7. The highlight of the year was a reunion of the men who had played in the Alabama-Washington game 50 years before in the Rose Bowl. The Tide beat tenth-place Penn State (led by all-American linebacker Greg Buttle) by the score of 13–6 in the first Sugar Bowl game played in the New Orleans' Superdome on New Year's Eve, but not before Bear Bryant got after some of his players who stayed out late before the game.

"Discipline is not what it used to be," moaned Bryant, but he still had a few words of advice for young coaches:

> If you're angry, don't take it out on the players.
> Don't talk too much or too soon.
> Don't over-coach the players. Let them play some.

Running records disappeared this year like free drinks at a bar. Some thought the 1972 freshmen eligibility rule gave everyone more experience; some believed it was due to the emphasis on offense. The change was greatest among runners as 28 backs averaged 100 yards a game, and 1,000 yards a season was commonplace.

Sportscaster Tom Harmon put it in perspective: "A thousand yards would have been nothing for Red Grange, Glenn Davis or Jay Berwanger. Give a guy like Grange the ball 40 times under two-platoon rules and he'd kill you. He might be running yet."

1976

Pittsburgh (12-0-0)			Southern California (11-1-0)		
31	Notre Dame	10	25	Missouri	46
42	Georgia Tech	14	53	Oregon	0
21	Temple	7	31	Purdue	13
44	Duke	31	55	Iowa	0
27	Louisville	6	23	Washington State	14
36	Miami (Florida)	19	56	Oregon State	0
45	Navy	0	20	California	6
23	Syracuse	13	48	Stanford	24
37	Army	7	20	Washington	3
24	West Virginia	16	24	UCLA	14
24	Penn State	7	17	Notre Dame	13
27	Georgia (Sugar Bowl)	3	14	Michigan (Rose Bowl)	6
381		133	386		139

Even as Archie Griffin was setting rushing marks, Tony Dorsett was overtaking him. While taking Pitt to the title, Dorsett gained 6,082 yards on

1,074 carries for a 5.66-yard average, tied Griffin's marks in consecutive and total 100-yard games, and won the Heisman. He also tied Glenn Davis' record of 59 touchdowns, became the only major collegian to reach the 6,000-yard plateau, and his two PAT's made him the all-time scorer with 356 points.

Johnny Majors was voted coach of the year. He gave Dorsett outstanding help with fullback Elliott Walker, who averaged 5.7 yards rushing in his career, and blocked for Dorsett in the veer offense Majors used. This two-fisted bombardment was helped by quarterback Matt Cavanaugh's tosses to tight end Jim Corbett and split ends Willie Taylor and Gordon Jones. At offensive guard was Tom Brzoza. The punter was Larry Swider. On defense were a couple of Kong-sized tackles, 6′6″, 248-pound Don Parrish and 6′6″, 242-pound Randy Holloway. Between them was middle guard Al Romano at 6′3″ and 235 pounds. In the rear were linebackers Jimbo Cramer and Arnie Weatherington. Defensive backs were Jeff Delaney, Leroy Felder, and Bob Jury, who had ten interceptions.

On the way to the rushing title, Dorsett gained 1,948 yards this year. He started off with 181 yards in Notre Dame Stadium, whose long grass Majors compared to the Iowa cornfields, and ran for 113 yards against Georgia Tech. In game three Dorsett had 112 yards, but returning quarterback Bob Haygood was out for the year with a knee injury. Cavanaugh came on with five touchdown passes to tame Duke, and Dorsett gained 129 yards. Dorsett had 130 yards against Louisville, but Cavanaugh left with a bad rib.

Tom Yewcic quarterbacked the Miami game, as Dorsett had 227 yards, and 180 more at Navy. Then in three home games he gained 241, 212, and 199 yards. At Three Rivers Stadium in the finale he had 224 yards, and Carson Long added a 47-yard field goal.

Pitt had been number two behind Michigan since September, but when the Wolverines lost in early November, Pitt moved into the top spot and held it until the end of the season. On New Year's Day the Panthers played SEC champ Georgia, which had ten wins and a loss to Mississippi, 21–17. Georgia was led by its all–American offensive guard, Joel Harris, and quarterback Ray Goff. But the Pitt tackles shut off Goff's dive plays, and ends Ed Wilamowski and Cecil Johnson helped Cramer and Weatherington jam the option on the corners, while Ramano and tackle Dave Logan caught the play from behind. Dorsett had 202 yards running and Cavanaugh had 192 passing. When it was over, Pitt was the only untarnished team, and Georgia was in tenth place.

Once again it was Trojans and Bruins in the LA Coliseum for all the marbles. Number-three USC lost its opening game but had eight wins in a row, while second-place UCLA had nine wins and a 10–10 tie with Ohio State. The Trojans took a 7–0 halftime lead when safety Dennis Thurman filched a Bruin fumble in midair and ran it back 47 yards for a score. Then the lethal Troy defense took over and allowed UCLA to get no closer than the USC 34-yard line. Linebackers Rod Martin, Dave Lewis, and Clay Matthews put a clamp on anyone who got past Gary Jeter at end, while

Pitt's Tony Dorsett is the only major collegian to break the 6,000-yard rushing mark.

Thurman, Ron Bush, Clint Strozier, and Mike Burns shot down anything deep.

With USC's clinic on defense taking over, quarterback Vince Evans directed three drives that put a lock on the Rose Bowl bid. Behind tackle Marv Powell, he pitched to Ricky Bell or handed it to fullbacks Dave Farmer or Mosi Tatupu. The first march of 57 yards ended in a Glen Walker field goal, but the second all-run drive of 61 yards made it 17–0 as the final period began. Evans ran 36 yards for the last Trojan tally, while all the points for new coach Terry Donahue's Bruins came at the end of the game on short runs by Theotis Brown and quarterback Jeff Dankworth.

Michigan was number one all year until they lost to Purdue, 16–14, in November. They got to the Rose Bowl with a 22–0 win over Ohio State which ended four years of frustration for coach Bo Schembechler. Ohio State beat Colorado 27–10 in the Orange Bowl, and finished in sixth place with a 9-2-1 record.

Led by its all–American offensive guard, Mark Donahue, the Wolverines verged on ostentation. They led in scoring with 38.7 points each game, in scoring defense with 7.4 points, in rushing offense with 362.6 yards, and in total offense with 448.1 yards.

The rushing duel between USC's Ricky Bell and Michigan's Rob Lytle did not materialize, as Bell left the game after his fourth carry, never to return. Lytle went over to cap a march from midfield, but tackle Walt Underwood blocked the Michigan conversion. Just before the half Evans scored on a rollout, and Glen Walker's point after put Troy in the lead at intermission, 7–6.

Coach John Robinson's Trojan defense shut off the Wolverine attack like a faucet. By the end of the game, Harlan Huckleby, Jim Smith, and Russ Davis had 155 yards rushing, and quarterback Rick Leach hit on 4 of 12 for 76 yards. Charles White, who took over for Bell, scored at the end of a 79-yard drive for a 14–6 USC win. Ten and two put Michigan third, while USC was second.

With two defeats in its first six games, 49–14 to Florida, paced by wide receiver Wes Chandler and halfback Tony Green, and to Arkansas, 14–7, the chances for Houston's fourth-place finish didn't look good. But coach Bill Yeoman cranked up the Cougars, and they claimed the SWC title in their first year as a member.

Included was a 21–10 win over defending champ Texas A&M, and a re-sounding 30–0 win over Texas. In the TCU set-to, split end Don Bass had four touchdown catches, three from quarterback Danny Davis. Clearing out the troops in the veer-T developed by Yeoman was guard Val Belcher, with running back Alois Blackwood lining up behind fullback Dyral Thomas. Leading the defense were all–American tackle Wilson Greenwood and Guy Brown, linebacker Paul Humphreys, and cornerbacks Anthony Francis and Mark Mohr. Houston's 30–21 Cotton Bowl win, the tenth, over Jerry Claiborne's Maryland squad, led by quarterback Mark Manges and defensive tackle Joe Campbell, put the 11-1-0 Terps eighth.

Two losses and a tie also made Oklahoma's fifth-place finish seem unlikely. After harsh words between Darrell Royal and Barry Switzer, President Ford tossed the coin before the OU-Texas game. It ended in a draw, as Russell Erxleben kicked field goals of 37 and 41 yards, and OU tied it with 1:38 left but did not convert the point after.

The Sooners lost to Oklahoma State as halfback Terry Miller scored on a 72-yard run, and then led the Cowboys to ten fourth-period points and a 31–24 win. A week later Colorado bested OU 42–31. The lead changed hands five times before the Buffs out-gunned Oklahoma, and Switzer had his first back-to-back losses.

OU threw no passes against Missouri, as quarterback Thomas Lott gained 126 yards, fullback Kenny King had 128, and halfback Horace Ivory rushed for 159. Ace-spoiler Missouri, victor over USC and Ohio State, 22–21, almost added Oklahoma to its victim list. Quarterback Steve Pisarkiewicz took the Tigers to the OU 15 with four minutes to go, but cornerback Terry Peters' interception saved a 27–20 win. Oklahoma beat number-nine Nebraska, 20–17, on Elvis Peacock's third score with 38 seconds to go, then got a ninth win in the Fiesta Bowl over Wyoming, 41–7.

Seventh-place Texas A&M had ten wins but lost to Houston and Texas Tech, 27–16. Barefoot Tony Franklin kicked a 65-yard and 64-yard field goal against Baylor and had five against Rice.

1977

Notre Dame	(11-1-0)		Alabama	(11-1-0)	
19	Pitt	9	34	Mississippi	13
13	Mississippi	20	24	Nebraska	31
31	Purdue	24	24	Vanderbilt	12
16	Michigan State	6	18	Georgia	10
24	Army	0	21	Southern Cal	20
49	Southern Cal	19	24	Tennessee	10
43	Navy	10	55	Louisville	6
69	Georgia Tech	14	37	Mississippi State	7
21	Clemson	17	24	Louisiana State	3
49	Air Force	0	36	Miami (Florida)	0
48	Miami (Florida)	10	48	Auburn	21
38	Texas (Cotton Bowl)	10	35	Ohio State (Sugar Bowl)	6
420		139	380		139

Notre Dame's climb to the top was long and arduous. In the opener with Pitt, Matt Cavanaugh passed the Panthers to an early lead, but went out with a bad wrist when defensive end Willie Fry fell on him. A fumbled punt in the end zone made it 9–0 Pitt.

Pitt's new quarterback couldn't get the rhythm down, and was penalized repeatedly. Irish quarterback Rusty Lisch hit on five straight passes, tight end Ken McAfee catching the last one for a score. Defensive end Hugh Green blocked the conversion for a 9–6 halftime Pitt lead, but Notre Dame came on for a second-half win.

Mississippi was the team which made Notre Dame's climb back a painful one. It was a seesaw tussle in which the Irish went in front, 13–10, on a pair of Dave Reeve field goals with 4:53 left. The Rebs retaliated in five plays on fullback Jim Storey's second scoring pass and Hoppy Langley's second field goal for the win.

It was in the third game that Notre Dame got on the championship path. Purdue quarterback Mark Herrmann had 270 passing yards at halftime and a 24–14 fourth-quarter lead when Joe Montana took over at quarterback for the Irish. In just eight minutes, he led them to ten quick points and a 24–24 tie. Montana then directed a final scoring drive of 70 yards for a 31–24 comeback win.

With Montana making his first start against Michigan State, the offense began to move. The defense also began to play like champions, as nose guard Bob Golik had 18 tackles, defensive end Ross Browner had 11, and cornerback Ted Burgmeier had 10. MSU was held to a pair of field goals in the gritty win. Army was also kept from a touchdown in the next game, as fullback Jerome Heavens became the first Irish back to gain 200 yards in a game.

The last three beatings by Southern Cal were avenged with a determined win over the Trojans. USC's Lynn Cain got the first rushing touchdown against Notre Dame all year, but the green jerseys which the Irish wore kept them high. The Green Machine rolled on as they shell-shocked Navy and

Georgia Tech. Against Tech, Dave Waymer took a short pass and ran 68 yards to a score.

Clemson almost halted the Irish climb back up, as they led at the end of three, 17-7. But Tiger quarterback Steve Fuller's 10-yard rollout and a one-yard plunge were the third and last time Notre Dame was scored on by rushing. Montana went in at the end of two long drives for a last-period win. Both scores came after Irish tackle Mike Calhoun recovered a fumble. Notre Dame closed with computer-counting victories over Air Force and Miami.

Rookie coach Fred Akers brought Texas through the year with a perfect record of 11 wins. Led by Outland winner Brad Shearer at defensive tackle and the nation's top rusher with 1,744 yards—Heisman-winning fullback Earl Campbell—Texas ended the regular season in first place. But Notre Dame forced four first-half turnovers and went on to a huge win in the Cotton Bowl. Irish coach Dan Devine said it all after the game: "This puts us where Texas was, number one." Both polls agreed; Texas went to fourth.

After an initial win, Alabama lost its only game to Nebraska at Lincoln. By the fourth game the defense began to congeal, and Roger Chapman's three last-half field goals helped catch Georgia.

Against top-rated USC in Los Angeles, two last-quarter Tony Nathan scores gave the Tide a 21-6 bulge. Quarterback Rob Hertel threw to wideout Randy Simmrin on two touchdown drives to make it close in the final minute. But Wayne Hamilton's rush brought an interception of Hertel's two-point toss, and Bama had it by one. The Tide defense held LSU to a Mike Conway field goal, and slowed down Charles Alexander's SEC season mark of 1,686 yards rushing.

Alabama trailed only once more during the season, as Auburn took a 7-0 lead on an 85-yard touchdown run by Joe Cribbs. Then the Tide methodically took the Tigers apart, including a 42-yard scoring pass from quarterback Jeff Rutledge to end Ozzie Newsome and a 12-yard pop up the middle by fullback Johnny Davis.

In the Sugar Bowl, Alabama met Ohio State, led by offensive tackle Chris Ward and linebacker Tom Cousineau. The Buckeyes had been beaten by Oklahoma, 29-28, as Uwe Von Schamann von-footed a field goal with three seconds showing, and been held to a pair of field goals by Michigan, 14-6, but were still tough. Alabama put the Bucks away easily, however, to finish in the runner-up spot.

In the Orange Bowl, it was Arkansas and Oklahoma. Both of them had lost to Texas, Arkansas by 13-9 and Oklahoma by 13-6. Barry Switzer said this was the best team he ever had at Norman, in spite of the 30 fumbles Oklahoma lost during the year. The Sooner fumbles were the best weapon Arkansas coach Lou Holtz had.

Two minutes after the kickoff, OU's Billy Sims fumbled the ball away on his nine-yard line. In two plays, Roland Sales sliced through the Sooner defense to score. Still in the first period, Kenny King fumbled again and Arkansas had the ball at midfield. Within minutes, quarterback Ron Calcagni scored to make it 14-0.

After the half, Steve Little added a 32-yard field goal for the Hogs. Before long, it was 24–0 on another Sales touchdown. Oklahoma, first in rushing with a 328.9-yard average, fumbled the game away and got beat up, 31–6. Ten-and-two Oklahoma dipped to seventh, while Arkansas was third with 11 wins and one defeat.

Penn State was the last of the first five teams to come in 11-1-0. Led by nose guard Randy Sidler, they lost only to Kentucky, 24–20, after a field goal and Jimmy Cefalo's 75-yard punt return gave them a 10–0 lead. Against West Virginia, Penn State scored three times in 90 seconds. Tackle Matt Millen scored on a blocked punt, quarterback Chuck Fusina threw 41 yards to Mickey Shuler, and Steve Geise had a seven-yard run. Three Matt Bahr field goals and a failed two-point conversion late in the game downed number-eight Pitt, 15–13, which had nine wins, two losses, and a 17–17 tie with Florida. The Lions ended the season with a 42–30 win over Arizona State on Christmas Day in the Fiesta Bowl.

Coach Fran Curci's Kentucky team finished the year in sixth place, highest ever for the Wildcats. After an opening day 10–7 victory over North Carolina on Joe Bryant's 22-yard field goal, Kentucky lost its only game of the season to Baylor, 21–6. All three Baylor scores came as a result of Youkay errors: a fumble near their own goal, a center snap over punter Kevin Kelly's head recovered on the UK 14, and a blocked punt which Mike Singletary scooped up and ran in for the Bears. Then the Cats got on track and won their last nine games, including wins over Penn State and Tennessee for the second straight time. In Kentucky's backfield were Derrick Ramsey at quarter, running backs Chris Hill and Rod Stewart, and Tom Dornbrook at guard. On defense for Youkay were Art Still at end and deep men Dallas Owens and Mike Siganos.

With ten wins and a 16–0 loss to Minnesota, Michigan still could not win in the Rose Bowl. Washington took a 17–0 halftime lead, and strung it out to 24–0 on a 28-yard touchdown pass from quarterback Warren Moon to wide receiver Spider Gaines.

Then quarterback Rick Leach began to throw for Michigan. He hit Curt Stephenson with a scoring pass good for 76 yards. Soon after Russ Davis scored, and Leach narrowed it to 27–20 with a 32-yard scoring toss to Stan Edwards. In the final 1:21, linebacker Michael Jackson stole one Leach pass and defensive back Nesby Glasgow pulled down another to clinch it for UW. Michigan ended in ninth place, and the Huskies were number ten. Standouts for the Wolverines were defensive back Dwight Hicks, center Walt Downing, guard Mark Donahue, and halfback Harlan Huckleby.

1978

USC came to Birmingham in September and bumped Alabama from first place. One win on the climb back was over Rose Bowl winner

Washington. The defense of middle guard Curtis McGriff, tackles Marty Lyons and Byron Braggs, end E.J. Junior, and Murray Legg at safety swarmed all over Husky runner Joe Steele and made him fumble the ball away twice. They beat Auburn for the sixth year in a row, as quarterback Jeff Rutledge set a school record of 30 career scoring passes with tosses to Bruce Bolton and Rick Neal.

Alabama (11-1-0)			Southern California (12-1-0)		
20	Nebraska	3	17	Texas Tech	9
38	Missouri	20	37	Oregon	10
14	Southern Cal	24	24	Alabama	14
51	Vanderbilt	28	30	Michigan State	9
20	Washington	17	7	Arizona State	20
23	Florida	12	38	Oregon State	7
30	Tennessee	17	42	California	17
35	Virginia Tech	0	13	Stanford	7
35	Mississippi State	14	28	Washington	10
31	Louisiana State	10	17	UCLA	10
34	Auburn	16	27	Notre Dame	25
14	Penn State (Sugar Bowl)	7	21	Hawaii	5
			17	Michigan (Rose Bowl)	10
345		168	318		153

Number-one Penn State met second-place Alabama in the Sugar Bowl. PSU led in rushing and total defense with 54.5 yards and 203.9 yards per game. On this knotty crew were nose guard Greg Jones, tackles Matt Millen and Bruce Clark, ends Larry Kubin and Joe Lalley, and linebackers Paul Suhey and Lance Mehl. Offensive linemen included Keith Dorney, Eric Cunningham, and Irv Pankey.

Both teams battled for almost a half. With 1:11 to go, the Tide went 80 yards in six plays to score. After one first down, Tony Nathan skirted right end for 30 yards to the State 37, and followed it up with seven more. Then Rutledge passed to split end Bolton for the take-the-lead touchdown at half-time.

In the third quarter, safety Pete Harris, who led everyone in interceptions, made off with a Rutledge pass near midfield. After Penn State marched to the Tide 17, Chuck Fusina tossed to Scott Fitzkee in the back of the end zone to even it at 7-7.

Alabama went ahead at the end of the third period following Lou Ikner's 62-yard punt return to the Lion 11. From the eight-yard line, Major Ogilvie took a pitch and ran in for a 14-7 Tide lead.

Midway through the last quarter, Penn State got the ball on a fumble on the Bama 19. An 11-yard run gave them a first down at the eight. On second down from the six, Fusina hit Fitzkee who was brought down at the one-yard line by Don McNeal. Matt Suhey tried the middle, but was stopped by Dave Hannah and Steve Wingo.

On fourth down Mike Guman tried the middle, but was belted by linebacker Barry Krauss for no gain. Krauss was knocked out on the play, but Penn State was knocked out of first place. The Tide was now number one, while Coach of the Year Joe Paterno's 11-1-0 Lions finished out of the money in fourth place.

Southern Cal came in second. In their offensive line were tackle Anthony Munoz, and guards Brad Budde and Pat Howell. At tailback, Charles White's explosive runs gained 1,760 yards, and quarterback Paul McDonald left-handed another 1,667 yards through the air. On defense were linemen Rich Dimler, linebacker Dennis Johnson, and Ronnie Lott and Dennis Smith in the backfield.

USC lost only to Arizona State, quarterbacked by Mark Malone and now in the PAC-10 with Arizona. They beat UCLA, led by linebacker Jerry Robinson and safety Ken Easley, and edged Notre Dame in a thriller. With McDonald hitting flanker Kevin Williams and handing to Charles White, USC was ahead 24-6 at the end of three.

Injuries to running backs Jerome Heavens and Vagas Ferguson forced Joe Montana to go upstairs. After he fumbled to start the last quarter, Montana unloaded a 57-yard touchdown bomb to split end Kris Haines. On the next possession, fullback Pete Buchanan scored to cap a 98-yard march, and it was 24-19 with 3:01 to go.

After the Irish held, Montana became a man in a hurry as he moved the ball to the Trojan two-yard line. With 46 seconds left, he hit flanker Pete Holohan on a slant-in pass for a 25-24 lead.

Now it was USC's turn to come back. From his 30-yard line, McDonald threw for ten yards. Then Calvin Sweeney broke free to the Irish 25, and Charles White's run positioned it for a field goal. Only six ticks remained as Frank Jordan kicked a 37-yarder, and 84,256 fans in the LA Coliseum cheered the garish finish.

Notre Dame ended its year with 23 last-period points in the Cotton Bowl to down number-ten Houston, 35-34, but losses 3-0 to Missouri and 28-14 to Michigan put the 9-3-0 Irish seventh.

For the third year in a row, Michigan beat Ohio State and earned the right to meet Southern Cal in Pasadena. Both teams had a left-handed quarterback and used a multiple-I attack. In the USC version Charles White did most of the running, while the Michigan offense used quarterback Rick Leach as a ball carrier.

After a Ronnie Lott interception, Paul McDonald threw nine yards to tight end Hobey Brenner for the first score. A 36-yard field goal by Greg Willner made it 7-3 at the end of a quarter.

White dived over the goal in the second period for Troy's next score. When he came down, White didn't have the ball. The Wolverines complained bitterly, but the line judge awarded USC a touchdown on the basis that the ball had crossed the goal line. Frank Jordan's 35-yard field goal lifted it to 17-3 at halftime.

Leach gave Michigan life after the half with a scoring toss to tailback Roosevelt Smith. But the USC defenders took over to hand Michigan its

Woody Hayes wound up his Ohio State career with a 238-72-10 record (a .759 average).

third straight Rose Bowl defeat. A 24–15 loss to Michigan State made them 10-2-0 for a fifth-place finish.

With its collection of chrome-plated performers, Oklahoma's torrid offense was first with 427.5 yards rushing and 40 points per game. Among its superstars were Outland winner Greg Roberts at offensive guard, running backs Kenny King and Heisman winner Billy Sims who led the nation with 1,762 yards rushing and 120 points, and quarterback Thomas Lott. On defense for the two-way terrors were nose guard Reggie Kinlaw, tackle Phil Tabor, linebackers Daryl Hunt and George Cumby, and safety Darrol Ray.

The only team to slow down Oklahoma in the early going was perennial hindrance, Kansas. But Uwe Von Schamann, called "Von Foot" by his team-mates, booted an 18-yard field goal to best the Jayhawks, 17–16. Then in the annual winner-take-all battle with Nebraska, coach Tom Osborne got his first win over the Sooners. Billy Todd kicked UN into a 17–14 lead with a 24-yard field goal early in the final quarter. It proved to be the winning margin, as the hard-hitting Huskers caused Sims to lose the ball twice on fumbles, the last one at the three-yard line with 3:27 remaining.

But Nebraska let the Big Eight title slip away with a 35–31 loss to Missouri. In an Orange Bowl repeat with the Sooners, OU won this time, 31–24. Oklahoma finished third with 11 wins and a loss, while the 9-3-0 Corn-huskers were number eight.

Clemson ended the year in sixth place with a 17–15 win over Ohio State in the Gator Bowl. It was their eleventh victory against one defeat, a 12–0 loss to Georgia in September. The Gator Bowl also ended the career of Woody Hayes, as he was asked to turn in his playbook. Ohio State almost tied it in the last period, but Art Schlichter's two-point run was stopped by Jim Stuckey.

Near the end of the game, Hayes emulated his military heroes once too often. Linebacker Charlie Bauman pilfered a Schlichter pass and was knocked out-of-bounds near the Buckeye bench. Hayes went after Bauman and punched him. Guard Ken Fritz tried to restrain his coach, but was also punched. Next morning Hayes was out as Ohio State coach, and the Gator Bowl replay got more TV exposure in the next few days than the exploits of Muhammad Ali.

"I hope that the next coach is just as good as he is," said Buckeye back Ron Springs, and he was not alone in his feelings.

With three losses, Texas came in ninth. Leading the Steers were quarter-back Randy McEachern, flanker Johnny "Lam" Jones, Jim Yarbrough at guard, and kicker Russell Erxleben. In the Sun Bowl the defense of tackle Steve McMichael, Dwight Jefferson at end, linebacker Lance Taylor, and defensive backs Johnnie Johnson and Glenn Blackwood stuffed Maryland for the Longhorn's ninth win, 42–0.

Another college coaching career ended in the Bluebonnet Bowl game between Stanford and Georgia. Behind 22–0 at the half, the take-charge vic-tory was a tribute to Stanford coach Bill Walsh, as the Cardinal adjusted at halftime and pulled it out, 25–22.

Walsh was a creative genius with the ability to communicate his ideas to others. His particular expertise was in developing a passing game and in training his quarterbacks to make it work. While others were teaching run-ners how many steps to take before cutting, Walsh spent whole afternoons teaching his quarterbacks the right amount of steps to take in dropping back. Hours more were spent making sure the quarterback's feet were pointed right when he threw. As a result, his quarterbacks led in passing two straight years: Guy Benjamin with 208 of 330 for 2,521 yards last year and Steve Dils with 247 of 391 for 2,943 yards this year.

At Stanford, Walsh had intelligent players who could implement his ideas. He departed from the time-worn dictum of making a passing game go by establishing the run. Stanford teams threw long and short and on first down and last. His disciplined pass routes were based on timing and execution, as decoys cleared out an area to free the prime receiver. Wide receiver James Lofton was often in the clear, and so was running back Darrin Nelson, who took short dump-off passes and turned them into big gains.

At Georgia Tech, Eddie Lee Ivery set a single-game rushing record of 356 yards on 26 carries in a 42–21 win over Air Force.

1979

Alabama (12-0-0)			Southern California (11-0-1)		
30	Georgia Tech	6	21	Texas Tech	7
45	Baylor	0	42	Oregon State	5
66	Vanderbilt	3	48	Minnesota	14
38	Wichita State	0	17	Louisiana State	12
40	Florida	0	50	Washington State	21
27	Tennessee	17	21	Stanford	21
31	Virginia Tech	7	42	Notre Dame	23
24	Mississippi State	7	24	California	14
3	Louisiana State	0	34	Arizona	7
30	Miami (Florida)	0	24	Washington	17
25	Auburn	18	49	UCLA	14
24	Arkansas (Sugar Bowl)	9	17	Ohio State (Rose Bowl)	16
383		67	389		171

The Tide was on top once again, as Bear Bryant's lettermen went through the year without much trouble. In the third game, quarterback Steadman Shealy ran 65 yards to score on the second play to destroy Vanderbilt with 471 yards rushing. Alabama had a chance to show its championship caliber in the Tennessee game by handing the Vols a 17-point lead and then coming from behind to win. Alan McElroy's 27-yard field goal stopped LSU. Led by halfback Major Ogilvie the Bama wishbone rolled on, but against Miami wide receiver Keith Pugh had seven catches. Another come-from-behind win defeated Auburn in the last game of the year.

With defensive ends Wayne Hamilton and E.J. Junior, tackle Byron Braggs, linebackers Don McNeal and Thomas Boyd, and Ricky Tucker and Tommy Wilcox deep, Alabama led in scoring defense with 5.3 points allowed per game. The Tide took over the top spot in October, but Ohio State edged them in the last regular-season poll by two points. "Being number one is like courting a girl," said Bear. "Once you get your hands on her, you don't like to let her go."

Two great coaching legends, Paul "Bear" Bryant and Wallace Wade, talk it over.

Alabama won back its number-one girl on New Year's Day in the Sugar Bowl against Arkansas. They showed why their defense was the best by stopping the Hogs six times on third down for no gain. Arkansas quarterback Kevin Scanlon was pressured so much that he was floored on every pass attempt except two.

After a 17–3 halftime deficit, Arkansas closed it to 17–9 with a third-period score. At the start of the last quarter, a Razorback punt was downed on the Tide two-yard line. On the next play, halfback Billy Jackson spun off 35 yards. Then he picked up 14 to midfield. Shealy swept left end for 22 yards. Behind the charge of tackle Jim Bunch, fullback Steve Whitman busted 12 yards straight ahead, and Bama scored on nine running plays.

Said Arkansas coach Lou Holtz, "Alabama's offense is fourth best in the nation, and it's the team's major weakness." With a 13–10 loss to Houston, the 10-2-0 Razorbacks finished eighth.

Before 106,255 spectators at Michigan Stadium, the largest crowd of modern times, Ohio State's new coach, Earl Bruce, did something Woody Hayes had not done for three years: he scored a touchdown against Michigan, beat them, and took Ohio State to the Rose Bowl. The score came in the third period when Michigan defensive back Mike Jolly tipped a pass into the hands of split end Chuck Hunter, who speared it with one hand in the end zone. The win came in the fourth quarter when Jim Laughlin blocked a punt which Todd Bell ran in for the winning points, 18–15.

Once-tied Southern Cal met unbeaten Ohio State in the Rose Bowl. USC was led by Heisman winner Charles White, the nation's leading rusher with 1,803 yards. White ended his career second only to Tony Dorsett in rushing with 5,598 yards gained on 1,023 carries for a 5.47 average. Back at quarter was Paul McDonald, with Hobey Brenner at tight end and Kevin Williams at split end. In the offensive line were guard Roy Foster and tackle Keith Van Horne. All-American guard Brad Budde spoke for those who fought in the pits: "Without us, you wouldn't hear of Charles White."

The Trojans broke on top with a 41-yard field goal by Eric Hipp. Later in that quarter, Art Schlichter fired a howitzer to split end Gary Williams, who took it on the 19 and ran to the USC two-yard line. Schlichter struggled for a yard on a keeper. On the next play, tailback Cal Murray was met by linebackers Dennis Johnson, Riki Gray, and Chip Banks. Then fullback Paul Campbell was held to no gain. On last down, defensive backs Dennis Smith and Ronnie Lott zeroed in on Schlichter and stood him upright.

USC scored on a long second-quarter pass, but Ohio State matched it with a field goal and long pass to make it 10–10 at the half.

Vlade Janakievski kicked second-half field goals of 37 and 24 yards for a 16–10 Buckeye lead. With 5:21 to go in the game, USC started a drive on its 17. White blasted four yards up the gut, three to the left, five on a slant. At the goal, he dived over Marcus Allen for the winning score. With an 11-1-0 mark, Ohio State fell to fourth, but Earle Bruce was coach of the year.

Oklahoma, paced by quarterback J.C. Watts and Billy Sims, finished third. Sims led the nation with 22 touchdowns and 132 points. Back on defense were linebacker George Cumby and safety Darrol Ray. After their only loss to Texas, 16–7, OU scored 38 points four weeks in a row and then downed Missouri, 24–22, and Nebraska, 17–14. In the Orange Bowl, Florida State took a 7-0 lead, but Oklahoma safety Bud Hebert's three interceptions were instrumental in stopping the Seminoles, 24–7, for OU's eleventh win.

Behind linemen Dennis Greenawalt and Melvin Jones, quarterback Delrick Brown brought Houston in fifth. They lost to Texas 21–13 and got a tenth win over Nebraska in the Cotton Bowl. On defense were tackle Leonard Mitchell and linebacker David Hodge. Jeff Quinn at quarter and halfback Jarvis Redwine took UN to ten wins but lost the last two by the same score to come in ninth.

Led by nose guard Ron Simmons, Bobby Bowden's Florida State team rolled through the year to 11 wins. Gary Henry started it off in the first game when he ran back a fourth-quarter punt 65 yards to quell Southern Mississippi, 17–14. But their unbeaten season terminated in the Orange Bowl, and they finished sixth.

After a 17-7 loss to North Carolina, Pitt beat Temple 10-9 on Mark Schubert's 46-yard field goal. Although they had defensive end Hugh Green, safety Jo Jo Heath, linebacker Jeff Pelusi, and offensive tackle Mark May, their attack stalled until freshman quarterback Dan Marino took over. Coach Jackie Sherrill's Panthers clawed Arizona 16–10 for their eleventh win on Christmas Day in the Fiesta Bowl to capture the number-seven spot.

With Keena Turner at linebacker, and Mark Herrmann's tosses to tight end Dave Young, Purdue mastered Tennessee in the Bluebonnet Bowl on New Year's Eve, 27–22, and was tenth at 10-2-0.

X. The Wide-Open Eighties

1980

Georgia (12-0-0)			Pittsburgh (11-1-0)		
16	Tennessee	15	14	Boston College	6
42	Texas A&M	0	18	Kansas	3
20	Clemson	16	36	Temple	2
34	Texas Christian	3	38	Maryland	9
28	Mississippi	21	22	Florida State	36
41	Vanderbilt	0	42	West Virginia	14
27	Kentucky	0	30	Tennessee	6
13	South Carolina	10	43	Syracuse	6
26	Florida	21	41	Louisville	23
31	Auburn	21	45	Army	7
38	Georgia Tech	20	14	Penn State	9
17	Notre Dame (Sugar Bowl)	10	37	So. Carolina (Gator Bowl)	9
333		137	380		130

November 1 was a bad day for unbeaten teams. Mississippi State deposed number-one Alabama 6–3, second-rated UCLA lost to Arizona 23–17, Oklahoma KO'd sixth-place North Carolina 41–7, and San Jose State beat number-ten Baylor 30–21. A week later, Notre Dame, led by linebacker Bob Crable, held Georgia Tech to a 3–3 tie, and Georgia was the only unbeaten and untied team. They moved in at the top, stayed there for keeps, and were the champs.

Georgia gave up a safety on a fumble recovered by fullback Jimmy Womack, but they rallied from a 15-point shortage to trim Tennessee before a crowd of 95,288, the largest in the South up to that time. Two weeks later, they overcame Clemson as Georgia cornerback Scott Woerner put them in front with a 67-yard punt return for a touchdown, and set up another score by stealing a pass and giving it a 98-yard ride to the two-yard marker. In the next two games, they built up halftime leads of 17–0. TCU fell easily, but Mississippi made it a game before losing by seven.

Tight end Norris Brown's 58-yard pass scored in the Vanderbilt game, and flanker Amp Arnold's 91-yard pass scored against Kentucky. Georgia led 13–0 over South Carolina and Heisman winner George Rogers on Rex Robinson field goals of 57 and 51 yards and a 76-yard Herschel Walker run. An Eddie Leopard field goal and Carl West's run scored for Carolina, but the Gamecocks fell short by three.

357

Against Florida, the Dawgs scored first on Walker's 72-yard run. Brian Clark's field goal made it 7–3. Then a scoring pass to fullback Ronnie Stewart was matched on a Gator throw by quarterback Wayne Peace to split end Cris Collinsworth. Robinson's two third-period field goals made it 20–10 for Georgia. Florida pushed ahead by one, but with 1:35 to go split end Lindsay Scott caught a pass from quarterback Buck Belue and went 93 yards down the sideline for the winning score. The win was secured by cornerback Mike Fisher's stolen pass. Against Auburn, cornerback Greg Bell blocked a punt which end Freddie Gilbert carried in.

Georgia Tech also trailed 17–0 at the half. Georgia's last score was on a 65-yard run by Walker, giving him 1,616 yards for the year, an NCAA mark for freshmen. Defensive leaders were end Dale Carver, linebacker Nate Taylor, guards Eddie Weaver and Joe Creamons, tackle Jimmy Payne, Jeff Hipp at safety, and guard Tim Morrison, tackle Nat Hudson, and flanker Chuck Jones on offense.

As President Carter watched in the stands, Georgia stopped 9-2-1 Notre Dame in the Sugar Bowl. A tie and losses to Georgia and USC, 20–3, made Notre Dame ninth. It was Dan Devine's last game as Irish coach, while Vince Dooley was coach of the year.

The Pitt Panthers, winner 11 times in 12 contests, finished in second place. Quarterback Dan Marino left the West Virginia game with a sprained left knee, but safety Rick Trocano came in and led the team for the rest of the season. In the next game against Tennessee, Willie Gault ran the kickoff back 100 yards for a Vol touchdown before the roof caved in. With its tandem quarterbacks, the passing attack averaged 268.4 yards each game and 3,185 yards for the year, best ever for a Pitt team. Making these passes click were ends Benjie Pryor, Julius Dawkins, and Dwight Collins. On offense were captain Russ Grimm at center, Outland winner Mark May at tackle, and fullback Randy McMillan.

The pride of Steeltown was its defense, which led the nation in both total defense with 205.5 yards and rushing defense with 65.3 yards per game. In Pitt's front wall was nose guard Jerry Boyarsky, tackles Greg Meisner and Bill Neill, and Ricky Jackson and Hugh Green as the iron wings. Green, a practitioner of the body-slam tackle, was warned by an official in the Florida State game to "quit tackling so hard." At linebacker was Sal Sunseri, who warmed up by banging his head on a door jamb. In the backfield were Lynn Thomas, Terry White, and Carlton Williamson who had an eye for the ball like Sherlock Holmes had for clues. At the end of the year, Green's jersey 99 was permanently retired.

The Penn State game was a study in defense. The Lions led on a field goal, but it was 7–3 at halftime on Trocano's 16-yard scoring pass to Pryor. On its first play after the half, Penn State fumbled. Eight plays later, Trocano went over on a nine-yard bootleg to the right. After a Pitt pass was purloined, freshman quarterback Todd Blackledge threw to flanker Kenny Jackson for a score to close within five. Then in the last minute, Williamson intercepted a Penn State pass to insure the win. Pitt ended the season in the

Gator Bowl with a victory over South Carolina and top rusher George Rogers, who had 1,781 yards. After losses to Nebraska, 21-7, Pitt, 14-9, and a 31-19 win over Ohio State in the Fiesta Bowl, Penn State was 10-2-0 and came in number eight.

Oklahoma got off to a bad start with two losses in its first four games. They lost five of six fumbles in the Stanford game, as quarterback John Elway threw three scoring passes to beat the Sooners, 31-14. Two weeks later, they gave away four fumbles and four interceptions to Texas and went down the drain, 20-13.

With guard Terry Crouch and tackle Louis Oubre leading the attack, the wishbone began to click, although two November wins were rough. Kansas lost 21-19 as Walter Mack's two-point run was stopped by end Orlando Flanagan. Against Nebraska, Oklahoma had the ball on its 20 with 3:16 to go, but trailed, 17-14. On the drive, Buster Rhymes took a pitch on the option and sped 43 yards to the Husker 14. Quarterback J.C. Watts threw 13 yards to Bobby Grayson at split end. Two plays later, Rhymes scored for a 21-17 win with 56 seconds remaining.

Nebraska's Jarvis Redwine and Andra Franklin powered them to the rushing title with 378.3 yards per game. They lost only to Oklahoma and Florida State, 18-14, but got a tenth win over Mississippi State, 31-17, in the Sun Bowl and finished seventh.

The Sooner wishbone was mobiling in high gear now. Leading it were Dave Overstreet, with Stan Wilson and Buster Rhymes as trailing backs. In the Orange Bowl rematch with Florida State, the Seminoles led throughout the second half, 17-10, when Oklahoma got the ball on its 22 with 3:19 left. Two minutes later, Watts tossed an 11-yard scoring pass to split end Steve Rhodes. Then Watts threw to tight end Forrest Valora for two points and win number ten, 18-17, and a third-place showing.

Michigan's start was even worse than OU's, as they lost two of their first three games. Notre Dame muzzled them 29-27 on the last play of the game, as Harry Oliver left-footed a 51-yard field goal. A week later, South Carolina's Eddie Leopard downed them on a 26-yard field goal. Then Michigan high-fived through its next eight games, including a 9-3 win over Ohio State. After swapping field goals with the Bucks, quarterback John Wangler hit Anthony Carter on a 13-yard touchdown pass. The Ohio field goal was the only points ceded by Michigan in the last four games, as their defense, led by linebackers Andy Cannavino, Paul Girgash, and Bob Thompson, had not surrendered a touchdown in 18 quarters.

The Michigan defense was just as grim in the Rose Bowl, as they gave Bo Schembechler his first Pasadena win in six tries. After tailback Butch Woolfolk sprinted 97 yards to give UM a 7-6 halftime lead, the offensive line took over. Led by tackles Ed Muransky and Bubba Paris, guard Kurt Becker, and center George Lilja, they ground out a 23-6 second half win over Washington. Ten wins and two losses put the Wolverines at number four.

Fifth-place Florida State was the fifth team to finish with ten wins and

BYU quarterback Jim McMahon set a flock of NCAA marks, then led the Chicago Bears to the pro title in 1985.

two losses. Besides their loss to Oklahoma in the Orange Bowl, the Seminoles lost to Miami 10–9 on quarterback Rick Stockwell's two-point pass failure at the end of the game. Led by tailback Sam Platt, FSU bounced back to defeat Nebraska, as punter Rohn Stark kept the Cornhuskers backed up all day, and Bill Capece kicked four field goals of 32, 27, 40, and 41 yards. After the last field goal with 3:27 remaining, the Huskers drove to the Seminole three-yard line. Then the Florida State line, with nose guard Ron Simmons in the pivot spot, gave a demonstration of its top-ranked scoring defense of 7.7 points per game. With 17 seconds left, linebacker Paul Piurowski decked Nebraska quarterback Jeff Quinn to run out the clock for the win.

A pair of field goals by Mississippi State's Dana Moore had ended Alabama's 28-game winning streak. Two weeks later, Notre Dame stopped them, 7–0. Led by a defensive unit which included E.J. Junior at end, nose guard Warren Lyles, linebacker Thomas Boyd, with Tommy Wilcox, Mike

Clements, Jeremiah Castille, and Ricky Turner in the backfield, the Tide blanked Kentucky, 45-0, and gave the Bear his three hundredth win. Veteran halfbacks Billy Jackson and Major Ogilvie, and freshman Linnie Patrick helped Alabama to ten wins and a sixth-place rating. In the Cotton Bowl, quarterback Don Jacobs led a sure-passing offense which downed Baylor, 30-2. Korean kicker Peter Kim added three field goals.

Coach Dick Crum's North Carolina team had 11 wins, lost to Oklahoma, and ended tenth. Linebacker Lawrence Taylor led them to a 16-7 win over Texas in the Bluebonnet Bowl. On offense were running backs Kelvin Bryant and Amos Lawrence, who tied Tony Dorsett's mark of rushing for 1,000 yards in each of his four years.

An hour's drive south of Salt Lake City, the Brigham Young Cougars were beginning to make football history. For the past two years, BYU led the nation in scoring, passing offense, and total offense. They averaged 40.6 points per game in 1979 and 46.7 points this year. They threw for 368.3 yards per game in 1979 and for 409.8 yards in 1980, an NCAA record. Their total offense averaged 521.4 yards last year and 535 yards this year.

BYU led in passing each year since 1976 except 1978, when offensive coordinator Doug Scovil was on leave to the Chicago Bears. In 1979, BYU passed for 4,056 yards, the first team to go over 4,000 yards. After winning all 11 games, they lost to Indiana in the Holiday Bowl, 38-37. Quarterback Marc Wilson directed one final drive, only to have a field goal go astray.

After a 25-21 loss to New Mexico, coach LaVell Edwards put even more bite in the Cougar this year. Quarterback Jim McMahon threw for 47 touchdowns and 4,571 yards, both NCAA marks. BYU's twelfth win was over Southern Methodist in the Holiday Bowl, 46-45, on a touchdown catch by tight end Clay Brown on the final play, and Kurt Gunther set a season record by kicking 64 extra points.

The climate near the Wasatch Mountains is clean in more ways than one. The BYU campus has no beer or cigarettes, no long hair or beards, and no vulgar T-shirts. With this in mind, the Cougar fans cheer their team with shouts of "Smite 'em, brethren!"

1981

Strength director George Dostal's sign hung in the training room all summer:

Clemson 11-0. In the Orange Bowl vs. Nebraska.

The football team pumped iron all year. Not only were they fit, but all offensive starters were back, including center Tony Berryhill, guard Bruce Clark, and tackle Lee Nanney. On defense were linebackers Jeff Davis and Danny Triplett, Terry Kinard and Tim Childers at safety, ends Andy

Headen and Bill Smith, tackle Jeff Bryant, nose guard Bill Devane, and 300-pound William Perry, called "GE" by the team because he looked like a refrigerator.

Clemson (12-0-0)			Texas (10-1-1)	
45	Wofford	10	31 Rice	3
13	Tulane	5	23 North Texas State	10
13	Georgia	3	14 Miami (Florida)	7
21	Kentucky	3	34 Oklahoma	14
27	Virginia	0	11 Arkansas	42
38	Duke	10	9 Southern Methodist	7
17	North Carolina State	7	26 Texas Tech	9
82	Wake Forest	24	14 Houston	14
10	North Carolina	8	31 Texas Christian	15
21	Maryland	7	34 Baylor	12
29	South Carolina	13	21 Texas A&M	13
22	Nebraska (Orange Bowl)	15	14 Alabama (Cotton Bowl)	12
338		105	262	158

The defense was tough as well as strong. After 18 quarters of not giving up a touchdown, Duke finally scored on a 21-yard pass from Ben Bennett to Cedric Jones. The Duke game also saw Clemson's offense come together, as quarterback Homer Jordan began to find receivers Jerry Gaillard, Frank Magwood, and Bubba Diggs. Against North Carolina State, fullback Jeff McCall scored on a 15-yard run in the final quarter to win it. In the Wake Forest game, the offense was awesome with 12 touchdowns and 756 yards total offense, both school records. Running backs Kevin Mack, Chuck McSwain, Craig Crawford, and Cliff Austin all scored, and flanker Perry Tuttle became Clemson's all-time receiver.

South Carolina was Clemson's next foe. The Gamecocks went out front 7–0, but cornerback Rod McSwain blocked a punt which linebacker Johnny Rembert recovered for a Tiger touchdown. Bob Paulling missed his first conversion attempt of the season, but kicked a 24-yard field goal to make it 9–6. Jordan turned left end for 11 yards, and Clemson had a 15–7 halftime lead.

South Carolina took the last-half kickoff and marched to a touchdown, but on the two-point try Jeff Suttle sacked Carolina quarterback Gordon Beckham to preserve the 15–13 lead. Clemson roared back with a score and added another in the final quarter, and the Tiger Rag was played all the way home from Columbia.

George Dostal's prediction had come true. Clemson was 11–0 and in the Orange Bowl against Nebraska. A Husker fumble on the third play resulted in a 41-yard field goal by Donald Igwebuike. Nebraska got on the scoreboard in the first quarter with a pitch from quarterback Mark Mauer to Mike Rozier, who then completed a 25-yard toss to Anthony Steels in the end zone. Kevin Seibel converted, Clemson added a field goal and second-period touchdown for a 12–7 halftime lead.

In the third quarter, Clemson scored on a 13-yard pass from Jordan to Tuttle, and a 36-yard field goal made it 22-7. Roger Craig high-pumped 26 yards around end in the last period for the final score. Clemson was the only undefeated team and national champ, and Danny Ford was coach of the year.

Texas finished second this year. After a win over a tough Miami team, they beat Oklahoma for the fourth time in five years. Oklahoma took a 14-3 lead, but Texas rallied on touchdown passes from quarterback Rick McIvor to wide receiver Maurice McCloney and 6'6" tight end Lawrence Sampleton. The Longhorns got blown out in the next game by Arkansas, but stopped SMU's Mustangs on 11 solo tackles by tackle Ken Sims and three field goals by Raul Allegre, the last one a 52-yarder in the final period. Southern Methodist, led by twin tailbacks Craig James and Eric Dickerson, lost only to Texas. With ten wins the Ponies came home in fifth place, but were home for the holidays because of NCAA violations.

The other setback for Texas was a tie with Houston. Behind 14-0 at the half, Bob Brewer took over for the injured McIvor and led the team to 14 second-half points. Allegre came through with a pair of field goals, a 45-yarder in the third quarter, and one of 47 yards in the fourth quarter to tie it with 3:27 remaining.

Brewer directed UT for the rest of the year. He was helped by halfback A.J. "Jam" Jones, and the previous year's quarterback, Donnie Little, now at split end. In the offensive line were guard Joe Shearin, tackle Terry Tausch, and center Mike Babb. Linebackers Doug Shankle and Bruce Scholtz made the defense respectable.

In the Cotton Bowl, Brewer led the Longhorns to win number ten, a comeback victory over Alabama. At the half, Texas found itself on the short end of a 10-0 score. Then Texas scored on a 30-yard quarterback draw which caught the Alabama defense off balance. UT's winning touchdown came in the final quarter on a smash by fullback Terry Orr with 2:05 to go. The Texas defense held, and when UT got the ball again they ran three quarterback sneaks, then gave up an intentional safety to run out the clock.

Penn State's high-rpm offense and firebrand defense brought them in third. Behind offensive linemen Sean Farrell, Mike Munchak, and Leo Wisniewski, quarterback Todd Blackledge tossed to flankers Kenny Jackson and Gregg Garrity, and Mike McCloskey at tight end. Curt Warner and Jon Williams made the ground game go. Against Nebraska, led by Outland winner Dave Rimington at center, Warner gained 238 yards. Bryan Franco kept pace with five field goals, but the lead changed hands seven times before the Huskers were outpointed, 30-24. Warner also rushed for 256 yards in the Syracuse game, while the defense contained Joe Morris and turned back the Orangemen, 41-16. Leading the defense were linebacker Chet Parlavecchio, tackle Greg Gattuso, and defensive backs Paul Lankford, Giuseppe Harris, Mark Robinson, and Roger Jackson.

Penn State lost to Miami, 17-14, and Alabama, 31-16, before they blasted unbeaten Pitt out of first place in the last game, 48-14. In the Fiesta

Soon after Earl Campbell of Texas set the SWC rushing mark of 4,443, SMU's Eric Dickerson (above) broke it with 4,450 yards.

Bowl, the defense held Marcus Allen to 85 yards rushing and beat USC, 26–10, for their tenth win.

Allen was the first to run for over 2,000 yards in a year, led with 23 touchdowns, and won the Heisman. He had 2,342 yards on 403 tries for a 212.9-yard average, all one-year marks. His 217 yards receiving gave him 2,559 yards in all-purpose running, another annual mark, and a 232.6-yard average, second to Whizzer White's 1937 record. "I've seen all the great ones," said Troy announcer Tom Kelly, "and I pick Marcus Allen as the best. He has the power of Ricky Bell, the durability of Mike Garrett, the versatility of O.J. Simpson—and the temperament of a saint."

Fourth-place Pitt led in defense for the second year in a row, as they were first against the rush with 62.4 yards and in total defense with 224.8 yards per game. In the middle of this steel-souled outfit, which held South Carolina to minus 52 yards rushing, were nose guard Jay Pelusi, tackles Bill Maas and Dave Puzzuoli, with Mike Woods and Chris Doleman on the ends. Behind them were linebackers Rich Kraynak and captain Sal Sunseri, and Tim Lewis, Pappy Thomas, and Dan Short in the backfield.

In the offensive line were center Emil Boures, guards Bob Fada and Ron Sams, and tackles Bill Fralic and Jim Covert. At quarterback was Dan Marino, who hit on 226 of 380 attempts for 2,876 yards and 37 touchdowns, all Pitt one-year records. On the end of his tosses were receivers Dwight Collins and Julius Dawkins. Fullback Wayne DiBartola and tailback Bryan Thomas, who rushed for 1,132 yards, added to the Panthers' 4,965 yards of total offense, another single-season Pitt mark.

The Panthers looked unstoppable as they ran up substantial scores on everyone. They took over first place in November, but lost it in the last game when Penn State decimated them. In the Sugar Bowl, they beat Georgia 24–20 on a 33-yard scoring pass from Marino to tight end John Brown with half-a-minute left for their eleventh win. Georgia, with losses only to Pitt and Clemson, finished with ten wins and a number-six ranking.

After a 24–21 loss to Georgia Tech, Alabama almost made it two in a row before they beat Kentucky in the last two minutes, 19–10. In the 28–7 win over Vanderbilt, the defense scored 16 first-half points: Benny Perrin ran back a stolen pass 78 yards to a score, tackle Jackie Cline blocked a punt for a safety, and end Russ Wood snared a midair fumble on the Vandy 33 and ran in.

Two games later, Southern Mississippi, whose 8.1-points per game topped the nation in scoring defense, slowed down the Tide, 13–13, on a 40-yard Steve Clark field goal with eight seconds to go. Then Terry Sanders, replacing injured Peter Kim, kicked a 28-yard last-period field goal to beat Mississippi State 13–10 and give Bryant his three hundred and thirteenth win, tying Pop Warner's record. Win number 314, tying Stagg's record, came against Penn State. Win number 315, giving Bryant the most coaching wins ever, was over Auburn, 28–17. The Tide scored twice in the last period, once on a 38-yard scoring pass from quarterback Walter Lewis to tight end Jesse Bendross, and once on a 15-yard run by Linnie Patrick. After its loss to Texas, Alabama was 9-2-1 and came in seventh.

Led by nose guard Tony Chickillo, linebacker Scott Nicolas, tackle Les Williams, and safety Fred Marion, 9-2-0 Miami, with losses to Texas and Mississippi State, 14–10, finished eighth. Dan "Bigfoot" Miller's 55-yard field goal with 40 seconds left beat Florida, 21–20. Then he kicked four more to down Houston, 12–7. On offense were flanker Larry Brodsky, halfbacks Smokey Roan and Speedy Neal, fullback Chris Hobbs, and quarterback Jim Kelly, who kept the job after the win over Penn State. In the 14–6 win over North Carolina State, Miami scored twice on passes from Kelly to tailback Mark Rush on its first two possessions.

Losses to South Carolina, 31–13, and Clemson brought North Carolina a number-nine rating. Injuries hobbled quarterback Rod Elkins and fullback Kelvin Bryant against Clemson, and a safety and two Brooks Barwick field goals could not catch the Tigers. UNC's tenth win was over Arkansas in the Gator Bowl, 31–27.

Tenth-place Washington also won ten and lost two. In spite of losses to Arizona State, 26–7, and UCLA, 31–0, UW was in the Rose Bowl against

Top ground gainer of the Trojans, Marcus Allen, now carries the ball for the Los Angeles Raiders.

Iowa. Tailback Jacque Robinson tallied on a second period pitch to put the Huskies in front. Then flanker Paul Skanski bagged two catches from quarterback Steve Pelluer, and fullback Vince Coby went over to make it 13–0 at the half.

UW's defense, led by linebackers Mark Stewart, Mark Jerue, Michael Collins, and Ken Driscoll, tackle Fletcher Jenkins, and backfield men Art Horton, Vince Newsome, and Derek Harvey stopped the Hawkeyes cold. Robinson's 34-yard scoring run and Tim Cowan's bootleg closed it out at 28–0. Iowa's Reggie Roley had a punting average of 49.8 yards, an all-time record.

Brigham Young again led in passing with 356.9 yards and in scoring with 38.7 points per game. Jim McMahon ended his career with 84 touchdown passes, still the record, and set records with 9,536 yards on 653 completions of 1,060 tries for 61.6 percent.

Stanford's Darrin Nelson closed his career with 6,885 yards all-purpose running on 966 plays (4,033 yards rushing, 2,368 receiving, 471 kickoff returns, 13 punt returns), the best so far.

1982

Penn State	(11-1-0)		Southern Methodist	(11-0-1)	
31	Temple	14	51	Tulane	7
39	Maryland	31	31	Texas El Paso	10
49	Rutgers	14	16	Texas Christian	13
27	Nebraska	24	38	North Texas State	10
21	Alabama	42	22	Baylor	19
28	Syracuse	7	20	Houston	14
24	West Virginia	0	30	Texas	17
52	Boston College	17	47	Texas A&M	9
54	North Carolina State	0	41	Rice	14
24	Notre Dame	14	34	Texas Tech	27
19	Pitt	10	17	Arkansas	17
27	Georgia (Sugar Bowl)	23	7	Pitt (Cotton Bowl)	3
395		196	354		160

After coming close often, Penn State finally made it to the top. In their first three games, quarterback Todd Blackledge hit on 12 touchdown passes. In the next win, Nebraska rolled up 472 yards total offense and held a 24–21 lead with 78 seconds to go. Blackledge directed a 65-yard drive and tossed a two-yard scoring pass to tight end Kirk Bowman to win it with four seconds left.

Alabama jumped off to a touchdown on a blocked punt, but the Lions came back on a 69-yard scoring pass from Blackledge to Curt Warner. Alabama took a 21-7 halftime lead, but the Lions clawed back to make it 27–21. Then a Penn State punt was blocked by one of their own men. Alabama recovered on the 12 and scored in two plays. On the first play after the kickoff the Tide scored on an intercepted pass, and in 90 seconds the game was out of sight.

The Lions came back to beat Syracuse, as Joe Paterno changed his defense. Steve Sefter and Walker Lee Ashley went to end, Ken Kelley, Scott Radecic, and Dave Paffenroth were linebackers, with Greg Gattuso, Dave Opfar, and Harry Hamilton as interior linemen.

The changes paid off. West Virginia was blanked and Boston College was stopped on six turnovers, but not before sophomore Doug Flutie threw for 520 yards. Another shutout victory came against North Carolina State. Allen Pinkett's 95-yard kickoff runback gave Notre Dame a 14-13 halftime lead before they lost in the last half. Pitt also led 7-3 at the half, but a 31-yard scoring pass from Blackledge to flanker Kenny Jackson gave Penn State the lead. Four field goals by Nick Gancitano and a 48.3-yard punting average by Ralph Giacomarro aided the Lion win.

Penn State coach Joe Paterno gets the treatment after his team beat Georgia in the Sugar Bowl for number one. Paterno is ninth with 199-44-2 for a .816 mark.

In only the sixth bowl contest between the two best teams, number-two Penn State met number-one Georgia in the Sugar Bowl. Blackledge opened the game with a 33-yard pass to tight end Mike McCloskey, and then tossed 27 yards to split end Gregg Garrity. Another pass to McCloskey was good for seven yards, and from the two-yard line Warner turned left end for the score with 2:51 gone. A Kevin Butler field goal pared it to four in the opening round.

A pair of Gancitano field goals and Warner's next touchdown made it 20–3 for PSU. Quarterback John Lastinger hit split end Herman Archie for a Georgia score and it was 20–10 at the half.

After the second-half kickoff, Georgia closed it to 20–17 on a Herschel Walker plunge. Early in the final quarter, Penn State escalated its lead to 27–17 on a 48-yard pass from Blackledge to Garrity. Georgia retaliated with a toss from Lastinger to tight end Clarence Kay to end the scoring. Coach of the year Paterno pointed his index finger into the night to proclaim Penn State number one, while 11-1-0 Georgia tumbled to fourth place.

After a successful career at Southern Mississippi, SMU coach Bobby Collins inherited a great team from Ron Meyer. The Ponies hit the trail at a gallop as Tulane was stampeded. On the second play of the next contest with Texas El Paso, Eric Dickerson took a pitch and scored on an 80-yard run. TCU led 13–6, but SMU tied it in the last quarter. Then defensive end

Curt Warner is Penn State's leading ground gainer with 3,398 yards.

Anthony Beverley fell on a fumble, and Jeff Harrell won it with a 19-yard field goal.

Against North Texas State, quarterback Jeff Courtwright hit on three touchdown passes, including a 96-yarder to Craig James, the longest in SWC history. Quarterback Lance McIlhenny overcame Baylor's 13–0 halftime lead on three scoring passes, two to tight end Rickey Bolden and one to flanker Jackie Wilson. In the next game a Fred Nichols steal led to SMU's first score, and a defense led by linebacker Gary Moten and linemen Michael Carter and Kevin Chaney held Houston to 0-for-7 on third down in the second half.

Texas erased a 10-0 lead as they tied it in the last period. Then split end Bobby Leach caught a deflected pass and raced 79 yards to score. An interception by safety Russ Carter led to a scoring pass by McIlhenny, who added another in the final minute.

Ricky Gann's field goal tied it for Texas Tech with 17 seconds left. Blane Smith bobbled the kickoff, then tossed a long lateral to Leach who ran 91 yards untouched to snatch it back.

Arkansas slowed down the Ponies in the last regular-season game with a tie. In the Cotton Bowl, Pitt led 3-0 on a 43-yard field goal by Eric Schubert, but SMU scored in the final period to win it and remain the only unbeaten team left in the nation.

Nebraska lost only to Penn State, missed the national title by four seconds, and finished third. Led by center Dave Rimington, who won the Outland Award again, the Huskers were first in scoring with 41.1 points, in total offense with 518.6 yards and in rushing with 394.3 yards per game. Against New Mexico State, they gained 883 yards and made 43 first downs, both NCAA marks.

In the annual battle with Oklahoma for the Orange Bowl, the Huskers held a 21-10 halftime lead. One touchdown was set up by the "Bounceroosky," a play designed for use on artificial turf. Quarterback Turner Gill tossed a long overhand lateral to Irving Fryar, who caught the ball on the bounce. When the ball bounced on the grass, the defense thought it was an incomplete pass and relaxed momentarily, but Fryar threw 37 yards downfield to tight end Mitch Krenk. The second half became a question of who would have the ball last in order to win. Marcus Dupree made it 21-17 on an 86-yard scoring run, then it was 28-17, and finally 28-24.

Nebraska's twelfth win was against LSU in the Orange Bowl. The Huskers scored first on Mark Schellen's five-yard burst, but a pair of touchdown runs by Dalton Hilliard and a 28-yard Juan Betanzos field goal gave LSU a 17-7 third-period lead. An 11-yard run by Mike Rozier and Gill's short dive gave Nebraska a 21-20 win.

With a hammer-hitting defense led by nose guard Karl Morgan, tackle Irv Eatman, and linebacker Blanchard Montgomery, UCLA held Wisconsin to 66 yards rushing. Trailing Michigan 21-0, quarterback Tom Ramsey took the Bruins to a 31-27 win on scoring passes of 46 yards to wide receiver Dokie Williams and a six-yarder to flanker Jojo Townsell. With Eatman shifted to offense for better pass blocking, Ramsey continued his hot hand with tosses to tight end Paul Bergmann and wideout Cormac Carney. Fullback Frank Bruno and center Don Dufour opened the holes for tailback Dan Andrews.

UCLA tied Arizona, 24-24, and lost to Washington, 10-7, but met Michigan in a Rose Bowl rematch. UCLA safety Don Rogers put quarterback Steve Smith out of the game with a sledgehammer hit, and Lupe Sanchez and Tom Sullivan double-teamed Anthony Carter to hold him in check.

John Lee's 39-yard field goal and a wedge by Ramsey gave UCLA a 10-0 lead. Michigan cut it to 10-7 on a Dave Hall pass to Eddie Garrett, but lost in the last half, 24-14, for UCLA's tenth win and a fifth-place rating. Ramsey was the year's top passer with 2,824 yards, while Carter set an all-time career mark of 17.4 yards gained per play (5,197 yards on 298 plays).

Led by linebackers Jimmy Williams and Greg Battle, Arizona State's 228.9 yards per game defense was the nation's best. Two of the points in the 15-0 win over California were on a blocked punt by safety Mike Richardson. Quarterback Tod Hons directed a quick-hitting attack. Behind 17-14 against Stanford with the ball on their 20 and 49 seconds left, Hons hit on four of five throws for 79 yards, fullback Dwaine Wright going the last yard for a 21-17 win. Then ASU fell behind Washington by ten points and lost, 17-13, as Darryl Clack's 50-yard touchdown run and a 47-yard field goal by Luis Zendejas were not enough to catch the Huskies. ASU also lost to Arizona, 28-18, but beat Oklahoma in the Fiesta Bowl, 32-21, and was sixth with a 10-2-0 record.

Seventh-place Washington was also 10-2-0 and smelled roses until a 43-31 loss to Stanford. UW blitzes backfired as quarterback John Elway connected on 16 of his last 17 passes. Wins over UCLA and ASU kept them in the hunt until they lost the last game to Washington State, 24-20. The WSU game also saw Chuck Nelson's record of 30 straight field goals snapped with his first miss of the season after 25 hits for 96.2 percent, a one-year mark. The Huskies closed with a 21-20 win over Maryland in the Aloha Bowl.

Clemson started with a 13-7 loss to Georgia and a 17-17 tie with Boston College. Injuries hurt key players from last year's champions, but they won the last nine games and finished eighth. North Carolina made it close but lost, 16-13. Clemson led Maryland 24-7 until Boomer Esiason directed two last-period drives to make it 24-22. NCAA curbs kept Clemson from post-season play, but they met South Carolina in Tokyo's Mirage Bowl and won 24-6.

Defensive ends Billy Ray Smith and Ron Faurot helped make Arkansas' 10.5-points per game scoring defense best in the land. Behind center Jay Benquette and Steve Korte at guard, quarterback Tom Jones' tosses to Derek Holloway and Gary Anderson led them to nine wins. They beat Florida 28-24 in the Bluebonnet Bowl, but a tie and losses to Baylor, 24-17, and Texas, 33-7, put them ninth.

Many of the Pitt players who won 42 of 48 games ended their college careers in the Cotton Bowl with SMU. Dan Marino became the Panthers' all-time passer with 626 of 1,084 tries for 7,905 yards, 74 touchdowns, and 57.5 percent. Nine wins and losses to SMU, Penn State, and Notre Dame, 31-16, made them number ten.

The Big Game between Cal and Stanford produced the wackiest play of the year. A Stanford field goal gave them a 20-19 lead with seconds to go. As the ball sailed downfield to the Bears, the Stanford band marched onto the field behind the kickoff.

Kevin Moen fielded the short kick at his 43 and crossed the midfield stripe to the Stanford 48. In the grasp of a tackler at the sideline, he lateraled to Rich Rodgers who in turn threw the ball back to Dwight Garner at the Cal 44. Garner ran a few steps to midfield, where he was stopped by three tacklers. As he was going down, he lateraled to Rodgers at the Stanford 48. Rodgers kept the ball alive with another lateral to Mariet Ford at the Cardinal 46. Ford made a big gain but was trapped at the Stanford 25. In desperation, he tossed the ball back over his shoulder. Trailing the play was Moen, who snatched the ball out of the air. By now the band was all over that end of the field. Moen picked his way past the saxophone section, gave the hip to a tuba player, and tromped on a trombonist in the end zone for a 25–20 Cal victory. No one complained too much, for it was just another weirdo happening in the Bay Area's fantasy land of Oz.

John Elway ended his Stanford career with 774 completions on 1,246 attempts for 77 touchdowns and 62.1 percent. Illinois' Tony Eason set a career record of 299.5 yards total offense per game with 6,589 yards on 1,016 plays.

Shortly after his Alabama team beat Illinois in the Liberty Bowl, 22–15, Bear Bryant died after a short illness. His record stood at 323 wins, 85 losses, and 17 ties for a .780 mark.

1983

Miami (11-1-0)			Nebraska (12-1-0)		
3	Florida	28	44	Penn State	6
29	Houston	7	56	Wyoming	20
35	Purdue	0	84	Minnesota	13
20	Notre Dame	0	42	UCLA	10
56	Duke	17	63	Syracuse	7
42	Louisville	14	14	Oklahoma State	10
31	Mississippi State	7	34	Missouri	13
17	Cincinnati	7	69	Colorado	19
20	West Virginia	3	51	Kansas State	25
12	East Carolina	7	72	Iowa State	29
17	Florida State	16	67	Kansas	13
31	Nebraska (Orange Bowl)	30	28	Oklahoma	21
			30	Miami (Orange Bowl)	31
313		136	654		217

Few people gave Miami a second look after Florida swamped them in their first game. Big wins over Houston and Purdue did not get them ranked in the top 20, but a 20–0 blitzing of Notre Dame, in which cornerback Reggie Sutton blocked two field goal attempts, moved them into fifteenth place by the end of September.

Coach Howard Schnellenberger's 57 freshmen and sophomores

matured quickly. Led by nose guard Tony Fitzpatrick, linebacker Jay Brophy, tackle Fred Robinson, and cornerback Rod Bellinger, their constant chattering was punctuated with a dogged defense. Duke got 32 yards rushing and quarterback Ben Bennett was sacked five times. West Virginia gained only two yards on the ground.

Lady Luck smiled on Miami in its last two games. An East Carolina player caught what would have been the winning touchdown with 1:04 left, but it was knocked out of his hands by a teammate. Against Florida State, a 19-yard Jeff Davis field goal won it on the last play of the game, and Miami finished the regular season number five.

Meanwhile, Nebraska built a record which was all-universe. Their scores were unreal, as they had a 52-point average and set a modern scoring mark of 624 points. Like Army in 1945, Nebraska was in first place all year. It wasn't a race but a runaway.

Nebraska's 6,560 yards total offense and 84 touchdowns are both one-year records. Heisman winner Mike Rozier led the Cornhusker attack with 2,148 yards rushing, only the second player to pass the 2,000-yard mark in one year. His 29 touchdowns and 174 points tied the one-year record. Rozier's 7.81 yards each carry this year is a record, and his 7.16-yard career average is second.

After downing defending champ Penn State, Nebraska drubbed Wyoming and gave Minnesota its worst licking. UCLA took a 10-0 lead, but Nebraska scored twice in each of the last three periods to give Tom Osborne his one hundredth coaching win. UN trailed Oklahoma State 10-7 at the half, and won it only after safety Bret Clark stole a Cowboy pass in the end zone on the last play of the game.

Five conference foes were flattened until UN met Oklahoma. The Sooners led twice in the first half and had a 14-14 halftime tie. OU was behind 28-21 when they moved to Nebraska's one-yard line in the final minute. Defensive end Bill Weber sacked quarterback Danny Bradley for a loss, and cornerback Neil Harris batted away two passes in a row to give UN its twenty-second straight win.

Nebraska got a rude jolt in the Orange Bowl. The pumped-up Miami defense upset the methodical precision in Nebraska's front wall of center Mark Traynowicz, guards Harry Grimminger and Outland winner Dean Steinkuhler, and tackles Scott Raridon and John Sherlock. Miami took a 17-0 lead on a field goal and two scoring passes from quarterback Bernie Kosar to tight end Glenn Dennison. After cornerback Dave Burke's interception, the Huskers scored in the second period on a fake called the "Fumbleroosky." Quarterback Turner Gill deliberately put the ball on the turf and ran to the right. Steinkuhler picked up the ball and went left 19 yards to a score. Another UN touchdown made it 17-14 at halftime.

Nebraska drew alongside on Scott Livingston's 34-yard field goal, and everyone settled down to watch the Husker machine go to work. Nebraska blitzed its backs to hurry Kosar, but they were picked up by Albert Bentley and Alonzo Highsmith, who each scored to give Miami a 31-17 lead. A

Husker score by Jeff Smith capped a 74-yard drive to make it 31–24 at the end of the third period.

Nebraska got the ball with 1:47 left. Gill took only a minute to lead the Huskers 74 yards to a touchdown. With the score 31–30 and the nation holding its breath, Gill tossed to wingback Irving Fryar on a two-point pass, but the ball was batted away by safety Ken Calhoun to claim the win. In their locker room, Miami knelt in prayer as they had done at halftime and before the game.

Auburn lost early in the year to Texas, 20–7, and finished third. In coach Pat Dye's wishbone, quarterback Randy Campbell gave the ball to backs Bo Jackson, Lionel James, and Tommie Agee, or threw to tight end Ed West. Nose guard Dowe Aughtman led the defensive front five, flanked by Doug Smith, Ben Thomas, Quency Williams, and Donnie Humphrey. The last two put the one-two on Maryland quarterback Boomer Esiason, as Williams belted him and Humphrey fell on the ball for a score. Linebacker Gregg Carr and cornerback Jimmie Warren plugged up the holes. Win number 11 was over Michigan in the Sugar Bowl, 9–7, on three field goals by Al Del Greco, the third one coming on the last play of the game.

Fourth-place Georgia was still a good team without Herschel Walker, now a pro. In the first game, safety Charlie Dean stole a last-second pass and returned it 69 yards for a score to down UCLA, 19–8. In the final game Tony Flack swiped a Georgia Tech pass with 1:22 left to save the 27–24 win. In between they lost to Auburn, 13–7, and tied Clemson, 16–16, on a 31-yard field goal by Kevin Butler with 38 seconds to go, after safety Terry Hoage had blocked two field goal tries. Behind offensive tackles Guy McIntyre and Jimmy Harper, quarterback John Lastinger led Georgia to ten wins, including a 10–9 win over Texas in the Cotton Bowl.

Texas had an 11-0-0 record at the end of the regular season and was number two, but the loss to Georgia dropped them to fifth place and helped Miami leapfrog to the top. They stopped Auburn after a Jeff Ward field goal and a 66-yard punt return by Jitter Fields gave them a 10–0 lead. Then the Longhorns rolled through the first half of the season with wins over Oklahoma, 28–16, and Arkansas, 31–3. Against Arkansas, quarterback Rob Moerschell hit wide receiver Bill Boy Bryant with a 56-yard touchdown toss, and threw scoring passes of 54 and 43 yards to split end Brent Duhon.

The last half was tougher. Two Ward field goals were needed to defeat SMU, 15–12. After Texas Tech took a 3–0 halftime lead, quarterback Todd Dodge led a 72-yard second-half drive and scored on a 12-yard bootleg for a 20–3 win. In the battle of the field goals, three more by Ward downed Houston, 9–3. TCU led 14–3 but lost, 20–14, as Fred Acorn's last-minute interception saved it. But the great year for offensive guard Doug Dawson, tailback Mike Luck, linebackers Jeff Leiding and Mark Lang, and defensive backs Jerry Gray and Mossy Cade missed by a point in the Cotton Bowl.

Number-six Florida, under Charley Pell, tied USC, 19–19, and lost to Auburn, 28–21, and Georgia, 10–9. Senior Wayne Peace at quarter and sophomore running backs John Williams and Neal Anderson led Florida to a ninth win over Iowa in the Gator Bowl, 14-6. Safeties Randy Clark and Tony Lilly, and linebackers Pat Miller and all-American Wilber Marshall riveted a sturdy Gator defense.

Quarterback Steve Young's tosses to receivers Gordon Hudson and Greg Peterson put Brigham Young first in passing with 381.2 yards and in total offense with an all-time mark of 584.2 yards each outing. Young threw 429 times, and connected on 306 passes for 71.3 percent, still a one-year record. After a 40-36 first-day loss to Baylor, BYU won its next 11 games, including a 21-17 win over Missouri in the Holiday Bowl and ended seventh. Linebacker Todd Shell led a defense which came on at the finish.

Nine-and-three Michigan was eighth. They beat Washington State 20-17, but Husky quarterback Steve Pelluer completed 14 straight in a 25-24 Washington win. Badger end Al Toon was kept in control, as Rick Rogers and Kerry Smith ran well in the wins over Wisconsin, 38-21, and Indiana, 43-18, but linebacker Mike Boren went out for the year with an injury. Linebackers Carlton Rose, Mike Mallory, Rod Lyles, and Tom Hassel took up the slack in the shutout wins over Michigan State, 42-0, and Northwestern, 35-0, Bob Bergeron's 45-yard field goal with 12 seconds remaining beat Iowa, 16-13, but the next weekend saw a 16-6 Illinois win. Split end Vince Bean caught seven passes in the 42-10 win over Purdue, and quarterback Steve Smith hit flanker Triando Markray with two scoring strikes in the 58-10 thumping of the Gophers. With five catches in the 24-21 defeat of Ohio State, tight end Sim Nelson became Michigan's top receiver. Toiling on offense were center Tom Dixon, guards Stefan Humphries and Jerry Diorio, and tackles Clay Miller and Doug James. In the defensive line were tackles Vince DeFelice and Kevin Brooks and nose guard Al Sincich.

Ninth-place Ohio State also had a 9-3-0 record. After wins over Oregon, 31-6, and Oklahoma, 24-14, they lost to Iowa, 20-14, and Illinois, 17-13. The fake fumble fluked against Michigan as Mike Hammerstein fell on it before Ohio's Kirk Lowdermilk got to it. Flanker Cedric Anderson took the ball away from safety Evan Cooper for the Bucks' last score, but halfback Brad Cochran's two interceptions helped seal the Buckeye defeat. Ohio State closed the year with a 28-23 win over Pitt in the Fiesta Bowl.

Illinois was tenth with ten wins. They lost the opener to Missouri, 28-18, and the last one to UCLA in the Rose Bowl, 45-9. The goal posts were torn down four times this year, as Illinois became the first Big Ten team to beat all nine conference foes.

Duke's Ben Bennett ended with a .596 completion mark. He hit on 820 of 1,375 tries for 9,614 yards, all new career records.

1984

Brigham Young was number one for the last three weeks of the regular season. Many people didn't agree with the vote because of BYU's schedule, even though they again led in passing offense with 346.2 yards and in total offense with 486.5 yards per game. But the Cougars were the only unbeaten team left with a string of 24 straight wins and were voted number one in the final poll.

Brigham Young	(13-0-0)		Washington	(11-1-0)	
20	Pitt	14	26	Northwestern	0
47	Baylor	13	20	Michigan	11
38	Tulsa	15	35	Houston	7
18	Hawaii	13	53	Miami (Ohio)	7
52	Colorado State	9	19	Oregon State	7
41	Wyoming	38	37	Stanford	15
30	Air Force	25	17	Oregon	10
48	New Mexico	0	28	Arizona	12
42	Texas El Paso	9	44	California	14
34	San Diego State	3	7	Southern Cal	16
24	Utah	14	38	Washington State	29
38	Utah State	13	28	Oklahoma (Orange Bowl)	17
24	Michigan (Holiday Bowl)	17			
456		183	352		145

During most of its games, BYU's offense moved like a two-minute drill. They overcame an 11-point deficit in the Pitt game, as quarterback Robbie Bosco zipped a 50-yard touchdown pass to Adam Haybert with 1:37 left for the win. After moving to a 34–7 halftime lead over Baylor, Bosco ended the day with six scoring passes, two each to Glen Koslowski and Kelly Smith, and one to Dave Mills. At one point in the win over Tulsa, BYU had minus three yards rushing but led 24-6, and moved up to eighth place.

BYU's defense of its conference crown began with a win over Hawaii. The Colorado State contest wasn't as close as the score indicates, as BYU scored on six of its first seven possessions. In the Wyoming game, the lead shifted back and forth until Bosco hit Dave Mills for his fifth touchdown pass with 4:16 remaining.

Against Air Force, Bosco threw four touchdown passes, three of them covering more than 50 yards. When New Mexico used only one down lineman and dropped off the rest as pass defenders, the Cougars ran for 217 yards. Bosco fired four touchdown passes to down UTEP, and BYU moved into the number-four spot. San Diego State was Western Athletic Conference win number seven, and BYU climbed to third behind Nebraska and Joe Morrison's South Carolina squad.

On the next weekend, Oklahoma beat Nebraska 17-7, and Navy gave South Carolina a 38–21 loss, thanks to five turnovers. With a win over Utah, BYU took over first place. In the season-ender with Utah State, Bosco was held to one touchdown pass. The BYU lead was only 24-13 early in the last period, but a 56-yard punt return by Vai Sikahema helped the Cougars to put it in the bag.

In the scoreless first quarter with Michigan in the Holiday Bowl, Bosco left the game with a sprained ankle. But he returned in the next period to direct an 80-yard drive for a 7–0 BYU lead.

Michigan scored twice on two BYU turnovers and led 14–10 at the end of the third quarter. After a 32-yard Bob Bergeron last-period field goal, BYU tied it on another 80-yard scoring caper. Then they won it on a Bosco pass at the end of an 83-yard march, and LaVell Edwards was chosen coach of the year.

"It was a heckuva way to go out," said senior tight end Dave Mills. Amen to that, brother! And all the saints said, "Amen."

While BYU was slowly inching its way to the top, other teams reached the peak only to slide back into the limbo of also-rans. No sooner was Nebraska number one when Syracuse knocked them off, 17–9, at the end of September. Texas took over first place for two weeks, but lost it after a 15–15 stalemate with Oklahoma.

In the OU–Texas tie, Oklahoma stopped Texas with a goal-line stand late in the game and took an intentional safety for a 15–12 lead. The Longhorns pounded back, but on the next-to-last play, Oklahoma's Keith Stanberry pocketed a pass and slid out-of-bounds from the waist down. The interception was not allowed, and Jeff Ward's 32-yard field goal tied it on the last play of the game.

Washington began with a win over Northwestern, as linebacker Tim Meamber picked off three Wildcat passes. Michigan went down as they scored one touchdown only in the last minute. The Houston veer offense faltered on two lost fumbles and two interceptions, and coach Don James had the Huskies on the title trail.

On the same weekend in which number-two Ohio State lost to Purdue 28–23, Jeff Jaeger kicked four Husky field goals to down Oregon State. Then Stanford threw five interceptions and lost a fumble near its goal, and the 6-0-0 Huskies were in first place.

Washington was number one for four weeks. They caught up with Oregon in the third period, as Tim Peoples blocked a punt which Mike Gaffney fell on for a score. The defense also put a stop on Arizona with six interceptions and four fumbles. Jacque Robinson scored three times against Cal, and Paul Sicuro, now at quarterback for Hugh Millen, promptly threw three touchdown passes.

Washington was turned out after a month. USC's Steve Jordan kicked field goals of 47 and 51 yards to make it 7–6 at the half. In the last period, Troy's Fred Crutcher crashed over and Jordan added a 46-yarder, as UW's weak attack fell before the Trojans.

Texas also lost its first game that day to Houston, 29–15. That same Saturday, Maryland rallied from a 31–0 halftime blowout to nip Miami, 42–40, the greatest comeback in college grid annals.

Washington ended the season as the leader in takeaways with 27 interceptions and 24 recovered fumbles. They beat Washington State and met Oklahoma in the Orange Bowl. UW surprised everyone with a 14–0 lead on Oklahoma's top-rated rushing defense of 68.8 yards per game, led by nose

Boston College's Doug Flutie was the first quarterback whose passing and total offense yardage exceeded 10,000 yards.

guard Tony Casillas. But the Sooners tied it at the half with two second-quarter scores, the last one a 56-yard pass from quarterback Danny Bradley to Derrick Shepard.

The OU fullback was "Okie from Muskogee" Jerome Ledbetter. At the start of the second half, starting halfbacks Steve Sewell and Spencer Tillman were replaced by Lydell Carr and Pat Collins. In the last quarter a penalty nullified a field goal, and OU was penalized for driving the Sooner

Schooner onto the playing field. Tim Lashar's 35-yard field goal later gave Oklahoma a 17–14 lead.

Quarterback Hugh Millen started the final quarter and led a 74-yard drive, capping it with a 12-yard touchdown toss to Mark Pattison for a 21–17 lead. Then Ron Holmes tipped a Bradley pass into the hands of linebacker Joe Kelly and fullback Rick Fenney punched over the last points. UW was number two, while Oklahoma, with a tie and losses to Washington and Kansas, 28–11, was sixth.

The Florida Gators lost their opening game to Miami, 32–20. Quarterback Bernie Kosar took Miami 72 yards in half a minute and tossed a 12-yard scoring pass to Eddie Brown with seven seconds to go. Then Tolbert Bain returned an intercepted pass 59 yards for a score on the last play of the game. On the next Saturday, LSU played the Gators to a 21–21 tie. In the third game, Galen Hall took over as coach and led Florida to nine straight wins.

Tennessee was beaten in win number four, 43–30. Cincinnati lost 48–17 on the Gators' 578 yards total offense, 111 by running back John Williams. Against Auburn, Neal Anderson broke a third-period tie with a 36-yard touchdown run and added another 15-yard scoring run in the final quarter to win, 24–3. Number-eight Florida then beat Georgia, 27–0, to end six straight Bulldog wins over them. In the Kentucky game they managed only one touchdown, but Bobby Raymond kicked six field goals in the 25–17 win and Florida moved to number four. Quarterback Kerwin Bell's two touchdown passes helped defeat Florida State, 27–17, and the Gators finished in third place with one of their best seasons.

It was the first time Florida was SEC champ. They had help from Mississippi State's Artie Cosby, whose 26-yard field goal on the game's last play beat LSU, 16–14, to give Florida the title. An NCAA rebuke for recruiting abuses kept Florida from bowl play.

After the loss to Syracuse, Nebraska defeated its next six conference foes. Kansas State lost 62–14 as Nebraska scored seven times in its first eight possessions. Iowa State was also beaten 44–0 with four touchdowns in the first seven minutes of the last period. In the 41–7 win over Kansas, quarterback Travis Turner and I-back Doug DuBose both scored twice. After the 17–7 loss to Oklahoma, UN still led in scoring defense with 9.5 points and in total defense with 203.3 yards each game. Against LSU in the Sugar Bowl, quarterback Craig Sundberg's nine-yard run after the half put Nebraska ahead, then he hit tight end Todd Frain twice to give UN its tenth win, 28–10, and a fourth-place finish.

Boston College was the year's most exciting team. Against Alabama, quarterback Doug Flutie led BC to 24 second-half points for a 38–31 win. After Temple took a 10–9 last-quarter lead, BC scored twice to win, 24–10. West Virginia finally grounded the BC Eagle. Down 20–6 at halftime, they held Flutie to no second-half points and won, 21–20. Against Penn State, Flutie became the first player to pass for 10,000 yards, but BC lost, 37–30.

By far the most exciting game for Jack Bicknell's club was with Miami, coached by Jimmy Johnson. In the first two drives Flutie hit 11 of 11 to give

BC a 14–0 lead. Bernie Kosar pulled Miami alongside at 21–21, but the Eagles led at the half, 28–21.

Miami took the lead on a touchdown and a field goal by Greg Cox, but a Kevin Snow field goal tied it at 31–31. Snow kicked another field goal at the start of the final quarter to make it 34–31. At midfield Mel Bratton turned right end for Miami, cut back, and outran everyone to the left corner for a 38–34 lead. A Steve Strachan touchdown put BC ahead again at 41–38.

Bratton's fourth score on a one-yard dive gave Miami a 45–41 lead with 28 seconds left. Then Flutie threw 19 yards to Troy Stradford and 13 yards to Scott Gieselman. With six seconds to go, Flutie faded back and uncorked the cannon that clinched the Heisman. Downfield one yard in the end zone was Gerard Phelan, who caught the 65-yard missile for the winning touchdown, 47–45.

Flutie led Boston College to a fifth-place finish with win number ten in the Cotton Bowl over Houston, 45–28. BC also led in scoring with 36.7 points per game, and Flutie's 3,454 passing yards led the nation. Flutie's 10,579 yards passing and 11,317 yards total offense were both all-time marks. His career totals were 677 hits on 1,270 tries for 67 touchdowns and a .533 average.

Ten wins and losses to Nebraska, 17–3, and Oklahoma, 24–14, made Oklahoma State number seven. Eighth-place SMU also had ten wins, but lost to Houston, 29–20, and Texas, 13–7. Ninth-place UCLA lost to Nebraska, 42–3, Oregon, 20–18, and Stanford, 23–21. UCLA's John Lee set a one-year mark of 29 field goals, then beat Miami in the Fiesta Bowl on a 22-yarder with 51 seconds left for win number nine, 39–37. Number-ten USC lost to LSU, 23–3, UCLA, 29–10, and Notre Dame, 19–7. Their tenth win was over Ohio State in the Rose Bowl, 20–17, as Cris Carter had a record 172 yards in receiving, and Rich Spangler kicked a record 52-yard field goal.

Ohio State's Keith Byars led in scoring with 144 points and rushing with 1,655 yards. Arizona State's Luis Zendejas became the all-time scorer with 368 points, and Western Michigan's Mike Prindle set a one-game mark of seven field goals. Rueben Mayes of Washington State ran for 357 yards against Oregon, a record, and tackle Bruce Smith of Virginia Tech won the Outland Trophy.

1985

Oklahoma fulfilled its preseason choice to be number one and wore the tiara. After a slow start against Minnesota, OU's speedy defense, led by ends Darrell Reed and Kevin Murphy, held off a late UM rush for the win. Minnesota scored on a 12-yard Rickey Foggie to Kevin Starks pass with 4:15 left, but two Tim Lashar field goals proved the winning margin. Then quarterback Troy Aikman led OU to a methodical win over Kansas State with eight straight third-period passes. Against Texas, Aikman pitched to Pat Collins, who went 45 yards to the winning score in the final quarter. The swarming Sooners, led by nose guard Tony Casillas and linebacker Brian Bosworth, stopped the Steers in the second half with no first downs and minus 26 yards rushing.

Oklahoma (11-1-0)			Michigan (10-1-1)		
13	Minnesota	7	20	Notre Dame	12
41	Kansas State	6	34	South Carolina	3
14	Texas	7	20	Maryland	0
14	Miami (Florida)	27	33	Wisconsin	6
59	Iowa State	14	31	Michigan State	0
48	Kansas	6	10	Iowa	12
51	Missouri	6	42	Indiana	15
31	Colorado	0	3	Illinois	3
27	Nebraska	7	47	Purdue	0
13	Oklahoma State	0	48	Minnesota	7
35	Southern Methodist	13	27	Ohio State	17
25	Penn State (Orange Bowl)	10	27	Nebraska (Fiesta Bowl)	23
371		103	342		98

Then quarterback Vinny Testaverde perforated the Oklahoma aerial defense with touchdown tosses of 56 and 35 yards and 270 yards passing. A four-yard bootleg by Testaverde and two Greg Cox field goals gave Miami a big lead which Oklahoma never overcame. Even worse, Aikman was lost for the year with a broken ankle.

Freshman Jamelle Holieway came in at quarterback and guided Oklahoma to six conference wins, including a victory over second-place Nebraska, whose kicker, Dale Klein, had tied the record of seven field goals in a 28–20 win over Missouri the month before. Tight end Keith Jackson scored on an 88-yard end-around to pave the way for OU's win over Nebraska. After downing SMU, Oklahoma was first in total defense with 193.5 yards, in pass defense with 103.6 yards per game, and second in rushing and scoring defense.

Third-place Oklahoma met number-one Penn State in the Orange Bowl. The Lions looked like champs as they swept down the field after the kickoff and fullback Tim Manoa scored from a yard out. OU came smashing back on Tim Lashar's 26-yard field goal and a 71-yard touchdown pass from Holieway to tight end Jackson. Two more Lashar field goals of 31 and 21 yards, each after thefts by defensive backs Sonny Brown and Tony Rayburn, and a 27-yarder by PSU kicker Massimo Manca made it 16–10 at intermission. Lashar's fourth field goal of 22 yards, an Orange Bowl record, and Lydell Carr's 61-yard touchdown run closed the scoring.

Michigan came in second. Notre Dame's John Carney had four field goals, but six sacks beat the Irish. Wideout Paul Jokisch had five catches against South Carolina, and after Maryland fell the UM goal was still clean, but guard Mark Hammerstein was lost with a broken arm. Michigan finally gave up a touchdown to Wisconsin, but Michigan State, led by top runner

Lorenzo White with 1,908 yards, had four turnovers which resulted in four scores, one a toss from quarterback Jim Harbaugh to tight end Eric Kattus.

Then Iowa stopped the Wolverines on four field goals by Rob Houghtlin, the last a 29-yarder on the last play. Harbaugh threw six yards to fullback Gerald White for the only touchdown of the game. Against Indiana, Harbaugh passed for 283 yards, a school mark, and tailback Jamie Morris had 179 yards rushing. Michigan survived a last-play field goal try by Chris White of Illinois, kicking for his dad, coach Mike White, as the ball hit the crossbar. Purdue was beaten down by 11 straight Harbaugh completions. UM's defense of nose guard Billy Harris, tackles Mike Hammerstein and Mark Messner, and linebackers Jeff Akers, Andy Moeller, Jim Scarcelli, and Mike Mallory, son of Indiana coach Bill Mallory, kept Minnesota from scoring until the final minutes. Harbaugh's three scoring passes against Ohio State, one a 77-yarder to John Kolesar, gave him a total of 18, another school record. His 139 of 212 for 1,913 yards and a .656 average was the country's best.

Michigan took its top-ranked scoring defense of 6.8 points per game to the Fiesta Bowl against Nebraska. Paced by tailback Doug DuBose and fullback Tom Rathman, the Huskers led in rushing for the fourth time in six years with an average of 374.3 yards per game. Trailing 14–3 at the half, Michigan turned two Husker fumbles into a 17–14 lead. A Pat Moons field goal and another touchdown made the spread 27–14 as the last quarter began. UN didn't score until there was only 2:39 remaining, and a minute later Michigan gave up an intentional safety. Cornerback Garland Rivers' interception in the final half-minute sealed the win, and cornerback Brad Cochran made most all–American teams.

Penn State was not impressive during the first part of the year due to injuries to tailback D.J. Dozier. The Lions blew a 17–0 lead over Maryland and trailed 18–17, but Massimo Manca's 46-yard field goal beat the Terps, 20–18. Penn State led Temple 14–0 at the half and hung on to win, 27–25. Two 17–10 wins over East Carolina and Rutgers followed, with fullback Steve Smith rambling 63 yards late in the last quarter to unseat the latter.

Four Massimo Manca field goals of 38, 44, 50, and 20 yards, and an 11-yard scoring pass from Matt Knizner, who replaced quarterback John Shaffer for one play, to tight end Brian Siverling gave State a 19–10 lead over Alabama with 6:12 to go. The Tide cut it to two with ten seconds left on a 14-yard touchdown pass from quarterback Mike Shula to tight end Thornton Chandler, then recovered the onside kickoff but lost it on a penalty.

Even the win over Alabama and a gutty defense of nose guard Mike Russo, end Bob White, linebackers Shane Conlan and Rogers Alexander, and defensive backs Mike Zordich and Ray Isom did not get them much of a following. Then they downed Syracuse 24–20, West Virginia 27–0, Boston College (led by Outland winner Mike Ruth at tackle) 16–12, and Cincinnati 31–10, and became the top team early in November. They closed with wins over Notre Dame, 36–6, and Pitt, 31–0, but the Orange Bowl defeat put them third.

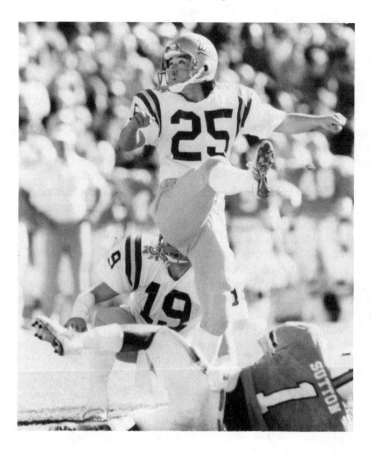

John Lee, UCLA's record-holding field goal kicker, watches another one split the uprights.

After a 26–26 opening tie with UCLA, Tennessee quarterback Tony Robinson's four touchdown passes beat Auburn, 38–20. A week later they were hard pressed to down Wake Forest, 31–29, and lost the next game to Florida, 17–10. Three Carlos Reveiz field goals clipped Alabama, 16–14, but Robinson went out with a serious knee injury. Then Georgia Tech's Black Watch defense, with black GT's on their helmets instead of white, kept Tennessee out of the end zone, but a 51-yard field goal by Reveiz with six seconds to go gained a 6–6 tie. With split end Tim McGee breaking almost every school passing mark for the Vols, they won their last five games and were eighth at the end of the season, but a strong 35–7 win over Miami in the Sugar Bowl vaulted them to fourth place.

Tennessee's defense of tackles Rich Brown and Marc Hovanik and linebacker Dale Jones pressured Miami's Vinny Testaverde and sacked him seven times. Daryl Dickey, who replaced Robinson at quarterback, defused the Hurricanes with short passes for UT's ninth win. All-American defensive back Chris White, who tied East Carolina's Kevin Walker with nine steals during the year to lead all comers, plucked another one from the ozone which led to the Vols' last score on a six-yard scurry by Charles Wilson. Miami had a chance to take it all if they won, but slumped to ninth with a 10-2-0 record.

Florida, which didn't play in a bowl game because of NCAA penalties, moved from sixth to fifth. The Gators opened with a 35–23 win over Miami, but were tied by Rutgers, 28–28, on a touchdown and two-point conversion with 35 seconds left. Six wins followed, including a 14–10 win over Auburn on quarterback Kerwin Bell's two scoring passes to wide receiver Ray McDonald. Florida held the top spot for one week until Georgia took the bite out of the Gators with a 24–3 win. The loss ended their unbeaten streak at 18 games, and was the first defeat for Galen Hall since he took over last year. A 15–13 win over Kentucky and a 38–14 whipping of Florida State gave the Gators nine victories a loss, and a tie for the second straight season.

Texas A&M also got off on the wrong foot with a 23–10 loss to Alabama, as Van Tiffin snapped a 10–10 fourth-quarter tie on field goals of 51 and 40 yards. Jackie Sherrill coached them to four wins before a 20–15 conquest by Baylor. A&M won its last five games, including a 19–17 win over Southern Methodist on Eric Franklin's 48-yard field goal with 1:46 remaining. For win nine, Texas got its worst beating by the Aggies, 42–10.

With a 36–16 Cotton Bowl win over Auburn, A&M ended sixth. Tackle Doug Williams led the Revolving Boar attack of 6'3", 221-pound Roger Vick, who had 764 yards rushing, and 6'0", 230-pound Anthony Toney with 856 yards. Split end Jeff Nelson caught 51 passes this year. In Dallas, it was quarterback Kevin Murray's 292-yards passing mark, mostly to tight end Rod Bernstine, which got A&M its points. But it was defense which beat Auburn in the last period. With A&M ahead 21–16 and Auburn at the Aggie three-yard line on fourth down, linebacker Larry Kelm dropped Heisman winner Bo Jackson for a loss. Cornerback Wayne Asberry did it again later on to put asthma in the Tiger growl.

Four field goals by John Lee helped UCLA bump Brigham Young 27–24 and end the nation's longest win streak at 25 games. The Bruins lost to Washington, 21–14, to USC, 17–13, got win nine at Pasadena, and their 70.3 yards per game rushing defense led all. Lee's 79 field goals and 85.9 percent were both career records.

Tackle Mark Walen led the Rose Bowl charge that sacked quarterback Chuck Long four times and caused four Ronnie Harmon fumbles. UCLA outshone Hayden Fry's Hawks, manned by nose guard Hap Peterson, linebackers Larry Station and George Davis, and safety Jay Norvell. Matt Stevens started for injured quarterback David Norrie, and Eric Ball, in for Gaston Green, scored four times to trip Iowa, 45–28, and put them tenth at 10-2-0 with UCLA seventh.

Coach of the Year Fisher DeBerry's Air Force squad had its finest year. One win was over Notre Dame, 21–15, as linebacker Terry Maki had 19 solo tackles and blocked a field goal caught by A.J. Scott, who ran it back 77 yards for the winning score. Using a flexbone attack, a wishbone with passes by halfback Kelly Pittman as well as quarterback Bart Weiss, their only loss was to Brigham Young, 28–21. Fullback Pat Evans took them to a twelfth win over Texas in the Bluebonnet Bowl, 24–16, and an eighth-place finish.

Quarterbacks continued to produce. Long Beach State's Doug Gaynor cracked the 300-yard per game total offense barrier with a 305-yard career average. BYU's Robbie Bosco completed 338 of 511 attempts, both new one-year marks. Bowling Green's Brian McClure joined the 10,000-yard club with 10,280 career passing yards, and Jim Everett of Purdue led with 6.93 yards gained on each play.

After 43 years at the same school (Grambling) Eddie Robinson became the winningest coach with 329 wins, both all-time highs, and Napoleon McCallum of Navy became the leader in all-purpose running with 7,172 yards.

Illegal financial help to athletes surfaced again. As far back as 1895, Duke gave up football for 25 years due to professionalism in the sport. Space does not permit a recital of the colleges which have brought in tramp athletes or been penalized in trying to field a winning team. Let it be sufficient to say that great teams are handmade just like great cars and shoes, and that some kind of policing agency is necessary because of the zeal of human nature. In the race to number one, football recruiting is a reflection of our society. Nobody likes someone looking over their shoulder, whether it's the policeman on the street or the Senate checking on the price of airplace parts, but it has to be done. The three-part division of our government is built on this idea.

The bottom line is that a college athlete should have financial help just like any deserving student, but like any student who can't cut it academically they should not be allowed to play unless they can make it in the classroom. Sane rules like the NCAA's satisfactory progress rule, which requires students who stay for a fifth year to declare a major and pass 24 hours of yearly credit toward that major, are basic, and so is a satisfactory grade-point average for all students. Football is an opportunity to step into the mainstream of American life just like any aspect of college, but if it is going to be done in college it should be done according to the requirements governing college life. Representative James Howard (D, N.J.) is sponsoring legislation to remove tax deduction status for contributions to college athletic departments that fail to graduate three-fourths of their scholarship athletes in five years. As far as fringe benefits are concerned, what deserving math or science student ever received a car or expense money?

1986

Penn State disarmed rivals with its plain uniforms and then beat them with defense. Behind center Keith Radecic, guards Dan Morgan and Steve Wisniewski, and tackles Stan Clayton and Chris Conlin, quarterback John Shaffer and fullback Steve Smith stood out in early wins. Dave Clark's run beat Cincinnati, Tim Manoa scored twice against Syracuse, and Alabama was stopped with five sacks and 44 yards rushing.

Penn State (12-0-0)			Miami (11-1-0)		
45	Temple	15	34	South Carolina	14
26	Boston College	14	23	Florida	15
42	East Carolina	17	61	Texas Tech	11
31	Rutgers	6	28	Oklahoma	16
23	Cincinnati	17	34	Northern Illinois	0
42	Syracuse	3	58	West Virginia	14
23	Alabama	3	45	Cincinnati	13
19	West Virginia	0	41	Florida State	23
17	Maryland	15	37	Pitt	10
24	Notre Dame	19	23	Tulsa	10
34	Pitt	14	36	East Carolina	10
14	Miami (Fiesta Bowl)	10	10	Penn State (Fiesta Bowl)	14
340		133	430		150

West Virginia was tough in close, so Massimo Manca kicked for field goals to down Don Nehlen's club. Three interceptions, one a 72-yard return by end Pete Curkendall held off Maryland. Terp play-caller Dan Henning hit wideout John Bonato late, but cornerback Duffy Cobbs tipped the two-point pass, and linebacker Pete Giftopoulos covered the onside kick to save the close win.

Lou Holtz, who replaced Jerry Faust this year at Notre Dame, had them in front until wideout Ray Roundtree's catch put PSU on top in the third quarter. Another Penn State score was equaled by Tim Brown's catch for Notre Dame. With 52 seconds left, the Irish moved to the six-yard line but end Bob White sacked quarterback Steve Beuerlein to save a second close win. Against Pitt, scores were made on a Blair Thomas 91-yard kickoff return, a Matt Knizner pass to wideout Eric Hamilton, and D.J. Dozier's 26-yard run.

On defense for Joe Paterno's Lions were end Tim Johnson and nose guard Mike Russo, linebackers Don Graham, all–American Shane Conlan, and Trey Bauer, roverback (or hero, in PSU parlance) Marques Henderson, safety Ray Isom, and cornerback Eddie Johnson.

In a game for the national title after the bowl games, Penn State faced Miami in the Sunkist Fiesta Bowl. Mel Bratton dived over for Miami, and Shaffer's scramble made it even at halftime. Mark Seelig's 38-yard field goal put Miami ahead, but after Conlan's second interception Dozier scored to make the final 14–10; then he knelt in prayer as Miami had done three years before.

Miami, under Jimmy Johnson, placed second. Linebackers Ron Carter, Winston Moss, and George Mira, Jr., led with four fumble recoveries and six sacks to beat Florida. Vinny Testaverde threw touchdowns to flanker Mike Irvin and tight end Charles Henry, and two to fullback Alonzo Highsmith in the shelling of Texas Tech.

In a repeat of last year's game, Testaverde beavered Oklahoma with 21 of 28 and no interceptions, one a toss to tight end Alfredo Roberts for a 7–3 lead at intermission and last-half win.

Darryl Oliver ran in for a yard against Northern Illinois, but Florida State turned the Hurricanes into a zephyr for three periods. A Tanner Holloman score for FSU was matched by Miami's Warren Williams. After a Testaverde touchdown throw, Keith Ross fed the kickoff to Dexter Carter who went 96 yards to tie it. Three Derek Schmidt field goals made it 20–14 at the half and 23–21 after three.

After Testaverde survived his fifth sack, two by nose guard Tom Harp, the pass blocking mended. Tackles Maurice Maddox and Scott Provin, guards Dave Alekna and Paul O'Connor, and center Gregg Rakoczy gave him time to throw darts to split ends Brian Blades and Brett Perriman and score once in the win. "He's like Babe Ruth coming to the plate," said Seminole coach Bobby Bowden.

The defense had tackles Jerome Brown and Dan Sileo, ends Dan Stubbs and Bill Hawkins, and backs Tolbert Bain, Don Ellis, Kevin McCutcheon, replacing injured Selwyn Brown, and interception King Bennie Blades, but there was a Lion in the way in the last game.

Oklahoma mauled UCLA, then against Minnesota scores came on Lydell Carr's 40-yard run and a Pat Collins 78-yard punt return. In the Miami game, linebacker Brian Bosworth, tackle Steve Bryan, and end Darrell Reed crowded Testaverde, but he won the game and the Heisman with 14 straight hits and three third-period scores.

OU was up for Kansas State on Eric Mitchel's 54-yard touchdown run, and Texas fell, 47–12. Pat Jones' Oklahoma State team was done in by linebacker Dante Jones' 55-yard scoring theft, and Keith Jackson's 69-yard touchdown catch helped sink Iowa State.

Earl Johnson's four scores beat Kansas, and Anthony Stafford scored on an 82-yard run in Missouri's worst loss, 77–0. Jamelle Holieway threw no passes to defeat Colorado, but he went 94 yards on three of four attempts to tie Nebraska with 1:22 left, and Tim Lashar's 31-yard field goal won it with six seconds to go, 20–17.

Oklahoma had all the numbers except the winning ones in the next lottery: total defense, 169.6 yards; rushing defense, 60.7 yards; pass defense, 108.9 yards; rushing, 404.7 yards; scoring defense, 6.6 points per game; and scoring, 42.4 points per game.

All-American guards Anthony Phillips and Mark Hutson led OU to a 42–8 Orange Bowl win over Arkansas to end third at 11-1-0. Halfback Spencer Tillman began the rout of the Razorbacks with a pair of touchdowns in the second period, the first a 77-yard run. It was Barry Switzer's 137th win against 25 losses and 4 ties for a .837 average and fourth-place rank. Arkansas' Greg Horne was the top punter with a 47.2-yard average.

Coach John Cooper took Arizona State to fourth place and a 10-1-1 mark. Anthony Parker's 65-yard punt return scored against SMU, and a catch by split end Aaron Cox led to the score which knotted Washington State, 21–21. USC lost on a Jeff Van Raaphorst touchdown toss to tight end

Jeff Gallimore, and Utah State was outdistanced on three Darryl Harris scores. The Rose Bowl came in sight with a win over Washington, linebacker Stacy Harvey intercepting two passes, and cinched in the thumping of Cal, as Bruce Hill scored three times, one on a 96-yard kickoff return. Fullback Channing Williams tallied four times to fade Wichita State, but Arizona's Larry Smith, who took over at Southern California at the end of the season, had their number for the fifth straight year, 34–17.

Behind their huge lines, all big enough to have electrodes in their neck, Van Raaphorst outsparred Michigan's Jim Harbaugh in Pasadena. After linebacker Greg Clark intercepted a pass at midfield, Kent Bostrom added his third field goal to end the scoring at 22–15. Safety Robby Boyd's last-minute theft sealed the win.

Sophomore quarterback Steve Taylor quickly found a place in Husker hearts with 139 yards rushing and 10 of 16 passes to down Florida State. Cornerback Brian Davis scored on a 32-yard interception in the first 12 seconds and Keith Jones, in for injured Doug DuBose, scored on a 78-yard scamper to begin the deluge of Illinois. Three first-half fumble recoveries by end Broderick Thomas hastened Oregon's downfall. South Carolina lost on Taylor's 11-yard toss to tight end Todd Millikan with 1:26 to go.

Dana Brinson's 58-yard kickoff return set up one score, and Rod Smith ran in a punt to put Oklahoma State behind early. Colorado, coached by Bill McCartney, gave UN its first loss, 20–10, as they scored on Jeff Campbell's 39-yard reverse, two Dave DeLine field goals, and O.C. Oliver's halfback pass to Lance Carl. Kansas State couldn't get by all–American tackle Danny Noonan, and Iowa State lost, as Ken Kaelin and Tyreese Knox each ran for 126 yards. Robb Schnitzler turned in a 70-yard punt return to conclude the scoring.

Quarterback Clete Blakeman made the most of his first start in a 70–0 worst-ever drubbing of Kansas, Nebraska took the Sooner land grabbers down to the wire before losing, and ended fifth at 10-2-0 after the 30–15 U.S. F&G Sugar Bowl win over LSU.

Auburn warmed up with a 42–14 win over UT-Chattanooga, 45–0 over East Carolina, and then beat Tennessee, 34–8. Against Western Carolina both tackles scored, Nate Hill on a fumble recovery and Malcolm McCary on an interception. Western Carolina's Bob Waters, ex-49er in Red Hickey's alternating quarterback shotgun with John Brodie and Billy Kilmer, coached despite the onset of Lou Gehrig's disease.

Tailback Brent Fullwood and linebacker Kurt Crain scored in the first two minutes against Vanderbilt. Auburn led Florida at the end of three, 17–0, but Bob McGinty's 51-yard field goal and a Kerwin Bell toss to wideout Ricky Nattiel cut it to one before Bell's two-point run won it. Chris Knapp kicked a 44-yard field goal in the win over Cincinnati, but Georgia decked Pat Dye's Auburn squad, 20–16.

As all–American Cornelius Bennett at linebacker and center Ben Tamburello eyed each other, a Tiger drive kept alive on Jeff Burger's toss to Trey

Gainous, and Tim Jessie's halfback reverse to end Lawyer Tillman beat Alabama with 32 seconds to go, 21–17.

Auburn and USC, with all–Americans Tim McDonald at safety but minus guard Jeff Bregel (who failed the drug test which went into effect this year) met in the Citrus Bowl. Auburn came away winner, 16–7, adding a last-period safety as tackle Tracy Rocker caught Rodney Peete behind his goal to come in sixth at 10-2-0.

Opening-game losses to Alabama, 16–10, and Washington, 40–7, ticketed Ohio State to Timbuktu. Pat O'Morrow got OSU going on a 19-yard field goal with 25 seconds left to beat Colorado, 13–10. Then Utah was defeated, 64–6, followed by seven conference wins, and once again it was Michigan and Ohio State for the Rose Bowl.

The Buckeyes had a 14-6 halftime lead on a four-yard pass from quarterback to Jim Karsatos to split end Cris Carter, and a 46-yard run by tailback Vince Workman. But Michigan scored on its first three second-half possessions to go ahead 26–17, as Jamie Morris worked the middle time after time. The Bucks closed it to 26-24, but lost when a long Matt Frantz field goal was no good.

Two all–American linebackers, Johnny Holland of Texas A&M and Chris Spielman of Ohio State squared off in the Cotton Bowl. When it was over Spielman had two interceptions, one for a touchdown, and linebacker Mike Kee added another in the 28–12 Buckeye win to give them a ten-and-three year and seventh-place finish.

Michigan turned back Notre Dame, 24–23, and Florida State, 20–18, with the help of two stolen passes by safety Ivan Hicks. Iowa tackle Jeff Drost did not play, but sore-armed Mark Vlasic came in to tie it with a pass to end Bob Smith. After Iowa fumbled in the final minute, Mike Gillette reversed last year's game on a 34-yard field goal down the pipe with no time left, 20–17.

Fullback Bob Perryman scored twice against Purdue, but the Gophers gave Michigan its first loss on Chip Lohmiller's 30-yard field goal as time ran out, 20–17. They rebounded to beat Ohio State for the trip to Pasadena, and downed Hawaii after the Rainbows, led by nose guard Al Noga, held them to a 3–3 halftime tie. Michigan was 11-2-0 and ranked eighth after the Rose Bowl loss.

With Wes Neighbors at center for Alabama, Gene Jelks scored on a 75-yard run against Vanderbilt, and Dave Casteal's touchdown put them ahead of Florida. Greg Richardson's 66-yard punt return and flanker Al Bell's two catches from Mike Shula overcame Notre Dame, but Penn State stopped them cold. Alabama also lost to LSU, 14–10, and Auburn, but was ninth at 10-3-0 after a 28-6 win over Washington in the John Hancock Sun Bowl. Van Tiffin never missed a PAT and had 135 in a row for a career mark. Bill Curry became coach at the end of the year when Tampa Bay claimed Ray Perkins.

Nine-and-three Louisiana State was tenth. Their hawk-eyed defense hijacked five Texas A&M passes, one each by linebackers Ron Sancho and

Mike Brooks, and cornerback Jim Pierson. Miami of Ohio dumped them, 21–12, but three Ronnie Lewis field goals beat Georgia, as Harvey Williams and Sam Martin both ran for over 100 yards. Eddie Fuller scored late to lock up the Kentucky game.

Mississippi came away with a 21–19 win on David Browndyke's missed field goal with nine seconds to go. Alabama was halted on two end-zone saves, one on safety Greg Jackson's interception, who later ear-holed Bobby Humphrey with a hit at the goal which caused a fumble covered by corner-back Kevin Guidry for a touchback. Tosses by Tom Hodson to split end Wendell Davis, flanker Rogie Magee, and tight end Brian Kinchen beat Notre Dame, 21–19, but only after the Irish missed a two-point pass with 3:32 left.

In their three-man trench were nose guard Henry Thomas, and tackles Karl Wilson and Roland Barbay. Coach Bill Arnsparger, a former defensive co-ordinator for Don Shula's Miami Dolphins, returned to Florida as its athletic director after the last game.

Brigham Young tackle Jason Buck won the Outland Trophy, and career marks were set in passing by Fresno State's Kevin Sweeney with 10,623 yards, and by Washington's Jeff Jaeger with 80 field goals. Temple's Paul Palmer had 2,633 yards all-purpose running for a season mark, and his 239.3-yard average is second annually.

Proposition 48 became NCAA bylaw 5-1-J. College athletes must have a "C" average in high school (2.0) in 11 core courses to eliminate easy classes, and pass the college entrance exam. The NCAA suspended football at Southern Methodist for a year due to repeated violations, the last one a slush fund for athletes. Kickoffs were also made from the 35-yard line this year.

Index to Names and Subjects

Entries in SMALL CAPS refer to subjects; **boldface** numbers indicate photographs.

Index to Colleges, Conferences, and Associations